Development and Semi-periphery

Development and Semi-periphery

Post-neoliberal Trajectories in South America and Central Eastern Europe

Edited by
Renato Boschi and Carlos Henrique Santana

ANTHEM PRESS
LONDON · NEW YORK · DELHI

Anthem Press
An imprint of Wimbledon Publishing Company
www.anthempress.com

This edition first published in UK and USA 2012
by ANTHEM PRESS
75-76 Blackfriars Road, London SE1 8HA, UK
or PO Box 9779, London SW19 7ZG, UK
and
244 Madison Ave. #116, New York, NY 10016, USA

British Library Cataloguing-in-Publication Data
A catalogue record for this book is available from the British Library.

Library of Congress Cataloging-in-Publication Data
Development and semi-periphery : post-neoliberal trajectories in South America
and Central Eastern Europe / edited by Renato Boschi and Carlos Henrique Santana.
p. cm. –
Includes bibliographical references.
ISBN 978-0-85728-440-2 (hardback : alk. paper)
1. Structural adjustment (Economic policy)–Europe, Eastern.
2. Structural adjustment (Economic policy)–Europe, Central.
3. Structural adjustment (Economic policy)–Latin America.
4. Europe, Eastern–Foreign economic relations.
5. Europe, Central–Foreign economic relations.
6. Latin America–Foreign economic relations.
7. Europe, Eastern–Politics and government–21st century.
8. Europe, Central–Politics and government–21st century.
9. Latin America–Politics and government–21st century.
I. Boschi, Renato Raul. II. Santana, Carlos Henrique.
HC244.D4298 2012
338.9437–dc23
2012002572

ISBN-13: 978 0 85728 440 2 (Hbk)
ISBN-10: 0 85728 440 1 (Hbk)

This title is also available as an eBook.

TABLE OF CONTENTS

LIST OF TABLES AND FIGURES

Tables

Figures

INTRODUCTION

Renato Boschi and
Carlos Henrique Santana

The trajectories of macroeconomic reforms and policies adopted in Central Eastern Europe (CEE) and South America (SA) have parallels that have been pointed out by the comparative political economy literature. There are countless approaches that emphasize influence of multilateral institutions such as the World Bank and the International Monetary Fund (IMF), which include the effect of external shocks – for example the debt crisis and the collapse of communist regime, the construction of democratic institutions, the role of regional integration etc. Within this variety of approaches, the prevalent perception is that the legacies of authoritarianism and economic crises in the 1980s set the stage for the adoption of institutional reform experiences that would produce long-term effects as to the capacity to implement a development agenda in these countries.

Such is the case with the recent discussions on the characterization of varieties of capitalism in the wake of the seminal study by Hall and Soskice. This brand of literature takes up central arguments produced about the characterization and changes in the capitalist system in the 1970s and 1980s – a period of turbulences in the global scenario with the oil shocks, debt crises and stagflation. Many of the aspects pointed out in previous analyses dating from that period already signaled a drastic reconfiguration occurring in the center/periphery (or semi-periphery relations), in particular the undermining of the socialist bloc, the rise of East Asian Tigers and even the future emergence of China as a possible capitalist power (Wallerstein 2004; Frank 1969).

Nowadays, the concern in the literature is that of characterizing some of the changes emerging out of the post-neoliberal period, the crisis of 2008 marking another divide in the center/periphery relations. Changes in center/semi-periphery relations and ensuing possibilities for relative changes for some countries appear now as a result of the crisis of deregulation. Such a crisis set productive regimes of advanced countries under drastic reconfiguration, including spatial redistribution of industrial production, loss of jobs and undermining of forms of social protection whereas in so-called emerging countries, a post-Keynesian scenario with demand-pulled investments, forms of social inclusion and expansions of internal markets seem to be the case. Changes are not the same for all these emerging semi-peripheral economies: the first difference concerns primarily Eastern European countries which can be set apart from their South American counterparts because of the modes of integration in the European Union (EU) and therefore the need to abide by rules affecting the performance of each country, left with very little maneuvering space in terms of macroeconomic policy. In addition, the option of expanding towards internal markets (which is open to the large South American economies) does not represent a real alternative to Eastern European countries. As a consequence, it is possible to notice differences between the two regions as to the response of their respective productive regimes to the crisis and to changes in the global capitalist system – which have prompted the recent characterization of Eastern European countries as "dependent market economies" (Nolke and Vliegenthart 2009) and "embedded neoliberalism" for Latin American countries (Brooks and Kurtz 2008). As a function of the degree of dependency and other structural factors – such as comparative advantages, size of population and size of territory – noticeable differences also exist between countries within the same region.

Forms of transition, forms of social protection and role of the state are the three main axes determining the reshaping of economies and their performance in recent times. The outcomes of the critical juncture represented by the transition towards more liberal market-based economies were not uniform in each case. In both regions, the active role of the state – in particular as a productive agent – was very central with the differences being a matter of degree, given the fact that in Eastern Europe, the extent of privatization was extensive to the economy as a whole. Another difference regards the social structure with extreme inequalities characterizing the South American region and much more equal societies characterizing the former socialist countries of Eastern Europe together with Russia. This, in addition, entails different forms of social protection when we compare the two regions: universal coverage in one case and stratified, limited forms of social protection in the other.

The pattern of transitions towards market-oriented economies in the realms of privatization and social policies are central aspects regarding the ways in which the production regimes between and even within regions can be analyzed. Comparative studies inform us that the past trajectories of each region consolidated perceptions which shaped the time and rhythm of reforms. Whereas during the national developmentalism period in Brazil (which coincided with the 30 golden postwar years) growth rates were second only to the Japanese, the same cannot be said about the rest of South America, where the adoption of the Economic Commission for Latin America (ECLA) program did not translate into continuous public policies able to bring about sustainable growth. In that sense, the experience of past trajectories was determinant to establish limits to the extent of reforms which began being adopted in the 1980s. A similar parallel can be observed in Central Eastern Europe (CEE). The comparative approaches related to CEE, which employ the perspective of the varieties of capitalism literature, stress the need to understand the determining character of past trajectories established since before the collapse of communism in order to identity the acceptable limits to market reforms (Feldmann 2006). More recent analyses in this perspective call attention to aspects such as the forms and degree of direct foreign investment as the mechanism of adaptation of productive regimes as market economies in the European context (Drahokoupil 2008).

Also, there is the important matter of how epistemic communities appropriate and interpret (in other words, how they diffuse) ideas, turning them into acceptable reform trajectories. Epistemic communities are transnational communities of professionals that supply, train and congregate cadres that occupy key political and policymaking positions whose function is to present programmatic solutions which help forge alliances between political forces and interest groups and, at the same time, respond to the necessities related to external restrictions. Restrictions and constraints to the construction of new agendas were quite strong around the 1980s, considering the high degree of indebtedness in South America in addition to the need for diplomatic recognition and international reliability that CEE demanded right after the collapse of the Soviet regime. In that sense, the notion of translation is considered highly relevant as it provides the concept which links abstract policy models to the modalities of their adoption in different countries. More recent studies on the topic have already advanced significantly both with regard to the empirical systematization as well as conceptual density of the debate (Fourcade-Gourinchas 2006; Bockman and Eyal 2002).

Another important element in the evaluation of the degree of continuity and rupture within the context of critical junctures is the identification of the variation of state capacities. Countries that consolidated a considerable degree of coordination of their productive regimes and welfare were more adverse to the abrupt changes in their institutions and at the same time, presented fewer oscillations in their policies. Comparative studies indicate, for example, that during the transition process an old nomenclature performed a crucial role in the production of a new productive regime, diminishing the costs of disruptive effects (Stark and Bruszt 1998). In South America, studies such as Sikkink's (1991) demonstrated how the continuity between policies was due to a more cohesive political system and institutions of development, such as public banks and professionalized bureaucratic arenas. For example, Brazil was able to guarantee a considerable degree of coordination and continuity of policies – something Argentina failed to do. All in all, the studies in the area of comparative political economy have advanced consistently, indicating that liberalization did not imply necessarily in the weakening of the state, but in the strengthening of its regulatory and fiscal capacities – producing something that some authors have called embedded neoliberalism (Kurtz and Brooks 2008).

As already mentioned, specificity of trajectories also appears in the modalities of welfare and productive regimes adopted in different countries. From that point of view, the pattern of commodification of the sphere of social rights and the demobilization of the state regulatory apparatus (which arose as a result of market-oriented reforms) affected the sustainability of public policies that could guarantee and broaden citizenship as well as the consolidation of development and technological innovation policies. Once again the comparative perspective indicates a landscape of significant variations. Whereas some countries underwent conspicuous declines in living standards, as for example the Baltic states, Argentina and the Andean countries, others such as Brazil and Slovenia maintained stable indicators with noticeable improvements during the last decade. On the other hand, although the global periphery's share in research and development (R&D) is still small, albeit increasing, there are arguably remarkable cases of persistent innovation policies, which perhaps justifies the use of a category such as the "semi-periphery" as the chapters in this book will argue.

The present volume brings together a set of articles which seek to evaluate the trajectories of past development, the role of transnational communities and the variety of state capacities, contrasting the experience of South American and Central and Eastern European countries. The aim of the different chapters is to comprehend how the scope of change of trajectories entailed by the market-oriented policies in the 1990s restricted the agenda and capacities of CEE in the context of financial crises and regional integration, while for South America the challenge was that of resuming state capacities and growth.

Understanding Trajectories

The varieties of capitalism literature have offered a broader and systematic analytical framework to understand the differences of reform trajectories and development among the countries. Although it does not satisfactorily take into account the dimension of state capacities and aspects related to institutional change over time, the model has contributed to the comprehension of the variation of institutional equilibriums and its importance to evaluate productive and welfare regimes. Nevertheless, the scope of this literature is more often than not restricted to empirical studies among Organisation for Economic Co-operation and Development (OECD) countries. Only more recently studies along this line have ventured into analyzing semi-peripheral countries (Schneider and Soskice 2009; Bohle and Greskovits 2007; Boschi and Gaitán 2008) or have raised the need for treating these cases in relation to more broadly defined ideal types. Even in these recent works a vision that articulates how the previous trajectories and the existence of inherited state capacities filtered the range of reform agenda in the so-called critical junctures is lacking. The endeavor of the present book is partially to fill this gap with analyses yielded by the contrasting experience of the two regions.

Many recent comparative political economy studies conclude CEE and SA countries have adhered to the market-oriented reform agenda due to the conditionalities imposed by multilateral organizations such as the IMF and the World Bank. This perspective repeatedly tends to emphasize the low bargaining capacity of countries. This kind of approach usually constructs analyses that bundle countries in homogeneous regional blocs, generally followed by equivalent demarcations in the so-called area studies. However, recent studies have demonstrated that mediation within the scope of domestic institutions is more meaningful than has normally been admitted. For example, these mediations occurred in welfare regimes changes in CEE (Hacker 2009) and in South America (Mesa-Lago 2007; Riesco 2009; Lautier 2009). Changes in the productive regimes, as is the case specifically with privatization, had to gain broader support and legitimacy through an agenda of cognitive translation associated with changes in the mechanisms of aggregation of preferences that, in turn, would provide support to the patterns of collective action of social actors with veto power (Fourcade-Gourinchas and Babb 2002; Kurtz 2004). In the case of Latin America, the coalitions between interest groups and state policymakers involved in the agenda of privatizations were crucial in capturing the main decision-making arenas related to the definition of macroeconomic policy and the implementation of a reform agenda (Schamis 2005). A similar process can be verified in relation to the nomenclature when inventing capitalism without capitalists becomes necessary (Eyal, Szelenyi and Townsley 1998). At the same time, CEE states positioned themselves strategically to reap the fruits of liberalization as zones of low cost production. And since they were relatively weak states, outsider liberalization represented an opportunity to exercise political economic leadership within the European Union (Orenstein 2008). In that sense, domestic mediations fulfilled a crucial role to understand the variety of trajectories, which are much richer than the literature normally suggests.

Chapters

The chapters of the book address many of the issues discussed above. Although no systematic comparisons are carried out, they were conceived in a way such that a comparative understanding of the two regions can be achieved. They collectively emphasize a variety of aspects associated with the transformations within the scope of production and welfare regimes. This brief introduction presents how they approached the institutional legacy, state capacities and the question of how within the context of critical junctures new trajectories can be legitimized. From different perspectives, the chapters analyze the impacts of financial liberalization and how they can be administrated by state regulatory capacities, implying a variety of ramifications concerning national state sovereignty. As we expand below, other chapters also show how investments and innovation patterns determine the insertion of these two regions in the international division of labor, while still others examine the decisive role of public policies sustained by states' capacities. Finally, other analyses examine in detail the recent transformations of political community with the historical trajectories of multiethnic societies in mind, and its effect on expanding the sphere of citizenship. While a set of chapters explore the transformations in the sphere of citizenship, others focus on the transformation of the welfare regime resulting from the commodification of social rights and public policies within the context of market-oriented reforms in the 1990s. They also try to evaluate the degrees of freedom for the return of social protection policies during the last decade and the possible constitution of new welfare regimes. Finally, a last set of chapters shows how the decision-making sphere was colonized by transnational professional communities that were engaged in the competition for hegemony in professional fields and contributed significantly to offer a cognitive and programmatic cohesion to the agenda of macroeconomic reforms.

Joseph Cohen emphasizes how states could mediate financial liberalization's pressures on developing countries, something he compares to the "management of a Faustian bargain." Since the Cold War's end, several major economic policy debates have hinged on whether countries should embrace today's liberal global capital markets. Proponents argued that accessing foreign capital markets provided immense opportunities to contain the widespread systemic financial problems of the 1980s, while allowing countries to build the physical and organizational infrastructure required to emulate the example of the Asian Tigers. International capital's critics often echoed the same kind of distrust expressed by Hilferding or Lenin during international capital's last great heyday in the late nineteenth and early twentieth centuries. They argued that these financial linkages ultimately served to expropriate wealth from the developing world to the world system's core, while keeping the former in a perpetual state of financial exposure that would undercut their policymaking autonomy and keep them peripheral. Cohen argues that this seemingly simple two sided argument is more complex: countries can employ a range of strategies to discourage or co-opt global capital's ability to discipline states. Through the analysis of five behavior patterns – incentivization, intervention, accumulation, coordination and dependence – Cohen offers an excellent approach to study the varieties of national state mediation within the context of financial liberalization. By observing how the CEE and South American countries have adjusted to this model, Cohen emphasizes that CEE is under the umbrella of the European Monetary Union with all the guarantees of macroeconomic stability but also dependency on the framework, where the member countries exercise asymmetric relations to fulfill the rules of membership. On the other hand, the integration of South America does not play a relevant role in the mediation of states with regard to financial markets, if at all. There is no commercial and financial integration in the region that could be compared with CEE. On the contrary, many countries adopted pegged exchange rate mechanisms aimed at providing maximum liquidity and opportunity to rapid exit of financial capital as a reward to attract these capitals.

Still within the approach associated with previous trajectories, David Lane emphasizes the historical aspects of the premarket reform era in CEE that would later play a significant role in the choices that countries adopted during the critical junctures of reforms. Unlike South American societies, the socialist bloc did not participate in the world economic system before 1986, but according to Lane there were already important differences among the socialist countries in terms of economic exchange before the end of the regime. These intrabloc variations have been identified by extensive comparative studies, both in terms of productive and welfare regimes (Feldmann 2006; Bohle and Greskovits 2007; Hacker 2009). Lane, however, takes a different route and shows this based on data relative to foreign direct investments and the contribution of aggregated value in the global production chain. From this point of view, CEE and Latin America are still positioned as part of a periphery – CEE being in a more favorable position in terms of production and export of value-added goods. Nevertheless, by taking into account some country level specificities within every bloc, it is possible to notice that the productive structure of some of them stands out in this zone of dependency, constituting what the author (following the literature of world systems) calls the semi-periphery. The positioning of the countries such as Brazil and Russia, for example, distinguishes them as suppliers of energetic commodities. As a result, they also stand out in trade negotiations within the scope of the Doha Round because of the potential of their domestic market as leverage in negotiations and also due to Russian and Brazilian participation in transnational enterprises – many of them state-owned or partially state-owned.

Within this same comparative approach, José Maurício Domingues builds upon a summary of the theoretical perspectives of dependency to come to the conclusion that there have not been enough significant transformations in the pattern of technological innovation and international insertion of these regions.

On the contrary, recent economic activities indicate a further deepening of the degree of dependency and marginalization. In fact, the economic dimension of CEE and South America, reflected in the gross domestic product (GDP) growth rates, have not translated into the improvement of positions within global competitive system and international division of labour. In that sense, Domingues pays less attention to distinct trajectories in the two regions, thereby providing a more homogeneous view concerning the consequences of recent economic transformations among the two regions.

Despite the rather pessimistic conclusion about significant structural change regarding the relative position of Latin America within the world system, the analysis proposed by Domingues has the advantage of dwelling on a theoretical premise treating development perspectives in terms of center/periphery relations. Throughout the analyses presented in this volume, a conception of center/periphery relations stand out as an underlying theoretical framework to understand how, when and where significant transformations in productive regimes can take place.

To some extent, the contributions of Rainer Kattel and Annalisa Primi overlap some arguments exposed by Lane and Domingues and further enrich the debate on the issue of technological innovation. When Kattel and Primi talk about some paradoxes of the periphery in their chapter focused on innovation policies in Latin America and CEE, they summarize the importance of state capacities in sustaining these policies while at the same time stress that the drive towards innovation is at times limited due to an aspect derived from the peripheral status itself. In other words, the paradox regards the fact that in peripheral areas it is not the lack of innovation efforts, but the fact that they seem to get trapped and do not yield cumulative effects because of lack of intrasector coordination and reduced demand that explains innovation lags. Focusing the differences of trajectories, the authors draw attention to the discontinuities of innovation policies as part of the reform trajectories in which learning, path dependency and cumulativeness affected political dynamics. By emphasizing Brazil and Slovenia as singular cases of sustaining innovation policies that avoided stop-and-go efforts, the authors remind us that the market-oriented reform agenda in these countries had to face the resistance of consolidated domestic policy legacy, whose established capacity was a valuable shield against agenda of reforms sustained by foreign direct investments.

If we consider the approaches employed by authors thus far, it is possible to affirm that the agenda of globalization with market-oriented macroeconomic reforms did not have a converging character. The states took advantage of previous trajectories and state capacities to establish degrees of adaptation to this agenda. Renato Boschi and Flavio Gaitán use the same approach in a more systematic manner, arguing more incisively, however, about the endogenous aspects of development trajectories. Local history, actors and institutions make a difference not only in understanding development, but also in being able to establish lines of comparison between a variety of productive and welfare regimes.

The set of chapters that follows concentrate on a different dimension of development trajectories, namely, that of social inclusion, identity formation, and political rights. They adopt a broad historical perspective in order to describe the construction of citizenship in multiethnic countries, as it is the case of several Baltic and Andean states. In the same perspective that takes into account the role of critical junctures and previous trajectories, two other analyses bring into consideration the impact of local identities in the process of nation building. The first examines the case of conflicting minorities and the enlargement of citizenship rights in Andean countries. By pointing out that the modernization process and national-state building in the Andes were consolidated through land reform, Xavier Albó shows how the indigenous population was incorporated into the sphere of citizenship through the broadening of state capacities in so far as the universal right to vote, universal access to education and the nationalization of natural resources, which have expanded the scope of state action, stifling ethnic differences under the idea of national peasant identity. The critical juncture of this period (the 1950s), influenced by the Mexican Revolution on one hand and by the conception of developmentalism, on the other hand, created the conditions to subsume indigenous movements into the conception of a "peasant society," which symbolically sustained and conferred a social sheen to nation building in Bolivia. The second study examines the process of identity erosion and recreation following the collapse of the Soviet bloc in the CEE region. In the case of the Baltic countries, the main historical element was Russian territorial domination and the attempt to forge a Soviet multinational identity.

At the critical juncture of the experiences of market-oriented reforms in the 1990s, Bolivia, Ecuador and the Baltic states were notoriously affected by the movement of deep deregulation, commodification of public services and social rights – but with different political consequences. While the indigenous peoples in the Andean countries began to abandon – from the 1990s on – the concept of national identity founded on a mestizo/peasant society, in the Baltic countries the non-Russian populations began to recover and develop the repertoire of symbolic belonging to the Western European societies, always in opposition to the legacy of Russia – whose population represents between 30–40 percent of the Baltic countries. In this way, liberalization destabilized a sense of earlier communitarian belonging. Thus, citizenship had to be claimed on the basis of the affirmation of an ethnic original condition.

The discrepancy with the political consequences of these processes is evident. In the Andean countries, the indigenous populations achieved greater political and associative empowerment in their effort to implement constitutional reforms, as occurred in Bolivia. In Baltic countries, the Europeanization of non-Russian "indigenous populations" was consolidated in parallel with successive barriers to access to citizenship for Russian populations, as described by Raivo Vetik's contribution to this volume. While indigenous peoples in the Andes – made vulnerable by the commodification of public services and social rights – were able to lead a countermovement of self-protection through the construction of a new constitutionally recognized polity in Bolivia, the Russian population in the Baltic countries was doubly vulnerable. They suffer more with the rising underemployment in a region with little social protection in relation to European standards, and, at same time, they have to face institutional barriers to access such diminished citizenship rights.

Within the debate on forms of reembedding through institutionalization of citizenship, Krista Lillemets offers the reader a fruitful Polanyian historical analysis which links the recent wave of social demands to the commodification of social relations engendered by market reforms in Brazil. In line with other contributions, which stress the emergence of new welfare regimes (Lautier, 2007; Mesa Lago, 2007; Hacker, 2009) and new developmentalism in Latina America, she identifies the elements of the modality of social protection and autonomous development policies that have been unfolding in Brazil. This modality social protection and new developmentalism is underscored by her description of the distinct *longue durée* of historical trajectory. The paper draws out the conclusion that the extent of freedom in bringing back new protection regimes and development policies is related with the trajectories of commodification of social rights, political and social democratization and the bureaucratic consistency of the institutions sustaining public policies. Thus, in order to understand the trajectory of Brazil, it is necessary to consider the past history and how the reform agenda was translated at the moment of critical junctures.

When put into comparative perspective then in the case of South America, the reform agendas came in response to the debt and inflation problems of the 1980s and therefore had a narrower focus. Comparatively, in the CEE countries, the agenda of market-oriented reforms had a broader scope as it intended to resolve not only macroeconomic problems but was also associated with the construction of democratic institutions – political independence in addition to the construction of market institutions.

In summary, tackling similar problems of adaptation to a market-based context in the case of Baltic countries was made more complicated in light of the implications of recent territorial independence and imminent integration. These multiple challenges of nation building added to the agenda of accelerated integration into the European community and openness to the experiences of institutional reforms advocated by multilateral agencies as the IMF and World Bank produced a spurious elective affinity between political autonomy, economic progress and the agenda of liberalizing reforms. Eyal, Szelenyi and Townley (1998) aptly demonstrated that at stake was a new cultural perception of belonging to the new order and the need to forge a subjectivity based on market rationality. From this standpoint, reforms could also be justified through resort to a cultural individual pedagogical meaning. However, such cultural legitimacy was not spontaneous, homogeneous, or quickly achieved. According to comparative research this was a process of long-term intellectual circulation and production, which finally stabilized in late 1980s (Bockman and Eyal 2002).

Considering the issue of belonging produced by the developments discussed above, the research of György Lengyel and Borbála Göncz presented in this volume adopts a constructivist approach to explore the symbolic and pragmatic aspects of the perception of the process of European integration by Hungarian elites. The aim of these authors is to explore the intensity of supranational bonding within Hungarian elites as a symbolic path of identification.

The authors thus provide an analysis that explains how social groups belonging to political and economic elites with veto power build policy preferences translated through a strong sense of belonging to a transnational community in Europe. With refined empirical research, Lengyel and Göncz provide substance to the translation mechanisms in contexts of critical junctures that we have stressed throughout this volume. At the same time, the authors explore possible changes in economic circumstances that prevent a homogeneous view on the aggregation pattern of group preference.

An opposite trend can be pointed out in the case of regional integration in Latin America, as indicated in a chapter authored by Juliana Erthal. Although her objective is not to analyze the circulation patterns of epistemic communities, the author pinpoints the differences in historical trajectories of institutionalization of European, Andean (Parlandino) and Central American (Parlacen) international parliaments. Unlike the European Parliament which has elected officials and legislative, control and communication powers, its Latin American counterparts (the Parlacen and the Parlandino) have fewer powers and attributions. According to Erthal, a number of issues related to the threats to national security, perceived democratic deficit as a consequence of creating supranational institutions, differences between presidential and parliamentary regimes, all create different incentive structures for the delegation of sovereignty.

Erthal's approach suggests a greater emphasis in historical institutional legacies and state capacities to understand the differences in trajectories of regional integration. Nevertheless, it is important to stress that previous unsuccessful attempts of regional trade integration in Latin America included a development agenda. However, the generation of intellectuals and policymakers that formulated this agenda was excluded from the decision-making process and from intellectual reproduction spaces as a result of their persecution by the military regimes in Latin America. This context of institutional rupture and generational exclusion established the region as a laboratory for cognitive wars.

This Latin American laboratory of epistemological competition is precisely the object of the work presented by Yves Dezalay and Bryant Garth. Through a historical analysis, the authors succeed in describing the institutionalization of professional fields of economics and law and their roles in the period of political and economic opening. Their research clarifies the international dimension of the reproduction of state peerage and the genesis of the international field of state power. The main actors of this scenario belong to a new global hierarchy in which North American economists appear at the apex of the reproduction of prestige in the field, attracting and allocating responsibilities in positions of power. The research of Dezalay and Garth indicates how the international transfer of expertise involves competition between disciplines in search of international credibility as it occurs between law and economics, and also represents a competition between professional networks structured around new hegemonic powers. This perspective has shed light onto the transnational alliance between the association of lawyers in the US and groups defending human rights during the democratic opening in South America. The same happened in the economic field, when orthodox minority fractions of the North American Academy (particularly the Chicago School of Economics) trained several generations of South American economists and transformed the continent in a laboratory for policies that served to reinforce their hegemony inside the field.

Also within this analytical framework that seeks to understand the mechanisms of translation in critical junctures, the chapter authored by Carlos Henrique Santana focuses on the current period of a renewed economic development agenda in Brazil. Through an approach that seeks to contextualize the comparative political economy literature, the author focuses on the role of an internationalized community of economists and attempts to identify (more systematically and within a more limited time span) the patterns of circulation of policymakers in the period of market-oriented reforms and the subsequent moment of resumption of coordinated policies by the state.

Furthermore, when observing the role of history in the delineation of policy options, Santana emphasizes certain state capacities that determined the differences of the reform model adopted in Brazil compared with other countries in South America. In the case of Brazil, such model has ensured a significant amount of flexibility in the resumption of development policies over the past eight years. In this respect, the coordination mechanisms of credit, like public banks and union pension funds, guaranteed a space for circulation of a new cognitive framework that allowed for the translation of a new development agenda.

Finally, the chapter by Fabiano Santos also concentrates on the impact of the political dimension in the production of a new development agenda. As in other chapters of the present book, this author also draws on the notion of trajectory effects to show changes in the content of the postreforms agenda. More specifically, the author addresses the effects of party competition along the capital/labor axis to understand the support for social policies in Brazil. Santos argues that the resumption of the conceptual and historical trajectory of social democracy is useful to understand the Brazilian case as well as to redefine our view of what happens in other parts of the South American continent. In this sense, two results of previous analyses should be remembered. First, it is essential to determine the past history and context of party competition, noting that it is premature and unhelpful to classify governments as populist or demagogic, as the case has been in some recent literature. More specifically, the strategies and rhetoric of the forces on the right of the political spectrum should be considered. In large measure, the Left in one country is not only a result of the societal model developed there, but also of political choices of their liberal opponents. Secondly, it is necessary to observe the public policies and alliances that are built around them. The author notices that policies aimed at benefitting the lower income strata and which are the objects of realignment of loyalties and voting behavior are the hallmark of the social democratic path. Therefore, wherever it occurs, the same historical processes of institutionalized dispute between labor and capital will also be part of the process to some extent.

The present volume assembles a wide range of themes which, without the explicit effort to carry out comparative analyses, constitute an important contribution towards understanding two regions of the capitalist semi-periphery as wide apart as South America and Central Eastern Europe. In so doing, similarities are pointed out in terms of the ways the crucial juncture of the economic reforms of the late twentieth century were undertaken in each context. Creating market institutions both in terms of achieving macroeconomic stability and in terms of establishing patterns of regulation was a common task these countries had to face. However, past trajectories – in particular the geopolitical dimension that characterized the political environment in each case – posed different constraints and challenges. In the South American region, the challenge was that of overcoming strong impositions by multilateral agencies in the wake of a fragile situation of indebtedness and high inflation inherited from the pursuit of an ISI development strategy over time. In the CEE region, the challenge brought about in a sudden way by the collapse of the Soviet bloc was that of recreating nations and creating a market economy almost from scratch. In particular, although the process of de-constructing a strong trajectory of state intervention existed in both regions, privatization and the activities of adaptation to a new economic order were much more dramatic in the latter, given the new impositions brought about by the integration in the European community in a subordinate position.

By contrast, if one thinks about the main axes of the new conjuncture – that of the state, welfare regimes and the nature of the transition itself – it is possible to notice in which direction the challenges for each region seemed to concentrate. For South America, it is certainly in the area of social policies and the creation of new forms of social protection to face historically ingrained inequalities and exclusion that these countries had to move more drastically. Here again, the nature of the transition (in most cases under the aegis of democratic institutions) sets the two regions apart. In South America, it was not until the advent of left parties in the government in the last decade, that policies of social inclusion and the possibility of relying on the internal market as an avenue for economic development became a reality. On the other hand, in the CEE region, commodification of social policies was not only intimately associated with the emergence of democratic institutions, but the transition meant the erosion of the previously existing socialist background of social equality and universal policies. From this point of view, however, these latter countries entered the new era with much better comparative advantages insofar as the degrees of education, qualification and standards of living were concerned.

Last but not least, the analyses carried out here raise some interesting questions concerning the prospects for development and future changes from the perspective of these two regions within the world capitalist system. Differences between countries aside, the semi-peripheral status that they enjoy in a lot of respects is attached to their previous trajectory of developing state capacities over time, having not fallen prey to the operation of market forces alone. In fact, the most fragile situations today primarily concern the countries that, given their pattern of integration in the aftermath of the reforms, became more dependent of and vulnerable to external dynamics. Such a remark concerns not only the financial dimension, but also areas in which endogenous processes and relative degrees of autonomy can be enjoyed and in which the joint operation of political institutions, elites and the capacity to think in terms of a broad project come into play.

Acknowledgments

This volume was the result of an international conference called "Comparative Perspectives of Development Experiences in South America and Eastern Europe." The meeting was held in the Estonian capital (Tallinn) in October 2008, and its program can be found at http://www.evi.ee/lib/south.pdf (accessed 16 January 2012). Organizing such a meeting was not an easy task. Professors from various research centers in Europe, South America and the United States were present at the conference. To bring everyone together, preparations began a year in advance and the meeting would have been unthinkable had it not been for the enthusiasm and support of Andres Kasekamp, professor at the University of Tartu and the director of the Estonian Foreign Policy Institute, which provided the financial support for the conference. Krista Lillemets who was in charge of the intercontinental coordination between researchers in Brazil and Estonia, had a crucial role in organizing and running the meeting. Moreover, we are grateful to Rein Raud, the former rector of the University of Tallinn, for offering us the excellent facilities of the university to conduct the conference.

The support and engagement of Renato Boschi, professor at the Institute of Social and Political Studies (IESP-UERJ), through the institutional involvement of the NEIC, contributed to consolidating the bridge between the researchers of both regions and created the conditions for publishing this book. This volume would not have been possible also without the support of Rainer Kattel, professor of Tallinn Technical University. Our recognition also goes to Thiago Nasser and the editorial team from Anthem Press, who made an invaluable contribution to language revision. Finally, we would like to thank the IESP-UERJ, for supporting the book project.

References

Bockman, Johanna and Gil Eyal. 2002. "Eastern Europe as a laboratory for economic knowledge: The transnational roots of neoliberalism." *American Journal of Sociology* 108.2: 310–52.

Bohle, Dorothee, and Bela Greskovits. 2007. "Neoliberalism, Embedded Neoliberalism and Neocorporatism: Towards Transnational Capitalism in Central-Eastern Europe." *West European Politics* 30.3: 443–66.

Boschi, Renato and Flavio Gaitán. 2008. "Empresas, Capacidades estatales y estrategias de desarrollo en Argentina, Brasil, y Chile." http://neic.iesp.uerj.br/textos/renato-wkshpniteroi.pdf (accessed 16 January 2012).

Drahokoupil, Jan. 2008. "The Investment-Promotion Machines: The Politics of Foreign Direct Investment Promotion in Central and Eastern Europe." *Europe-Asia Studies* 60.2: 197–225.

Eyal, Gil, Ivan Szelenyi and Eleanor Townsley. 1998. *Making Capitalism without Capitalists: Class Formation and Elite Struggles in Post-Communist Central Europe*. London: Verso.

Feldmann, Magnus. 2006. "Emerging Varieties of Capitalism in Transition Countries: Industrial Relations and Wage Bargaining in Estonia and Slovenia." *Comparative Political Studies* 39.7: 829–54.

Fourcade-Gourinchas, Marion and Sarah Babb. 2002. "The rebirth of the liberal creed: Paths to neoliberalism in four countries." *American Journal of Sociology* 108.3: 533–79.

Fourcade-Gourinchas, Marion. 2006. "The construction of a global profession: The transnacionalization of economics." *American Journal of Sociology* 112.1: 145–94.

Frank, Andre G. 1969. *Latin America: Underdevelopment or Revolution*. New York and London: Monthly Review Press.

Hacker, Björn. 2009. "Hybridization instead of Clustering: Transformation Processes of Welfare Policies in Central and Eastern Europe." *Social Policy and Administration* 43.2: 152–69.

Lautier, Bruno. 2007. "Les politiques sociales au Brésil durant le gouvernement de Lula: Aumône d'Etat ou droits sociaux." *Problèmes d'Amérique latine* 63: 51–76.

Kurtz, Marcus. 2004. "Dilemmas of Democracy in the Open Economies – Lessons from Latin America." *World Politics* 56: 262–302.

Kurtz, Marcus and Sarah Brooks. 2008. "Embedding neoliberal reform in Latin America." *World Politics* 60.2: 231–80.

Mesa-Lago, Carmelo. 2007. "Social Security in Latin America – Pension and Health Care Reforms in the Last Quarter Century." *Latin American Research Review* 42.2: 181–201.

Nölke, Andreas and Arjan Vliegenthart. 2009. "Enlarging the Varieties of Capitalism: The Emergence of Dependent Market Economies in East Central Europe." *World Politics* 61.4: 670–702.

Orenstein, Mitchell A. 2008. "Out-liberalizing the EU: Pension privatization in Central and Eastern Europe." *Journal of European Public Policy* 15.6: 899–917.

Riesco, Manuel. 2009. "Latin America: A new developmental welfare state model in the making?" *International Journal of Social Welfare* 18: S22–S36.

Schneider, Ben Ross and David Soskice. 2009. "Inequality in developed countries and Latin America: Coordinated, liberal and hierarchical systems." *Economy and Society* 38.1: 17–52.

Schamis, Hector. 2005. *RE-Forming the State: The Politics of Privatization in Latin America and Europe*. Ann Arbor: University of Michigan Press.

Sikkink, Kathryn. 1991. *Ideas and Institutions: Developmentalism in Brazil and Argentina*. Ithaca, NY: Cornell University Press.

Stark, David and Laszlo Bruszt. 1998. *Postsocialist Pathways: Transforming Politics and Property in East Central Europe*. Cambridge: Cambridge University Press.

Wallerstein, Immanuel. 2004. *World-System Analysis: An Introduction*. London: Duke University Press.

Part I

DEVELOPMENT, MACROECONOMIC POLICIES AND VARIETIES OF CAPITALISM

Chapter 1

POSTSOCIALIST STATES IN THE SYSTEM OF GLOBAL CAPITALISM: A COMPARATIVE PERSPECTIVE

David Lane
University of Cambridge

David Held and Andrew McGrew, in a widely accepted definition, refer to globalization as "the historical process which transforms the spatial organisations of spatial relations and transactions, generating transcontinental or interregional networks of communication."[1] One might distinguish between the economic dimension, made up by transnational and international corporations,[2] and the cultural ideological sphere, embracing a market ideology and a consumerism ethic.[3] This chapter is restricted to the economic dimension of global transformation of the countries of Eastern Europe and the former USSR, and comparisons are made with the advanced Western countries, Latin America and China. After outlining the role the state socialist countries played in the world system, I consider the place of the economies of the postsocialist countries in the world economy. The focus of this chapter is on the extent of economic globalization of countries and their economic corporations. Since 1989, important differences have developed between the postsocialist states with respect to economic penetration and exposure to the world market. Greater participation in the global economy is a characteristic of the Central European states and Estonia; whereas Russia has a hybrid social formation containing elements of state economic control, national capitalism and global capitalism. The outcomes have not fulfilled the expectations of those advocating entry into the world economy. There has been a decline in their relative economic and welfare positions, though some countries have fared worse than others. While there are important differences between the countries of Central Eastern Europe and Latin America, it is concluded that they have many common features distinguishing them from the core capitalist countries and China and Russia. It is contended that some countries of the "semi-periphery" have possibilities for development without being part of the core states of the world system. To substantiate these viewpoints, I evaluate the global presence of the former state socialist societies. My focus is on the transnational companies in a comparative perspective of the core capitalist countries. Transnational influences are also surveyed in terms of foreign investment dependency on foreign company affiliates. Innovation and economic advance is measured by the spending on research and development (R&D). Finally, the effects of transformation on human development are considered.

State Socialism and the World System

The world system orientation conceptualizes the world economy in three main sectors: the hegemonic core (the dominant "Western" capitalist countries), the periphery (developing countries of the South) and the semi-periphery – countries with industrial capacity and national capital outside the capitalist core. The semi-periphery is regarded as a transitionary formation.

State socialist countries were part of the semi-periphery; there were no "socialist economies." Wallerstein claims that the world capitalist economy included the "entire world, including those states ideologically committed to socialism."[4] It is contended that state socialist systems were not socialist modes of production, but interacted with the capitalist world economy. The socialist state, which exhibited some features of socialism (e.g. employment security, comprehensive welfare provision) nevertheless became a major player in capitalist accumulation, which in turn provided a basis for reintegration into the world capitalist system[5] beginning around the 1970s. Following the World War II, such writers argued that international capital had penetrated the socialist bloc and had undermined it.[6] This line of reasoning would lead to grouping the socialist states with those of the dependent countries of the South, such as Latin America. It also carries the implication that the transformation itself was not a qualitative change from socialism to capitalism, but rather a shift between different forms of capitalism.

There are two main economic arguments put forward in support of the thesis of incorporation into the world economy. First, the increasing levels of imports – and consequent high levels of foreign debt – created dependency on the Western capitalist system. Second is the growth of communist transnational corporations, which led to an internal capitalist dynamic. I discuss these in turn and conclude that the Soviet bloc was not part of the world capitalist economy.

From the 1950s to 1985, the socialist countries increased their trade at a higher rate than developed capitalist economies.[7] But these developments do not, as contended by world system theorists, involve a high level of dependency on the world capitalist market. If we disaggregate the trade by different blocs, we find that the state socialist societies were far from being included into the world economic system. Consider data for 1983, before Gorbachev's perestroika policy. The highest share of trade turnover was between the socialist countries themselves, by far. Capitalist countries played a relatively minor role; even for the highest traders with the capitalist world, (Hungary, USSR and the GDR) turnover was a third or under and for most Comecon members it was under 20 percent.[8] The scale of imports from capitalist countries, moreover, was not great. In 1984, imports from nonsocialist countries constituted only 1.39 percent of gross national product for the USSR, 4.2 percent for Hungary and 2.1 percent for Poland[9] – the latter two being the largest importers. The dollar value of imports expressed as an average per capita of the population was only $97.7 for USSR, though a considerable $307.2 for Hungary.[10]

A second development was the growth in debt to Western governments and financial institutions. By 1973, gross indebtedness was some $17.6 billion[11] and had risen to $48.8 billion by 1985.[12] However, it was distributed very unevenly: of the total Eastern European (excluding USSR) debt in convertible currency, Poland accounted for over half ($25.7 billion) and the second largest debtor country was Hungary; both financed their Western imports through loans from the West. Some scholars extrapolating from the example of these two countries come to quite the wrong conclusion. As a whole, the Soviet bloc was not in any serious financial difficulty. Eastern Europe and the USSR's total export earnings covered imports, with a large positive trade balance in 1984 and only a 2 percent deficit in 1985.[13] One could not argue that the Soviet bloc as a whole was in a financial crisis, which precipitated the transformation entailed by perestroika. The Soviet bloc was a relatively independent autonomous economic entity.

A critical component in the globalization of capitalism is the interpenetration of companies between nation-states – the rise of international corporations. For globalization to be a component part of the former state socialist economies in any significant way, one would expect to find the presence of global companies. Studies of developments before 1985, however, show that inflows and outflows of investment capital were not very significant on a world scale.

Outward investment from the state socialist countries went to the advanced capitalist nations and to the Third World. It included the setting up of offices of companies abroad (such as Aeroflot and Moscow Narodny Bank) which were registered in the host states. Carl H. McMillan estimates that by 1983 some 500 companies in OECD countries had equity participation from state companies in the Council for Mutual Economic Assistance (Comecon/ CMEA) countries.[14] But the scale of such investment was small: a total of

$550 million in 1983, and more than half of this was capital in banks and financial companies.[15]

The Third World accounted for approximately a third of outward investment which was directed to resource exploitation and was in small local companies. Even relatively medium sized transnational corporations (TNCs) like Pepsi Cola – 55th in world rank – had a greater share in the world stock of foreign investment than did all the state socialist countries combined. In 1985, the socialist countries (excluding China) accounted for only between 0.1 and 0.2 percent of the world stock of foreign direct investment, whereas IBM alone had 3.32 percent.[16] Moreover, one must take into account the political factor. The socialist economic corporations were controlled by the home governments; they did not operate with the freedom of capitalist firms and they exerted little pressure over governments. Essentially (and what is missed by many world system theorists), economic coordination was bureaucratic in nature – not performed through markets.

Direct foreign investment into the socialist states was relatively low before the mid-1980s. The loans mentioned above were the financial side to the growth of East–West trade agreements which enabled the exchange of licenses and designs and coproduction ventures (usually Western firms providing key components).[17] But there were few transnational corporations in the socialist countries. Until 1975, only five joint ventures had been established between enterprises in the Comecon countries and the West.[18]

However, there were already important differences between the socialist countries. Poland and Hungary had small but significant Western investments from the 1970s.[19] By 1986, Hungary had given enterprises the right – with relatively few restrictions – to engage in foreign trade. The object of the reforms was "…a fuller integration of the national economy in the world economy."[20] In Poland 695 foreign enterprises were in operation by 1986.[21] They were, however, a relatively small contribution to the economy; such enterprises accounted for about 1 percent of sales even in 1987 and employment was only 0.4 percent of the total.[22]

In the USSR, strong controls were exercised over foreign companies; some (such as Pepsi Cola and Fiat) were given licenses to produce under government control and there were limitations on the foreign owners. Only in the mid-1980s did the government encourage foreign direct investment (FDI), and under Gorbachev, liberalization of trade took place, special areas of joint entrepreneurship were established and free economic zones were set up – though they were not very successful.[23]

Moreover, they were not dependent on the world capitalist system in the same way as were Latin American countries which had a long and continuous history of European and American investment (as well as their own indigenous entrepreneurs and land owners). The state socialist semi-periphery was a relatively independent autonomous economic entity not closely linked to – let alone integrated into – the world economic system. Superstructural institutions (such as ideology and a dominant communist party) are beyond the scope of this chapter, but they too were not supportive of capitalistic market forms of accumulation. The centrally directed system, which operated on a country level as well as regionally through Comecon, greatly limited the extent of interaction with the world capitalist economy. Hence, the context in which capital accumulation occurred was quite different from that of modern capitalism. A qualitative shock, a transformation, was required to push the state socialist societies into the world system. This came with the reform program of Gorbachev.

Gorbachev recognized the importance of the world economy. "The world economy is a single organism, and no state, whatever its social system or economic status, can normally develop outside of it… This places on the agenda the need [for]…a new structure of the international division of labor."[24] Exclusion from the global economy, Gorbachev contended, had a detrimental effect on the development of the USSR and the socialist bloc.[25] He had no doubts that the USSR should (and would) join the core nations of capitalism, returning to its European home.

The Consequences of Reform: The Shift to a Global Economy

After 1989, the move to markets and private property strongly impacted on the shape of foreign trade, foreign investment and the place of the postcommunist countries in the world global order. The global dimension of change is usually regarded positively as part of the victory of liberalism and democracy. In this perspective, globalization empowers people through the development of wealth, communications (travel, networks) and culture. Others contest this judgment and contend that globalization has negative connotations. Global corporations and political organizations disempower individuals and weaken the responsibility of states because the processes of government – previously answerable to polyarchic interests – have been superseded by global (and nonaccountable) decision making by transnational organizations. Asymmetric relationships develop between the core industrialized and militarized countries and the periphery.

The reformed Central and Eastern European countries (CEECs) of the former socialist bloc have joined the world economic system through their membership of the European Union (EU). In doing so, they have become absorbed into the economic mechanisms dominated by the hegemonic old member states of the EU. The countries of the CIS, while moving towards the world economic system, have remained in many respects in the semi-periphery. They now share some of the economic features of the Latin American countries. Putin, Medvedev and others claim that Russia has not only survived, but is now sufficiently strong to be considered as one of the world's leading states and economies. I will argue below that, on the contrary, Russia's power (unlike that of China) has declined and the economy has inherent weaknesses which preclude it from becoming a major world power – at least in the foreseeable future.

Following the collapse of Comecon and the opening of markets to the West, capital flowed to the former state socialist societies. However, in comparison with advanced countries of the West, such flows were relatively small. As the amount of FDI can vary greatly from year to year, reflecting foreign purchases or investments of a "one off" nature, the European Bank for Reconstruction and Development (EBRD) has aggregated the inflows over the period of transformation (1989 to 2005).[26] The average for the CEECs was $2,714 per capita; for the Czech Republic the sum came to $5,000. For the CIS states, the average was only $643 per head. The FDI stock in 2006 for Russia came to $197.6 billion – by comparison, for China it was $292.6 billion; this places Russia just above Ireland which had a stock of $179.0 billion, and China is just below Italy which had $294.8 billion. Western European countries are in a different league: the comparable figure for Germany is $502.3 billion and UK $1,135.3 billion.[27] These figures represent purchases of assets in the host countries as well as capital investments in private companies. To what extent then, did the privatization of companies in the postsocialist countries lead to the growth of corporations having a world ranking?

The economic power of capitalist companies is evaluated in two ways: by measuring their revenue and by their market valuation. On the basis of these measures, the postsocialist countries have very low rankings. *Fortune* magazine publishes a list which is based on revenue.[28] This list has the advantage of including 500 companies not quoted on the stock exchange (and therefore having no market valuation). In the July 2008 edition (data for March 2008)[29] of the *Fortune* 500 top global companies, the United States has 153 companies followed by Japan with 64; France (38) and Germany (39) were also significant and in Latin America, there were just 10 companies divided equally between Mexico and Brazil. The only postsocialist country to have any significant number of companies is China with 29. Russia had only five, four in the energy sector and one bank; the postcommunist countries in the EU had only one representative: Poland with one company. The total revenue and profits of these companies is relatively small in comparison to the top Western corporations. Gazprom – the highest postcommunist earner – had a smaller profit than Exxon Mobil, though a much higher proportion of its revenues, in 2008.

A similar picture appears when we consider companies by market value.[30] The *Financial Times* global 500 allocates companies to a parent country on the basis of "incorporation, stock market listing and market perception." On this basis, in 2008, there were 169 companies with American ownership, followed by UK with 35, Japan with 39 and the postsocialist countries including China and Russia with 25 and 13 respectively; of the EU postsocialist member states, Poland had 2 and Czech Republic 1. The whole of Latin America had 17: 11 from Brazil, 4 from Mexico and one each from Argentina and Chile.[31]

The sum of revenues earned by companies in the top 500 globally for USA, UK, China, Russia, Brazil and Poland is shown in Figure 1.1. Data here illustrate the vast qualitative gap between the USA and Russia and China. In terms of market value, these data put in perspective the economic wealth of the two major postcommunist countries; in terms of revenue, the companies in the United States earned 31 times more than Russian ones. In this respect, Russia is comparable to a country like Spain. The postsocialist new EU member states (as illustrated by Poland) hardly come into the picture. Brazil is comparable in company earnings to Russia.

Even with reservations about inadequacies in the data bases, the evidence shows quite conclusively that the economic power of Russia and China, as measured by the presence of large scale companies, is at a lower level than the advanced Western states – particularly the USA. China is an emerging

Figure 1.1. Total revenue in top 500 world companies located in the USA, the UK, China, Russia, Brazil and Poland (2008)

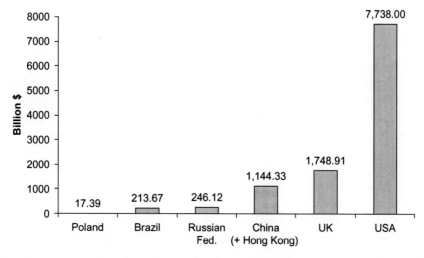

Note: Earnings of companies in the world top 500 as published by *Fortune* magazine, 2008. http://money.cnn.com/magazines/fortune/global500/2008/countries/US.html (accessed 13 September 2008). Calculated by author.

power and has a stronger profile in terms of economic sectors with Russia being limited to companies in the primary sectors – oil and gas and materials – and is particularly lacking in high-tech industries. The countries of CEE and Latin America (with exception of Brazil, which is more comparable to Russia) form a separate grouping outside the core capitalist countries, having an insignificant number of large nationally based global companies.

The Distribution of Transnational Companies

A crucial feature of the relationship a country has to the world economic system is the extent to which its economy is penetrated by foreign corporations. TNCs are a major economic instrument of international business and are constituted of parent enterprises and foreign affiliates.[32] The top 100 companies (ranked by foreign assets) include only those with affiliates in majority ownership.[33] In 2005, they accounted for 10 percent, 17 percent and 13 percent respectively of foreign assets, sales and employment of all TNCs.[34] Eighty-four of the companies have headquarters in the EU, Japan and the USA – the largest cluster of which is the USA with 24 corporations. The TNCs have immense economic (and consequently political) power. In 2005, 54.5 percent of the assets of the world's 100 largest TNCs were located outside the home of the corporation, as were 55.5 percent of sales and 53.1 percent of their employees.[35] Profits, of course, were repatriated to the owners in the home countries and thus wealth was transferred to the hegemonic states.

The companies formed after the collapse of state socialism have little presence in the world of such transnational companies. In the United Nations Conference on Trade and Development (UNCTAD) *World Investment Report 2007*, there is not one former European communist country in the top 100 nonfinancial companies. China also has no company, though Hong Kong has one (Jardine Matheson Holdings Ltd) in 97th place.[36] In the whole of Latin America, there was only one company: Cemex Sab De CV from Mexico, ranked 63rd.[37] Even if one considers companies only from developing countries (in which Latin America is included), there are only 4 in the top 100, all from Mexico (three of which are food companies and one metal products); in this grouping China has only 5.[38] In the top 100 companies by geographical spread, Lukoil is the only European postsocialist country, ranked 90th with affiliates in 19 host countries. It is followed by the Lenovo group from China, ranked 94th with affiliates in 15 countries; the only Latin American country with a company was, again, Mexico's Cemex SA with 35 affiliates. The spread of these countries is not very imposing: Royal Dutch/Shell (UK and Netherlands), ranked second, has 96 affiliates.[39]

A similar situation is found for TNCs: of the top 50 (ranked by geographical spread, which essentially is a measure of the number of foreign affiliates), there is only one communist or postcommunist country – China – with the Bank of China occupying 40th place.[40] The Latin American countries did not have any companies in this category.

These data would confirm the earlier findings: the dominant financial and nonfinancial companies, by number of foreign affiliates and global reach are dominated by the USA and the leading Western European countries. China, Russia, Brazil and Mexico have some presence, though this is relatively small in comparison to the core industrial and Western states.

Affiliates and Global Reach

A second measure of economic dependence is the extent to which companies in a country are owned by foreigners. The growth of capitalism has led to foreign affiliates[41] playing a particularly significant role in the economies of the postcommunist countries in the EU. Table 1.1 details the number of foreign affiliates in terms of the postsocialist, some Latin American and other countries. There are over 71,000 in the Czech Republic alone. As one would expect (given the much lower level of foreign direct investment noted above) in the CIS countries, foreign ownership is much less: of the 10,782 firms, 4,004 are in Kyrgyzstan (data only available for 1998); as of 2004, Russia has 1,176 firms, Belarus has 52 affiliates and Ukraine with only a few hundred. Given the larger size of its economy, Brazil (with 3,549 firms) has relatively few foreign affiliates. Mexico is also exceptional, having attracted many American companies through the North American Free Trade (NAFTA) agreements. China seems a special case, hosting approximately a third of all foreign affiliates of TNCs on a world scale. As China has a small share of world inward investment (2 percent in 2006), these foreign affiliates must be small in size.

Figure 1.2 brings out the significant differences between the areas of the CEECs, CIS and South America. The new member states possess an enormous number of foreign affiliates; South America has even fewer than the CIS. Proximity to the USA and membership of NAFTA accounts for the much larger number of foreign owned companies in Central America, in which Mexico accounts for nearly 90 percent of the affiliates. The breaking down of national borders, through membership of economic organizations such as the EU and NAFTA, encourages the spread of affiliates.

Transnational companies themselves vary in the extent to which they have foreign exposure and global reach. The Transnationality Index (TNI) of a company is the average of three ratios: foreign assets to total assets, foreign sales

Table 1.1. Number of foreign affiliates in postcommunist countries with comparisons to other countries (2006 or latest available year)

New EU members	Foreign affiliates*
Czech Rep. (1999)	71,385***
Hungary	26,019
Poland	14,469
Slovakia	2,780
Slovenia (2000)	1,617
Lithuania	2,877
Latvia	603
Estonia	2,858
Other former communist countries	
Bulgaria (2000)	7,153
Albania	16
Romania (2002)	89,911**
Croatia	2,532
CIS total	10,782
Of which:	
Belarus	52
Ukraine	367
Russia	1,176
Kazakhstan	1,837
Kyrgyzstan (1998)	4,004
Moldova	2,670
Latin America	
Brazil	3,549
Argentina	1,558
Mexico	25,708
Others	
USA (2002)	24,607
Turkey	14,955
UK	13,667
China (excluding Hong Kong)	280,000
World Total	777,647

Source: UNCTAD, *World Investment Report 2007* (New York and Geneva: United Nations, 2007), 217–18. Data based on national sources.
Note: *Number of foreign affiliates in the economy shown. **These figures appear abnormally high, but are given in the source. ***The high figure for parent corporations in Czech Republic probably accounted for by splitting of former Czechoslovakia; of this figure 53,775 are fully owned foreign affiliates.

Figure 1.2. Affiliates of foreign corporations: South America, EU new member states and CIS

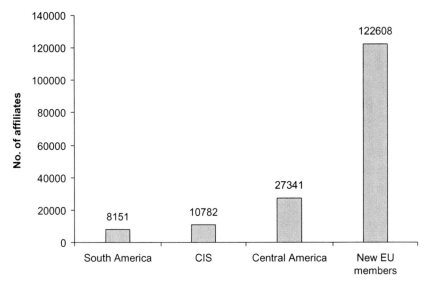

Source: UNCTAD, *World Investment Report 2007*, 217–18.

to total sales and foreign employment to total employment. Of the top 100 companies, those located in Japan had the lowest TNI in 2003 (42.8), those in the USA 45.8, while smaller European countries had higher exposures: Britain was 69.2 and "small European countries" 72.2.[42] The top TNCs in Southeast Europe and the CIS are below the averages cited above, being only 36.6. Their global spread is much less.[43] The average for a company like Lukoil in 2004 was only 37.8 (most derived from its foreign sales) and Norilsk Nickel's index was 32.3.[44] In 2005, the top company ranked by foreign assets, General Electric, had a TNI of 50.1, and the number two world company – Vodafone – 82.4.[45] Clearly such companies were much more dependent for sales and profits abroad than the small TNIs of the postsocialist countries. Repatriated profits play an important role in sustaining the wealth of large corporations. The postsocialist countries have entered the core of industrialized nations, but on different terms to the dominant countries. The Latin American countries, as well as the former socialist countries, accrue relatively little in the form of repatriated profits.

These data show that the expectations of those reformers who conceived of integration into the world economy have been fulfilled to some extent. The new EU members and China have certainly attracted investment from foreign corporations and have an even larger number of foreign affiliates than many established Western capitalist countries. The large numbers of take-overs has led to a growing preponderance of foreign companies in some of the Central European states, though not so in the CIS and even in Latin America (Mexico excepted). In all the postcommunist countries, there has been a lack of capacity to form large capitalist companies able to complete in the world economic system. The only exception is a small number of Russian companies exploiting natural resources (detailed below). Like the Latin American countries, the new EU member states have been integrated into the world economic system; it would be perverse to argue that membership of the EU does not confer core status on a country. But they are not equal members of the core nations.

While traditionally the core refers to the dominant European countries (and USA) and the periphery to the South, changes in the production chain involving the spread of manufacturing through outsourcing have led to differentiation within the capitalist core. Namely, the emergence of a hegemonic bloc (USA, Japan, Germany and UK) among the core countries and others (the new members of the EU among them), which constitute a subordinate group. The CIS countries have remained on its semi-periphery. This becomes clearer when we shift the focus from companies to consider the exposure of the postsocialist countries to global influence.

Globalization of the Postsocialist Countries

The global reach of corporations impacts on countries differentially. The TNI for a country measures the extent to which its economy is subject to foreign influence. It is calculated as the average of four ratios: FDI inflows as a percentage of gross fixed capital formation for the past three years; FDI inward stocks as a percentage of gross domestic product (GDP) in a given year; value added of foreign affiliates as a percentage of GDP in a given year; and employment of foreign affiliates as a percentage of total employment in a given year. For a country, a high index indicates a significant economic dependence on foreign companies. In 2004, the average for all developed countries was 24. There is a great range between the exposure of developed economies: lowest was Japan with an index of just 1, the USA had a low index (6), while the UK had one of the highest of the core countries (47). As one might expect from the earlier discussion, the new postcommunist members of the EU have very high exposures: Estonia 47, Bulgaria 39.6, Slovakia 35.4, Hungary 32.8 and Czech Republic 27. Russia had a fairly low exposure of 12 (though in 2002 it was 18 due to the disproportionate contribution of FDI stock as a percentage of GDP in that year); Ukraine 14 and Belarus was only 5, making it one of the lowest in the world. China also had a low ratio, only 8.[46] Comparisons between EU new member states, CIS and Southern America are shown on Figure 1.3. (Countries are selected as not all countries are given in the source.) The new member states have very high foreign penetration. With the exception of Chile, Latin America is higher than the CIS and China, though

Figure 1.3. Transnationality Indexes for selected EU new members, CIS, China and Latin America (2004)

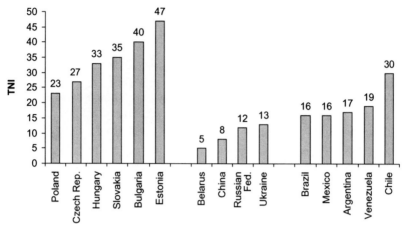

Source: UNCTAD, *World Investment Report 2007*, 13.

foreign penetration and dependency is far less than in the postsocialist new EU member states.

The international division of labor gives rise to specialization in different types of production, which in turn shape the occupational structure and source of foreign earnings. Figure 1.4 depicts the types of exports (primary,

Figure 1.4. Structure of exports, selected countries by sector (2004)

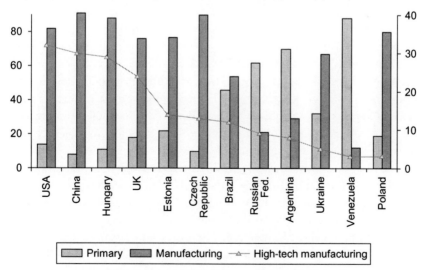

Source: UNDP, *Human Development Report 2006* (New York: Palgrave Macmillan, 2006), 339.
Note: Primary and manufacturing measured on left axis (percent), high-tech exports (percent of manufactured exports) measured on right axis.

manufacturing and high-tech manufacturing) of selected postsocialist, Latin American countries and, for comparison, the USA, UK and China. The countries are arranged by the weight of high-tech exports (the line graph with the axis on the right).

Study of Figure 1.4 illustrates the significantly different trading profiles of the postsocialist countries compared to those of the leading capitalist states. It brings out the asymmetric relationship of the type of exports between the postcommunist countries and UK and USA. Russia has a particularly skewed distribution of exports, its energy sector exports accounting for 62 percent of merchandise exports in 2004.

The "high-tech" component in manufactured exports is extremely low for all the CEECs, except for Hungary. By value in the period 2002–3, Hungary's top exports were in the commodity groups of: telecom equipment (12.1 percent), combustion piston engines (9.3 percent), automatic data processing equipment (5.6 percent), and motor vehicles (3.9 percent). These were derived mainly from foreign companies hosted in Hungary and were relatively small in scale; its telecom equipment, for example, only accounted for some 2.13 percent of world output.[47] By comparison, the USA's production was in high-tech commodities: 17 percent of the world's transistors and valves and 36 percent of aircraft; the UK produced 4.7 percent of the world's passenger vehicles and 9 percent of pharmaceutical products.[48] The only major industrial postsocialist power is China. Eight percent of its exports are in automatic data processing equipment, 6.3 percent in telecom equipment, 4.5 percent in office machinery, 3.53 in toys and sporting goods and 3.3 percent in footwear. Importantly, automatic data processing equipment came to 15.56 percent of world exports, and telecom equipment 11 percent.[49] Russia's top three exports in terms of value (2003–4) were: crude petroleum (27 percent), natural gas (14 percent) and "special transactions" (arms) at 12 percent. For Latin American countries, primary products are a major component of exports and they have relatively low shares of high technology products. Brazil's most important exports (in value terms) were seeds and soft fixed oils, iron ore and meat. Chile's were copper, base metals, and fruit, and for Venezuela: crude petroleum, aluminum and pig iron.[50]

The conclusion to be drawn from this analysis is that – with the notable exception of China and Hungary – the postsocialist societies have entered the global system, but they have joined the Latin American countries at the lower value added place in the world production chain. An important difference between the EU new member states and Latin American ones is that the former produces and exports more manufactured goods. CIS members, on their turn, are less integrated into the world economy; they have relatively less foreign direct investment (and hence fewer foreign companies) and their exports are not only in low-tech manufacturing but in primary products – timber, ores, minerals and particularly energy. Russia is exceptional as a major energy exporting country.

Intellectual Capital

An important determinant of the type of economic production is the level of intellectual capital. This gives rise to invention and, consequently, ownership of intellectual property through patents. One expectation of optimistic reformers of state socialism, made explicit by Gorbachev and Castells, was that entry of the USSR to the world economy would speed up the process of innovation and development. This has not happened. The advanced Western states (particularly the USA and Japan) dominate R&D – and therefore intellectual property.

The World Intellectual Property Organization (WIPO) collects national data on patent registration which may be used as one index to compare innovation in different countries. (Patent registration is a complex subject – only one index is utilized here which I believe is indicative of trends.) In 2006, patent applicants from Japan, the United States of America, the Republic of Korea and Germany accounted for 76 percent

Figure 1.5. Patent filings by country of origin (2006): Core countries, new EU members and South America

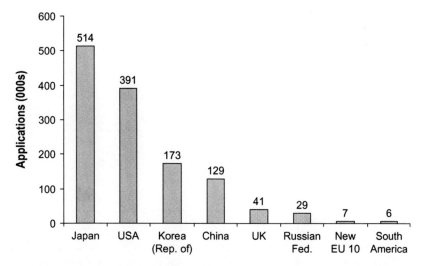

Source: IPSO, *World Patent Report 2008*, 62–4. Online: www.wipo.int/export/sites/ipstats/en/statistics/patents (accessed 22 Sept 2008).
Note: Filings by country of origin in 2006.

of total world patent filings.[51] The only significant other player was China with 7.3 percent of filings in 2006. Figure 1.5 illustrates (for comparative purposes) the shares of Japan, USA, UK, Korea, China, the 10 new postsocialist EU member states and South America. The latter two groupings are relatively similar in total, though Brazil accounts for four fifths of South American patents.

R&D investment, which underpins technical advancement and innovation, again is most uneven on a world basis. In Figure 1.6, the total expenditure on R&D by county and groups of countries (EU new members and South America) and the proportion of GDP on average spent of R&D between 2000 and 2004. The USA greatly outranks the remainder (though Japan, not shown here, is also a leading player.) The world's top ten countries account for 86.9 percent of world R&D.[52] The postcommunist and Latin American countries are in a completely different league than the Western major powers. To bring home the significance of the differences: the Ford Motor company spent $7.2 billion on development R&D, whereas the total for the Russian Federation was $4.3 billion – the same as Volkswagen. Poland spent $1.1 billion –

Figure 1.6. R&D: Selected states, South America and EU new members

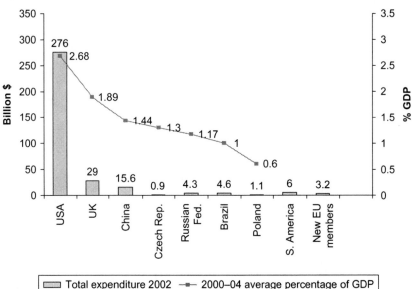

Sources: Total expenditure on R&D figures are drawn from UNCTAD, *World Investment Report 2005* (Geneva and New York: United Nations, 2005), 105, 267–8. Percentage of GDP figures are drawn from the World Bank, *2007 World Development Indicators* (Washington DC: World Bank, 2007), 308–10.
Note: GDP on right-hand axis, total expenditure on left-hand axis.

about half that of Hitachi.[53] As the largest companies are located in the Western countries, it is suggested that they will dominate R&D spending. Of the 700 largest R&D spending firms, 296 are located in the USA and account for 42 percent of the spending, followed by Japan (22 percent), and Germany (7.6 percent).[54] South American spending is higher than that of the EU postsocialist new members; again Russia and Brazil are at roughly the same level.

We might conclude that the core industrial states of the world system not only own and control its major financial and nonfinancial companies, but also dominate R&D which – through patenting – gives ownership and control of intellectual property. The postsocialist countries and South America have a similar profile, poles apart from the core states.

The Impact on Human Development

In the study of economic trends above, I concluded that the state socialist societies have entered the world economic system – though with different economic consequences. We now consider how the economic changes have influenced human development. It might be contended that human development (the well-being of the population) might not be causally connected to the differences in economic endowments and developments noted above. The benefits of membership of the world economic system might accrue equally to its members.

Human development trends are captured by the Human Development Index (HDI) constructed by the United Nations Development Programme (UNDP). The index is a composite measure of life expectancy at birth, adult literacy, mean years of schooling and real purchasing power (at PPP).[55] The index ranks all the countries in the world, the highest having a ranking of 1. At the start of the transformation process in 1990, all the European socialist countries (except Romania) were in the "high human development category" – comprising 53 countries. Czechoslovakia, ranked 27, followed by Hungary at 30 and by the USSR at 31, had the highest levels of human development among socialist countries. (In 1987, the German Democratic Republic (GDR) had the highest score of 15, when the UK had an index of 17.) It will be remembered that at this time, the USSR included many rural undeveloped republics of Central Asia, and the rankings of the European republics (the Baltic states and the Russian Federation) would certainly be higher than 31. Non-European socialist countries were in the medium development echelon: Cuba 62, North Korea 74 and China 82. The Latin American states were clustered below the European socialist states, the highest ranking being: Uruguay 32, Chile 38 and Costa Rica 40, followed by Argentina 43, Venezuela 44 and Mexico at 45; Brazil's score was 60.

Figure 1.7a. Human Development Indexes: Postsocialist and Latin American countries, original rankings (1990 and 2005)

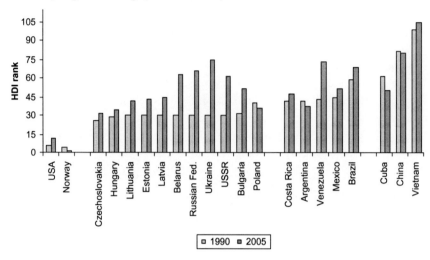

Figure 1.7b. Human Development Indexes: Postsocialist and Latin American countries, adjusted HDI ratios (1990 and 2005)

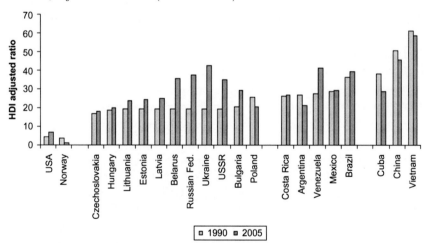

Sources: UNDP, *Human Development Report 1991* (New York and Oxford: Oxford University Press, 1991), 119–21; UNDP, *Human Development Report 2007/2008*. Online: http//hdr.undp.org/en/media/hdr_20072008 (accessed 13 September 2008).
Notes: There were a total of 160 ranked states for 1990, 177 for 2005. The rank for Czechoslovakia in 1990 is replaced by that of the Czech Republic in 2005. The index for USSR in 2005 is an aggregate of former republics.

How then did the transformation process affect human development? Did the post-Soviet European countries close the gap on the advanced capitalist states? Figure 1.7a compares the rankings of the former state socialist societies to other states (including Latin American ones) in 1990 and 2005. The countries of the former USSR have suffered a considerable relative decline in levels of human development. The USSR ranked 31 in 1990, yet the republics of the former USSR had fallen to an average of 83 in 2006. The Central Asian republics and Ukraine all had positions lower than 60 (Ukraine, 78 and Tajikistan, 122). In 2006, the Russian Federation was ranked at 67 and Belarus 64. Compared to their relative position in 1990, only Estonia and Lithuania had survived relatively well – though below the previous USSR ranking. Bearing in mind that the Baltic states had the highest levels in the USSR, one might charitably conclude that they just maintained their relative position. The Caucasus has also fallen well below even the level of the Russian Federation; Armenia in 2006 was ranked 83 (just below Grenada) and Georgia 96 (just below Paraguay). Georgia had a particularly significant decline, as it was one of the most developed republics in the USSR. Poland had risen slightly from 41 to 37, whereas the CEECs had fallen – Hungary from 30 to 36. With the exception of Argentina which had risen from 43 to 38, the Latin American countries had also fallen in their rankings, particularly Venezuela from 44 to 74 and Brazil from 59 to 70.

While these rankings show that neither the post–state socialist nor the Latin American countries had risen, one might object that there is an in-built bias in the statistics as the number of country units increased between the two dates. In order to adjust for this problem, Figure 1.7b shows the rankings converted into ratios (i.e. 1990/160 × 100; 2005/177 × 100). This correction makes no difference to the relative rise and fall of the rankings. The core Western industrialized countries constitute those with the highest human development scores; of the top 20, all are Western and Northern European countries plus Japan, USA, Canada, New Zealand and Australia. The new EU member states fall below these levels and have not reduced the gap in any significant way. The post-USSR European societies have fallen in rankings and as of 2005, are similar in profile to those of Latin America.

Conclusions

Unlike the societies of Latin America, state socialist societies before 1986 were not part of the world economic system. At best, only two European countries (Poland and Hungary) had significant links with it but were not dependent on it. Transnational corporations played no role in the economies of state socialism. Economic coordination was bureaucratic, and was not conducted through market exchange.

Following the demise of the socialist system, the newly constituted capitalist countries have developed different economic structures. Global capitalism has made greater progress in the new member states of the EU (and China) than in the CIS. The former are much more closely integrated into the world system of trade and production; they have become part of the global division of labor. This is illustrated by the greater globalization of production through inward FDI and the hosting of foreign companies. Czech Republic, Hungary and Estonia are highly dependent on foreign direct investment for capital formation, and their economies are substantially penetrated by foreign capital. They are becoming integrated into the economies of old EU states on the terms of the latter. They are bound to the political economy of the EU of which – while enjoying its freedom of movement – they are likely to remain relatively poorer members. While the level of human development has improved somewhat in absolute terms, the relative position of these countries in relation to the core world states has not.

The predicted rise in wealth and living standards, as a consequence of a movement into the world economy, has not materialized. Moreover, in many respects the CIS states are not fully incorporated into the world system, as their economies have a high level of state ownership and foreign companies have little presence. Their military and political elites (not discussed in this chapter), unlike those of the new EU member states, are not integrated into those of the Western hegemonic societies, and membership of the EU is not on the political agenda. In many ways they remain in the semi-periphery, though their autonomy from the world system is less than in Soviet times. For the non-EU postsocialist states of the former USSR, movement to the world market system has led to an overall decline in human development; in some cases – Ukraine, Georgia, Kazakhstan and Russia – to a precipitous degree.

Russia must be distinguished from the other European postsocialist societies. It has the largest economy and is the only one with any global economic presence. Russia is becoming a hybrid economy with a large primary exporting sector, and declining manufacturing and agriculture. Its energy sector is integrated into the world economy and significant transnational companies are emerging, though they have a relatively low global reach, and are dependent on sales. Its economic global presence is restricted to a small number of energy companies with few affiliates. In this context, there is an option for a type of national corporatist capitalism – similar to that developed in China – as an alternative to participation in the global economy on the terms of neoliberalism. Though there is a considerable presence of foreign companies in China, its membership in the World Trade Organization (WTO) somewhat limits its trade options. For China and Russia, economic coordination has become a task for the state, rather than markets, in directing resources to support technically advanced industries and research. This provides a base for the notion of "self-determination" and "sovereignty" currently advocated for Russia.[56] The key to successful policy is the correct utilization of economic rents (earned from materials' export industries) for innovation and renewal.

The economies of Latin America share similar characteristics with the postsocialist states. They have one large country (Brazil) that is distinguished from the rest, as Russia is from the European postsocialist states. But both blocs lack a global economic presence comparable to the core industrial countries of capitalism (USA, Japan, Germany and the UK). In the past 20 years, both groups of countries have suffered a relative decline in their ranking in terms of world human development. Again, like all the former state socialist countries, they have a low component of high-tech industries in their export profiles; they are at a qualitatively lower level of research and industrial innovation than the core Western countries. One difference between Latin America and most of the post-Soviet states, particularly in the CIS, is that the latter still retain elements of the state socialist system, particularly a greater role of the state and greater state ownership.

But Latin America and the postsocialist countries cannot be considered to be two homogeneous blocs. Rather, they are composed of different groups of countries, the sizes of Russia and Brazil respectively separate these countries from the others. The postsocialist EU member states have found that the EU gives not only opportunities but also constraints, and limits economic and political choices. In contrast, in Latin America only Mexico is part of a larger institutional area economic association, NAFTA, which is not comparable economically and politically to the EU. While the CEECs are becoming absorbed into the world economic system through the EU (and NATO), Russia and Belarus are moving to a different type of corporate capitalism. For Latin American societies, there is not one alternative model. Mexico is more closely integrated with Canada and the USA through NAFTA. Brazil and Venezuela could possibly constitute part of a separate economic bloc composed of Russia, India and China.

The assumptions of many who advocated entry into the world economy, both before and after the fall of state socialism, is that participation benefits all. Castells's conclusion that the situation of countries in the Soviet bloc prevented development and retarded its members' "fundamental sources of economic and military power"[57] would appear not to have been changed very much after following the fall of the Soviet system. What is lacking in these accounts is recognition that the world economy is composed of a range of states differentiated in terms of economic, political and social resources. The state socialist political economy may have had a braking effect on developments leading to public disenchantment and calls for reform. But other factors (the extent of a market, type of economic endowment, geographical location and the stock of cultural as well as economic capital) also hinder growth and development and limit military power. These are common factors affecting Latin American as well as postsocialist states.

The economic power of the hegemonic core states is perpetuated through their dominant corporations, financial dominance and their high level of development and research as well as military forms of enforcement. The world system approach envisages a polarization of interests between core and periphery. The core countries extend their lead and keep research, design and development, finance and ownership of intellectual and physical property. Their economic power is constitutive of their political hegemony. The quality and quantity of their weapons of mass destruction cannot be matched. The peripheral states provide contract manufacturing as well as the provision of primary and secondary products at the lower end of the production chain; they experience an outflow of profits and labor in return for FDI and manufactured products. There is an asymmetric relationship both economically and politically. As the chief executive of Rolls Royce has put it (though with respect to the UK economy): "It is pretty obvious that if businesses are not from a particular country, and the brand, and the routes to market and the intellectual property and everything else are vested somewhere else, then any decisions that are made about investments and the dis-investments will have a national flavour."[58]

Many nations on the periphery, when confronted with the economic, political and military power of the core states, have little alternative than to accede to their policies. There were some good reasons for the CEECs to join the EU rather than to stay outside it. But some countries (Russia, China, India and Brazil) of the semi-periphery may have more options than assumed by world system theorists and those who envisage a "one world" economy regulated by the hegemonic model of Anglo-American capitalism. The emerging power of the semi-periphery in the form of Brazil, China and India is becoming evident in WTO Doha discussions, at which they have been able to assert their interests against the demands of the core countries. There are divergences as well as convergence in the world economy.[59] The assumptions shared by transitologists and world system theorists that the semi-periphery is a transient category may be mistaken. Whether the CIS states and China remain "transitionary" societies which will eventually become integrated into the world system in the same way as the new EU member states is highly problematic. Undoubtedly, a new type of state corporatist capitalism is developing in China and Russia which is currently lacking in Latin America, outside Cuba and Venezuela.

The semi-periphery may lead to the rise of alternative groupings of states which interact with the core but are not part of it – in the same way as the state socialist societies before their collapse. As evidenced by data on levels of transnationalization, the economies of many countries have production which is local in character, and regional companies and political actors have considerable scope for action independently of the global economy.

Notes and References

1 David Held and Andrew McGrew, "The End of the Old World Order? Globalization and the Prospects for World Order," *Review of International Studies* 24.5 (1998): 220. This might be contrasted with a narrower version of globalization defined as international economic networks operating independently of any country. See Paul Hirst Paul and Grahame Thompson, *Globalization in Question*, 2nd ed. (Oxford: Polity Press, 1999).

2 An international corporation is one with subsidiaries that extend the firm's production beyond the boundary of one country.

3 Leslie Sklair, "The Transnational Capitalist Class and Global Capitalism," *Political Power and Social Theory* 12 (1998): 3.

4 I. Wallerstein, *The Capitalist World Economy* (Cambridge: Cambridge University Press, 1979), 271.

5 Others, such as Christopher Chase-Dunn and Alex Callinicos, point to other forms of integration in the capitalist world economy which may be decisive. To survive, "...global military competition compelled the subordination of production within the USSR to the goal of capital accumulation." A. Callinicos, *The Revenge of History* (Oxford: Polity Press, 1991), 25.

6 Terry Boswell and Christopher Chase-Dunn, *The Spiral of Capitalism and Socialism* (London and Boulder, CO: Lynne Rienner, 2000), 135.

7 The index of turnover in value terms rose some 95 times for Bulgaria, 43 times for Hungary, 49 for GDR, 39 for USSR and 24 times for Poland. For detailed statistics in ten yearly intervals, see *Statisticheski ezhegodnik stran chlenov soveta ekonomicheskoy vzaimomoshchi* (Moscow: Goskomstat, 1988), 339–40.

8 For details, see *Statisticheski ezhegodnik stran chlenov soveta ekonomicheskoy vzaimopomoshchi* (Moscow, 1984), 297.

9 Author's calculations based on *Statisticheski* and GNP data from CIA, *The World Factbook 1986* (Washington DC: US Government Office, 1986), 227.

10 Value of commodities expressed in 1975 dollar prices. Source: "Recent Changes in Europe's Trade," *Economic Bulletin for Europe* 37.4 (1985). Population data, *Statisticheski ezhegodnik* (1998), 16. GNP data derived from *World Factbook 1986*. CIA calculations for per capita income in 1984 are: Hungary, $7,200; Poland, $6,190; USSR, $7,120.

11 Data refer to USSR and Eastern Europe. "The European Economy in 1975," in United Nations, *Economic Survey of Europe in 1975* (New York: United Nations 1975), 144.

12 "Economic commission for Europe," in United Nations, *Economic Survey of Europe in 1985–86* (New York: United Nations, 1986), 255–6.

13 For details of the 1970s see J. Wilczynsky, *The Economics and Politics of East–West Trade* (London: Macmillan, 1969), 382–3. See also the discussion in A. Gunder Frank, *Crisis in the World Economy* (London: Heinemann, 1980), 194–202.

14 There were 116 from the USSR; followed by Hungary with 107, Poland with 102 and Bulgaria with 48. The following companies had investments in foreign

countries, after the collapse of the socialist countries officials in these companies were well placed to procure and deal in foreign assets. For instance, from the USSR, Gosbank had 20 investments, Soyuznefteexport 18, Vneshtorgbank 20, Sovracht 23, Exportles 14, Stankoimport 15, Mashpriborintorg 10 and Soyuzchimexport 12. For a full list see Carl H. McMillan, *Multinationals from the Second World* (London: Macmillan, 1987), 53–5.

15 McMillan, *Multinationals from the Second World*, 43.

16 "Socialist Countries' Enterprises Abroad: New Trends," *CTC Reporter* 24 (Autumn 1987): 18.

17 Again, For details of the 1970s see Wilczynsky, *The Economics and Politics of East–West Trade*, 382–3. See also the discussion in Frank, *Crisis in the World Economy*, 194–202.

18 Data cited in "Socialist countries' enterprises abroad": 22.

19 For data see Leslie Sklair, *Globalisation* (Oxford University Press, 2002), 226.

20 On Hungary, see J. Matonyi, "The Legal Framework for Joint Ventures in Hungary," CTC Reporter 23 (Spring 1987): 52–3. Quoted in Sklair, *Globalisation*, 226.

21 Ireneusz Nawrocki, Ireneusz, "Foreign enterprises in Poland: Ten years of experience," *CTC Reporter* 24 (Autumn 1987): 49.

22 Fifty-three percent of the foreign enterprises employed less than 50 employees and only 5 percent over 500. Nawrocki, ibid.

23 See Sklair, *Globalisation*, 226 and I. Ivanov, "Joint Ventures in the Soviet Union," *CTC Reporter* 23 (Spring 1987): 49–51; "Socialist countries enterprises abroad: New trends," *CTC Reporter* 24 (Autumn 1987): 21.

24 M. Gorbachev, "Address to the United Nations." Cited in Manuel Castells, *The End of Millennium* (Malden and Oxford: Blackwell, 1998), 5.

25 Here he follows writers such as Castells, who has argued that the exclusion of the USSR from world developments in information technology led to stagnation. Manuel Castells, *The End of Millennium*, 9.

26 *Transition Report 2006* (London: EBRD, 2006), 32, 38.

27 UNCTAD, *World Investment Report 2007* (Geneva and New York: United Nations, 2007), 255–7. Hereafter *WIR 2007*.

28 The data include companies that "publish financial data and report part or all of their figures to a government agency."

29 "Top Five Hundred Companies," *Fortune Magazine*, 21 July 2008. http://money. cnn.com/magazines/fortune/global500/2008/countries/Russia.html (accessed 13 September 2008).

30 The *Financial Times'* "Global 500" lists companies which have at least 15 percent of shares in "free float"; it therefore may underestimate some corporations which have very large state or family holdings.

31 *Financial* Times, "Global 500," data for March 2008. http://media.ft.com/cms/8ebb955e (accessed 21 September 2008).

32 A formal definition of a transnational corporation (TNC) is that it is "an incorporated or unincorporated enterprise comprising parent enterprises and their foreign affiliates. A parent enterprise is defined as an enterprise that controls assets of other entities in countries other than its home country, usually by owning a certain equity capital stake." A foreign affiliate is an incorporated or unincorporated enterprise in which an investor, who is a resident in another economy, owns a stake that permits a lasting interest in the management of that enterprise (an equity stake of 10 percent for an incorporated enterprise or its equivalent for an unincorporated enterprise). In *World Investment Report* (*WIR*) subsidiary enterprises, associate enterprises and branches are all referred to

as foreign affiliates or affiliates. UNCTAD, *World Investment Report 2005* (Geneva and New York: United Nations, 2005), 297. Hereafter *WIR 2005*.

33 *WIR 2007*, 231, Note C.

34 Ibid., 24.

35 Ibid., 25.

36 Ibid., 231.

37 Ibid., 230–1, Table A.I.13.

38 Ibid., 233–4, Annex Table A.I.14.

39 Ibid., 236. The geographical spread index is calculated on the basis of the number of foreign affiliates, divided by the total number of affiliates and multiplied by the number of host countries.

40 For a definition see *WIR 2007*, 26. Data on page 235.

41 Definition: "An equity capital stake of 10 percent or more of the ordinary shares or voting power for an incorporated enterprise…is usually considered as the threshold for the control of assets. A foreign affiliate is an…enterprise in which an investor, who is a resident in another economy, owns a stake that permits a lasting interest in the management of that enterprise." The threshold is 10 percent of equity state or equivalent. Definition from *WIR 2005*, 297–8.

42 Ibid., 18.

43 Ibid., 19.

44 *WIR 2007*, Annex Table A, A.I.13.

45 Ibid., 229.

46 Ibid., 13.

47 UNCTAD, *Handbook of Statistics* (Geneva and New York: United Nations, 2005), 168.

48 UNCTAD, *Handbook of Statistics*.

49 Ibid., 163.

50 Ibid., 162, 163, 179.

51 IPSO, *World Patent Report 2008*, 7. www.wipo.int/export/sites/ipstats/en/statistical/patents (accessed 22 September 2008).

52 *WIR 2005*, 105.

53 *WIR 2005*, 120.

54 *WIR 2005*, 121.

55 In the following tables, the issues for 1991 (referring to the year 1990) and 2007/08 (referring to 2005) have been utilized. UNDP, *Human Development Report 1991* (New York and London: Oxford University Press, 1991). Note that later editions have revised some of the rankings as more has data become available. *Human Development Report 2007/2008*. www.hdr.und.org/en/media/HDR_20072008 (accessed 13 September 2008).

56 See the discussion in *Grani globalizatsii* (Moscow: Alpina, 2003), esp. chapter 9, and V. Yu. Surkov, *Osnovnye tendentsii I perspektivy razvitiya sovremennoy Rossii* (Moscow: Sovremennaya gumanitarnaya akademiya, 2006).

57 Castells, *The End Of Millennium*, 43.

58 Sir John Rose, quoted in *Financial Times*, 10/11 February 2007. He then contends that it "was the responsibility of government and industry to provide a clear 'road map' of industrial sectors in which the UK wanted to compete… this had not yet been done."

59 For further discussion see H. Kitschelt, P. Lange, G. Marks and J. D. Stephens, "Convergence and Divergence in Advanced Capitalist Democracies," in H. Kitschelt, P. Lange, G. Marks and J. D. Stephens (eds), *Continuity and Change in Contemporary Capitalism* (Cambridge: Cambridge University Press, 1999), 427–60.

Chapter 2

POLITICS AND DEVELOPMENT: LESSONS FROM LATIN AMERICA

Renato Boschi
Instituto de Estudos Sociais e Políticos, IESP-UERJ

Flavio Gaitán
Universidad de Buenos Aires

Desarrollo es un término de azarosa biografía en América Latina. Sus promesas arrastraron a todos los sectores de la sociedad y de algún modo encendieron uno de los más densos y ricos debates de toda nuestra historia, pero fueron eclipsándose en un horizonte cada vez más esquivo y sus abanderados y seguidores fueron enjaulados por el desencanto.
—Anibal Quijano

Introduction

Since the beginning of the century, the tendency in Latin America has been that of extraordinary ideological turns followed by the reversing of the direction of public policies. Considering the degree of the metamorphosis going on in the states of the region, electoral victories of formulas that proclaimed (in a more or less clear way) their distance from the neoliberal ideology, have taken place in a fairly short period of time with renewed state intervention in the economy.

This turn has given new energy to the discussion of the new public agenda and the key components of the emerging development project being constructed by political scientists and economists. In other words, a new space for politics was opened up. The 1980s was a period of relative freedom for the governments of peripheral countries, given the deep fiscal crisis inherited after the debt crisis and the neoliberal ideological policies. The combination of the renowned Washington Consensus and fiscal constraints were key for governments to carry out a handbook of structural reforms forced, mostly, by short-term emergencies. In recent years, the process of reverting the countries' conditions to carry out their autonomous development pathways has been accelerated. Furthermore, changes in the domestic and global scenario strengthened the freedom and autonomy of politics in national projects.

This geopolitical climate change is essential for the analysis of sociopolitical alternatives for the countries in the region. Contemporary discussions on development alternatives take into account the premises of neoliberal thinking and consider the possibility of carrying out development projects within the framework of a capitalist extended system which is increasingly interdependent and globalized, with a surprising degree of wealth concentration in the axis of the rich countries of the North. Until the crisis of 2008, alternatives were constrained by the fact that capital flows took place mostly between the three subsystems that compose such system: the North American bloc, the European Community and the ensemble of Southeast Asia Pacific countries, led by Japan. Since then, deregulation that affected financial markets in the North paradoxically opened up new avenues for some of the emerging countries of the capitalist semi-periphery, the so-called BRICS (Brazil, Russia, India, China and South Africa) in particular. The new context provides opportunities for endogenous choices as a result of the increased influx of direct foreign investments on one hand, and an enlarged space in international governance as suggested by the role of G20 countries in different arenas, on another hand. Given these changes – both at the domestic and international levels – questions regarding the alternatives available for some countries arise. This is especially prevalent in Latin America which, throughout the twentieth century, had historically shown through a series of interventionist policies within the framework of a model of protectionism and industrialization by import substitution, a reasonable performance indicated by the steady average growth rates in that period despite the absence of redistribution through social policies.

In this paper, we try to focus on the role of institutions and politics in the creation of a new development agenda and its function as a breeding ground for the components of that agenda. First, we consider development to be an endogenous process which takes place within states in the globalized framework of a power struggle vis-à-vis other states, regions and multilateral agencies. In this context, the importance of politics – rather than being diminished – is amplified, since any project aiming to become hegemonic and diffused through epistemic communities must be translated at the national level in the form of laws, regulations and other forms of public policy. Moreover, elites do not lose their strategic importance, and politics retains its fundamental role (Diniz 2008).

We will focus on some general processes taking place in South American countries and Mexico. While differences between countries in the region are quite marked, it is possible to identify similarities in the contemporary socioeconomic changes affecting them. With differences in the degree of intensity and timing of implementation, all countries have gone through a process of transition from protected economies to systems based on the neoclassical paradigm. In recent years, the opposite phenomenon, the shift towards greater state involvement typical of a new development model, is taking place in the region as a whole, with few exceptions. This chapter is organized as follows: first, we will present the theoretical framework of institutional legacies and their impact on the possibilities of implementing the new developmental agenda which is still under construction. Next, we will analyze the role of institutions and the relationship between market and state, or between the public and private sectors. Finally, we will try to draw some conclusions from this recent historical experience of Latin America.

New Development Agenda for Latin America

Concerns about development are not new (Cooper 2005) and represent the quest for favorable conditions to generate the modernization of societal dynamics, which lead to economic progress and social transformation (Ferrer 2001; Stiglitz 2001). In Latin America, studies on development and underdevelopment were stimulated by structuralist thought, through the creation of the Economic Commission for Latin America and Caribbean (ECLAC) in the late forties, and then excluded from the public agenda after the crisis of the interventionist model of import substitution. Nevertheless, during the last decade a remarkable change in the ideological orientation of the vast majority of governments in the region has taken place, partly in response to the economic and legitimacy crisis caused by the neoliberal project. This unforeseen breakthrough revitalized the discussion of key concepts in the field of development studies such as: the role of the state and of economic, political and social actors in socioeconomic projects; the relationship between politics and economics; and the role of institutions in development prospects, among others. In other words, even though it is still taking place, this transformation which started with the election of governments that label themselves as anti-neoliberal and prointerventionists, opened a new era in the long debate on alternative development perspectives that have taken place in Latin America since the postwar period (Bresser Pereira 2006).

Even though the current development model retrieves elements of the ECLAC's poststructuralist discourse (Boschi and Gaitán 2008) it is undoubtedly different and combines the value of state intervention with recognition and observance of the importance of macroeconomic stability, largely because of the specter of the inflationary spiral which the region suffered in the eighties. The notion of stability implies resorting to instruments of exchange control, interest rates and fiscal surplus (or at least balance) as tools in the intended process of economic growth. In open opposition to the neoclassical idea which denies space for the national state, the neodevelopment speech revitalizes the role of the state apparatus as a primary agent of development. The profound crisis that hit the global capitalist system in late 2008 was faced by some of the countries in the region through the adoption of a series of countercyclical measures which were effective in sustaining the level of employment and economic activities as a whole. In other words, facing the crisis required an effective combination of state intervention capabilities and the maintenance of macroeconomic stability (ECLAC 2011a).

This neodevelopmentalist discourse was born out of academic debates as well as historical experience. It grows out of the controversies between the advocates of the neoclassical view, who tended to naturalize the orthodox perspective in terms of the benefits of coordination through the market, emphasizing, at the same time, the thesis that poor growth performance was due to the fact that reforms were not carried out completely. In this context, the new outlook (which is still shaping itself) faces opposition, on one hand from the neoclassical sectors, autistic before the poor results of the neoliberal experiences, and on the other hand, from the radical left who criticizes the supposed continuity of policies. The argument in favor of recovering state capabilities as a development factor is still a matter of controversy in the public debate.

Thus, it is possible to observe a contradiction between a market-friendly perspective – generally associated with economic efficiency and supported by those who defend the rigidity of monetary stability – and a developmentalist tradition – related to the need to recover state capacities – which in orthodox tradition tends to be associated with archaism, protectionism and corruption. The new discourse recognizes the importance of good governance (the role of the state in the promotion of development) but is definitely more limited in this sense than the one held in the classical developmental vision. In particular, the overall state's role in production, central in the old view, is replaced by a mitigated version of the state's presence in strategic sectors combined with the state's function in regulation.

A key aspect of the new agenda is production diversification and expansion of trading markets. There is a growing recognition that the scale of the struggle between countries on global trade is so strong that investment in science and technology[1] becomes necessary not only to put Latin American countries in the path of development but, above all, not to lose the small share that countries in the region have in international trade. International trade is the key variable to consider in assessing the distance of the Latin American countries with respect to those of the economic center. International trade is growing year after year and in spite of the fact that national boundaries still define the scope of intermediation, the importance of trade relations between countries is undeniable. Rodrik (2001, 26) states that "no country has succeeded by turning its back to international trade." If Latin America has historically specialized in the production of agricultural and livestock products – and its participation in these areas was crucial – changes in international trade over the past 35 years led to deep adjustments. During this period, agricultural products went from being 30 percent of world trade to 10 percent. As a result, Latin America's accumulated share of world exports is falling.[2] Two observations are in order: first, the existence of an export boom of commodities can be taken as the reversal of the previous developmental thesis of the structural inequality of exchange terms; second, the built-in technological content in agricultural production leads to reconsider the traditional views on the role of the agro-export sector. Nowadays, growth in production is both related to technological innovations and the expansion of the agricultural frontier in some countries like Brazil, Argentina and Paraguay.

The Brazilian experience under PT administration shows the importance of the state's action in the diversification of the foreign trade. Since 2000, a reversal of the trade deficit has been occurring and was explained in a first stage by the devaluation of the Real (the currency unit) caused by the implementation of a floating exchange rate. In a second stage (and in a fundamental way) after the Real began recovering its value, currency no longer explained the pattern of trade – especially after 2002. Neither has it represented an obstacle in

---

1 Brazil is the country in the region that has made the most progress in institutionalizing its science and technology system. In this process, synergy between state and private sector seem to be a central factor in the successful developmental experiences. In this sense it seems to be an advantage in the Brazilian experience. While in Argentina the government represents 72.7 percent of financing and higher education institutions 3.68 percent leaving a 22.5 percent to companies, in Brazil the government support 44.49 percent of investments in research and development while universities finance 1.61 percent and the remaining 53.89 percent are from the government. In Chile, institutions of higher education represent 17.2 percent of R&D expenditure while government is 33.76 percent. Firms are responsible for 43.72 percent of research investment (RICYT 2010).

2 In 1960 it accounted for 8 percent, in the 1980s it was reduced to less than 6 percent and in 1990 it reached 3.3 percent (Lopez Segrera 1998). Currently, South and Central America have a 3.8 percent share of world exports (WTO 2011). Of that portion, the largest country in the region, Brazil, represents 1.3 percent.

view of more recent overvaluation of the Real in the wake of the 2008 crisis. A better explanation lies in the policies pursued since Lula's administration, particularly those included in the Industrial, Technological and Foreign Trade Program (PITCE) and Growth Acceleration Program (PAC) and more recent industrial policies such as the Program for Productive Development (PDP) implemented by the Brazilian National Development Bank (BNDES) since 2008. In addition, Brazil has a comparative advantage in terms of the strength of some existing local financing institutions (especially public but also private) and differs in this respect from the rest of the countries in the region. Furthermore, as part of its South–South strategy introduced in 2003 by the Lula administration, Brazil strengthened its embassies, mostly in Latin America and Africa, which led to an increase in exports.

Certain branches of knowledge such as biotechnology, threaten the comparative advantages of some traditional exports. The development of financing systems, especially those focusing on production diversification and innovation, are vital to the new developmental strategies. The Brazilian state reform maintained certain clusters of technical excellence. Bureaucratic institutions such as BNDES were kept. This institution, due to its importance, strategic role and the nature of its activities, has no parallel in any other Latin American country. Indeed, currently it plays a much larger role than it did during the country's developmental phase, in particular acting as the agency implementing countercyclical policies in hard times in addition to fostering the competitiveness of the Brazilian capitalist system. In other countries, although in a much smaller scale, a few other development promotion agencies such as the Chilean Corporación para el Fomento de la Producción (CORFO) or Banco de Industria y Comercio Exterior (BICE) and Banco de la Nación, in Argentina, assume a strategic role in creating favorable conditions for private investment.

Finally, social issues are another key factor in the new interventionist models. The social agenda has a significant level of importance in the neodevelopment model. Latin American countries have been unable to combine growth and equality. Between 1970 and 2006, Latin America grew as a whole at an average rate of 3 percent, yet the proportion and number of poor people remains constant. Today, 32 percent of its population is classified as poor (about 180 million) and 12.9 percent as indigent (72 million). This is not to deny that progress has been made. In the last decade, the poverty rate dropped and social policies were expanded (ECLAC 2010, 2011b). One of the main aspects of the post-neoliberal agenda in terms of development challenges in the current globalization phase involves not only economic aspects, but more than ever, its social dimension as well. Essentially, this regards the ability to extend development to society as a whole. This concern for social inclusion appears both in the academic debate and on the neodevelopmental experiences which have expanded the instruments for social intervention. 18 countries in Latin America implemented conditional income transfer programs, such as Programa Oportunidades in Mexico, Bolsa Família in Brazil and Asignación Universal por Hijo in Argentina (ECLAC, 2011c). These programs have substantive consequences, including their impact on poverty and particularly extreme poverty reduction, increase in school enrollment and sanitary control.

Path continuity, legacies and development possibilities

The task of identifying the elements of the new developmental agenda is complex, but it is just part of studying the dynamics of development. One of the main questions in the extensive literature on the subject regards the conditions which allow for the establishment of policies for a new agenda.[3]

Entering a development path involves exploring the possibility of a variety of ways that do not necessarily imply a radical break with the past. It also implies exploring some other previous alternatives which constrain future choices (Boyer 2005; Amable 2003). In the institutionalist perspective,[4] the successful adoption of a new institutional framework depends on the context and historical trajectories that have shaped the national state and institutions in each country. The generation of virtuous cycles of development would be connected – among other factors – to a process of successive stages involving the establishment of institutions capable of reducing transaction costs and increase efficiency (North 1990, 1998; Crouch 2005; Pierson 2004). In the case of Latin America, such an effort implies the consideration of the post–market reforms scenario.

There has been no single model of neoliberal adjustment, but different models of transition to market-oriented economies. Thus, for example, it is possible to identify neoliberalism with state coordination in Chile, a model

---

3 As an ongoing process which reassesses some of the ECLAC's structuralist elements combined with a new direction some of the legacy of the neoclassical paradigms, the identification of the neodevelopmental agenda is not simple but includes new form of social policies, investment in education, science and technology, industry promotion and the diversification of the productive matrix, among other aspects (Boschi and Gaitán 2008).

4 Hall and Taylor (1996) point out the existence of three neoinstitutionalist lines: a first one continues public choice theory emphasizing institutions as rules that define the frame within which strategic interactions will take place as rational actors maximize utilities; a second one refers to the sociology of organizations and seeks to interpret the role of institutions in terms of standards of behavior and, finally a third one that also uses a broader definition and draws attention to the historical trajectories that resulted in certain institutional arrangements (Schmidt 2007).

which disguises complex processes, which are far from the anti-interventionist practice usually associated with this experience.[5] In Argentina, the process of implementation of structural adjustment was radical, based on neoliberal orthodoxy with productive regression. The dismantling of the interventionist model of the postwar period was fairly extensive. Uruguay and Brazil are examples of countries that did not experience extreme neoliberal adjustments; they can be described as having applied a development model with macroeconomic orthodoxy rather than as having followed classic neoliberal model.

It can be said that the countries which advanced less in the implementation of structural reforms are precisely those that were reluctant to copy models and therefore had more freedom to apply a neodevelopment agenda following their own paths (Chang 2007; Kholi 2004). The literature on Asian cases of successful *catching-up* indicate: (i) the importance of relatively autonomous paths, doing away with "handbook" implementations of reforms; (ii) the key role that political components and technical officials can exercise in defining the path for a particular national project; and (iii) the centrality of coordination mechanisms and interest intermediation structures. In fact, some studies, among them Evans (2005, 2008) and Weiss (2003), present the so-called emerging Asian Tigers as examples of the capacity of bureaucracies to create market-oriented elites converging with the capacity of markets in establishing an interface with state bureaucracies, leading their respective trajectories away from predatory processes. If autonomy is an important factor, Latin America seems to be treading this path in the sense of doing without the surveillance of multilateral financial institutions for the first time in a long time, as the cases of Argentina and Brazil in recent times demonstrate.

Identifying institutional legacies and the role of institutional arrangements capable of overcoming vicious cycles commonly regarded as obstacles to development is not a simple task. Actually, although the successful postwar development experiences of Latin American countries show that state institutions played a key role in creating favorable conditions for socioeconomic

---

5 Beneath a neoliberal facade that characterized the Chilean model of development, mechanisms closer to a developmental form of state interventionism operated. State coordination activities included public support for the major export sectors such as fishing, fruit and timber would have been the catalysts for the boom in certain exports. The preservation of state coordination mechanisms, in conjunction with the reorganization of businessmen towards economic reforms gave way to a frame in which even the preservation of the mining sector under the protection of the state and capital control mechanisms operated. Elements that led to a strategy that was able to account for the problems of market failures and space associated with them for a positive state intervention (Kurt 2001).

development, the way in which institutions are ultimately generated and become efficient instruments for state intervention is not clearly delineated. Such a task calls for a distinction between the strictly economic level and political factors that outline – on the whole – the alternatives for future development, together with other variables that assure institutional comparative advantages. In other words, if institutions matter, it is also important to show how they make a difference.

State, markets, and politics as key elements of development models

Nonetheless, the recognition that institutions play a central role is just a starting point for a larger problem: the conditions for the creation and maintenance of such organizations. The task of creating them is not easy (North 1994). Institutions are more than simple rules of the game and procedures that must be followed. As is known, their efficacy depends on the possibility of influencing individual or collective behavior and incorporating values, preferences and expectations of human beings.

In terms of a development platform, the problem concerns the possibility of making government institutions incorporate a developmental orientation in their daily operation, thus triggering a virtuous cycle of growth. In this sense, there must be institutions in place that are capable of effectively dealing with the interaction between individuals and groups with opposing interests. Also, a shared frame of reference among elites is necessary to guarantee productive results in a fairly stable manner over time. Elites with influence over the public agenda have a key role in this process. In this regard, emphasis is put on the political and bureaucratic component (the existence of Weberian bureaucracies with *esprit de corps*) and on coordination between the public and private sectors (the existence of arenas for cooperation between entrepreneurs and the state).

The state's ability to build strong administrative-bureaucratic machinery is vital in creating the path towards development. Cases of more integrated or cohesive patterns of state intervention, such as Brazil and Chile, have relied on the existence of these bureaucratic nuclei. On the other hand, the state must be capable of taking into account interest group actions, both from capital and labor, especially when they pursue conflicting alternatives. Brazil has comparative institutional advantages in this respect: the creation of various councils since President Lula's administrations, as well as preexisting mechanisms of private/public interface opened up a space for a kind of societal corporatism which has proved to be instrumental for the creation of consensus as to development strategies (Boschi 2010).

The instruments for achieving growth targets are varied and the choice of a particular set of instruments involves the mobilization of social support, the formation of coalitions, the diffusion of values favorable to the different options and the organization of collective action in different institutional formats (political parties, business associations and trade unions), among others. The challenge is that of putting the state apparatus in motion to create an inclusive development project (Gourevitch 1986).[6] Having in view that the neodevelopment agenda is being built upon the state structure that survived the aftermath of neoliberal reforms, the task at hand is that of generating consensus around the idea of national development. At this point, consideration must be given to the fact that the neodevelopment agenda is still not the wining choice. The epistemic community identified with the open market theories remains strong and the tendency for these orientations to prevail as a filter in the elites' world views is proportional to the time the corresponding policies were in place. The same would be true of the legacy of state interventionism, affected as it was by the reforms. In some cases, the reversal of this previous trajectory encountered obstacles and it took longer for neoclassical views to take hold.

Disparities in Latin America are remarkable in this regard. In Chile, where neoclassical ideas flourished in an almost unique manner, the coalition government that emerged with the process of democratization (the Concertación de Partidos por la Democracia) was greatly constrained by the social commitment to neoclassical principles. In Brazil, a latecomer to neoliberalism, the full implementation of a neoliberal platform never occurred and expressions of a strong developmental state remain. In Argentina, where the dismantling of state capabilities and productive regime was radical, coalitions were also constrained by neoliberal legacies. The transition to a post-neoliberal project was possible only after the profound crisis which hit the country late in 2001 causing the gross domestic product (GDP) to drop about 20 percent and jacking poverty rates to above 55 percent of population.

In the Brazilian case, even though business elites were among the first to support neoliberalism, the deepening of the developmental model generated sectors more critical to the opening of markets. Later on during Fernando Henrique Cardoso's second government, they adopted a critical position regarding the maintenance of the fundaments of monetary stability: high interest rates, high primary surpluses and mainly, the high tax burden.

---

6 This author argues that cyclical capitalism crises lead to changes of economic policy (laissez-faire, mercantilism, centralized planning, demand stimulation, industrial policies) and that the resulting nature of the state is going to depend not only on those choices but also on the probability these will constitute the dominant model.

Since the Lula government, there seems to be a certain preference for a developmental model centered on the need for productive investment and infrastructure, while simultaneously enhancing stability as a public good (Diniz and Boschi 2007).

As analyzed in detail in Boschi (2008b, 2009) significant differences also exist in the way Latin American parliamentary elites perceive the role of the state in development policies and also in their views regarding the state-market dichotomy. Based on data from a Parliamentary Elites in Latin America survey coordinated by Alcantara (2005) at the University of Salamanca, it becomes clear that there are significant differences in the perception and views of parliamentarians from various countries. Thus, it appears that the Chilean parliamentary elites are more favorable to market regulation (53.4 percent), a position that could be explained by the depth and longevity of the market reforms. In Brazil, the proportion of parliamentarians friendly to market regulation is smaller than the Chilean case (43.3 percent). On the other hand, in Mexico, 57.3 percent of the elites prefer the highest degree of statism and 28.2 percent prefer a high degree of statism, with a total absence of preferences in the promarket category. The data presented in this work is revealing of the almost dichotomous way that choices are framed in the public debate about development alternatives. It is also indicative of the still preliminary nature of a neodevelopmental perspective as a policy preference in the region. The perceptions of potential support coalitions for a development platform based on new forms of state interventionism with different degrees between countries has yet to be constructed, diffused and consolidated (Boschi 2010).

Differences in the perception of elites about the state in each country are stressed in the revealing analysis of Dezalay and Garth (2002, also in this volume) of the contending perceptions of lawyers and economists in the process of Latin American state building. Centered in the Brazilian, Chilean, Argentinean and Mexican cases, the work underlines how the elite fragmentation in Argentina and Mexico led to a less consensual position on the role of the state and a more outward-looking perspective with lower propensity to accumulation of state capacities. On the other hand, Brazil is closer to the Chilean case for reasons ranging from the preservation of a law-based tradition of control of the state apparatus to the progressive creation of institutional capacities of state interventionism. In other words, in the latter cases, the presence of more cohesive elites that took possession of the state apparatus through a tradition of thought linked to the law acted as a deterrent to the projected state minimalist perspective of the economists.

Therefore, with regard to the role of elites, it is necessary to stress the importance of previous visions about the state as instrumental in the diffusion of new prodevelopmental networks of professionals articulated in epistemic communities. Very often, the state versus market polarity blurs the identification of new trends. As already mentioned, beneath the façade of the market reforms, the vision of the Chilean model as a beacon of neoliberal success, hides the preservation of significant coordination activities and patterns of state intervention, as a result of previously shared views regarding the strategic role of the state (Kurt 2001).

In other words, history, actors and local decisions matter. The point is to recognize that regardless of any factors that limit the integration of these peripheral countries into the world economy, development remains an endogenous process and, in this sense, is based on the creation of a national project leading to cooperation among various social actors (employers, workers, politicians and government technicians). The implementation of a developmental agenda and the generation of stable institutions is the result of broad agreements that require consensus among the players representing the social, political and economic life. Such agreements must be honored by its participants, with the collaboration of various sectors to achieve relative stability and maintenance in the short and medium term. The political system becomes the key dimension in this respect. The various mechanisms for handling the conflict are crucial, as already stated. As stressed in socioeconomic analyses, a project implies a certain direction, choice between alternatives in which different actors and social groups are influenced in dissimilar ways. That is, projects generate adjustments in social stratification and will find support on groups that are favored; at the same time they will be rejected by those who perceive the process as a threat to their interests (Faletto 1996; Becker 2007). Therefore, the greater or lesser ability political systems possess to deal with conflicting situations and generate consensus on at least a few issues is a central feature in any development model.

Governance in this sense is crucial, especially in terms of the nature of the coalitions that come to power and seek to implement a more developmental platform. This situation is quite different in each given context. Political and institutional factors shaping the productive regimes generally make a difference in terms of economic performance. For instance, the governmental coalition led by Argentinean president Fernandez de Kirchner was more homogeneous, structured on the momentarily hegemonic field of the Partido Juticialista and was able to incorporate dissenters from opposing parties, thus not facing any strong or articulated opposition. On the other hand, Lula's first term coalition was highly fragmented and made up of parties both on the right and left of the ideological spectrum. Pragmatism and dogmatism made the task of defining and obtaining support for a long-term development project more difficult. Even so, the government managed to assure political support amidst some turbulence and institutions have been reasonably effective in terms of assuring governability.

Chile and Uruguay can be listed as examples of coalitions compromising towards the center. Overcoming the authoritarian regime of Pinochet in Chile made it possible for the creation of a more centrist, homogenous coalition which revealed itself as fairly pragmatic and efficient. However, since the government of Ricardo Lagos (2000–6) under the leadership of the Socialist Party, the stability of the coalition was affected because of conflicting ideological pressures. The adoption of more progressive public policies proposed by the Socialists was met by resistance on the part of Christian Democrats. Higher levels of conflict within the coalition eventually contributed to the election of Sebastián Piñera.

The nature of the political coalition is part of a broader axis that includes not only the players who are in the government but also in the broader framework of the political system (pluralism, fragmentation, division of powers, etc.). The most significant difference between countries lies in their institutional capacity to breed conditions for cooperation. In this sense, experiences where political parties are the key actors in electoral dynamics contrasts with those in which the distinctive feature is the mutual exclusion of parties as legitimate actors leading to a zero-sum game which makes room for an active role of social movements in the political arena. This tends to be the case in the Andean countries, especially Ecuador, Bolivia and Venezuela where the most outstanding feature is the clear difficulty of channeling conflict through political institutions.

On the other hand, Uruguay, Chile, Brazil and to a lesser extent Colombia and Peru, combine a party system that introduces alternation in the exercise of power, legitimacy of the actors in the political game and an active role of parliament. Argentina represents a case in which, while legitimacy of the actors in government is undeniable, political institutions are incapable of creating conditions for cooperation among actors. In addition, there appears to be no strong opposition with potential to become a real alternative of government.

Conflict management requires clear rules which involve not only political, but especially economic actors. A development proposal which, in a capitalist system involves competition for resources, investment, technology and human capital, requires a strong business sector. The role of business associations constitutes, in this respect, another institutional aspect in the construction of such an agenda (Sicsu 2005; Diniz and Boschi 2006; Boschi 2006).

Albeit crucial, cooperation between businesses and public sector also depends on how the state creates conditions for such cooperation. Coordination between state and market is affected, in the first place, by the existence of planning mechanisms and of coordination between the two areas and, in second place, by effective means of implementation which brings us back to the subject of state capacities. In fact, as already emphasized, the basis of any possibility of a developmental proposal implies a basic agreement between politics and economy, or between economic and political actors. The issue is not only that of public administration paying attention to market signals, but also that of knowing when these signals are positive and the administration is still able to preserve the power to control and to coordinate. As long as these signals act as a positive link between public goods distribution and users' preferences, they can improve the performance of public institutions (Evans 2005).

This pattern of relations between business and an autonomous yet responsive bureaucratic core would be critical to explaining the virtuous paths of "recovery" in the wake of market reforms. Resistance from bureaucratic elites, business and unions has been a key factor in the neoliberal slowdown and in the late implementation of reforms in some cases. In contrast with cases of Argentina and Chile where privatization was almost total, in Brazil, the privatization of "Vale do Rio Doce," emblem of the Fernando Henrique Cardoso's administration, faced resistance from business and trade-union sectors which acted as a brake on future privatizations.

The role of business is fundamental in the analysis of the formation of a developmental platform. One important line of study can be identified by authors that emphasize the relationship between business sector and state as a decisive factor of certain development experiences. Focusing on East Asian and Latin American countries, these studies show that economic performance is strongly related to collaboration between private sector interest groups and the state. Among other things, class associations contribute to correct market failures, apart from being functional in solving coordination problems (Schneider and Maxfield 1997; Schneider 2004, 2009).

Corporatism, sometimes understood as a form of representation of interests opposed to liberal democracy because it implied working class control in its inception, can in fact be reinterpreted in terms of its positive effects as ground for cooperation between social sectors and the state. In Latin America, there have been experiences of strong (Mexico, Brazil) or weak (Chile, Venezuela) corporatism, which have generated different paths of transition to market-centered coordination, and from there towards a new developmental orientation (Boschi 2006). State corporatism is essential to counteract the tendency for business and corporate fragmentation such as in Brazil and Mexico. In cases of weak state corporatism such as in Chile and Venezuela, corporate hegemony was achieved through the operation of strong peak associations. Above all, as has been analyzed (Boschi 1994; Diniz and Boschi 1991) in Brazil, the development and consolidation of an official structure of representation[7] constituted a major asset at the time of shaping the collective identity of the private sector vis-à-vis the state and was essential in terms of keeping the relative integrity of the domestic private industrial sector in the immediate postreforms scenario.

Conclusions: Uncertainty and the Development Process

Even recognizing the role of institutions in creating the conditions for a broad agreement around the idea of national development this is still a project under way. In this sense, attention should be directed towards the micro public policies and towards the behavior of policymakers with the ability to influence key policies of the new agenda.

Development may also be a product of certain unplanned decisions. Uncertainty surrounds the production of public policies from the moment of their conception down to the stages of implementation and evaluation. Unpredictable outcomes may also change the prospects for economic growth and performance along a development path. The discovery of two vast oil fields in Brazilian jurisdictional waters that could turn the country into a producer is an example of how imponderables may open up new scenarios. The current Brazilian experience also illustrates how an apparently irreversible trajectory of social inequality was changed in the direction of broad social inclusion through political decisions which ended up opening opportunities for an inward-oriented process of economic growth.

Development is a long-term process. Certain policies can be successful in creating productive dynamics, but only when evaluated in the long-run. A seemingly stable period of growth assuring development in one moment of time can also be interrupted. For example, mid-twentieth century Argentina had a relatively advantageous position and could be considered a developed country in terms of social and economic achievements as compared to all the remaining countries of the region. Yet, that condition was not guaranteed of a sustained or continuous development process, entering the second half of the century in stop and go cycles.

That said, a negative evaluation of some processes or institutions made on a limited time span can eventually change in due time. Patrimonialism

---

7 The degree of organization and strengthening of business associations has also been fundamental for moving forward processes of structural adjustment. For example, privatization progressed much less in the Brazilian case, partly because of opposition from organized sectors that managed to mitigate their impact. The fragmentation of Argentine businessmen and a better organization of their Brazilian counterparts characterized by strong pragmatism and organized into corporate associations and other organized bodies related to them, were generally receptive to reforms, despite the fact that they had differential impact upon the various segments of the industry.

and corporatism, which have been viewed in negative aspects as forms of elite domination of public arenas, can be positively reinterpreted when examined in retrospective. Patrimonialism, which in the Brazilian experience expressed the extension of private oligarchic domain into the public arena, was based on a sort of competition between various regional groups over control of the state apparatus, with the unexpected result of the preservation state capacities over time. Also seen in perspective, the policies carried out by the military governments can be positively reinterpreted not only in their ability to generate sustained growth rates and potential for development, but also in their consequences in terms of nation building. In brief, the Brazilian experience illustrates a case of solid capitalist growth in which the process of creating an interventionist state, beginning with the 1930 Revolution of Getúlio Vargas, can be analyzed in terms of the presence of imponderable elements, combining uncertainty with determination of some elite sectors.

The specific nature of development processes in Latin America clearly shows, on one hand, the role that the state can play, and on the other hand, the concern with structural inequalities determining factors in the dynamics of development. It is in this space between the state and the process of overcoming structural inequalities that development can take place.

State intervention is the basis for breaking with long-prevailing negative complementarities that occur at the level of firms. In other words, policies have to be devised so as to fill gaps in research and development, training and qualifying labor, in addition to basic social policies that the private sector does not or cannot carry out. Yet, the return to the omnipresent role of the state of the past is not the real alternative. Neither would it be possible to continue denying the role of the state in creating favorable conditions for development, as it became clear from the poor results of the economic reforms of the 1990s. Thinking the state nowadays implies taking into account not only endogenous processes but also the regional arena. Strategies of regional integration in this sense could enhance Latin America's possibilities to enter a cycle of sustained development. In sum, the more inclusive a developmental project is from the political and social standpoint, the greater the chances that it will be viewed as a national task worth fighting for and the more the possibilities for region as a whole to make important advances in its lasting peripheral status.

References

Alcantara Saez, Manuel. 2008. *Proyecto de Elites Latinoamericanas (PELA)*. Universidad de Salamanca 1994–2005.

Amable, Bruno. 2003. *The Diversity of Modern Capitalism*. Oxford: Oxford University Press.

Becker, Uwe. 2007. "Open Systemness and Contested Reference Frames and Change: A of the Varieties of Capitalism Theory." *Socio-Economic Review* 5.2: 261–86.

Boschi, Renato. 2006. "Setor Privado, Reestruturação Econômica e Democratização na América Latina," in *América Latina Hoje*, ed. José Maurício Domingues and María Maneiro. Rio de Janeiro: Civilização Brasileira.

―――・ 2008a. "Capacidades Estatales y Políticas de Desarrollo en Brasil: Tendencias Recientes," in *La Democracia Brasileña: Balance y Perspectivas para el Siglo XXI*, ed. Manuel Alcantara Saez and Carlos Ranulfo Melo. Salamanca: Ediciones Universidad Salamanca.

―――・ 2008b. "Elites y Desarrollo en América Latina: Trayectorias Recientes en Chile y Brasil," in *Elites y Desarrollo*, ed. Alejandra Salas-Porras and Viesca Valverde. Mexico City: UNAM.

―――・ 2009. "Elites Parlamentares e a Agenda Pós-neoliberal: Brasil e Chile," in *Elites Parlamentares na América Latina*, ed. Fátima Anastasia, Magna Inacio, Araceli Díaz and Marta Rocha. Belo Horizonte: Editora Argumentum.

―――・ 2010. "Corporativismo Societal, a Democratização do Estado e as Bases Social-Democratas do Capitalismo Brasileiro." *Insight Inteligência* 12.48: 1–20.

Boschi, Renato and Flavio Gaitán. 2008. "Gobiernos Progresistas, Agenda Neodesarrollista y Capacidades Estatales: La Experiencia Reciente en Argentina, Brasil y Chile," in *Desempenho de Governos Progressistas no Cone Sul*, organized by Maria Regina Soares de Lima. Rio de Janeiro: IUPERJ.

Boyer, Robert. 2005. "How and Why Capitalisms Differ." *Economy and Society* 34.4: 509–57.

Bresser, Pereira and Luiz Carlos. 2006. "O Novo Desenvolvimentismo e a Ortodoxia Convencional." *São Paulo em Perspectiva* 20.3: 5–24.

Chang, Ha Joon. 2007. *Bad Samaritans: Rich Nations, Poor Policies and the Threat to the Developing World*. London: Random House.

Cooper, Richard. 2005. "A Half Century of Development." Center for International Development Working Paper 167, Harvard University.

Crouch, Colin. 2005. *Capitalist Diversity and Change: Recombinant Governance and Institutional Entrepreneurs*. Oxford: Oxford University Press.

Dezalay, Ives, and Bryant Garth. 2002. *The Internationalization of Palace Wars, Lawyers, Economists and the Contest to Transform Latin American State*. Chicago: University of Chicago Press.

Diniz, Eli. 2008. "Depois do Neoliberalismo, Rediscutindo a Articulação Estado e Desenvolvimento no Novo Milenio." *Ponto de Vista* no. 2 (September 2008). Rio de Janeiro: NEIC-IESP. http://neic.iuperj.br/pontodevista/ (accessed September 2011).

Diniz, Eli, and Renato Boschi. 2007. *A Difícil Rota do Desenvolvimento: Empresários e a agenda pós-neoliberal*. Belo Horizonte and Rio de Janeiro: Editora UFMG/IUPERJ.

―――・ 2004. *Empresários, interesses e mercado: Dilemas do desenvolvimento brasileiro*. Rio de Janeiro: Editora da UFMG.

―――・ 1991. "O Corporativismo na Construção do Espaço Público." *Corporativismo e Desigualdade: A Construção do Espaço Público no Brasil*, organized by Renato Boschi. Rio de Janeiro: Rio Fundo Editora/IUPERJ.

ECLAC. 2010. "Panorama Social de América Latina y el Caribe." http://www.eclac.cl/cgi-bin/getProd.asp?xml=/publicaciones/xml/9/41799/P41799.xml&xsl=/dds/tpl/p9f.xsl&base=/tpl/top-bottom.xsl (accessed September 2011).

―――・ 2011a. "Políticas contra-cíclicas para una recuperación sostenida del empleo." http://www.eclac.cl/publicaciones/xml/0/43690/2011-355-CEPAL-OIT-No_5-WEB.pdf (accessed September 2011).

————· 2011b. "Pobreza en América Latina cae en 2010 y retoma tendencia pre-crisis." Press release. http://www.eclac.org/cgi-bin/getProd.asp?xml=/prensa/noticias/comunicados/8/41798/P41798.xml&xsl=/prensa/tpl/p6f.xsl&base=/tpl/top-bottom.xslt (accessed October 2011).

Evans, Peter. 2005. "Harnessing the State: Rebalancing Strategies for Monitoring and Motivation," in *States and Development: Historical Antecedents of Stagnation and Advance*, ed. Matthew Lange and Dietrich Rueschemeyer. Basingstoke: Palgrave MacMillan.

————· 2008. "In search of the 21st Century Developmental State." Centre for Global Political Economy Working Paper No. 4, University of Sussex.

Faletto, Enzo. 1996. "La CEPAL y la Sociología Del Desarrollo." *Revista de La CEPAL* 58: 191–204.

Ferrer, Aldo. 2004. "Globalización, Desarrollo y Densidad Nacional, un abordaje de la experiencia de América Latina." Mimeo.

Gourevitch, Peter. 1986. *Politics in Hard Times: Comparative Responses to International Economic Crises.* London and Ithaca, NY: Cornell University Press.

Hall, Peter and David Soskice. 2001. *Varieties of Capitalism: The Institutional Foundations of Comparative Advantage.* Oxford and New York: Oxford University Press.

Hall, Peter and R. Taylor. 1996. "Political Science and the Three Variants of New Institutionalisms." *Political Studies* 44: 936–57.

Kholi, Atul. 2004. *State Directed Development: Political Power and Industrialization in the Global Periphery.* Cambridge: Cambridge University Press.

Kurt, Marcus. 2001. "State Developmentalism without a Developmentalist State: The Public Foundation of the 'Free-Market Miracle' in Chile." *Latin American Policies and Society* 43.2: 1–25.

Lopez Segrera, Francisco. 1998. *Los Retos de la Globalización.* Caracas: UNESCO.

North, Douglass. 1990. *Institutions, Institutional Change and Economic Performance.* Cambridge: Cambridge University Press.

————· 1998. "Economic Performance Through Time," in *The New Institutionalism in Sociology*, ed. M. C. Brinton and V. Nee. Stanford: Stanford University Press.

————· 2005. *Understanding the Process of Economic Change.* Princeton: Princeton University Press.

Pierson, Paul. 2004. *Politics in Time, History, Institutions and Social Analysis.* Princeton: Princeton University Press.

RICYT. 2010. "El Estado de la Ciencia en América Latina." http://bd.ricyt.org/explorer.php/query/submit?excel=on&indicators[]=GASFIN&syear=1990&eyear=2009& (accessed October 2011).

Rodrik, Dani. 2001. *The Global Governance of Trade: As if Development Really Mattered.* Paper presented at a UNDP conference on trade and development, October. http://www.wcfia.harvard.edu/sites/default/files/529__Rodrik5.pdf (accessed September 2011).

Rodrik, Dani and Ethan Kaplan. 2001. "Did the Malaysian Capital Controls Work?" JFK School of Government Working Paper RWP01-008, Harvard University. http://papers.ssrn.com/paper.taf?abstract_id=262173 (accessed October 2011).

Schmidt, Vivien. 2007. "Bringing the State back into Varieties of Capitalism and Discourse back into the Explanation of Change." Centre for European Studies working paper, 7 March. http://aie.pitt.edu/9281/1/Schmidt.pdf (accessed September 2011).

Schneider, Ben. 2004. "Business, Politics and the State in 20th Century Latin America." New York: Cambridge University Press.

———· 2009. "Hierarchical Market Economies and Varieties of Capitalism in Latin America." *Journal of Latin American Studies* 41: 553–75.

Schneider, Ben and Sylvia Maxfield. 1997. *Business and the State in Developing Countries*. Ithaca, NY: Cornell University Press.

Sicsu, João, Luiz Fernando de Paula and Renaut Michel. 2005. *Novo-Desenvolvimentismo: Um projeto Nacional de Crescimento com Equidade Social*. São Paulo: Manole.

Stiglitz, Joseph. 1998. *A New Paradigm for Development: Strategies, Policies and Processes*, 9th Raul Prebisch Lecture. Geneva: UNCTAD.

Weiss, Linda (ed.) 2003. *States in the Global Economy. Bringing Domestic Institutions Back In*. Cambridge: Cambridge University Press.

WTO. 2011. "International Trade Statistics." http://www.wto.org/english/res_e/statis_e/its2010_e/its10_toc_e.htm (accessed September 2011).

Chapter 3

MANAGING THE FAUSTIAN BARGAIN: MONETARY AUTONOMY IN THE PURSUIT OF DEVELOPMENT IN EASTERN EUROPE AND LATIN AMERICA

Joseph Nathan Cohen
City University of New York

Globalization and economic liberalization promised developing countries improved opportunities for capital investment and, in turn, accelerated economic development. These promises helped cultivate a rush across the developing world to create favorable conditions for capital investors. Increased inward capital flows did occur but frequently retreated rapidly, helped spark systemic volatility and, for many countries, ultimately resulted in a disappointing development record (Rodrik and Subramanian 2008). By the turn of the millennium, there emerged a strong sense that the interests of capital investors and national economic development could diverge and even oppose one another. Governments increasingly saw global capital markets as a potentially destructive force and sought ways to manage the perils of modern financial capitalism.

Today's enlarged, mobile and powerful global capital markets present policymakers with a tightrope. These markets can undermine development efforts as easily as they help, but there are many means by which governments can insulate their economies from these adverse effects. This chapter focuses on how governments can manage capital markets strains with a special focus on monetary policy. Strains occur when there is a rapid or sustained flight of resources from a national economy, which can create a range of policy problems when it occurs, including currency devaluation, inflation, government insolvency and bankruptcy epidemics. When a monetary system becomes especially unstable, it can hurt economic prosperity and, in extreme cases, undermine general political-economic order.

Under many circumstances, opening one's markets to global capital flows creates increased risk of monetary problems that policymakers can attempt to mitigate by various means. Five generic strategies for insuring one's economy against capital market strain are considered. *Incentivization* attempts to discourage capital flight by making one's economy maximally attractive for capital investors. *Intervention* attempts to impede capital flight by using the state's legal powers and resources to restrict or manipulate the movement of capital. *Financial accumulation* is a strategy in which governments attempt to arm themselves with access to large pools of financing that can be used to act against market sentiment on markets themselves. *Cooperation* involves coordination among states that pool resources to act against markets. *Dependency* is an arrangement in which a weaker country surrenders economic sovereignty to a stronger one in exchange for the latter's sponsorship of monetary stability. Each of these strategies face practical difficulties and potential problems.

Countries in Latin America and Eastern Europe will have to consider the blend of monetary defense strategies to use in the years to come. Many European countries have sought refuge in the European Monetary Union (EMU). This arrangement offers first-rate monetary protection, but places them in a position in which the strains of dependency could eventually be strong, although the system's current workings seem to be more cooperative in nature. Concerns that political shifts may change the Euro bloc into something that serves the interests of its core countries – perhaps at the expense of the newly admitted – is an issue that policymakers in that region will have to confront. In Latin America, these choices are more complicated. Cooperative and dependency arrangements look less desirable and accumulation somewhat less practical. The region seems stuck with blends of incentives and interventions, which are likely to be less effective than European options. What may help the region most is a change in attitudes among the world system's core countries on their role in fostering global development.

Managing Money under Financial Capitalism: Some Preliminaries

Policymakers embraced financial liberalization for many reasons, among them the belief that it would rescue them from the economic quagmires of the 1970s and 1980s. By engaging markets, these countries exposed their economies to financial pressures that affected economic stability, policymaking autonomy and in turn, the social infrastructure by which their economies were organized. Capital flows grew to be large and volatile, often overwhelming governments' ability to maintain financial order and sustain economic progress. The destructive side of the global financial boom is a force that policymakers now respect, and present an important consideration that should be integrated into any national economic strategy.

The rise of financial capitalism

After World War II, the Western allies sought to embed financial markets in a web of stringent, cooperatively enforced regulations institutionalized in the Bretton Woods Accord of 1944. This accord established a regime of coordinated exchange rate fixing, mutual macrofinancial insurance and active public sector control of financial markets. It was pursued in part as a result of the practical difficulties involved in reestablishing the liberal prewar international economic regime, in part to insulate governments from the tumult that resulted in the Great Depression and in part in an effort to protect government policymaking from pressures from financial markets (Bordo 1993; Helleiner 1994; Ruggie 1982; Sachs and Warner 1995). By controlling capital's ability to shake exchange rates, price system stability or government solvency, private financiers' ability to sanction governments for enacting anticapital policies were limited, thereby helping states institute the interventionist policies of the mid-twentieth century (Cohen 2008). The participation of the world system's core members suppressed financial volatility globally.

This system faced a slow chipping-away in the 1950s and 1960s and then a breakdown by 1971 (see Block 1977; Helleiner 1994). The 1973 oil shock created a dangerous combination of widespread stagflation and a sovereign lending bubble which culminated in states weathering economic crises through deficit spending. Governments accumulated massive debts, culminating in a financial crisis in 1982. While financially imperiled governments faced an inability to finance their operations, political gridlock proved to be a hurdle to aggressive financial restoration and many policymakers addressed this situation through the practice of seigniorage. The result was severe inflation and chronic stagnation throughout the 1980s, amounting to a "lost decade" of development for many countries. What seemed to be the patent failure of governments' macroeconomic management delegitimized the postwar portrayal of the state as a prudent safeguard against market excesses and helped usher in a range of policy initiatives designed to cut the state's size, scope of operations and regulatory hold on markets. The collapse of the Soviet system by the 1990s solidified sentiments that opposed government interventionism and brought many of the world's developing states into this rising liberal system.

Excitement about the Cold War's end and opportunities for capital infusion-led economic development triggered an "emerging markets" investment boom in the 1990s. Global financial flows soared vertiginously. Median gross foreign direct investment (FDI) and gross private capital flows grew by factors of almost four and seven respectively, as a percentage of gross domestic product (GDP) at the median between the 1980s and 2000s. Among the top quartile of wealthier countries, market capitalization of listed companies almost tripled from the 1980s to 2000s, as more of their countries assets were channeled to equity markets. Through government and private sectors, capital poured into developing countries introducing capital inflows on a previously unseen scale and for which unprepared regulatory authorities and immature financial institutions had not been ready. The degree to which these doors were opened to capital varied (see Taylor 2006), but everywhere emerging capital markets were a force that took root in economic life.

Liberalization not only opened the doors to financial inflows but also outflows, and the 1990s showed that money could flee a country easily and sometimes in ways that suggested indiscriminate panic or sanction. These crises could occur unexpectedly and for reasons not directly tied to identifiable underlying problems, for example as the result of financial communities' self-fulfilling prophesies of impending panic (Obstfeld 1996) or as a form of collective punishment resulting from general flights from all developing markets when particular countries or regions fell into problems (Fratzscher 2003; Kaminsky and Reinhart 2000). The economic costs of such crises could be profound, sparking exchange rate drops, inflation, trade disruption, credit crises and severe recessions. In extreme cases – such as Indonesia in 1998 or Argentina in 2001 – financial crises unleashed political crises, undermined social order and destabilized states.

Financial pressures under economic liberalism

Contemporary economic history shows that adverse reactions by capital markets can hurt an economy and in turn, threaten political stability. Capital flight's destructive capacity is a well-known threat that has shaped economic policymaking. As a result, some argue that financial liberalization undercuts the autonomy of policymakers who are pushed to tailor policies to the interests of international capital holders (Andrews 1994; Haggard and Maxfield 1996). Financial pressures' encroachment on policy is most visible when countries fall into crisis. Under these circumstances, victims have sometimes found themselves having to make policy concessions to external bailout financiers, for example through the International Monetary Fund (IMF) conditionality (reviewed in Dreher 2008) or in bilateral negotiations (e.g., see Kirshner 2006 on South Korea's concessions to the US after its 1997 crisis). Even in the absence of crisis, governments might anticipate the desires of capital markets and implement policies that prioritize catering to that sector's demands – even at the expense of other national economic priorities.

Such an encroachment on autonomy made sense after the 1980s when governments appeared to use their power over the regulatory environment to make patently misconceived (or even politically expedient) financial decisions, often in ways that seemed to entail damages to the economy-at-large. Giving capital markets power over the economy makes sense as long as we assume that there is an affinity between the interests of capital investors and general economic prosperity. Given the overall questionable outcome of financial globalization's effect on development, assuming such an affinity seems hasty. Certain kinds of policy concessions reduce regulation or maximize the ease with which they can flee an economy – precisely the kinds of reforms that make countries more vulnerable to strain. In some cases, financial concerns can lead governments to enact policies that disadvantage other economically important sectors. For example, artificially inflating a country's exchange rates can reduce the risk to which locally denominated debt holders are exposed, but it also hurts exports. Providing tax inducements to foreign investors shifts the tax burden to local enterprise and consumers and does nothing to help bolster government finances if liberalization does not help spur strong development. At best, the development benefit of financial liberalization appears to be mixed (Kose et al. 2006).

Seeking a defensive posture

Over the past decade, perspectives on the ultimate benevolence of free international capital markets have changed. Rodrik and Subramanian (2008) argue that the net development effect of capital market liberalization has been "disappointing," and suggest that part of the problem is that opening the doors to capital does not mean that investment opportunities in the potential recipient country will be good. A mere welcoming of capital as a solution to economic problems does nothing to help the many underlying institutional conditions that influence investment viability, and trying to bring about wholesale institutional change and liberalize a wide range of markets all at once is likely an impractical endeavor. History suggests that any multitude of underlying problems can make a country vulnerable to the flight of the capital upon which they come to depend, and prominent analysts have argued that capital markets are something against which countries should defend themselves (Feldstein 1999). How can a country achieve such insulation? Countries have pursued numerous strategies in the twenty-first century, each of which has its own costs and benefits. We turn to a typology of these strategies next.

Maintaining Monetary Autonomy: Five Generic Strategies

Monetary autonomy refers to a situation in which government policy is not pressured by financial markets, thus does not have to grapple with the threat of economic crisis and is not pushed to implement pro-financier policies (see Cohen 2008). As recent events in the US suggest, no country is fully insulated from these pressures, but differences in exposure to these forces exist. A policymaker seeking to mitigate international financial markets' encroachments on the policymaking process has several potential strategies at his or her disposal. Below, I present a typology of five such strategies: incentivization, intervention, accumulation, coordination and dependency. Each strategy has its own costs and benefits.

Incentivization

Strictly speaking, government can have its hands tied in situations that policies themselves have created. This occurred in the 1980s when monetary systems confronted a myriad of problems, many of which were government policy's own making. Political forces sway the state and this context ushered in policy directives that served to erode general economic order and formal economy participation, often leaving these countries with largely ungovernable economies. Morales and Sachs's (1989) discussion of Bolivia's Siles administration is an illustrative example. Given this paper's basic premise that the threat of capital flight is a key pressure on policymakers, such a strategy might seem wrong-headed at first glance. In order to perceive this underlying logic one must separate conceptually the state from a country's political forces and acknowledge that certain political environments can cripple a state's ability to manage its own economy. Financial systems represent social orders, and such orders can fall into a kind of chaos that neither the government nor private enterprise can control well.

A reestablishment of governments' control over economic activity requires a restoration of price stability and public finances. One way to do this is to privatize the economy and chase global capital, which can infuse an economy with hard currencies, shed costly and politically charged public enterprises, help alleviate pressures on balances of payments and fiscal deficits, and perhaps most importantly, undercut bad governments' policymaking autonomy. The Washington Consensus and similar reforms can be seen as a cover for the tough decisions that seemed impossible through strictly domestic deliberations. Although some portray economic liberalization as a choice that was an imposition for foreigners' will on developing countries, closer examinations suggest that domestic constituencies have also favored such reforms (e.g., Armijo and Faucher 2002).

Many of the policies implemented under the wave of liberalization in the early 1990s could be described as *incentivization*, a means of asserting state economic control by attempting to reestablish financial order through attracting needed capital inflows by maximizing the incentives international financiers have to transfer resources into a developing country. Some of these reforms include basic elements of the original Washington Consensus – privatization, deregulation, tax and expenditure reduction, easing restrictions on foreign inward investment and the reinforcement of property rights, though the liberalization of capital outflows was not part of this consensus (Williamson 1990). Once basic reforms were implemented, however, capital outflow liberalization was soon argued to help inflows and was ultimately implemented (Labán M. and Larraín B. 2001; Schadler et al. 1993).

The chief benefits of these liberalization strategies is that they help countries make difficult decisions by externalizing the cause of politically difficult decisions (Przeworski and Vreeland 2000) like unloading money-losing public enterprises or cutting government expenditures. They also help establish basic environmental conditions that are likely to be necessary if a country wants to enjoy any of the benefits conferred by First World financial systems, such as strong property rights or effective contract enforcement. The global investment boom and the fact inflation was quelled in many countries during the 1990s (see Cohen and Centeno 2006) suggests that liberalization can provide governments and economies with the resources to reverse stagflation. It also seems clear that regardless of the financial pressures faced by governments since 1990s, states in developing countries have dramatically enhanced their ability to exert fiscal and monetary power within their own economies.

Problems with this strategy emerge when a country is no longer mired in general economic crisis, and there are actually large amounts of circulating capital to flee. At such a point, the interests of the state and international capital markets can diverge. States may want to regain lost control of privatized strategic sectors, as many countries did with their oil deposits over the past decade. They might want successful foreign-owned enterprises to help fund public initiatives and try to raise the taxes levied on them. Once capital flight emerges as a threat to national prosperity, governments may want to restrict capital mobility to retain its existing capital or prevent disruptions from hot money. All of these solutions are problematic. In one sense, they can amount to a violation of an implicit contract with capital markets, who often assume the risk of entering troubled markets in hopes of large future profits. Changing these terms can lead to reputation damage and perhaps future prospects for attracting investment. Some reassertions of state ownership can amount to serious violations of property rights, like the recapture of oil rights by Russia, Venezuela or Bolivia. Also, opening the door to international capital markets creates entrenched interest groups and institutions, and undoing these policies can spark serious political conflict and strain relationships with investors' home countries.

Incentivization appears to have been used as a crisis strategy, which comes at the cost of lock-in to external vulnerability and control over strategically important parts of the economy. At some point the interests of international capital markets and domestic development may diverge, making countries vulnerable to many of the problems that came up during the 1990s. In this sense, one can characterize incentivization as a kind of Faustian bargain: to sell control over one's economy to international markets to alleviate crisis but then have to live with their potentially negative influence once the crisis has passed.

Intervention

Intervention is a means of asserting a government's economic power by using legal power and prerogatives to constrain or influence the choices available to international investors. While the 1990s have been characterized here as an era of rapid liberalization and financial deregulation, it is important to note that most governments engaged in piecemeal reforms, holding on to many mechanisms of regulatory control. Examples of such interventions include capital flow restrictions, regulated direct investment, restrictions on foreign borrowing or exchange rate manipulations. These strategies, and these were employed in various combinations across the developing world (see Taylor 2006).

As noted earlier, governments resorted to strong capital controls during the mid-twentieth century, although many observers argue that they were poorly conceived and often circumvented (Bruton 1998; Isard 2005). More generally, tight financial regulation is thought by many laissez-faire proponents to eschew some of the free market's primary benefits. They make capital allocation subject to purely political pressures, can suppress the information transmission that takes place through price changes and saddle policymakers with the impractical task of fine-tuning a capital allocation system that must fund something as staggeringly complex as an aggregate economy. Such regulations may also shift the attention of enterprises away from innovation and productivity enhancement towards lobbying (Krueger 1974). Furthermore, they have a record of not working well, and have been dismissed by some observers as relics of a worn-out political ideology (Dornbusch 1998). Finally, such regulations may discourage the inflow of capital that provides a key incentive for engaging these markets in the first place.

Since 1997, analysts have become more skeptical about the development-related benefits of capital market integration. Attitudes towards capital controls have become more positive – particularly with respect to restrictions on short-term flows (e.g., Montiel and Reinhart 1999). Regulation has also become more topical given recent financial problems in the United States, which was itself an important source of advocacy for the benefits of unfettered financial markets. Overall, there is a deep ambivalence among policy experts concerning the use of regulation to steer financial market outcomes. This uncertainty reflects the view that many forms of financial market regulation can be undermined even while actors nominally adhere to the letter of its policies (Healy and Palepu 2003). Americans have shown an inclination to deal with financial problems by enacting policies designed to maximize transparency in financial reporting (like the Sarbanes–Oxley Act), although such redresses have been criticized as ignoring fundamental problems associated with financial systems that still leave much financial power in the hands of private actors, thus remain vulnerable to the systematic failing of laissez-faire systems (e.g., Soederberg 2008). A central problem with intervention is that policy is much less nimble than capital markets, and private actors can find a myriad of ways to circumvent them. Nevertheless, regulation remains a practical option for coping with perceived problems in the financial system, given that governments can implement them unilaterally.

Financial Accumulation

Countries that wish to insulate themselves from financial market *pressures* need not insulate themselves from the financial markets entirely. Financial strategies can be used to insulate oneself from such pressures, although doing so generally comes at the cost of other policy goals. One such strategy is *financial accumulation*, in which countries acquire large reserves and deploy these reserves to buy against market sentiment in times of financial panic. The idea here is that many strains are a product of herd-like behavior and unwarranted panic. One way to insulate a country from the early onset of financial strain is to buy up excess supplies of one's own currency on markets, or, failing that, use reserves to finance strategically important imports or debt obligations. This is a delaying tactic (B. Cohen 2006), and is premised on the idea that many strains are essentially short-lived, unless the momentum of a currency crash and extended crisis leads to sustained losses of faith in a country's currency.

Should a government help its own currency weather the storms of a panic, other market actors might begin to speculate in favor of currency appreciation, or, if unsuccessful, governments are given the time to find longer-term bailout financing to start the process of financial recovery. This tactic is not likely to be sustainable over a longer period of time, as currency market turnover dwarfs most countries' capacity to hoard reserves. In 2005, daily global forex (foreign exchange) turnover was estimated to be $1.8 trillion (Bank for International Settlements 2005), while most countries bank less than $100 billion in reserves (International Monetary Fund 2008).

Reserve accumulation is typically explained as the result of currency sterilization, although time-series data suggests that reserve hoarding accelerated after the 1994 Mexican peso crisis and intensified after the 1997 East Asian crisis (Cohen 2008). During this period, reserve holdings rose across the world, even in countries that were suffering from balance of payments deficits. In a recent study, I show that developing countries that have banked reserves experience faster economic growth, and that this relationship holds up in regression analyses (Cohen 2008). Reserve accumulation appears to be a strategy that pays off perhaps by smoothing the chronic boom-and-bust cycles that have plagued economic development in the late twentieth century, and much of the world's policymakers appear to be cognizant of these benefits given that such a wide range of countries have stocked reserves that are huge by historical standards.

A key benefit of this strategy is that it attempts to control the excesses of markets without violating the basic logic of them. Banking reserves does nothing to threaten property rights, nor presents any problems to the original terms of investment in which capital first entered the developing world. It need not create calcified rules that distort economic allocation. Reserve banking is unlikely to attract the ire of the world system's most dominant players, especially the US, particularly because America relies on this reserve hoarding to sustain its own large budget deficits. Some argue that America's reliance on this reserve banking helps developing countries gain influence over US policy (Dooley, Folkerts-Landau and Garber 2003, 2004). This strategy may be a difficult option in practice for many countries as it requires a form of savings from governments that are already hard-pressed to find financial surpluses. Furthermore, although some evidence suggests that it is effective, the strategy may face practical limits once it is seriously tested.

Cooperation

A fourth option for countries seeking insulation from international capital markets is *cooperation*, in which countries engage in a form of mutual insurance against capital market strain. This strategy's the basic idea is that individual countries may lack the reserves, regulatory power and other resources to contain the vast majority of strains on a currency, but their chances improve as their resources are pooled. Arguably, the Bretton Woods Accord (which successfully contained capital market excesses for roughly two decades) was such an arrangement, whereby the victorious Allied countries pooled resources and capacities to ensure that financial pressure would not inordinately affect the accord members' efforts to reform their economies after WWII. More recently, the EMU can be seen as a form of coordination, in which its countries jointly face strains to the euro, and do so within a governance framework that gives reasonable influence to smaller countries.

The euro illustrates some of the benefits of coordination among strong players. Together, EMU members command large reserves, hold regulatory jurisdiction over many important private sector actors and have been able to create a strong currency that commands a significant proportion (roughly one-third) of international currency market turnover. This last feature of the euro is especially important, because the integrity of the global financial order is reasonably dependent on a stable euro. Serious threats to this currency will likely pose problems across the world system, meaning that it is likely that Europe would benefit from cooperation with a range of non-EMU countries and perhaps major nongovernmental actors, should a serious threat emerge.

As with any form of insurance, there is always the threat of a free rider problem, whereby a particular member feels empowered to make financially irresponsible decisions – like running large budget deficits – in effect, passing the burden of monetary stabilization to others. Within the euro framework the imposition of financial discipline seemed reasonably successful until recently, but has since been shown to be illusory. As in other regions, particularly those with a history of chronically resorting to deficit spending or inflationary policy like Latin America, it is not be as easy to find the political will to impose such discipline for the purposes of fortifying a mutual insurance pact given that they often cannot find the will to insulate themselves.

Moreover, some regions are unlikely to be able to pool enough economic power and resources to control the impact of markets effectively. Regions like Latin America or Africa are populated by financially strained governments that hold regulatory power over relatively minor players in the global financial system. Furthermore, efforts to unionize have reportedly been met with opposition from the United States – for example in its opposition to the formation of the Asian Monetary Fund proposal after the 1997 East Asian crisis (Kirshner 2006). Coordination among developing countries may represent a threat to US financial dominance, and the country may be willing to squash efforts that erode their influence if it is able to do so.

Even without formal pacts, there is a possibility that de facto coordination exists among some countries. Benjamin Cohen (2006) argues that, beyond the power to delay the effects of monetary strain, countries may also be able to defend themselves from shock by "deflecting" their impact by enlisting the help of other countries that are likely to suffer should the afflicted economic system collapse. For example, it seems unlikely that the advanced industrial countries would allow one of its own currencies to collapse, given the amount of interdependency that exists among them and the broader geostrategic implications of allowing a key ally to fall into critical crisis. America's rapid response to Mexico in 1994 suggests that, when confronted with a financial threat that could cause severe problems, the United States is ready to help quickly. Other central banks have been quick to extend credit to the US during the present mortgage crisis. Coordination may be effective for wealthy countries, but has been difficult to implement elsewhere.

Dependency

There is a fine line between cooperation among mutually defending countries and dependency relationships that act as a means by which powerful countries can coerce or exploit minor ones. *Dependency* is a monetary defense strategy in which an economically weaker country submits to the bargaining terms of a larger power in hopes that it will stabilize a financial system. Jonathan Kirshner (1995) offers comprehensive discussions of monetary dependency. Given that it is rare for countries in an economic pact to have the kind of financial parity that exists between, for example, France and Germany – one might expect that any political arrangement designed for mutual defense may also provide stronger countries with opportunities to wield power over smaller countries that are more dependent on such agreements.

Dependency can be a helpful strategy for coping with monetary strain, provided that these dependent relationships benefit (or at least do not exploit) the weaker country. A transnational monetary relationship is rarely a clear manifestation of dependency or cooperation (as most official discourse will describe such relationships as if they were the latter) and may even be seen by its participants in such terms. There are clear examples of power plays that expose the vulnerabilities that can inhere in dependency relationships. Kirshner (1995, 121–40) offers an extended discussion of how 1930s Germany was able to exploit currency difficulties in Southeastern Europe to bind these countries to a stabilization plan that relied on the Reichsmark – thereby creating a sense of common economic fate among these countries and Germany – and perhaps increased economic and political influence from the former to the latter. Thacker (1999) presents evidence that countries are more likely to receive IMF help if they support the United States in other international political matters such as aligning their UN votes with America. Monetary politics is a tool of statecraft, and countries always try to pressure each other to advance their own geopolitical agendas. By embedding one's country in a dependency relationship, a developing country leaves itself vulnerable to such power plays.

Choices for Latin America and Eastern Europe

Financial pressures are a perpetual concern for governments – particularly during historical periods in which international capital is mobile and powerful, as is the case today. In our current context in which the capitalist system is experiencing financial instability at its core, the prospect of turbulence seems especially strong. Governments in Latin America and Eastern Europe will have to find ways to buffer themselves in this environment. However, these regions face particular circumstances that influence the viability of different strategies.

In Eastern Europe, policymakers have sought protection by embedding their systems in the EMU, thereby placing themselves under the auspices of Western Europe's major continental powers. Such a solution presents gold-standard protection from market pressures and a range of clear nonmonetary benefits to member countries (like lower transaction costs with Western Europe, a friendlier investment environment for enterprises that serve the euro area or the reduction of exchange rate uncertainty). Furthermore, the regulations governing union membership encourage monetary discipline, thus conferring some of the benefits sought in the post-1980s pursuit of liberal incentivization strategies.

Here, the long-term concerns of such an arrangement are the other means by which such an arrangement ties the hands of government. The EMU can be a coordinative or dependency relationship depending on the tenor of the policies adopted by its central bank, which is itself constrained by the politics of its powerful countries. Such a change can occur in situations where the interests of the union's core members see a divergence from those of the East. By adopting the euro, Eastern Europeans are foregoing an ability to tailor monetary and exchange rate policies to suit the exigencies of the particular local pressures they face. In effect, adopting the euro is a solution that foregoes governments' political control over the money system to combat nonmonetary pressures. Before 2008, governments were far more concerned with things like capital flight or currency market panics, and the ECU helped buffer Greece, Italy and Spain from the types of meltdowns that afflicted South Korea or Russia in 1997. When sovereign credit markets dried up after 2008, the downside of these protections became obvious: these less-wealthy countries' inability to print money or devalue their exchange rates became immense economic handicaps.

The lingering question here is whether Eastern Europe is entering another kind of Faustian bargain, in which it becomes entrenched in a system that ultimately does not treat the region's development as a key priority. The current situation of Italy is an instructive example, where the country could benefit from exchange rate devaluations to spur its struggling export sector. Under the EMU, Germany, France, Finland and Belgium have enjoyed enhanced competitiveness as a result of differential inflation, while price disadvantages have been accruing to high inflation countries like Italy, Portugal and Spain (Fischer 2007). This does not suggest that the EMU systematically disadvantages weaker or more financially troubled countries. One can easily find policies that suggest embattled European countries are in a situation for which they are partly responsible. However, it does highlight the difficulties that can occur when a country is deprived of locally responsive exchange rate and monetary policies. A second potential concern is the use of a monetary union as a vehicle for transferring economic burdens from strong to weak countries. For example, France and Germany have repeatedly breached the terms of the Stability and Growth Pact (SGP), and the EU repeatedly failed to implement the sanctions laid out by the accord (Annett and Jaeger 2004; Wypolsz 2006). In fact the EU's large countries have been the worst fiscal offenders in the Union, leaving the burden of fiscal discipline to its smaller, SGP-compliant members.

I do not wish to suggest that Eastern Europe should adopt a strong dose of Euroscepticism in matters related to money. In fact, most observers believe that the benefits of EMU integration are large (for example, improved within-continent trade) and that some of the stresses (like asymmetry of shocks) will diminish in the long-term (Frankel 2005). However, pure economics are not the sole determinant of central banking policy. Bretton Woods itself became mired in problems when the US used its monetary power to finance the Vietnam War. Also, local political currents in the core EMU countries have the capacity to pressure EU policy if a strong enough will develops. The point being made here is that integration into the Euro zone entails deep institutional changes that cannot be undone easily, and those that make the leap will have to remain cognizant of (and develop explicit economic and political strategies for) the dependency relations that will develop.

In Latin America, no such gold standard insulation from international market forces seems to be available. Monetary union – either among themselves or with the US through dollarization – looks like a poor option. The former choice, by many analyses, does not seem to make economic sense. Latin American countries do not trade much with each other and different parts of the region experience an asymmetry of economic shocks, implying that there are few gains resulting from economizing on transaction costs and a unified response to shocks would probably always make someone unhappy (Belke and Gros 2002; Edwards 2006; Hochreither, Schmidt-Hebbel and Winckler 2002). The second option – dollarization – is likely to produce a monetary policy that is completely unresponsive to local economic conditions and makes less sense as Latin America trades more with other countries. America's economy has little exposure to Latin American fortunes (except perhaps Mexico), and a long history of indifference to that region's development compared with what seems to be Western Europe's current attitudes towards the East.

Barring any serious concerted effort to bring the real economies of Latin America together, the countries of this region are forced to seek monetary autonomy on their own. Incentivization remains an important part of such a strategy, because the region generally lacks the public finances or robust trade sectors to forego foreign investment. Furthermore, financial governance in that region has been – and often continues to be – loose and in need of some sort of discipline. For some observers, finding ways to constrain monetary policy is paramount for the financial stabilization of Latin America (Mishkin and Savastano 2000). Some countries (notably Brazil) do look strong, and have been able to generate potentially strong export markets and accumulate Asian-style massive reserves. Others like Venezuela appear to be stuck in policies that led to the continent's financial demise in the 1980s.

To a great extent, Latin American countries have sought to deal with their problems through intervention, resorting to technically clever policy devices like flexible pegging or inflation targeting, and these policies are believed to have helped fight inflation (e.g., Corbo and Schmidt-Hebbel 2001). Latin America has never had a lack of economic expertise and most cutting-edge strategies ultimately have a limited shelf life. A key question is whether the region's recent successes were context-dependent – a product of general tranquility in international capital flows and a global commodity boom – or whether these successes are the result of rock-solid strategies with real long-term viability. If we conceptualize this region's financial dealings as the product of economic power rather than flows and balances, this region does not command the strength wielded by other middle-income regions. They remain economically dependent, although recent distancing from IMF or US export market reliance may be helpful. True autonomy probably requires political changes on a range of issues, like enhancing regional trade or fortifying individual national finances. This is hardly a new perspective, but the issues still remain pertinent.

References

Andrews, David M. 1994. "Capital Mobility and State Autonomy: Toward a Structural Theory of International Monetary Relations." *International Studies Quarterly* 38: 193–218.

Annett, Anthony and Albert Jaeger. 2004. "Europe's Quest for Financial Discipline: Will the Stability and Growth Pact Help Europe Find the Right Balance Between Fiscal Discipline and Flexibility." *Finance and Development* (June): 22–5.

Armijo, Leslie Elliott and Philippe Faucher. 2002. "'We Have a Consensus': Explaining Political Support for Market Reforms in Latin America." *Latin American Politics and Society* 44: 1–40.

Bank for International Settlements. 2005. "Triennial Central Bank Survey: Foreign Exchange and Derivatives Market Activity in 2004." Basel: Bank for International Settlements.

Belke, Ansgar and Daniel Gros. 2002. "Monetary Integration in the Southern Cone: Mercosur is Not Like the EU?" Central Bank of Chile Working Papers, No. 188. Santiago: Central Bank of Chile.

Block, Fred. 1977. *The Origins of International Economic Disorder: A Study of United States International Monetary Policy from World War II to the Present.* Berkeley: University of California Press.

Bordo, Michael D. 1993. "The Bretton Woods International Monetary System: A Historical Overview," in *A Retrospective on the Bretton Woods System: Lessons for International Monetary Reform,* ed. Michael D. Bordo and Barry Eichengreen, 3–98. Chicago: University of Chicago Press.

Bruton, Henry J. 1998. "A Reconsideration of Import Substitution." *Journal of Economic Literature* 36: 903–36.

Cohen, Benjamin J. 2006. "The Macrofoundations of Monetary Power." in *International Monetary Power,* ed. David M. Andrews, 31–50. Ithaca, NY: Cornell University Press.

Cohen, Joseph Nathan. 2008. "Financial Capitalism's Elusive Quest: Macrofinancial Autonomy and Economic Growth in the Developing World, 1990–2005." Unpublished manuscript.

Cohen, Joseph Nathan and Miguel Angel Centeno. 2006. "Neoliberalism and Patterns of Economic Performance, 1980–2000." *Annals of the American Academy of Political and Social Science* 606: 32–67.

Corbo, Vittorio and Klaus Schmidt-Hebbel. 2001. "Inflation Targeting in Latin America." Central Bank of Chile Working Papers, No. 105. Santiago: Central Bank of Chile.

Dooley, Michael P., David Folkerts-Landau and Peter Garber. 2003. "An Essay on the Revived Bretton Woods System." NBER Working Paper No. 9971. Cambridge, MA: National Bureau of Economic Research.

———. 2004. "The Revived Bretton Woods System: The Effects of Periphery Intervention and Reserve Management on Interest Rates and Exchange Rates in Center Countries." NBER Working Paper No. 10332. Cambridge, MA: National Bureau of Economic Research.

Dornbusch, Rudiger. 1998. "Capital Controls: An Idea Whose Time Has Passed," in *Should the IMF Pursue Capital-Account Convertibility? Essays in International Finance No. 207,* ed. Stanley Fischer, Richard N. Cooper, Rudiger Dornbusch, Peter M. Garber, Carlos Massad, Jacques J. Polak, Dani Rodrik and Savak S. Tarapore. Princeton: Princeton University Press.

Dreher, Axel. 2008. "IMF Conditionality: Theory and Evidence." KOF Working Papers, No. 188. Zurich: Swiss Federal Institute of Technology.

Edwards, Sebastian. 2006. "Monetary Unions, External Shocks, and Economic Performance: A Latin American Perspective." NBER Working Paper No. 12229. Cambridge, MA: National Bureau of Economic Research.

Feldstein, Martin. 1999. "Self-Protection for Emerging Market Economies." NBER Working Paper No. 6907. Cambridge, MA: National Bureau of Economic Research.

Fischer, Christoph. 2007. "An Assessment of the Trends in International Price Competitiveness among EMU Countries." Discussion Paper Series 1: Economic Studies, No. 08/2007. Frankfurt: Deutsche Bundesbank.

Frankel, Jeffrey. 2005. "Real Convergence and Euro Adoption in Central and Eastern Europe: Trade and Business Cycle Correlations as Endogenous Criteria for Joining the EMU," in *Euro Adoption in Central and Eastern Europe*, ed. Susan Schadler, 9–21. Washington DC: International Monetary Fund.

Fratzscher, Marcel. 2003. "On Currency Crises and Contagion." *International Journal of Finance and Economics* 8: 109–29.

Haggard, S. and S. Maxfield. 1996. "The Political Economy of Financial Internationalization in the Developing World." *International Organization* 50: 35–68.

Healy, Paul M. and Krisha G. Palepu. 2003. "The Fall of Enron." *Journal of Economic Perspectives* 17: 3–26.

Helleiner, Eric. 1994. *States and the Reemergence of Global Finance: From Bretton Woods to the 1990s*. Ithaca, NY: Cornell University Press.

Hochreither, Eduard, Klaus Schmidt-Hebbel and Georg Winckler. 2002. "Monetary Union: European Lessons, Latin American Prospects." Central Bank of Chile Working Papers, No. 167. Santiago: Central Bank of Chile.

International Monetary Fund. 2008. "Time Series Data on International Reserves and Foreign Currency Liquidity: Official Reserve Assets." Washington DC: International Monetary Fund.

Isard, Peter. 2005. *Globalization and the International Financial System: What's Wrong and What can be Done*. New York: Cambridge University Press.

Kaminsky, Graciela and Carmen Reinhart. 2000. "On Crises, Contagion and Confusion." *Journal of International Economics* 51: 145–68.

Kirshner, Jonathan. 1995. *Currency and Coercion: The Political Economy of International Monetary Power*. Princeton: Princeton University Press.

———. 2006. "Currency and Coercion in the Twenty-First Century," in *International Monetary Power*, ed. David M. Andrews, 139–60. Ithaca, NY: Cornell University Press.

Kose, M. Ayhan, Eswar Prasad, Kenneth Rogoff and Shang-Jin Wei. 2006. "Financial Globalization: A Reappraisal." IMF Staff Papers WP/06/189. Washington DC: International Monetary Fund.

Krueger, Anne O. 1974. "The Political Economy of the Rent-Seeking Society." *American Economic Review* 64: 291–303.

Labán M., Raúl, and Felipe Larraín B. 2001. "Can a Liberalization of Capital Outflows Increase Net Capital Inflows?: Latin America in the 1990s," in *Capital Flows, Capital Controls, and Currency Crises*, ed. Felipe Larraín B., 19–37. Ann Arbor: University of Michigan Press.

Mishkin, Frederic S. and Miguel A. Savastano. 2000. "Monetary Policy Strategies for Latin America." NBER Working Paper No. 7617. Cambridge, MA: National Bureau of Economic Research.

Montiel, Peter and Carmen Reinhart. 1999. "Do Capital Controls and Macroeconomic Policies Influence the Volume and Composition of Capital Flows? Evidence from the 1990s." *Journal of International Money and Finance* 18: 619–35.

Morales, Juan Antonio and Jeffrey Sachs. 1989. "Bolivia's Economic Crisis," in *Developing Country Debt and the World Economy*, ed. Jeffrey Sachs, 57–80. Chicago: University of Chicago Press.

Obstfeld, Maurice. 1996. "Models of Currency Crises with Self-Fulfilling Features." *European Economic Review* 40: 1037–48.

Przeworski, Adam and James Raymond Vreeland. 2000. "The Effect of IMF Programs on Economic Growth." *Journal of Development Economics* 62: 385–421.

Rodrik, Dani and Arvind Subramanian. 2008. "Why Did Financial Globalization Disappoint?" Cambridge, MA: Harvard University.

Ruggie, John Gerard. 1982. "International Regimes, Transactions, and Change: Embedded Liberalism in the Postwar Economic Order." *International Organization* 36: 379–415.

Sachs, Jeffrey D. and Andrew Warner. 1995. "Economic Reform and the Process of Global Integration." *Brookings Papers on Economic Activity*, vol. 1995, no. 1: 1–95.

Schadler, Susan, Maria Carkovic, Adam Bennett and Robert Khan. 1993. "Recent Experiences with Surges in Capital Inflows." IMF Occasional Paper No. 108. Washington DC: International Monetary Fund.

Soederberg, Susanne. 2008. "Deconstructing the Official Treatment for 'Enronitis': The Sarbanes-Oxley Act and the Neoliberal Governance of Corporate America." *Critical Sociology* 34: 657–80.

Taylor, Lance (ed.) 2006. *External Liberalization in Asia, Post-Socialist Europe, and Brazil.* New York: Oxford University Press.

Thacker, Strom. 1999. "The High Politics of IMF Lending." *World Politics* 52: 38–75.

Williamson, John. 1990. "What Washington Means by Policy Reform," in *Latin American Adjustment: How Much Has Happened?*, ed. John Williamson. Washington DC: Peterson Institute for International Economics.

Wypolsz, Charles. 2006. "European Monetary Union: The Dark Sides of a Major Success." *Economic Policy*: 207–61.

Chapter 4

DEVELOPMENT AND DEPENDENCY, DEVELOPMENTALISM AND ALTERNATIVES[1]

José Maurício Domingues
Instituto de Estudos Sociais e Políticos, IESP-UERJ

Introduction

Reflecting on development in the course of one of the most major crises ever faced in the modern world allows us to put things in perspective. Perhaps neoliberalism is finally going under – along with global economic prosperity and growth – regardless of the relative strength of the emerging East. In any case, while it is doubtful whether deeper changes will alter neoliberal economics and social policy as well as the widening inequality they entailed, a finance-led model of accumulation has proved untenable and will have to be changed in order to unburden the "real economy" processes wherein technological change and capital accumulation have proceeded apace in the last two decades. This is, in a more oblique way, the object of the present discussion which concerns the policies adopted thus far as well as the alternatives in respect to development in the contemporary world, with particular attention to the issue in the periphery and the semi-periphery.

This chapter will proceed through the following steps: first, I will briefly define the field of development and some basic issues to be investigated. Next, I will take up such issues in relation to Latin America. Economic development, underdevelopment and dependency, along with social conditions and social policy, will be outlined and discussed in both general and specific terms. Backwardness in technological terms as well as a dependent insertion in the

---

1 Presented at the conference on the "Comparative Perspectives of Development Experiences in South America and Eastern Europe, Development and Semiperiphery," Tallinn University, Estonia, October 2008.

world economy (increasingly via the export of primary products, but also to some extent due to a turn towards development sustained by increasing internal demand and targeted social policies with some improvement of overall social conditions) will be encountered. Finally, I will concentrate on the situation of Brazil in particular, raising a number of more far-reaching issues from its examination. Alternatives to this problematic situation will then be briefly considered. The overall conclusion is not especially positive, although it evinces mixed reflections and feelings; pessimism is certainly not the motto of the chapter.

Development: In General and in Latin America

Development is a large field and is presently facing a crisis. The issues this field has dealt with can be cast in several manners; from the perspective of "colonial economics" and the issues raised by latecomers to industrialization – especially through modernization and dependency theories as well as of developmentalism, present-day neoliberalism and the proposals to surpass it – and, finally, the human development approach along with the "alternative" and "post"-development perspectives. Lately in the so-called "South," the failure of development policies has gone hand in hand with a "profound impasse of development thinking." Neoliberalism was an answer to the impasses of global Keynesianism and the developmental state's limited success in Latin America (though not in Asia), while other approaches on their turn have tried to grasp issues beyond economic growth. This is the case of alternative development perspectives or approaches based on human needs and social problems, such as the 1970s "basic needs" doctrine or the United Nations (UN) Human Development Index (HDI) which includes basic welfare measures as a yardstick of development (Pieterse 2001, 94–110; Domingues 2008, ch. 2).

It cannot be denied that at a general, absolute and very basic level, there have been improvements in the conditions of life of the poor in most of the world (especially in urban areas). Eastern Europe and especially Russia, a sharply negative exception, do not share this positive outlook, while on the other hand, improvements are arguable in relation to rent and surely are not occurring in relation to global inequality.[2] In any case, access to some basic

---

2 The data used by the UN for its Millennium Development Goals, especially rent, consumption and poverty, are partly provided by the World Bank (see United Nations 2003b, 1–11). They are obtained with a very arguable perspective, which several authors (cf. Kiely 2007 chap. 7) discard as biased and excessively optimistic, stating that in fact, if China and India are excluded, there would have been an increase in world poverty at least until 2003.

public services, vaccination, health care, nourishment, child mortality, gender equity, etc., have somewhat improved such as envisioned and projected by the UN Millennium Development Goals (MDG) as well as documented by the global evolution of the HDI, although a number of problems do not bode well for the future. Examples include the spread of slums (wherein one third of the world's population dwells) and the slow pace of changes, especially in addition to the fact that recent changes for the better relied heavily on a favorable economic scenario for growth based on the rise in the price of commodities. This, however, seems to be coming to a halt at the same time as other challenges arise – such as the climate changes potentially provoked by global warming, which will disproportionately affect the poor. All in all, the millennium project will not live up to the "commitments" (United Nations 2003, 2008a) it set out to achieve. Moreover, the power of finance capital and of transnational corporations as well as the specialization of so-called "Southern" countries in (primary or even industrial) products of low aggregate value brought back to the forefront the issues dependency theory once underscored (Roitman Rosenmann 2008, ch. 2), although the theories which had criticized this state of affairs thirty years ago have not really made a comeback.

Development implied to a great extent (and in particular, in its most articulated versions or at least in the Latin American context) a shift in the power balance within countries as well as between countries in the global arena (Sunkel and Paz 1974). Neoliberalism has effectively displaced this view, which was underpinned by the structuralist outlook of the UN Economic Commission for Latin America (ECLA) and has amounted to a return of classical political economy. Neoclassical economics, with the supposition and celebration of perfect markets and unfettered economic development (meaning simply growth), now has the upper hand – or at least had it until the recent global financial crash. Although it has produced a rephrasing of development which goes beyond its previous conceptualization as something tantamount to gross domestic product (GDP) and thereby proposed a more "human face" to actual neoliberal practices, namely the human development approach and its HDI. Based on Sen's capability approach, this method however does not question and in fact sits comfortably aside economic orthodoxy and its "best practices." A close alliance has been forged with it, targeting the poverty of the poorest people and merely providing them with a future in which they might become a little less poor. This stems from Sen's and similar views of development, which are specific and highly individualistic and are accompanied by a fragmenting notion of freedom, which simply gives a philosophical sheen of legitimacy to such a political strategy (Sen 1999; and, for a critical argument, Domingues 2006b). Increasing inequality, both internal and global – whose evolution is totally independent from absolute and minor positive evolutions of the HDI – disappear in this picture, as do the attempts to overcome them.

In any case, this has been the world in which we have been living for two decades and we are likely to remain there. This is what (to take examples which do not actually involve the former "Third World" or the "South") we see in post–real socialist Eastern and Central Europe: patrimonial, underdeveloped capitalism (such as in Russia), plus perhaps a sweatshop economy based on cheap labor (as in Estonia), or something more developed but still "associated and dependent" capitalism driven by transnational corporations (with a good technological level and good jobs) for the happy few which made it through the transition due to particularly lucky conditions (the Visegrad countries, especially the Czech Republic, Hungary, Poland, Slovenia) are the paths taken in the course of their transition back to capitalism. Social conditions vary accordingly, being significantly better in the latter (King 2001; Bohle and Greskovits 2007). While the central countries of capitalism – the US, those in Northwest Europe, Japan – carry on as the engines of innovation and accumulation within the global system despite the recent financial crisis and a possible shift of the capitalism axis toward Asia (China and the Southeast region), much of the world follows on without any actual change in its relative position in the international division of labor. Worse still, perhaps, it is devolving in this regard with the evolution of social conditions in principle replicating economic prowess, although this is not always the case given that it can vary independently to some extent (Castells 2000; RICYT 2005). The periphery dreamt of catching-up with the West. Perhaps in East Asia this will be the case through its varied but mostly successful developmentalist states (Amsden 2001), and some Eastern European countries can perform well, albeit dependently, so as to get closer to a central or a very strong semi-peripheral condition. In most of the world since the 1980s, however, this is clearly not possible – at least in the foreseeable future. Small wonder, therefore, development thinking is in such a bad shape.

Things do not look bright either when we focus on one of the foremost innovations in the field in the last decades: "sustainable development." This began as a general prospect that questioned the possibility of reconciling the well-being of the planet with development and population growth in the Club of Rome 1972 *Limits to Growth* document and came to a conclusion in the 1987 Brutland Report for the United Nations, titled *Our Common Future* with an accommodation between the two terms of the pair, sustainability and development. They had to be brought together due to the desires and demands of developing countries, but also of course thanks to the expansive dynamics of capitalism. A rather vague notion resulted from the whole discussion and was institutionalized without greater impact over actual economic and social developments in global terms (Nobre and Carvalho 2002). And, as the MDG themselves show, the single most dramatic symptom of the pressure growth has been upon the Earth's living infrastructure, global warming, which has not deserved the resources and the necessary changes in order to be averted (United Nations 2008a).

That said, how does Latin America as a specific region fit into this frame? The basic hypothesis of this chapter regarding contemporary Latin America runs as follows. Modernity has, in the subcontinent as well as in the center of the global system, evolved thus far through three phases in which the latter has been the main dynamic force. After a liberal restricted phase and a following one organized by the state (in Latin America's typical case, a weak developmentalist state), we have globally entered a third phase in which high technology and networked firms (often with state sponsorship) leads the process of capitalist accumulation. Economic growth has indeed been steadily in the region from 2004 to 2008, in average above 3 percent per year, something that has not happened since the late 1960s. However, in contrast to important parts of Asia, Latin America has been once again confined to the role of a peripheral or semi-peripheral economy, often stuck by and large, in the position of primary commodities exporters. This has been in fact reinforced more recently and is true even in the case of industrially stronger Brazil, as we will see below. While Mexico is dependent for its exports on assembling industries – the "maquiladoras" – which usually add little value to the parts brought together there, drawing upon cheap labor, Argentina and especially Chile were deindustrialized by the military dictatorships of the 1970s–80s and export basically primary products. Brazil's exports are also highly dependent on commodities (soya beans, iron, steel, meat, etc.), which are completed by low added value industrialized products. Overall, social conditions have improved recently whereas pressure over natural resources has steadily intensified (Domingues and Pontual 2009, passim, especially ch. 2; CEPAL 2008b, 13, 19).

Thus we can even speak, despite the recent wave of growth, of the reentrenchment of (dependent) "underdevelopment" if we are to recover Cardoso and Faletto's (1970, especially 25ff.) classical statement of the issue. This is plausible if we conceive underdevelopment as the lack of differentiation of the economy in comparison with developed ones within the encompassing system; in other words, if we take into consideration the gap between the central countries and the periphery or even the semi-periphery, where "associated (and dependent) development" originally occurred – in Latin America in particular – via the transplantation of relatively old Fordist industries catering mainly for the middle classes. Even these more advanced countries lag behind today, insofar as such industries of the 1970s–80s are no longer in the forefront of global processes of accumulation (in fact when transplanted they were about to exhaust their expansive drive). Whereas this was due to the lack of industry and especially of a sector based on the production of means of production (a thesis supported by the contemporary Regulation School, cf. Boyer and Saillard 2002), today the same can be said in relation to the lack of technological development in the periphery and even in much of the semi-periphery in contrast to what goes on in the center of the system – especially in relation to microelectronics, information technologies and telecommunications, the dynamic core of contemporary capitalist accumulation (Castells [1998] 2000).

The gap has actually been widening in this regard, since investment in science and technology (S&T) and research and development (R&D) is concentrated in the US, Western Europe and some parts of Asia (including China, which departs from a very low position, though). In 2003, global spending in S&T and R&D reached $860 billion, an amazing 82 percent increase in relation to 1994. While Latin America slightly increased its expenditure, its share of global expenses decreased from a tiny 3.1 to 2.5 percent (using purchasing power parity terms (PPP) which improves this picture slightly). In 2005 (again according to PPP terms), North America as a whole invested 35.1 percent of the total worldly expenditure in S&T and R&D; Europe declined to 25.7 and Asia improved its share to 34.4 percent. Latin America's position worsened, decreasing to 2.5 percent – an almost residual value indeed. Other data further color this picture: while in 2005 the US invested 2.6 percent of a huge GDP and Japan 3.33 percent in the field with Europe reaching 1.74 and China 1.34 percent, the Latin American countries came far behind. Brazil, at the regional top, invested 0.82, Chile 0.68, Cuba 0.51, Argentina and Mexico both 0.46 percent – a steady average for the former despite a difficult period in 2001–2 due to its major economic crisis, and with such numbers meaning an increase in fact in the latter's resources for research and formation. Latin America's average was 0.54 percent. The private sector is largely absent from the picture, contrary to what happens in central countries. The ratio of researchers to inhabitants is low even in those countries: 0.7, 0.8 and 1.7 for 1,000 people respectively for Mexico, Brazil and Argentina – where qualification is lower however – compared for instance, to 6.9 in France and 9.0 in the US (all data here has been extracted from RICYT 2005, 2008). There are very few innovation clusters in the region (basically, only in Brazil) and universities by and large remain distant from productive processes (Bortagaray and Tiffin 2002). Moreover, there is virtually no cooperation between Latin American countries, albeit Argentina and Brazil within the Mercosur constituting a small exception to this. High technology sectors are nonexistent, aside from a few exceptions, mainly in Brazil, in activities often linked to agriculture.

The dynamic centers of global accumulation remain the US, Western Europe and, to a smaller extent, some Asian countries. Dependency is reproduced through a renewed international division of labor. Industrialization via import substitution and state-led development was abandoned. Dependency is now reproduced through a renewed division of labor, specifically by the power of transnational corporations, finance capital, international financial organizations and entities such as risk assessment agencies. Latin America remains in a subordinate position in all these dimensions (Kiely 2007; Domingues 2008, 61–4). This has all further worsened if we consider that the Latin American countries have opted to open themselves up to transnational corporations, which they have tried to attract – especially since the 1990s – to operate in their territories without these firms investing locally in R&D and without this ever being demanded of them (in fact, by 2000, such firms invested almost nothing outside their domestic basis). Moreover, insofar as "knowledge" is kept exclusive through property rights in a strict manner (since it generates "technological rents") – in particular when it is produced through science and technology and can be only partially codified and formally transmitted – the lack of national control over processes based on innovation implies an even more disadvantaged position and relative loss of power. As the figures show, the contrary has happened and carries on happening with something of an actual trend of neodevelopmentalism appearing in Southeast Asia and in China in the public as well as in the private sector, sometimes via joint ventures with transnational firms. Formerly (and still today) these countries have emulated the Japanese model (see Amsden 2001, in particular 2–7, 14, 191).

In any case, social conditions have improved in terms of education, nourishment, sanitation, gender equality and so on, according to HDI measures. Latin America does not perform too badly in these terms in international comparison, having achieved 87 percent of Goal 1 of the Millennium Agenda in 68 percent of time. Some of its countries are among the better off (Argentina, Chile, Uruguay, Costa Rica, Cuba, Mexico and Brazil) while most of them are in the intermediate layer (Venezuela, Colombia, the Dominican Republic, Peru, Ecuador, Paraguay, El Salvador, Nicaragua, Honduras, Bolivia and Guatemala), although the pattern for comparison and classification includes countries so deprived – especially in sub-Saharan Africa and South Asia – the picture becomes highly contestable (United Nations 2008a, 2008b; CEPAL 2008a, 64, which suggests the goals established by the UN globally should be broadened for the subcontinent). Poverty and extreme poverty clearly increased under neoliberal governments, especially in Argentina and Bolivia, but began decreasing sharply after changes in economic policy in the former (with no data available as yet for the Evo Morales government in Bolivia), while Uruguay alone has been prey to a long-term systematic decay in living conditions and income (CEPAL 2008a, 56–8).

Thus, although Latin America is still the region of the world with the highest levels of inequality, the income of the poor has increased along with an improvement of social conditions. The former is directly coupled with economic growth, rode atop the wave of strong worldwide economic performance for some six years until 2008 and can be linked to social policy, which has a lot to do with targeted programs. These originally derive from the World Bank's schemes of compensation for neoliberal "structural reform," Sen's perspective (though this is hardly acknowledged) and the need to face up to the fact that an extremely large number of people in Latin America live in destitution and hunger, whose eradication was explicitly the goal of Luis Inácio Lula da Silva's Zero Hunger program (Brazil's main social program), although its original outline owes much to the Fernando Henrique Cardoso government. While this and similar programs might rather be seen as a form of managing poverty, which does not actually aim at overcoming it (Lautier 1995), other governments in the region have implemented them – for instance, Morales and his anti-neoliberal, leftwing administration in Bolivia launched the Juancito Pinto Bonus (Hardy 2003; Domingues 2008: 21–3; CEPAL 2008a, 110–7). Nevertheless, whether or not this decrease of inequality can follow a sustainable path beyond the immediate favorable economic situation, and the rise to government after the radical period of neoliberal reforms of mostly center-of-the-left or leftist political forces is yet to be seen. Although commodity exports have played a crucial role in these economies, the internal market has been aided by sustained growth and perhaps, to a varying extent, by such programs of direct income transfer, implying some synergy between the expansion of GDP and the improvement of popular income.

In addition, it must be said that "sustainable development" (the proposal of which was somewhat shaped by Latin American proposals in the course of the debate on how to reverse environmental degradation and reconcile it with economic growth) is not in good shape in the subcontinent. There has been a lot of legislation – specifically in Brazil, but also in Mexico and Venezuela and now Bolivia, Ecuador and Argentina – but when push comes to shove, development has usually gained the upper hand vis-à-vis sustainability and environmental protection. The development of agribusiness and the exploration of the regions' mineral resources, as well as of its oil and gas, has increased the pressure upon its natural infrastructure (Domingues and Pontual 2009).

The meaning of this improvement of market conditions for labor and especially the very poor, along with the backwardness of technological developments and a renewed pressure on natural resources, will be taken up with particular attention to the case of Brazil below. Contradictory trends will emerge from this discussion. The situation is problematic for both of them. However, they may not remain so and converge due to political decision and appropriate policy outlines.

Development in Brazil

Similarly to what happened all over the world, development was conceived of in Brazil during the second phase of modernity – when the country's industrialization really took off – as based on a relatively weak developmental state due to political reasons, especially if compared with those that emerged in Asia, but still more powerful than those in most Latin American countries and elsewhere in the world. In other words, the process relied on a "collective subjectivity" capable of mobilizing resources in a centralized manner. From the 1930s to the 1970s Brazil grew steadily and in some periods very strongly, without land reform and via a model of "conservative modernization." A reasonably solid industrial basis was developed and Brazil became – along with India – the only Third World country to have built a means of production (or capital goods) sector, although this was less than sophisticated. The 1980s were a decade of deep crisis and economic paralysis, followed by neoliberal reforms. These, which implied structural adjustment and privatization, were however relatively mild if compared to what happened in other Latin American countries. Noteworthy is the fact that, contrary to Chile and especially Argentina, Brazil never deindustrialized. Poverty, and in particular inequality, remained deeply entrenched in Brazilian society throughout the period although to a great extent agribusiness sorted out the agrarian problem in a capitalist direction. Since the 1980s – and especially with the 1988 Constitution – democracy and the full range of rights have become key factors in the political dynamics of the country. While the 1990s, under two Cardoso governments, advanced moderate neoliberal reforms and Lula's first term in office did not change anything significantly; except for the refashioning and broadening of targeted social policy through the Bolsa Família program, state investments have grown and efforts at the development of S&T and R&D have been made without so far resulting in an actual breakthrough in terms of steady as well as more far reaching innovations. No actual rupture with that paradigm has emerged – in fact agribusiness and primary exports in general have been strengthened, although the growth of the internal market has also gained some momentum in the last couple of years. Pressure upon these countries' natural environments has also deepened recently (see Domingues 2006a, 2008). Let us examine this more closely.

With respect to S&T and R&D, the most important figures have already been mentioned above. While investment is concentrated in government hands, the private sector does not perform well at all: it channels very little money into innovation, large and export firms respond for most of the investment and there is virtually no cooperation between firms let alone between firms and university research centers –even because this network is possible only if companies themselves have an internal structure geared towards research (De Negri and Salerno 2005). The government has actively sought to change this with funding especially through its Financiadora de Estudos e Projetos (FINEP) and by laws and policies facilitating and stimulating technological innovation and partnerships. Outcomes have been real, but still limited.[3] For policymakers, intellectuals and even entrepreneurial leadership, Brazil faces daunting challenges in this field, especially considering the country's well-known deficiencies in microelectronics sector – a deadlock hard to overcome although Brazil has fared little better in the software industry (Schueler and Lessa 2008).[4] In cognizance to "sustainability," problems have been plenty. Although Brazil has enacted very advanced legislation and to some extent has a reasonably strong administrative body to deal with the issue, the growth of agribusiness (especially encroaching upon the Amazon region, partially caused by the expansion of sugarcane plantations for the production of ethanol, a cleaner energy source) and megascale development projects have had a negative impact in this regard in a country perceived as an extension of Eden and where natural resources have been seen as basically inexhaustible – our prosperous future often taken as a given due to this particular and blessed endowment (Schueler and Lessa 2008; Domingues and Pontual 2009).

It is perhaps with respect to developments in the internal market that there have been a greater number of novel developments since 2007. As noted by the Applied Economic Research Institute (IPEA) of Brazil, 2008 data reveals both a continuous process of gross capital formation (fixed as well as stocks) and a strong growth of "domestic demand" for a couple of years now, which includes the regular increase of family consumption due to a steady rise in levels of employment and especially formal jobs, minimum wage increases above inflation, unemployment benefits and direct income transfer social policies, bringing into market consumers with low levels of income who happen to

---

3 There are evidences that governmental policies have had some impact on innovation in recent years (cf. De Negri and Kubota 2008).

4 There has been in fact a relative involution in terms of technological content of the Brazilian industry in the last decades – hence of its particularly important effect in the impulse towards innovation in the economy as a whole (Nassif 2008). Such conclusions would certainly look worse with a methodology that made clear that the electric-electronic sectors in the country too often perform merely assemblage and that microelectronics is practically inexistent. Not by chance do the Lula government industrial and innovation policies give special attention to capital goods.

also be most prone to consume (IPEA 2008, 8). It is true that durable goods (such as cars, whose exports declined) and imports due to the dollar at a low exchange rate have caused a rise in middle class consumption, which adds credit expansion to the list of effects created by greater consumption at the lower income level (according to the Brazilian Institute for Geography and Statistics' data (IBGE), cf. Folha online).

A conceptual digression is important here for the elaboration of the argument. Under the impact of the Club of Rome 1972 report on the environment and engaged in a dialogue with dependency theories, Furtado stated the impossibility of a generalization of Western patterns of consumption and discussed what he called "the myth of economic development," opposing "modernization" and "development." The former was based on the diffusion of the consumption patterns typical of the center, as opposed to the process of capital formation in the periphery, implying strong research in R&D to the detriment of the consumption patterns of the poorest strata of the population. This gave rise to dependency – whose core was actually "cultural colonization." While initially high consumption was financed by primary exports, the substitution of imported goods by internal production of the same products for the "modernized" minority which were the allies of the powerful in the center, engendered and also became dependent on income concentration, eventually leading to the displacement of national by foreign firms which ultimately control technological advancements. Actual "development" as such would be based on the diffusion of goods for mass consumption produced with simpler technology and a much better distribution of income (and perhaps a local or state bourgeoisie) (Furtado 1974, 78–97).

In order to eschew terminological problems, let me first note that we can approach what Furtado calls modernization and development as two distinct processes of modernization based on distinct "modernizing moves" by collective subjectivities, in a more or less intended manner (cf. Domingues 2008). Furtado's view is in this regard perhaps dated by his refusal of the notion of modernity such as conceptualized by the old and teleological modernization theory. At any rate, some sort of modernization necessarily comes about, with contingency playing a strong role. Modernization is activated by political will but also by more encompassing and less intentional social dynamics, in one direction or another, of the two possibilities he discussed. We will also come back to his problematic – and in my view false opposition – between advancements in S&T and R&D, on the one hand and development proper, on the other. But to some extent, he was perhaps on the right track when he stressed the role of the increase in consumption of basic goods for the masses. This was of course related to the strengthening of the internal market, which should embrace not only the upper and middle classes, but workers as well. even the poorest ones, in its dynamics, whereby a sort of growth linked to the overcoming of poverty, income distribution and in the end a change in patterns of consumption could be achieved – a global necessity indeed, although this poses thorny issues, especially for the center.

This may have something to do with programs similar to the Brazilian Bolsa Família. A sort of Keynesianism of the poor would emerge from this, a demand-led outcome, even though what was originally envisaged was perhaps not a demand-led economic policy but rather simply a program to feed people decently. While the middle classes are part of the story since durable goods are of course consumed by them in higher levels than by the popular classes, food, clothing and other basic, nondurable and simplest goods have been increasingly produced for workers who have been earning more and have suffered less from unemployment thanks to economic growth, and especially for the very poor, in which the Bolsa Família program has played a key role. A twist to development has somehow been achieved in this regard, although this has been limited and its scope is arguable since the whole present situation has been dependent on global growth, whose immediate future is uncertain at best. This view, moreover, is perhaps more realistic, insofar as it does not project into a desired future the actual processes of the present, rather than thinking about the program as the avenue for a universal politics of minimal income or something similar to start with because there is already a multiplicity of targeted income policies which are not necessarily synchronized and in line with the Bolsa Família (Lautier 2007; Domingues 2008, 19–20).[5]

Hence, we have three aspects of development in contemporary Brazil, each of which follows distinct trajectories. First, there is the issue of technological development in which the subcontinent is clearly and acutely lagging behind; second, the increased pressure over natural resources which is being addressed by a sustainable development project that is but a pale reflection today of what it proposed in the heyday of its idealization; and finally, the social policy-dependent economic growth which in the last years has especially helped bring the poorest strata into the market. Inequality has decreased also in the last years – although speaking of a huge new middle class, just because people earn and consume more, is so nonsensical that such a claim barely deserves discussion. In Furtado's view, the first and the last aspects would be at odds, whereas he did not perceive any alternatives for the second. But is this really

---

5 In a global situation in which industrial products face, according to some (Brenner 2006), a permanent crisis of overproduction, tapping on the internal market has helped the accumulation of capital in Brazil and in this sense, contributed to its development. I leave aside here the discussion of the bureaucratic form of clientelism that may be seen as crucial for this programme.

the case? At the risk of reproducing the problematic "structural heterogeneity" that Pinto (1976) identified as typical of the Latin American productive tissue, both must be emphasized regardless of whether targeted social policies are at the root of the increase in popular consumption, or whether more universal and inclusive measures are sought for. A change in the paradigm of production vis-à-vis nature should by no means disappear from the agenda, but it certainly depends much more on scientific development than Furtado seemed capable of appreciating (cf. Beck [1986] 1992).

If fighting inequalities in the course of development hinges on dealing with the relative position of social classes whereby the fight against poverty can take on a new meaning, tackling it globally entails the overcoming of the devastating gap that is today inherent to the relations between the center and the periphery as well as the semi-periphery with regard to science and technology. It does not necessarily mean that (especially if we are to take into account the complexity and manifold possibilities that this situation has posed to all contemporary societies) all countries must dominate the productive and technological capacities that can be identified at present. But if small and medium-sized countries can somehow specialize in a number of specific niches of production – either in services or industry – a country as large as Brazil cannot give up on controlling the main sectors of science and technological development as well as means of production, even when inserted within regional blocs and partnerships. Right now all we can do is keep trying to if not catch up with the central countries, at least establish patterns of development with which we can control our destiny and move towards overcoming or reducing international inequalities. It may be that a neodevelopmentalist model will eventually emerge, combining macroeconomic stability and the power of market mechanism inherited from the neoliberal phase with state intervention, which depends on an increase of state capacity of coordination in addition to a stronger internal market (Boschi and Gaitán 2008). Some initial steps have been taken in this direction, with Brazil standing out in this regard. But according to the arguments of this chapter, even this country still has a long way to go. For Latin America as a whole, the situation is even more difficult.

An Excursus on "Alternative Development" or "Alternatives to Development"

The shortcomings and often violent outcomes of development have also led to its questioning. Let me briefly explore in which directions this has been carried out. With regard to Latin America, this is strongly expressed theoretically by Escobar's (1995, especially 222ff.) poststructuralist approach, within a postdevelopment outlook, in which alternatives to mainstream development are seen as local and having been put forward basically by indigenous peoples in forest areas. Not only are claims in this regard exaggerated, they also leave most people in the region absolutely marginalized from public debate and policies being that in this sort of argument, the role of the state is usually neglected and the local connections are undertheorized.

This is the case even of Nandy's (2003, 9–10, 158–70, 171–81) insightful if exaggerated propositions, especially about India. Drawing upon a critique of modernity that stems from dissenting views within Western modernity – especially the condemnation of the drive towards homogenization of its mainstream project by the Frankfurt School – Nandy is too quick to establish a connection between development in general, with no distinctions allowed for within it and a brand of colonialism in search of a new "civilizing mission." He then jumps to another unqualified affirmation that development equates underdevelopment to "insanity," "immaturity" and "irrationality." "Alternative development" and "beyond development" perspectives would be appropriate answers to that, pitching the concrete, nonmodern traditions against development as pathways to a "desirable" society. Development must have its universalistic claims denied. Besides, it appears as an authoritarian project and practice – science dismissing all other forms of knowledge and the state playing an ill-fated role in the top-down mobilization of society, as it is usually parasitic and self-concerned. Examples in this regard include Brazil, China, Japan, Taiwan and to some extent India and Sri Lanka, due to recent choices taken in these countries.

But what are the alternatives beyond development? For Nandy it seems that resistance is what is actually at stake, as if there was no reason to be discontent with that. He disregards both the allure of development for most of the population and the unchecked power of the state and market insofar as no actual alternative – beyond circumscribed situations and localized resistance – is offered as a platform through which a dispute over the general direction of the process could be staged, regardless of how hard this is of course. It is strange that Nandy denounces the state and science, being critical of consumerism and fetishism but is not really concerned with the advance of neoliberalism, which jettisoned the state and sits comfortably together with local projects and the work carried out by nongovernmental organizations (NGOs). It makes no sense either to denounce an alleged collusion of authoritarianism and development: many countries (take for instance contemporary Brazil and India) defy such simplistic arguments, whatever limitations one may point out in the dynamics of their democracies let alone the implicit thesis that modernity is intrinsically and exclusively oppressive and the fact that the collusion of authoritarianism and underdevelopment is just too easy to locate in many instances.[6] In addition, while the diversity of knowledge that characterizes humanity should be welcome and acknowledged, it is unlikely that we can go very far – given the problems we face – without the widespread use of advanced science, however sensitive to the density of social life and democratic politics it must become. Should we be content with staying at the margins of actual processes of development, appeased by the wholesome denunciation of its evil designs, or can and should we go further than that?

In fact, after more than one or two decades of debate, such moves have not really offered an alternative paradigm. To be sure, one may argue that the goal was not (or should not be) such a blueprint, since it is locally and by specific populations that things should be worked out. However, concretely alternative and beyond development perspectives may end up as merely local projects that well fit the dominant neoliberal paradigm which has dictated economic and social policies around the world, since they do not tackle large-scale problems (Pieterse 2001, 49–74, 104–7). Of course there may be more radical perspectives which do not necessarily involve discredited forms of socialism, opening up to social experimentation with social life and economics. But they too have not gone past the stage of theoretical proposals (see Unger 2006.)[7]

Thus, if "alternatives to development" or "alternative development" are not to be simply discarded, especially as they imply social experiment with economics, social policy and forms of life, the issues that concretely involve the majority of the population of the world today relate to the position of their countries and regions within the global system, to social conditions and inequality and finally, to the relation of development and growth with the survival of the planet and the human species. They cannot

---

6 One argument is, however, especially insightful and powerful in his analysis: while all human cultures have been aware of individualism, achievement drives and competitiveness but produced checks against such impulses, modernity has unleashed and elevated them to a superior position, with development drawing upon the same sources (Nandy 2003, 166–7). A political program should readily emerge from this.

7 In his discussion, Unger proposes to "rebel" against ruling orthodoxies. Changes in internal markets and global trade and institutions, cooperation and innovation in a large-scale and the freeing of labor are the main elements of his program. They are to be sustained by a working class seen as both very general (not the unionized industrial proletariat) and more individualist than socialists and social democrats ever imagined, without – on the contrary – antagonizing the petty-bourgeoisie. Reformed nations and styles of development, however always implying energized and institutionally open-ended democracy, feature prominently too. Experimentalism and the faith in the individual as an earthly god go hand in hand. The interest of the discussion and the brightness of the alternative have as their counterweight the disconnection of the program from social movements and their extremely encompassing demands.

be tackled merely with reference to local issues. In this chapter the situation was reviewed with special reference to Latin America and although no particularly good prospects were identified, a few elements may point to improvements especially of living conditions in absolute, not relative terms. It seems that as tiresome and somewhat dismal as it can be, we must carry on searching intellectually and practically for ways to break through the present situation.

Conclusion

According to the analysis carried out in the preceding pages, the balance sheet of development for Latin America and Brazil in particular is not at all convincing, despite substantial changes for the better which occurred in some dimensions in the last years. Economically, growth has not translated into improved positions for these countries within the global system and division of labor. In fact, "underdevelopment" has been regaining ground, since internal differentiation vis-à-vis the economies of central countries has not only stagnated but actually retreated, given the absence of the most sophisticated scientific and technological advances (let alone the absence or limitations of industry in many Latin American countries, with the traditional means of production – specifically capital goods – sector remaining underdeveloped even in Brazil). Nature has been mistreated too, with no greater improvement in this area and renewed pressure over natural resources creeping in, despite efforts by activists and sometimes by governments and advances in legislation. Alternative development or alternatives to development do not seem very far, although some of the ideas that come up in the debate may still have a role to play. Socially there has been some progress, but still limited both in infrastructural terms and in terms of income distribution and in the struggle to eliminate extreme poverty and hunger. Can neodevelopmentalism lead to an inflection to this process? This is still to be seen.

In any case, it is a good thing that the period of conformism is on the wane in Latin America. While Eastern Europe willingly embraces its new semi-peripheral or peripheral position within the global system and even the European Community (EC), Latin America and other parts of the world have at least raised criticisms in relation to its own development (Boatca, 2006). Those neodevelopmentalist themes are gaining some ground in the debate. I will bring this article to a conclusion by advancing one specific suggestion. While the first phase of modernity enshrined the liberal market and the second phase of modernity which corresponds to the golden years of development had the state as a central agent of this modernizing project, the third phase has made the market its sacred cow, with all virtuous developments depending on its unhindered workings, although networks have also played a role especially in high technology areas, which is not even often recognized. Neoliberalism been hegemonic thus far, but this does not need to be the case forever. We can envision a more complex pattern leading to networked modernizing moves in which state, market and specific particular social agents come together and negotiate directions for development, with no damage done to a more universalistic and encompassing perspective (Domingues [1999] 2003, 2008). There is no way to get rid of the market today, nor is getting rid of the state more than a rhetorical move. Democratization and complexity need greater participation and flexibility (not excluding but certainly not privileging NGOs). The national and the regional levels remain crucial for the overall perspective and we cannot be sure that *realpolitik* games will not be played and large shifts will never occur. In any case the local level, inclusion and debate must be given pride of place in this outline of new developmentalist practices, beyond any homogenizing perspective. Networked development, in its political, social and economic aspects, would be probably the most interesting and viable way to lend a progressive and emancipatory twist to the third phase of modernity and build a more "moderate" state (as demanded by Nandy 2003, xii, 12–14). It does not cease to be an activist state capable of mobilizing resources, but it deals with its far-reaching challenges and demands – searching for innovation and new relations with nature, fighting inequalities both internally and globally – through subtler and cooperative links with multiple collectivities. Universalism and the inclusion of particularities, underdevelopment and dependency, sustainable development and widespread creativity, inequality and social policies, social pluralism and a more homogeneous diffusion of advanced technology would all have to be tackled within such a framework, stretching from the global to the local level.

The strong push Latin America has produced in relation to democracy since the 1980s, with the unfolding of a "molecular revolution," a powerful modernizing move against the neoliberal "transformist" project, another such move that was implemented at the same time provides ground for hope (Domingues 2008). This is precisely the case as new ideas and policies can potentially be put forward in connection with popular struggles and coalitions, perhaps allowing us to resume development in a different and more radical basis, tackling the problems and deadlocks that often seem impossible to overcome. This does not mean that intellectual effort is not needed. On the contrary, new, fresh thought is badly required. Of course, the world may not change significantly or even change for the worse. But the last word on development, let us hope, has not yet been said.

References

Amsden, Alice H. 2001. *The Rise of the "Rest." Challenges to the West from Late Industrializing Economies.* New York: Oxford University Press.

Beck, Ulrich. [1986] 1992. *Risk Society.* London: Sage.

Boatca, Manuela. 2006. "Semiperipheries in the World-System: Reflecting Eastern European and Latin American experiences." *Journal of World-Systems Research* 12.2.

Bohle, Dorothee and Béla Greskovits. 2007. "Neoliberalism, Embedded Neoliberalism, and Neocorporatism: Paths Towards Transnational Capitalism in Central-Eastern Europe." *West European Politics* 30.3: 443–66.

Bortagaray, Isabel and Scott Tiffin. 2002. "Innovation Clusters in Latin America," in *Technology Policy and Innovation*, vol. 1, ed. M. Heitor, D. Gibson, and M. Ibarra. New York: Quorum Books.

Boschi, Renato and Flavio Gaitán. 2008. "Empresas, capacidades estatales y estrategias de desarrollo en Brasil, Argentina y Chile." *Ponto de Vista* no. 3 (October 2008). Rio de Janeiro: NEIC-IESP. http://neic.iuperj.br/pontodevista/ (accessed September 2011).

Boyer, Robert and Yves Saillard (eds). 2002. *Théorie de la regulación. L'État des saviors.* Paris: La Découverte.

Brenner, Robert. 2006. *The Economics of Global Turbulence. The Advanced Capitalist Economies from Long Boom to Long Downturn, 1945–2005.* London and New York: Verso.

Cardoso, Fernando Henrique and Enzo Faletto. 1970. *Dependência e desenvolvimento na América Latina.* Rio de Janeiro: Zahar.

Castells, Manuel. [1998] 2000. *The Network Society. The Information Age: Economy, Society and Culture, Volume I.* Oxford: Blackwell.

———· 2000. *End of Millennium. The Information Age: Economy, Society and Culture, Volume III.* Oxford: Blackwell.

CEPAL. 2008a. *Panorama social de América Latina 2007.* http://www.eclac.org/cgi-bin/getProd.asp?xml=/publicaciones/xml/5/30305/P30305.xml&xsl=/dds/tpl/p9f.xsl&base=/tpl/top-bottom.xslt (accessed 17 January 2012).

———· 2008b. *Estudio económico de América Latina y el Caribe, 2007–2008.* Santiago, Chile: CEPAL.

De Negri, João Alberto and Sérgio Salerno (eds). 2005. *Inovações, padrões tecnológicos e desempenho das firmas industriais.* Brasília: IPEA.

De Negri, João Alberto and Luis Claudio Kubota (eds). 2008. *Políticas de incentivo à produção tecnológica no Brasil.* Brasília: IPEA.

Domingues, José Maurício. [1999] 2003. "Desenvolvimento, modernidade, subjetividade," in *Do ocidente à modernidade. Intelectuais e mudança social.* Rio de Janeiro: Civilização Brasileira.

———· 2006a. "Modelos de desenvolvimento e desafios latino-americanos," in *Aproximações à América Latina. Desafios contemporaneous.* Rio de Janeiro: Civilização Brasileira.

———· 2006b. "Amartya Sen, Freedom and Development: A Critical View," in *The Plurality of Modernity: Decentering Social Theory*, ed. Sérgio Costa, José Maurício Domingues, Wolfgang Knöbl and Josué Pereira da Silva. Mering: Hampp.

———· 2008. *Latin America and Contemporary Modernity: A Sociological Interpretation.* New York and London: Routledge.

Domingues, José Maurício and Andrea C. Pontual. 2009. "Environmental Responsibility and the Public Sphere in Latin America," in *Critical Turns in Critical Theory: New Directions in Political and Social Thought*, ed. Seamus O'Tuama. London and New York: I.B. Tauris.

Escobar, Arturo. 1995. *Encountering Development. The Making and Unmaking of the Third World.* Princeton: Princeton University Press.

Furtado, Celso. 1974. *O mito do desenvolvimento*. Rio de Janeiro: Paz e Terra.

Hardy, Clarisa. 2003. "Una nueva generación de reformas sociales en América Latina," in *La cuestión social: superación de la pobreza y política social a 7 años de Copenhague*, ed. Rolando Cordera, Leonardo Lomelí, and Rosa Elena Montes de Oca. Mexico City: UNAM, IETD and INDS.

IPEA. 2008. *Carta de conjuntura*. September.

Kiely, Ray. 2007. *The New Political Economy of Development. Globalization, Imperialism, Hegemony*. Basingstoke and New York: Palgrave.

King, Lawrence P. 2001. "Making Markets: A Comparative Study of Postcommunist Managerial Strategies in Central Europe." *Theory and Society* 30.4: 494–538.

Lautier, Bruno. 1995. "Citoyenneté et politiques d'ajustement," in *La citoyenneté sociale en Amérique latine*, ed. Bérengère Marques-Pereira and Ilán Bizberg. Paris: L'Harmattan.

———. 2007. "Les politiques sociales au Brasil durant le gouvernement de Lula: Aumône d'État ou droits sociaux." *Problèmes d'Amérique latine* 63: 51–76.

Nandy, Ashis. 2003. *The Romance of the State and the Fate of Dissent in the Tropics*. New Delhi: Oxford University Press.

Nassif, André. 2008. "Estructura y competitividad de la industria brasileña de bienes de capital." *Revista de la CEPAL* 96: 221–237.

Nobre, Marcos and Maurício de Carvalho. 2002. *Desenvolvimento sustentável: A institucionalização de um conceito*. Brasília: IBAMA/São Paulo: CEBRAP.

Pieterse, Jan Nederveen. 2001. *Development Theory. Deconstructions/Reconstructions*. London: Sage.

Pinto, Aníbal. 1976. "Heterogeneidade e padrão de desenvolvimento recente," in *América Latina. Ensaios de interpretação econômica*, ed. José Serra. Rio de Janeiro: Paz e Terra.

RICYT. 2005. *El Estado de la Ciencia*. Buenos Aires: RICYT.

———. 2008. *El Estado de la Ciencia*. Buenos Aires: RICYT.

Roitman Rosenmann, Marcos. 2008. *Pensar América Latina*. Buenos Aires: CLACSO.

Schuler, Paulo and Rogério Lessa. 2008. "Para onde vai o Brasil?" *Rumos. Economia & Desenvolvimento para os Novos Tempos* 239.

Sen, Amartya. 1999. *Development as Freedom*. New York: Knopf.

Sunkel, Osvaldo and Pedro Paz. 1974. *Os conceitos de desenvolvimento e subdesenvolvimento*. Rio de Janeiro: Forum and Hachette.

Unger, Roberto Mangabeira. 2006. *What Should the Left Propose?* London: Verso.

United Nations. 2003. *Human Development Report 2003*. New York and Oxford: University of Oxford Press.

———. 2008a. *The Millennium Development Goals Report*. New York: United Nations.

———. 2008b. *Human Development Report 2007/2008*. http://hdr.undp.org/en/media/HDR_20072008_EN_Complete.pdf (accessed 17 January 2012).

Part II

POLITICAL CULTURE, IDENTITY POLITICS AND POLITICAL CONTENTION

Chapter 5

INDIGENOUS MOVEMENTS IN BOLIVIA, ECUADOR AND PERU

Xavier Albó
CIPCA, La Paz

Ecuador, Peru and Bolivia are the three countries with the largest relative and absolute indigenous population in South America. Along with Mexico and Guatemala, these countries concentrate the majority of "witness" peoples (as Brazilian anthropologist Darcy Ribeiro named them) throughout the American continent. Given the historical and cultural significance of these groups, examining how they live today and how they are willing to play an active role in the political arena of their countries is of the utmost importance.

In this chapter, I will focus on Bolivia, Ecuador, and Peru: the three Central Andean countries which share centuries of history, first as part of the Tawantinsuyu (Inca Empire), and afterwards as part of the same Spanish Viceroyalty before they became modern independent states in the nineteenth century.

After a brief summary of some basic facts concerning their indigenous population, this chapter will narrate the intertwined history of these countries with special emphasis on more recent developments, taking into account the impact of subsequent waves of globalization in their territories, resources and ways of life as well as the main proposals and also the achievements of these movements in relation to the political role of indigenous populations in the state.[1]

Basic Data

The geographical backbone uniting these three countries together from north to south is the Andean mountain range, which centuries ago, was also the part of the domains of the Inca Empire (Tawantinsuyu), the capital of which was Cusco, in Peru. At that time, this Andean area was also highly populated and developed and to this day remains the region with the highest concentration of indigenous population, most of which have retained their ancestral Quechua and Aymara languages. Their settlements are mainly located at altitudes from 1,500 to 4,500 meters, sometimes along sharp slopes of mountains that soar up to 5,000 or even 6,000 meters, but can also be found in deep valleys and canyons. Developing one of the main historical world civilizations amidst these corrugated and difficult ecological environments was indeed a unique achievement.

The second main region is the narrow Pacific Coast, which was also densely populated before the conquest, especially in the area which is now Peru, as its rich archaeological remnants testify. The Spaniards arrived there first in 1532 from Panama and established their own capital in Lima as the head of a viceroyalty which covered all the area of these three modern countries and beyond. Open to the seas and to global immigrations and influences since colonial times, this region is now the most populated and prosperous one both in Ecuador and Peru – but not in Bolivia, since it lost its coastal territories to Chile in the 1879 War of the Pacific. In coastal regions most indigenous local population was rapidly assimilated, making this region less relevant for the purposes of this chapter except for the continuous immigration of highlanders (called *serranos*), many of which were once again assimilated after a few generations.

Eastwards the three countries also have a flat and warm tropical lowland region located either within the Amazonian basin or, as in southeast Bolivia (the Chaco region) within the La Plata Basin (LPB). Hundreds of smaller indigenous groups from a great variety of cultural and linguistic groups lived there; only a few of them developed some kind of local "kingdom." The colonial invaders were less interested in these regions as they offered little in terms substantial mining or manpower resources. Besides cattle and agricultural farms, the main effort in this region came from Jesuit, Franciscan and other missionaries inspired by the well-known experience of "Christian *reducciones*" originated in nearby Paraguay. European and other entrepreneurs did not become truly interested in this region until the late nineteenth century when new international commodities became attractive such as quinine, rubber, timber, new commercial crops and, more recently, oil.

The sharp cultural differences between these three regions sometimes resulted in the discrimination of the *serranos* by coastal populations. In Bolivia this sort of discrimination is mutual and opposes highlanders, known also as *collas*, to Amazonian lowlanders, also called *cambas*.

Applying universal criteria in defining the size of an indigenous population is still a controversial issue, as we will see in the following recent census data.

The 2001 Bolivian census shows that 62 percent of the 8.3 million total population claim to belong to some indigenous group: 31 percent are Quechua,

25 percent Aymara (both in the Andean region) and 6 percent belong to about 30 small groups in the eastern lowlands. This is the highest concentration in South America.

In Ecuador the 2001 census asked the question differently, through more generic categories usually applied by the nonindigenous to indigenous. Out of a population of 13 million, 77 percent identified themselves as *mestizo* (mixed blood) and only 7 percent as indigenous, while the local indigenous organizations claim that the real figure for the latter should be between 35 and 45 percent.[2] Most of them are Quichua,[3] both in the Andean and Amazonian regions, plus nine other minority groups in the lowlands.

The 2005 Peruvian census (with 26 million people) decided not to include this kind of question; Mexican anthropologist Bonfil Batalla would call that a "statistical ethnocide." Therefore we can only rely on a 2001 national sampling survey which, using a self-definition question similar to that in the Bolivian census, shows that 30 percent consider themselves Quechua, 4 percent Aymara and 3 percent members of other 65 small lowland ethnic groups.

Most people assume than all these indigenous groups live in their rural territories, and as a matter of fact many local censuses count them only in these places, especially in the lowlands. However this assumption is misleading. Nowadays, as a result of migration, there are more indigenous in the cities (including those in the coastal region) than in their rural territories; quite a few, including many indigenous leaders, keep moving along both locations.

Entangled Processes

Although these indigenous groups belong now to three different countries, their common history, culture, language and political ruling before and during the colonial era both in the coast and in the Andean region, make it possible to intertwine their histories into a single narrative connecting the past to the present.

Colonial period

The generic labeling and leveling of all these peoples as "indigenous" is the result of the earlier globalization which took place with the discovery, conquest and advent of colonial regime after 1492. Columbus's confusion as to where his ships had arrived led to giving the generic name of "Indians" to all the indigenous of America, as if all they had come from distant India. Their previous identifications as Shuar, Guarani, Qulla, etc. were progressively reduced and diluted into such generic and discriminating labels. As a result, under the impact of this first wave of globalization, they were no longer regarded as specific peoples with their own particular histories, cultures and identities. Their deeper identities were camouflaged and their gradual decimation further mystified the "Indian" quid pro quo. According to Wieviorka, this was the beginning of modern racism.

However, indigenous peoples were not fully dominated. Besides frequent local rebellions, the general uprising which occurred from 1780 to 1783 and extended from Cusco to northern Argentina and Chile shook the colonial system. It was led in Cusco and its environs by traditional authorities such as Tupaj Amaru and his wife Micaela Bastidas in the La Plata (Sucre) and Potosí region by Katari brothers near, and by plebeian leaders like Julian Apasa, who took the war name of Tupaj Katari, and his wife Bartolina Sisa, around La Paz. They were ultimately defeated by Spanish and creole forces, but this uprising awakened the conscience of local creoles and made them realize that their independence from the Spaniards was possible. To this day the memory of this uprising is quite alive in all indigenous mobilizations. Among the many smaller tropical lowland groups, while some were fully colonized, a few – mainly the Shuar in Amazonian Ecuador and the Guarani in Bolivian Chaco – were part of the "war frontier" which was never fully conquered (as the Mapuche in southern Chile as well), and not a few remained "undiscovered" or at least isolated until the mid-twentieth century or even later.

Neocolonial republics

Independence, accomplished between 1810 and 1830, did not truly liberate these indigenous populations in spite of the fact that they constituted the great majority of the three new republics. Moreover, during the mid-nineteenth century a new "liberal" globalization wave further worsened the indigenous situation. Communal lands were "liberated" to the market in the name of individual freedom which, according to the new liberal ideology, also implied private property. So, appealing to "liberty," big new private landholdings appeared and their former communal owners became hacienda servants under neofeudal labor arrangements. Social Darwinism added a pseudoscientific façade to racism and discrimination: indigenous peoples were supposed to be racially less fit than whites and therefore the best way for them to progress was under a white landlord. Furthermore, new international markets required alpaca wool, rubber (connected with the new automobile industry) and other items, and this allowed the new white-mestizo creole elites to claim for themselves even more indigenous lands. In colonial times, communities were the last rampart for the survival of indigenous cultures and ways of life. Yet at that time, in the name of liberty, even this bastion began to collapse.

As a result, in the late nineteenth century indigenous rebellions multiplied and in some cases they fostered temporary alliances between the indigenous and new political parties. Yet, when the latter succeeded and came to power, they behaved like their predecessors, claiming more communal lands. Bolivian history is filled with examples of turnarounds such as these from 1850 to 1932.

Related to the processes just described is the emergence of the new socialist left, after the Mexican and Russian revolutions both in 1917. At the beginning these new urban revolutionaries – led by Peruvian Mariátegui, father of the first communist parties in South America – set their eyes on indigenous peoples as the poorest and the most exploited ones within the poor lower class. This provided some good support for this exploited indigenous population. Thanks to these efforts, the first indigenous/peasant organization was born among the Quichua of Ecuador in 1926 (Federación Ecuatoriana de Indios or FEI) and in 1936 the first Quechua "peasant" unions appeared in Cochabamba. In spite of Mariátegui's pioneering discourse, this trend did not reach coastal Peru until 1946 and only expanded to its Andean region the late 1950s.

There were however two shortcomings in this new approach. The first one was that the specific cultural and ethnic identity of these various peoples was not sufficiently acknowledged. In spite of some early rhetorical statements,[4] the indigenous were considered relevant exclusively or mainly from a class perspective. For this very reason some of these new organizations preferred the category "peasant" even if their affiliates were also Quechua. The second limitation was that the communist or socialist parties which supported these organizations and movements became dependent on the Soviet Union (or later, on the Chinese) Communist Party, and therefore international issues and struggles from the top took priority over local issues such as the indigenous question.

From Indians to peasants

The main evolution under these constrains was the quest for agrarian reforms, first in Bolivia, in 1953, and much later in Ecuador and Peru.

These timing differences require an explanation. Whereas in the 1920s Peru and Ecuador led the formation of socialist-oriented indigenous-peasant organizations, in the next decades Bolivia headed more radical changes as a result of its defeat in the Chaco War (1932–5) against Paraguay. This was fuelled by the economic disputes between two oil multinationals, one allied with Paraguay and the other with Bolivia. Bolivia lost the war and as a result there was a deep identity crisis leading to a kind of refoundation of the state. The main lines of such a change had already been laid out by the 1938 Constitutional Assembly but its implementation was much slower, following an unstable trajectory as the conservative status quo and the innovators fought through elections, coups and finally the bloody 1952 National Revolution led by the Movimiento Nacionalista Revolucionario (MNR), which combined Marxist, nationalist and populist approaches.

As a result, Bolivia institutionalized several major social, political and economic structural changes much earlier than the other Latin American countries except Mexico. The more significant ones were the nationalization of mines (which at the time accounted for about 80 percent of all exports), the agrarian reform, universal suffrage (including women, the illiterate and indigenous populations) and the broadening of basic education for all. The central state gained substantial strength both economically and politically and most of the popular population segments finally felt included for the first time since independence and hence became proud, or at least conscious, of being an active part of the Bolivian nation. This was the beginning of the "State of 52," as it is known, which survived until 1985, although since 1965 the main democratic rights and institutions were suspended by a chain of military coups and regimes.

Indigenous groups, which in the 1950s comprised about three-fourths of the total population, were among the main winners, at least in the western Andean region, and therefore became very fond of the MNR. But, inspired by the Mexican Revolution and in accordance with mainstream sociological and political trends of the 1950s, the MNR rhetoric avoided the "indigenous" and ethnic concepts and proposed instead *campesino* (peasant) as the politically correct one. Likewise, the main goal of the reform was not to restore communal lands but rather to return or grant family and individual plots of land to "peasants." In the same vein, communities became *peasant syndicates* (a particular kind of trade unions) within a nationwide confederation which was very active in the implementation of the agrarian reform. All rural education and the obligatory military service were offered only in Spanish as the key tools to "civilize" the "Indians."

One decade later, Ecuador had its "decaffeinated" agrarian reform in 1964 and an even weaker second one in 1973. Peru had its own, led by a military group somehow inspired by the Yugoslavian model, in 1969. But these were already late responses, supported by the US, to Fidel Castro's revolution in Cuba in 1959.

In all cases, this kind of modernization was seen then as the right approach to overcome discrimination based on racial criteria. At that time most social scientists and politicians, from both the right and left, feared that claiming specific rights for "Indians" was too dangerous, because class conditions could be changed whereas the "racial" one could not (as it happened with the black movement in other countries). Except for anthropologists, the distinction between "ethnic," "cultural" and "racial" was either misunderstood or unacceptable. The best way to build the nation-state in these multicultural countries was considered to be through the fiction of the new "mestizo" state and society. But mestizo meant that indigenous should adopt the cultural traits of the dominant white-mestizo segments and not vice versa.

...And back to indigenous peoples

However, indigenous peoples had other feelings. At the beginning, many did expect that becoming "peasants" and just "Bolivian," "Peruvian" or Ecuadorian" would rid them of humiliation and racial discrimination. Yet in the late 1960s, some Aymaras began to question these assumptions; by neglecting their indigenous condition they were "throwing the baby out with the bath water." They rediscovered that they were and wanted to remain Aymaras (they preferred this denomination rather than the generic "indigenous" or "Indian" ones). Restoring the memory of past rebellions, they adopted the name *kataristas* in a reference to the anticolonial rebellion of 1780. Soon afterwards, in 1972, Quichuas from the Ecuadorian Andes also created a new organization called ECUARUNARI a Quichua syllabic acronym that means "the rising of Ecuadorian Indians" (literally: *runa-kuna* "persons").

At the other edge, peoples from the Amazonian forests who had not been submitted to this process of becoming "peasants" also started gaining consciousness and organizing themselves in new ways to react against the invasion of their territories by new extractive enterprises. This began in 1964 with the Shuar in Ecuador and with the Amuesha/Yánesha in Peru in 1968; by 1980 all the Amazonian groups had joined this effort and formed the Confederation of Indigenous Nationalities of the Ecuadorian Amazon (CONFENIAE) and the Interethnic Association for Development in the Peruvian Jungle (AIDESEP). Also in 1980, ECUARUNARI and CONFENIAE joined forces and formed a national organization originally called the Coordination of Indigenous Nationalities of Ecuador (CONACNIE) changed in 1986 to CONAIE. Indigenous peoples from the Bolivian lowlands followed the Peruvian model and in 1982 – when military dictatorships ended and democracy returned – created the Indigenous Confederation of Eastern Bolivia (CIDOB).

The new paradigm was already everywhere except in the Peruvian Coastal and Andean regions where both the state institutions and many local people still preferred to call themselves either peasants or sometimes *serranos*. Two main factors seem to explain this. The first one is the long internal war that this country and region suffered in the 1980s and early 1990s between the leftist armed group Sendero Luminoso (The Shining Path) and the Peruvian army. About 70,000 people were killed – 75 percent of them speakers of Quechua, Ashaninka or other native languages – and many escaped from their communities. Survival was the key issue during all these years rather than thinking of new conceptual identifications and organizations.

The second factor, which began much earlier but whose effects were accelerated later by the first factor, is the massive migration to Lima and the coast, where local identities easily became diluted. When these migrants came back to their former rural communities in the highlands, they tried to persuade their relatives and friends to be "modern" and to forget their indigenous origins.

It is worth noting that, except for the Peruvian Andes, all this ethnic awakening appeared years before ethnic issues gained high visibility around the world after the fall of the wall in Berlin (1989), the end of the socialist model in Eastern Europe and also before the ILO and the UN approved their documents in favor of indigenous peoples in 1989 and 2007. All these innovations as well as other issues raised by the feminist movement and others that advocate the right to be "different," or by the Green Movement and others concerned with environment, contributed with arguments and allies to the indigenous movements here described. But, given this chronology, these recent innovations at the international level cannot be considered the cause of our indigenous emergence.

In the following years both in Ecuador and Bolivia indigenous organizations consolidated and their influence within the state grew to the point that they came to be parts of government and congress and even became one of the main actors in the state reform through constitutional changes.

In Bolivia, since the fall of military dictatorships and the return to democracy through a confused period from 1978 to 1982, *kataristas* became the hegemonic group within the National Peasant Confederation, renamed CSUTCB[5] in 1979. This renewed organization became more independent from governments and, without losing its previous class approach, added a new and strong ethnic profile to it. *Kataristas* argued that their reality and struggle should be seen and taken care of with "two eyes": as peasants who were a substantial portion of the "exploited *class*," along with miners and other labor movements; and as Aymaras, Quechuas, etc., along with all the other "oppressed *nations*" within the neocolonial state. They also formed the first indigenous parties, still more symbolic than real, and through them elected their first national deputies.

The "insurgent" and the "tolerated" Indian

At a continental level, a substantial breakthrough occurred in the 1990s, when the international context was already somehow more favorable. It can be seen as a permanent dialectical struggle between the *indio alzado* (insurgent) and the *indio permitido* (tolerated), to use two common Latin American metaphorical expressions.

As for the insurgent Indian, in 1990 some similar events occurred both in Ecuador and in Bolivia. In Ecuador, CONAIE was already well-established throughout the country and, in response to the general lack of attention to indigenous claims, on 28 May 1990 they produced a predictable yet still surprising "ethnic earthquake," as some analysts later called it. That morning a multitude of indigenous established a sit-in occupying one of the main churches in Quito and during the next days, thousands and thousands began to blockade all the main roads throughout the Andean region and held massive assemblies in several cities. They did not have a very specific issue to negotiate but it was a general and diffused expression of disgust for the lack of sensibility on the part of society and its authorities. Their main slogan then referred to their need to be accepted and included: "Never again a country without Indians." This was the first of eight or more similar events in the following years, with demands becoming more and more specific.

Bolivia (and even Peru before the Shining Path war) had established blockades before in previous years, with varying degrees of effectiveness. In the late 1980s the main conflict in Bolivia was between repressive forces and coca leaf producers (who had migrated from the highlands in search of an alternative way of survival) in the tropical area of Cochabamba, and who, without being cocaine producers, were caught in the middle of an ambiguous international "war on drugs" as its first (weaker and less guilty) target. Their mottos were "Coca is not cocaine" and – in Quechua –"*Kawsachun coca wañuchun yanki*" (Long live coca, death to Yankees). In 1990 another "first" happened in Bolivia: the 40-days march "for territory and dignity" of about eight hundred lowland indigenous men, women and children from twelve ethnic groups all the way to La Paz. Since then this issue remains high a priority in the national agenda. In 1992 Amazonian Indians from Ecuador did something similar.

All these mobilizations happened shortly before the well-publicized official celebrations for the fifth centennial of Columbus's arrival to this continent (in October 1492). Indigenous organizations everywhere wondered whether they had anything to celebrate or they should rather complain and protest. But in their first continental gathering in Quito, Ecuador in June 1990, they finally decided that this event could be a good launching pad to share experiences and to strengthen their identities and organizations nationally and internationally. Hence, along with other peasant, black, urban worker and other grassroots organizations, they adopted the slogan "500 years of resistance." 1992 thus became a landmark for a more continental and even global approach to their movement.

All these events had an unexpected positive reaction in several governments, partly as a result of the new international context mentioned above. This is the *indio permitido* (tolerated Indian) perspective. As a result, during the 1990 march for territory in Bolivia, President Paz Zamora decided to meet with them accompanied by other high-level authorities in the jungle. He finally accepted their demands and even ratified the ILO Convention 169, approved just two years before in Geneva. His quick response was partly justified by the need to avoid international criticism as he negotiated substantial grants abroad.

From 1993 to 1997 a new government led by "Goni" Sánchez de Lozada, made further concessions. Along with Jeffrey Sachs, Goni had been one of the key executers of a thorough structural change initiated in 1985 meant to implement a "shock" program for the introduction of the globalized neoliberal model in Bolivia, This signified the end of the "State of 52." Eight years later he was facing the need to make this model "more human" and, advised by a US political marketing company, he selected the Aymara *katarista* Victor Hugo Cárdenas as his vice presidential candidate. This created a new image which proved crucial in winning the elections and in starting a government able to promote structural reform that was palatable to the indigenous and other popular groups. For instance, in 1994 the constitutional modifications which would acknowledge Bolivia as a "multiethnic, pluricultural" bilingual state, and which established intercultural education and decentralization, granting power to small rural municipalities ("Popular Participation" Law) were approved; and in 1996, the INRA law formalized the legal status of indigenous territories (or TCO).

In Ecuador, CONAIE had another successful general uprising in 1994 as an immediate reaction to right-wing president Sixto Duran and his parliament's decision to approve hastily and without any previous consultation a rural development law which favored big landowners and endangered the property of indigenous families and community-owned lands. Under intense pressure from the *indio alzado*, Duran had to share the negotiation table with a small Indian lady – Nina Pacari – and she, supported by her organization, made the government change the law again. Following this experience, in 1995 the CONAIE, along with other nonindigenous allies, decided to create their own political party called Pachakutik, the name of a precolonial Inca king, which also means "the one who changes time-and-space." Ecuadorian indigenous organizations therefore combined both insurgence and reform strategies, or – as they termed it – civil "disobedience" and "obedience." The main challenge these newly tolerated indigenous had to face was their participation in a constitutional assembly convened in 1998, after a national political crisis. In spite of the general conservative atmosphere of that convention,

Pachakutik was able to join forces and establish consensus, and prepared its proposals through a mobile "Alternative Constituent Assembly" throughout Ecuador. The party elected 10 percent of the constituents and the treatment of indigenous issues in the new constitution was much better than expected. At that time, this text was considered the best ever approved on this topic in Latin America.[6]

Nothing similar has happened in Peru so far, except in the Amazon where local indigenous groups and organizations never questioned their ethnic identities. The Shining Path conflict lost its strength after its main leader, Abimael Guzman, was captured in 1992 by Fujimori. But this president had an authoritarian, populist and modernizing approach which did not allow for significant openings to the indigenous questions. However – and significantly enough – this same Fujimori was the first one to mention the "pluri-cultural" quality of the state in his 1993 Peruvian Constitution (something explicit now in practically all Latin American constitutions). In that case this was no doubt a reaction to the new international atmosphere and perhaps even part of a strategy within the neoliberal economic model: provided that the global economy is well-controlled from above, something has to be granted to the nearly extinct indigenous peoples to keep them pacified. This established a minimum of concessions, able to satisfy the *indio permitido*. Otherwise, the general rule remained from above and below to "civilize Indians," except for a few local expressions mainly in the Aymara region next to Bolivia.

Coming to Power within the State

In the 2000s, further steps up were taken. Victor Hugo's vice presidency in Bolivia and the successful role of Pachakutik in the new constitution of Ecuador made it clear for insurgent indigenous movements and elites alike that it was possible for the former to become part of the state structure.

Bolivia

In Bolivia, insurgent coca producers, led by a young Aymara – Evo Morales – were the first ones to realize that the Popular Participation Law of 1994 created a new scenario in which it would be possible to gain formal recognition and power within the state. They quickly organized a new party, skillfully dribbled around the Electoral Court's moves to stop them and, in 1996, won elections in most municipalities not only in the coca producing area but also in other rural areas of Cochabamba. In 1997 they tried again at the national level and obtained four deputies, Evo among them. The next elected government, headed by former military dictator Banzer, tried to ensure US support with his "*zero coca*" program which was followed up by his successor Tuto Quiroga when in 2001 Banzer became sick and had to step down from power. Repression escalated in the tropical coca-growing areas, but so did organized resistance.

Since 2000 the neoliberal economic model, in place since 1985, began to collapse mainly due to increasing popular reactions against the lack of social sensibility of local and multinational enterprises in the way they were handling natural resources. The first general protest concerned the drinking water service in Cochabamba. Natural gas came next. From a long time land, wood and other natural resources were at the center of conflicts in the lowlands. Social protest was mounting. Each protest generated a chain reaction, and Morales – along with his new political party, the Movimiento al Socialismo (MAS) – became the main generators of dissent even among other social and political sectors both rural and urban, including the main traditional left-wing parties.

In January 2002, there was a general rebellion started by Cochabamba coca producers after an unfortunate decree by President Quiroga, forbidding access to any legal internal coca market for them. Some people were killed and this was the argument for the main traditional parties who alternated power since 1985 to expel Evo from his parliament seat. But this had the effect of strengthening him to the point that five months later, he and his party MAS received a share of votes only 1.5 percent below Goni Sanchez de Lozada, the winner. However, in late 2003, Goni had to renounce and escape from the country after he tried to stop a general popular rebellion (linked with the natural gas issue) particularly strong in El Alto (which is 74 percent Aymara and is the poor urban counterpart of La Paz) killing 70 unarmed civilians, most of them rural and urban Aymaras. After two short interim constitutional presidencies, new elections were called and the Evo and MAS coalition won with an unheard of 54 percent of votes, far ahead the second most voted former president Quiroga who reached only 28 percent. Evo Morales became the first elected indigenous president in all America.

After almost three years, this experience remains something unique and creative but also conflictive in many ways. A systematic analysis of it would require much more time and space. I will only shortly summarize the political issues at stake. The fact that Evo was the first indigenous president at the beginning acquired him much symbolical capital, raised hope and pride among the poor and indigenous, attracted international curiosity and solidarity but also galvanized internal enemies among the traditional elites which felt endangered by this new outcome.

The main bet to ensure structural change in the political scene was a constitutional assembly in Sucre from August 2006 to December 2007.

Its 255 elected members represented the multicultural reality of Bolivia better than ever, but only a few were lawyers and many were not shrewd politicians. 56 percent came from indigenous groups, 54 percent were MAS affiliates, while the main opposition force controlled only 24 percent of the assembly and the other 22 percent belonged to 14 minor political groups. At the beginning, the majority tried to push their view by all means, even without having two-thirds majority legally required to approve the final text. By forming alliances, the majority reached 62 percent and the opposition 29 percent. Too much time was lost in long and slow – sometimes productive other times sterile – discussions. In the last months there were frequent conflicts near the assembly's facilities due to militant outsiders who, associated with wealthier nonindigenous elites mainly from Santa Cruz (the largest city in the lowlands), tried everything to abort the assembly. At the end, constituents moved to other saver locations and approved the text with the legal majority but without the participation of the radical opposition, which had walked off two months before.

The constitutional text is like a newborn infant which had to be extracted by force from its mother's womb. The baby remains alive but still needs intensive care. Up to now (mid-2008) the referendum for its final approval has been postponed once and again because of open and growing conflict with opposition forces, particularly strong in Santa Cruz and the other three lowland departments that they control. Their main goal is to obtain "full autonomy" in their strongholds mainly for political and economic reasons: they lost the political hegemony but still have control over the main economic resources of the country and fear to lose their privileges if they have to share their wealth with the rest of the population. Their economic grievances are now amplified by the regional, social and even racial undertones that oppose them to the rest, since they are "white, tall and speak English" (as their beauty miss candidate explained some time ago).

On the other side, according to the new constitution's founding statement, Bolivia is a "unitarian plurinational state." It is plurinational because it is constituted by many "indigenous-originary-peasant peoples and nations" which existed since precolonial times who have now achieved full recognition. The name "nation" here should not be understood as if each of these peoples would be willing to become a separate state, as is the case in several new European countries. But it could imply certain collective rights for each people. For example: partial internal autonomy within their territories to develop their cultural ways of living, acknowledgment of juridical pluralism and other features already recognized by the recent UN Declaration of the Rights of Indigenous Peoples (September 2007) – which in Bolivia has already been accepted as a national law. On the other hand, the state declares itself unitarian (as has always been) and takes measures to make it strong as the only way to keep the country together. It promotes well-living (*suma qamaña*, in Aymara) and internal equity, ensures sovereignty in the control and use of its strategic natural resources – which its solemn preamble describes as part of Pacha Mama (Mother Earth) – which cannot be sold out nor profaned. This emphasis and a strong unitarian state show that former MNR's "State of 52" is still a source of inspiration for the government and its constituents. These are some of the main concepts of this constitution. The present text maintains the popular and sometimes baroque flavor of the constituents rather than abstract conceptualizations that only initiated professional lawyers could understand. Moreover, it reflects the haste of its approval, with many parts still requiring a final polishing. Yet aborting this constitution to begin all over again as if nothing had happened would be a political and historical error.

However, each time the government tries to convoke the pending referendum on the new constitution, the lowland autonomist leaders, known also as *cívicos*, answer with a new move. In May–June 2008 they held and won with high percentages four illegal and therefore uncontrolled local referendums for their audacious statutes of autonomy, which would require constitutional changes to be applicable. The government answered with a legal referendum in August to ratify or revoke (a) the president and vice president's mandate and (b) the highest authority in each department. The president and vice president were ratified by 67 percent, including "yes" scores from between 41 and 53 percent in rebel departments, where their local authorities were also ratified but with lower scores (53–63). In other words, most people want some sort of agreement between both political projects.

With such broad support, the government once again tried to summon its pending referendum and this time the autonomist "civic" leaders of these four departments began a systematic and simultaneous occupation and even destruction of government institutions sometimes followed by intense fighting, persecution and, as in Pando, violent action culminating with the September 11 massacre of marching MAS peasant and indigenous groups. The conflict became so serious that the presidents of the newly founded the Union of South American States (UNASUR) met immediately to show their support of the Bolivian government and to condemn blatantly the anti-institutional "civil coup d'état," as they called those violent actions. As a result, several international missions came to Bolivia and with their support and that of other local facilitators, high-level talks were conducted to reach an agreement.[7]

Ecuador

In the 2000 elections, CONAIE and its political party the Pachakutik improved its electoral record by receiving 14 percent of votes and coming in fifth in the race, in alliance with a secondary candidate. But the winner – Jamil Mahuad – failed in his attempt to implement the neoliberal model. Several banks broke down, the country adopted the US dollar as the national currency and a popular/military rebellion (massive but peaceful) ousted the president from office, installing instead a triumvirate which included Antonio Vargas, then president of CONAIE who had played an important role in the rebellion along with a group of low rank military led by Lucio Gutierrez and several urban leftist groups. As a result, an Amazonian with indigenous origins had become co-president. However, only a few hours after the chief commander of the army rejected this solution and handed the presidential banner to the former vice president, a wealthy entrepreneur who continued and deepened Mahuad's model.

The indigenous felt betrayed but resumed organizing their forces. A few months later in the next local elections they claimed victories in 5 out of 22 provinces nationwide and the absolute majority of rural *juntas parroquiales* (the lowest ranking municipalities). In January 2001, CONAIE along with all other rural organizations – indigenous and nonindigenous – staged their largest and more harshly repressed uprising under the new inclusive slogan "nothing only for indigenous." At the end it was able to get the government to make important concessions not only for them but for the general population as well.

With its success in the 2003 general elections, the Pachakutik struck a deal with presidential candidate Lucio Gutierrez (the military leader who led the 2000 rebellion). They won the election and were part of a coalition government, in which it occupied four important ministries, two of them headed by indigenous members: Nina Pacari as chancellor and Luis Macas as minister of agriculture. However, once in power, Gutierrez changed his discourse and continued the previous economic model, albeit within a more populist approach. This caused a deep and lasting division within the party and the indigenous movement. The main Andean historical leaders but Antonio Vargas abandoned the coalition; several local leaders and most of the Amazonian branch of CONAIE remained with Gutierrez (who was also Amazon-born). In this region, this was the beginning of a long and serious split between two branches known as the *vía empresarial* (for their support and joint ventures with the oil enterprises) and the *vía de resistencia* (for their opposition to such enterprises). Some time later, this split generated a similar division within CONAIE and the Coordination of Indigenous Organizations of the Amazon Basin (COICA), the highest mechanisms of coordination among the indigenous organizations of eight lowland countries. Multinational oil interests supported by the populist neoliberal government succeeded in dividing the previously powerful indigenous organization.

CONAIE and especially Pachakutik never fully recovered from this traumatic experience. Even when Gutierrez faced a huge urban popular rebellion in 2005, CONAIE's participation was almost null and some Amazonian indigenous groups remained loyal to him. By the end of 2006, new general election gave the presidency to formerly unknown candidate Rafael Correa, a leftist economist from the coast but with considerable experience in the Andes who could even speak some Quichua. Correa was committed to social change in favor or the poor but he became suspicious of indigenous organizations partly due to his political and theoretical approach, partly due to their meager performance with Gutierrez and perhaps as a result of some personal misunderstandings. As a candidate, Correa offered the vice presidency to Luis Macas, the main historical leader of CONAIE. But Luis, still wary of his bad experience with Gutierrez, refused and suggested rather that Correa should be his vice president.

Correa is very close to Evo and several other presidents on the left side of the current Latin American political spectrum. He is aware of and keeps in mind recent innovations in Bolivia but at the same time tries to learn from its mistakes. Soon after his inauguration, he also summoned a new constitutional assembly which has successfully been concluded and approved in a referendum without the problems faced in Bolivia. Given the crisis of indigenous organizations mentioned above, the participation of CONAIE in this assembly was – paradoxically – less visible than in the previous one of 1998. However, the new text made improvements relative to the 1998 constitution in terms of indigenous topics. Echoes of the Bolivian one appear already in Art. 1: "Ecuador is a…unitarian, intercultural and plurinational… State." It appeals also to a vital relation with "Mother Earth" and summarizes its utopia of harmonic development as *Sumak kawsay*, the Quichua equivalent of Aymara *Suma qamaña*: "well living" – that is, in harmony with nature and among all humans with inclusion and equality. It maintains and complements the collective rights of indigenous "communities, peoples and nationalities" in the same line established by the 1998 constitution. The list of such rights climbed from 15 to 21. It included, for instance, the recognition of indigenous custom law. But, for the reasons already mentioned, all these topics are less central and developed than in the new Bolivian constitution.

Peru

Obviously the country of Peru does not have the level of indigenous presence in the state structure achieved by Ecuador and Bolivia. Yet, in the 2000s, some relevant yet still minor signs towards the recovery of indigenous conscience could be noticed. No doubt changes in the neighboring Andean countries are an influence, at times a rather explicit one through invitations and exchanges. Four issues are particularly relevant concerning this subject.

The first one is in the democratic strengthening of the municipal level of government, which is occurring by means comparable to the Bolivian Law of Popular Participation. This process began with Fujimori in the 1990s but was deepened during the next decade with Alejandro Toledo, elected in 2002. Two innovations contributed: opening the political spectrum to local associations and the acknowledgment of three local municipal levels. These instruments made the role of the local population and their demands more visible and relevant. In turn, they allowed their deep identities to flourish again.

The second one is the unforeseen reaction of many communities to the unrestricted privileges granted by Fujimori to numerous international extracting enterprises. In the Amazon, AIDESEP led the local reaction to the penetration of oil companies. But the main novelty was the expanding opposition of Andean communities against powerful mining companies which started intruding in their daily lives. Between 1990 and 1997, mining revenues in Peru increased 2,000 percent, second only to Chile in Latin America. Several local organized protests joined their forces and in 1999 they founded the National Confederation of Communities Affected by Mining (CONACAMI) which represents the complaints of about one thousand communities. The interesting point is that demands are made not only in terms of technical environmental issues but also based on their rights as indigenous communities framed by the ILO Convention 169. They rediscovered the fact that they were better off trying to protect themselves based on their indigenous rights rather than as regular citizens or peasants. This allowed CONACAMI and the AIDESEP, with the support of some international NGOs, to become the spearhead of the national recovery of indigenous conscience at the national level and they are also leading a new five-national alliance of indigenous organizations called the Coordination of Andean Indigenous Organizations (CAOI). This becomes another outstanding example of *glocalization*, that is, of conflating global and local interests and of a new alternative globalization from below, from local grassroots organizations.

The third issue has recently started to influence the state sphere as such. In the 1990s the World Bank and other international agencies became more interested in the question of the indigenous and other specifically endangered groups and started two projects in Ecuador and Peru especially targeted to eliminate poverty among indigenous and black populations. As a response, in 1998 Fujimori finally created a state agency first called Technical Secretariat for Indigenous Affairs (SETAI), later renamed the National Commission for Andean-Amazonian-Afroperuvian Peoples (CONAPA) by Toledo. This was designed as the national counterpart of the World Bank designed to channel international resources. After his inauguration, Toledo – himself with clear Indian physical but not cultural traits – made a symbolic trip to the top of the world famous Machu Picchu ruins and, wearing Inca garb, promised to improve the conditions of indigenous peoples in Peru and throughout the Andean countries. The first lady, a Belgian anthropologist who speaks Quechua, was put in charge of implementing this policy and of encouraging the creation of new indigenous organizations. This official support plus several administrative problems hindered the development of a good relationship between these and other grassroots organizations mentioned in the previous paragraph. However, the "indigenous" issue had been included into the official state agenda.

The fourth sign appeared in the 2006 elections, when Ollanta Humala surprisingly won the first electoral round with sweeping successes in the Andes and Amazon regions. Humala, a military with Andean roots and a millenarian Inca rhetoric, cannot be fully compared to the Aymara grassroots leader Evo Morales in Bolivia (who explicitly supported him). But this success symbolizes a shifting tide in Peru. In the second round, all forces joined against him and former APRA leader, and President Alan Garcia became president for a second time. He is now a newborn neoliberal closer to the US and to the right-leaning Latin American regimes and unlikely to foster indigenous movements in spite of what is happening in neighboring Ecuador and Bolivia.

But this is not the end of history...

Notes and References

1 This chapter summarizes my book *Movimientos y poder indígena en Bolivia, Ecuador y Perú* (La Paz: CIPCA, 2008).
2 See the 2006 UN *Rapport on Ecuador* by the special reporter on the situation of human rights and fundamental liberties rights of the indigenous.
3 Dialectal variations explain why in some places this name is spelled *quichua* and, in others, *quechua*.
4 For instance, the 1931 Peruvian Communist Party Program (one year after Mariátegui's premature death) acknowledges the Indians' right "to create their own culture, to be educated in their own languages" and even "to organize themselves as independent governments – the Quechua and Aymara republics – in a tight alliance with workers."
5 Confederación Sindical Única de Trabajadores Campesinos de Bolivia.
6 Cletus Gregor Barié, *Pueblos indígenas y derechos constitucionales en América Latina. Un panorama* (Mexico City: Instituto Indigenista Interamericano y Comisión Nacional para el Desarrollo de los Pueblos Indígenas; Quito: Abya-Yala; La Paz: Banco Mundial, Fideicomiso Noruego, 2003), 283–320, 548–59.
7 This was indeed the case. In January 2009, the new constitution, with some amendments agreed upon with the opposition, was finally approved by a wide margin of 61 percent. In December 2009 Evo was also reelected by an even wider margin, 64 percent, along with the new "Asamblea Legislativa Plurinacional" (the new name of the Congress) for which his party, MAS, earned a two-thirds majority (as of August 2010).

Chapter 6

PATH DEPENDENCE VERSUS ADAPTATION IN ESTONIAN ETHNOPOLITICS

Raivo Vetik
Tallinn University

Introduction

This chapter will discuss how, despite two decades of democratic transformation, Estonia still faces massive statelessness. It will be argued that both social and political factors explain such a state of affairs. On the one hand, national integration remains a complicated issue for Estonian society, while on the other hand, there is strong path dependence in the way the issue of citizenship is framed in a still divided political landscape. The discussion will be based mostly on two datasets compiled by the author and his collaborators – a public opinion poll, conducted in spring 2008[1] and an in-depth interview study connected to the poll carried out in April 2008.[2]

---

1 The integration monitoring survey of 2008 was a statewide poll in which oral interviews and the proportional random cohort method were used to question 1,505 people aged 15–74 in March and April of 2008. Among the respondents, 83 percent had Estonian citizenship, 8 percent had Russian citizenship, 2 percent citizenship in another state and 7 percent of the cohort was stateless. In the cohort, there were 992 Estonians and 513 other nationalities. Among the latter, 51 percent had Estonian citizenship, 23 percent were Russian citizens, 5 percent citizens of another state and 21 percent were stateless persons. In compiling the sociodemographic characterization of the model, population statistics data from 1 January 2008 were used. To reduce the differences that arose when comparing the model and the representativeness of the poll results, the results obtained were considered according to the following sociodemographic features: place of residence, gender, age, religion and education.

2 In April 2008 in connection with the integration monitoring, ten in-depth interviews were conducted with stateless persons who had children younger than the age of 15 with undetermined citizenship. Among the ten interviews, five were carried out with

The analysis will be divided into two sections: the first part will focus on the reasons of statelessness as the stateless persons themselves see it; the second part will discuss the relationship between citizenship status and socioeconomic as well as sociocultural adaptation among Estonian Russians, aiming to highlight broader structural obstacles to overcoming the statelessness status.

In the literature on Estonian ethnopolicy two diverse trends can be identified. One trend is based on the concept of nation building and holds that "the historical need to define the position of the Estonian nation concerning the position and future of the new Russian minority in the country has accelerated the transformation of Estonia from an ethnic nation (characterized by the historically dominant position of defensive nationalism) to a modern civic nation" (Lauristin and Heidmets 2002). The other trend is much more critical, holding that the Estonian ethnopoliticy has the effect of reenforcing interethnic alienation (Brosig 2008). Gregory Feldman describes, along these lines, the Estonian ethnopolicy as a power strategy pursued by certain political forces and demonstrates how the invocation of national security concerns is used to justify the denial of citizenship to Soviet-era Russian-speaking migrants (Feldman 2005). David Laitin interprets the Estonian ethnopolicy in light of the terms of domestic party competition, external relationships with the EU as well as Russia, and the desire of the Estonian political class to provide a public good (Laitin 2003). The critical trend in this literature is also represented by Vello Pettai and Klara Hallik, who argue that restricting automatic citizenship exclusively to pre-1940 citizens and their descendants represent an attempt to marginalize the non-Estonian minority. They argue that such a policy should be understood in terms of ethnic control (Pettai and Hallik 2002).

This article is based on the normative assumption that "the denial and deprivation of citizenship and the creation of statelessness undermines

---

respondents from Tallinn, two from Narva, and one from each – Jõhvi, Sillamäe and Kohtla-Järve. In Tallinn, people from different parts of town were interviewed (three from Lasnamäe, one from Õismäe and one from the city-center area). The basis for the sampling procedure was the impersonalized list provided by the State Chancellery, where residents with undetermined citizenship who also had children below 15 were listed (the list included 2,437 cases). The gross sample was determined to be ten times bigger and the stratified sample (N=100) chosen from the total population was divided into strata on the basis of residence areas and the children's age. In each stratum, simple random sampling was employed after that. The people included in the sample were sent contact letters, introducing them to the research and asking for their consent for participation. 18 people demonstrated their willingness to take part in the study, of whom 10 where chosen for the interview according to the initially stipulated condition for residential variety as well as accounting for variety in gender, age and one's status as a single or joint parent.

the promotion of human security understood in the broadest sense" (Blitz and Lynch 2009). It will be argued, based on the analysis, that there is an urgent need to reconsider the presumptions of the ethnopolicies reproducing statelessness in Estonia.

Historical Context of the Statelessness Issue in Estonia

After regaining independence in August 1991 and reintroducing the Citizenship Act of 1938 half a year later in February 1992, about one-third of the population of Estonia became stateless. The most controversial consequence of the 1992 Citizenship Act lies in the fact that although it was presented in an ethnically neutral language, the law nonetheless affected above all the Russian-speaking minority, who had migrated to Estonia during the Soviet period (Kionka and Vetik 1996). The law was based on the idea of the "legal continuity" of the prewar Estonian Republic, which means that only those persons who were citizens before Estonia's incorporation into the Soviet Union in 1940 and their descendants were entitled to automatic citizenship. By contrast, migrants from the Soviet period and their descendants had to go through the process of naturalization.

Naturalization requirements in the Estonian law can be regarded as rather liberal compared to most other countries (Smith et.al 1998). However, what makes the Estonian citizenship issue exceptional is the fact that at the moment the citizenship law was brought into force, it left a considerable part of the population without citizenship. Such an exclusive move should be seen in the context of the high level of perceived threat and mistrust between the Estonian majority and the Russian-speaking minority populations at the beginning of 1990s. This can be illustrated, for example, by the fact that in the 1991 independence referendum, while a majority of Estonians voted in favor of Estonian independence only 25 percent of the Estonian Russians did the same (Vetik 1993). Thus, only six months before actually regaining independence, the Estonian society was fundamentally polarized as to one of the most existential political issues, which inevitably evoked strong mutual fears regarding the future.

This was the psychological context in which the ideology of "legal continuity," proposed by the "Citizens' Committees" movement, gained support among most ethnic Estonians in contrast to alternative options for devising citizenship policy proposed by other political forces and supported by most Estonian Russians. This ideology assumes that acquiring Estonian citizenship involves first of all the question of loyalty, i.e. if a person successfully passes the Estonian language and citizenship exams, this accomplishment proves loyalty and thus makes the person worthy of Estonian citizenship.

It then follows that according to Estonian citizenship ideology: first, citizenship status is something which should be earned by the internal migrants who have settled in Estonia during the Soviet period; second, those who acquire Estonian citizenship demonstrate that they have adopted the "Estonian mindset" and would like to be integrated into Estonian society (Steen 2006).

The two alternatives of citizenship policy Estonia was facing in the beginning of 1990s can also be described in terms of "integration through participation or integration for participation" (Semjonov 2002). The "integration for participation" option was based on the assumption that loyalty is not an issue in Estonia and that interethnic issues should be handled in terms of general human rights and equality. The "integration for participation" option, on the contrary, was based on the assumption that there is a deep existential disagreement in Estonian society regarding its future as an independent state, and this is reason enough to deny automatic Estonian citizenship to those who were presumed to be anti-independence, i.e. the migrants from the Soviet Union. The independence referendum of March 1991 demonstrated that the majority of the Estonian Russians did not support Estonian independence, thus providing grounds for the second option, which eventually emerged as the winner in the citizenship debate.

As of 31 December 2009, there were 104,813 persons with undetermined citizenship in Estonia, indicating that the statelessness issue is far from being resolved in Estonia. Naturalization of stateless persons has been

Figure 6.1. The changing citizenship status of the Estonian population, 1992–2008

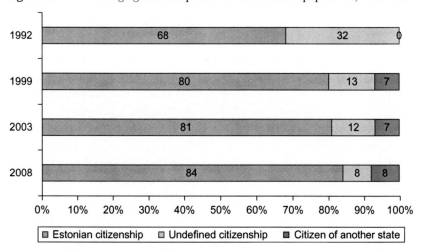

Sources: 1992 and 1999 statistics from the Citizenship and Migration Board; 2003 and 2008 data from the Ministry of Internal Affairs population registry; "Estonia Today" citizenship fact sheet, April 2008. Published by the Ministry of Foreign Affairs.

comparatively active in the first half of the 1990s, but has since slowed down. The dynamics of the naturalization process is represented in Figure 6.1, where it can be seen that by 1999, the percentage of Estonian citizens within the population had risen to 80 percent and by 2008 to 84 percent. As a result, currently about 16 percent of the population still does not hold Estonian citizenship – about half of them are stateless and another half are citizens of foreign states, mainly Russia. Thus, from 1992 to 2008 about 150,000 persons were naturalized in Estonia, while about 100,000 persons became citizens of Russia.

Perception of Reasons of Persistent Statelessness

The in-depth interview study of stateless persons carried out in April 2008 reveals that the reasons for persistent statelessness can be divided into four groups: difficulties in learning the Estonian language and passing the citizenship test; emotional aversions to applying for citizenship, related to the fact that many Estonian Russians feel that – similarly to ethnic Estonians – after independence was restored in Estonia they should have been granted citizenship automatically; various reasons related to Russia such as travel opportunities, visiting relatives, considerations regarding the education of children, etc. and finally, the consideration that the lack of citizenship does not affect a person's daily life.

The stateless respondents consider difficulties in learning the Estonian language to be the most significant reason for not applying for citizenship. Six out of ten respondents in the interview study mentioned the language issue as one of the reasons for not obtaining Estonian citizenship thus far. The significance of the problems related to learning Estonian is affirmed by the integration monitoring survey of 2008, conducted in parallel with the in-depth interviews, in which over 90 percent of Estonian Russians named difficulties with learning the Estonian language as the reason why many Estonian Russians still had not acquired Estonian citizenship. In the interview study, the main obstacles mentioned by the respondents were the absence of contacts with Estonians as well as the cost of the courses, which they consider should be free of charge.

I cannot speak Estonian sufficiently to pass the language exam. Estonian is very hard to learn, because there are so few contacts between the two ethnic groups in our country. Some people do communicate in Estonian at work, but I worked at a place where everybody was Russian. So, I use Estonian only at shops, about 5–10 minutes per day. But this is not sufficient... We have not been provided proper conditions for studying

Estonian. That is the first reason why I have not applied for Estonian citizenship. (Female, 37 years, Tallinn)

Estonian language courses cost an immense amount of money. I cannot afford to pay 1,500–2,000 kroons per month for it, because I have two children and one of them, besides, is ill. And so a vicious circle unravels: if I do not know Estonian, I cannot find a well-paying job, and therefore cannot pay for the courses. (Female, 37 years, Tallinn)

The second group of reasons is related to emotional aversions, which stem from the opinion that the Estonian citizenship policy is unjust by its very nature. Many respondents of the interviews felt bitter for not receiving citizenship unconditionally like most ethnic Estonians did in the beginning of 1990s, despite being born and raised in Estonia and living there for their entire life. The need for applying for citizenship was considered demeaning by most respondents; according to their judgment, the state should care about its all residents and not grant privileges to one ethnic group. In the integration monitoring survey of 2008, two-thirds of the Russian-speaking respondents also agreed with similar claims explaining the reasons behind statelessness. Besides the fact that applying for citizenship is considered demeaning and unfair, some respondents said they felt as second-rate persons in the eyes of Estonians and the Estonian state.

But overall, it is all so strange that second or third generation people, born here, are not offered citizenship. In the USA, they offer citizenship even if a person was born in the airplane, provided that the airline was American. But overall, I think that our country is still young and the attitude towards citizenship is still not so serious. (Female, 37 years, Tallinn)

We have not applied, and do not intend to apply for citizenship in the future. I was born here and have lived here for over 40 years. I already have two children here. And I consider applying for citizenship a big humiliation for myself. No such thing exists in any other state of the European Union. (Male, 41 years, Jõhvi)

The second reason why I do not wish to apply for citizenship lies in the fact that I do not want to become a so-called second-rate citizen. Because I will be considered as this person who has become a citizen through naturalization. But why acquire citizenship then? Anyway, these feelings that I have now will remain the same, my attitude will not change as well. I seriously do not like this differentiation: you have received citizenship through naturalization, but I am a true citizen. It happens that there are first and second rate citizens. But we are all, in fact, equal... All people must be regarded as equals. There is no sense in wasting time, money and emotions to become a citizen, if in the end you do not gain anything, because their attitude will stay the same. But the color of the passport does not mean anything, if the attitude towards me will stay the same. (Female, 35 years, Tallinn)

The third group of reasons for statelessness has to do with various issues related to Russia. Some respondents said that applying for the Russian citizenship is easier than applying for the Estonian citizenship, which is why they decided to go for Russia over Estonia. Other people said that they need to travel to Russia to visit relatives or to do business, which is the reason for not applying for the Estonian citizenship. In the integration monitoring survey of 2008, the reasons related to Russia were mentioned by 70 percent of the respondents. It is important to note that applying for the Russian citizenship has abruptly increased in Estonia in recent years (Kase 2008).

Being a noncitizen is very difficult. Also, some people have relatives in Russia. Some apply for Russian citizenship because they have tried, but not succeeded in obtaining Estonian citizenship. Some elderly people take the Russian citizenship only because they are unable to learn the language. (Female, 35 years, Tallinn)

Maybe, because it is cheaper and good for business as well. The cigarettes and lots of other things, like children's clothes, are cheaper there. This is how many people probably reason. On the other hand, many have relatives on the other side. I also have relatives there. If you want to visit, you need to apply for a visa and so on. (Male, 41 years, Jõhvi)

The fourth group of reasons has to do with the pragmatic consideration that the lack of citizenship does not affect a person's daily life. About three-fourths of the respondents agreed to this type of claim in the integration monitoring survey of 2008. In the in-depth interview study we encountered the following answers to the questions of how not having the Estonian citizenship affects their life:

He [the respondent's husband] does not intend to apply for Estonian citizenship, because he knows that he already came here at a more mature age and cannot learn Estonian language in any way. He doesn't apply for some other state citizenship because he also feels comfortable with the gray passport. My husband does not feel that he is discriminated here in any way. He has not encountered that either. He has his own business here. He is very loyal to Estonia, but as his business here is doing well and the lack of citizenship does not bother him, he does not feel that applying for some country's citizenship is necessary. (Female, 33 years, Tallinn)

I think that those people who want citizenship do everything to receive it, but those who do not wish for it will never get it. Citizenship is not important to some, because they are satisfied with their lives and also have a good income. So – they don't even have time to think about citizenship. (Female, 33 years, Tallinn)

The pragmatic reasons also included the following types of considerations of stateless parents regarding the future of their underage children:

But my second child is a boy. And I don't want anyone to send him into the army, no matter if it's the Estonian or Russian one, to fight in some strange place without him agreeing to it. I want to leave him the right to choose which country's citizenship he wants. (Female, 37 years, Tallinn)

My son wants to go study in Russia and that is hard to do with a Russian visa. The language barrier is also a problem. It's easier for him to study in Russian in his native language, than in Estonia in a foreign language. But my daughter is applying for the Estonian citizenship, since she is planning on continuing her studies in Estonia. (Male, 41 years, Jõhvi)

The dynamics of the attitudes described above can be studied using the data of integration monitoring, which have been conducted on four occasions over the past ten years (in 2000, 2002, 2005 and 2008). Comparisons of the monitorings provide an opportunity to place the statelessness issue into a broader perspective and to examine the trends in attitudes. Let us compare, for example, the list of reasons of statelessness the Estonian Russians mentioned in the integration monitoring of 2000 and 2008. The factors listed in Figure 6.2 can be divided into three groups – difficulties in fulfilling citizenship requirements, pragmatic reasons and a sense of belonging to Estonia. Several significant conclusions bearing upon citizenship policy can be made based on the data. First, Russian Estonians consider the factors related to meeting citizenship requirements to be the most important reasons for remaining in the condition of statelessness. For example, in the integration monitoring survey of 2008, 34 percent of the respondents considered the inability to learn Estonian to be the reason for their continuing statelessness and 23 percent stated that the reason lies within the humiliating nature of the citizenship requirements. The second

Figure 6.2. A comparison of reasons of statelessness from 2000 and 2008 (% of the response "definitely")

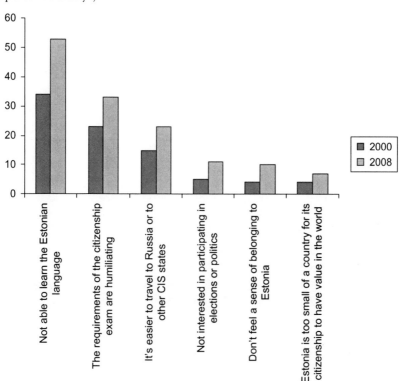

Sources: Integration monitoring surveys of 2000 and 2008.

conclusion is that the reasons related to the sense of belonging to Estonia are considered the least important – for example, in the integration monitoring survey of 2008, only 11 percent of the stateless respondents agreed to the statement "not interested in elections or politics," 10 percent "don't feel a sense of belonging in Estonia," while 7 percent felt that "Estonia is too small of a country for its citizenship to have any value in the world."

The third conclusion is that the internal structure of the Estonian Russians' attitudes has not changed over the course of time, i.e. the sequence of the outlined factors along their significance has remained the same. At the same time, however, there has been a significant change in the intensity of the attitudes during these eight years, as the negative scores of all factors have increased. Evidently the data showing that in eight years, learning Estonian has supposedly become more difficult (since the percentage of Estonian Russians who considered their inability to learn Estonian to be a reason for

Table 6.1. "Which citizenship would you like to have?" (% of stateless respondents, 2000–8)

	2000	2002	2005	2008
Estonian citizenship	60	65	74	51
Russian citizenship	5	6	11	19
Citizenship in another country	7	9	5	14
No citizenship at all	16	14	7	16
Hard to say	12	6	3	–
N	170	109	102	105

Sources: Integration monitoring surveys, 2002–8.

statelessness went to from 34 percent in 2000 to 53 percent in 2008) can't be taken at face value. Instead, one could argue the tendencies revealed in the table expresses increase of general negativity towards ethnopolicies in Estonia. Such an argument is corroborated by comparing the data on citizenship preferences gathered during the four integration monitoring studies. Table 6.1 shows that preference towards the Estonian citizenship started following an upward trend in 2000, which lasted until 2005 (74 percent). Then in 2008, the number of those who wanted Estonian citizenship dropped to only half (51 percent) of all noncitizens. Similarly, if in the year 2000 there were 16 percent of noncitizens who didn't want any kind of citizenship, and by 2005 the share of this category of people in the cohort dropped to 7 percent; then by 2008, their share rose again to 16 percent. Finally, while in the year 2000 5 percent desired Russian citizenship and 11 percent desired it in 2005, by 2008 this percentage had climbed to 19 percent of the stateless respondents.

The Citizenship Status and Adaptation of Estonian Russians in the Estonian Society

Socioeconomic adaptation

Research data confirms that the socioeconomic indicators of adaptation of Russian-speaking population have gradually improved in Estonia. For example, the differences in the salaries of ethnic Estonians and Estonian Russians have been steadily decreasing during the past decade (Leping and Toomet 2008). The integration monitoring survey of 2008 reveals that the main reason for the existing differences in earnings is the smaller representation of Russian-speaking people who have a higher education in the higher income groups, which means that they have less access to the highest paying jobs (Kasearu and Trumm 2008). The monitoring also shows that evaluation of personal material

Table 6.2. An evaluation of personal material situation, separated by nationality and citizenship (%)

Evaluation of economic situation	Estonian-speaking respondents	Russian-speaking respondents			
		All	Incl. Estonian citizens	Incl. Russian citizens	Incl. stateless persons
I am/we are living well with my/our current income	15	9	13	4	5
I/we can manage with my/our current income	58	53	56	48	52
It is hard to manage with my/our current income	19	26	23	37	21
We are struggling to manage with our current income	6	13	9	12	22

Source: Integration monitoring survey, 2008.

well-being of the Estonian citizens is relatively similar, regardless of ethnicity. However, there is a significant difference in this regard between Estonian citizens and those who do not have Estonian citizenship. Table 6.2 shows that 15 percent of Estonian-speaking and 13 percent of Russian-speaking Estonian citizens live comfortably with their current wages, while only 6 percent and 9 percent respectively say that they are struggling to get along. The figure for Russian citizens and stateless persons who responded they live comfortably with their wages was 3.5 percent and 5 percent, respectively, while 12 percent and 23 percent responded that they are struggling.

The integration monitoring survey of 2008 shows that the socioeconomic stratification among Estonian Russians is closely related to their citizenship status (Lauristin 2008). Compared to Russian citizens and noncitizens, the group of Estonian Russians with Estonian citizenship is characterized by a greater share of young and educated people; they are better speakers of Estonian and foreign languages and have a higher employment status. They are also characterized by greater social confidence and optimism about their future and are more prepared to protect their rights. In contrast, among noncitizens, the prevalent sentiments are rejection, inferiority and passivity. Evaluation of social competence among the Russian-speaking Estonian citizens is similar to that of Estonian-speaking Estonian citizens, and positive attitudes towards changes in the Estonian society are more prevalent among

Table 6.3. Differences in satisfaction evaluations of Russian-speaking respondents with various citizenship statuses, compared to the Estonian-speaking population (%)

Satisfied with...	Work	Security	Living conditions	Economic situation	Life overall
Estonian citizens	4.6	4.1	2.2	30.9	0.5
Russian citizens	28.0	29.0	2.5	59.4	17.2
Stateless	32.2	24.6	23.9	60.5	15.3

Source: Integration monitoring survey, 2008.

them compared to the other groups of Estonian Russians. Table 6.3 shows that the satisfaction evaluations of Russian-speaking Estonian citizens in relation to their work, security, living conditions and life overall are, as a rule, very close to those of Estonians and differ significantly from those of Russian citizens and stateless persons. The only important difference between Estonian-speaking and Russian-speaking Estonian citizens is related to the evaluation of their economic situation, where the difference is still 31 percentage points. However, the Russian citizens and stateless noncitizens differ from ethnic Estonian citizens by as much as 60 percentage points in this regard.

Thus, the Estonian citizens among the Russian-language population represent those who have been better able to adapt in the postcommunist condition. On the contrary, people with the Russian citizenship are older and less educated than average, their Estonian language skills are the lowest and they tend to live in Eastern Estonia where the Russian language is predominant. At the same time, their socioeconomic situation is somewhat better than that of stateless noncitizens. Among Russian citizens there is a rather large group adapted very successfully to a market economy, who hold active ties with Russia, as the Russian citizenship guarantees them the freedom of movement and business opportunities. Finally, among the stateless noncitizens there are more middle-aged people with secondary education whose Estonian language skills are somewhat better compared to the Russian citizens, although their socioeconomic status is ranked lowest among the three groups. Among the stateless noncitizens passiveness, low self-esteem and bitterness are the highest ranked attitudes, according to the data of integration monitoring.

Sociocultural and identificational adaptation

Command of the Estonian language among the Estonian Russians has gradually improved over the last decade and has become functionally more diverse (Vihalemm 2008). However, it is important to differentiate between two opposite tendencies with regard to their sociocultural and identificational integration. First, the utilitarian significance of learning Estonian has become stronger over the years, meaning that more Estonian Russians say that the Estonian language is important for them and they need it in labor market. On the other hand, the integrative meaning of learning the Estonian language has decreased as it is less and less considered to be sufficient for achieving mutual trust in society and an equal standing compared to ethnic Estonians. This is why in the integration monitoring survey of 2008, for example, only 38 percent and 23 percent of the respondents, respectively, agree that learning Estonian increases their confidence and helps achieve an equal position with ethnic Estonians. This is considerably less compared to the 2005 monitoring, in which 68 percent and 64 percent of the respondents agreed to the respective statements (Vihalemm 2008).

As such, it appears that while major indicators of Estonian Russians' structural integration have gradually improved, the indicators of their identificational integration, which are supposed to express the so called "Estonian mindset," have instead worsened over the recent years. For example, their trust towards Estonian state institutions has decreased over the recent years, as has the share of those who feel that they are accepted as part of the Estonian people (Vetik 2008b). Figure 6.3 indicates that, compared to ethnic Estonians, the level of trust is extremely low among Estonian Russians, with the generalized trust in the state at 20–25 percent, and with trust in institutions such as the government, the parliament and the president at 5–15 percent. This is more than two and in some cases even three times lower compared to the trust of ethnic Estonians towards the Estonian state institutions. However,

Figure 6.3. Trust in the Estonian state and its institutions (%)

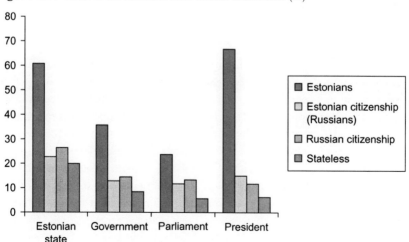

Source: Integration monitoring survey, 2008.

as Figure 6.3 also indicates, in the internal comparison of Estonian Russians the groups with different legal statuses have relatively similar attitudes. It is interesting to point out that the trust of Russian citizens is even greater than that of Estonian citizens, which may seem paradoxical at first glance. It can explained by the large share of older and retired people among the citizens of Russia, whose more positive attitude towards the Estonian state may be connected to their lesser expectations, and, at the same time, the relatively good social security provisions they experience in Estonia when compared to the situation in Russia (Lauristin 2008).

The analysis of the integration monitoring trends indicates that the negative tendencies described above have started in recent years – up until 2005 the attitudes of Estonian Russians were becoming more positive, yet after that has been an abrupt decline. In the literature, such a change has been explained by the politization of interethnic relations in the internal power-politics of recent years. The issue of conflicting historical memories of ethnic Estonians and Estonian Russians has been particularly utilized in recent electoral campaigns. The most vivid example is the so-called "Bronze Soldier crisis," which occurred in the context of the electoral campaign for the Estonian Parliament and which has led to the arrest of more than 1,000 young Russians in April 2007 who were protesting against the removal of the Soviet-era war memorial from downtown Tallinn (Burch and Smith 2007; Hackmann and Lehti 2008; Wertsch 2008). One of the results of the ethnic polarization of the society has been the increase of negative mutual attitudes and the framing of integration in terms of the fulfillment of particular demands by the other group and not as a mutual adjustment (Vetik 2007).

Conclusion

The analyses above reveal that division of the Russian-speaking population in Estonia into three legal categories – Estonian citizens, stateless noncitizens and Russian citizens – reflects their socioeconomic adaptation to postcommunist Estonia. The data shows that those who acquired the Estonian citizenship tend to be better off compared to the other two categories in the labor market as well as in terms of demographic characteristics. It appears that the citizenship policy strengthens the tendencies of neoliberal market ideology, which have been dominant in Estonia since regaining independence, as it favors those who are already in a better situation and undermines the opportunities of those who, for various objective or subjective reasons, are worse off. However, despite better socioeconomic adaptation, Estonian citizens share the concerns of their ethnic peers over the issues of equal rights between ethnic groups and the importance of preserving their own language and culture. Level of trust towards state institutions is equally low among all three categories.

Hence, one can argue that those who have not managed to naturalize do not exhibit a specific mindset compared to the other groups, as presumed in the citizenship ideology. Their lack of Estonian citizenship is not the result of unwillingness but mostly the reflection of certain socioeconomic and demographic factors. Such a finding highlights the need to reconsider the presumptions of the citizenship policy. However, the Estonian political class has demonstrated remarkable path dependency in framing the citizenship issue despite the fact that the external context and the challenges Estonia currently faces have changed. Political forces arguing for the reframing of the citizenship issue have not been able to win a parliamentary majority at any time during the last two decades (Lauristin 2009) and even the dialogue over the statelessness issue has not been seriously on the agenda (Ivanov 2008).

It has been argued in academic literature that the long-term statelessness of a remarkable share of permanent residents is eroding the interest in Estonian nationality (Vetik 2007). The argument holds that the challenges Estonia is facing have changed considerably, compared to the time when the Citizenship Act was adopted. In the context of withdrawal from the USSR and restoring of the Estonian nation-state at the beginning of the 1990s, it was presumed that the effort to acquire Estonian citizenship by those who relocated to Estonia during the Soviet era was proof of their loyalty to the Estonian state and their willingness to integrate into the Estonian society. By now the Estonian nation-state has been restored and Estonia has become a member of the EU and NATO, which means that the context of framing of citizenship issue is completely different. There is no evidence supporting the view that the noncitizens in Estonia are hostile to the idea of the Estonian independence, as was presumed in the beginning of the 1990s. Inversely, a large body of literature indicates that a vast majority of stateless noncitizens wishes to be a part of the Estonian nation and to contribute to the development of the country (Vetik et al. 2008). The analysis carried out in this paper supports the view that engaging all permanent residents and creating a favorable legal context is an urgent need in Estonia. In a globalizing and increasingly multicultural world, integration is a key factor in ensuring sustainability of the Estonian nation-state. In such a context the institution of citizenship should no longer be regarded as an award for "successful" integration, but rather as an instrument helping to achieve better integration of the society and particularly of those, who are less fortunate (see also Teder 2009 in this respect).

References

Blitz, B. and M. Lynch (eds). 2009. *Statelessness and the Benefits of Citizenship: A Comparative Study.* Oxford: Oxford Brookes University.

Brosig, M. 2008. "A Plan for the Future? The Estonian State Integration Program on National Minorities 2000–2007." *Journal on Ethnopolitics and Migration Issues in Europe* 7.2: 1–19.

Burch, S. and D. J. Smith. 2007. "Empty Spaces and the Value of Symbols: Estonia's War of Monuments' from Another Angle." *Europe-Asia Studies* 59.6: 913–36.

Eesti Koostöö Kogu. 2008. *Estonian Human Development Report 2007*, ed. M. Heidmets. Tallinn: Eesti Ekspressi Kirjastuse AS.

Feldman, G. 2005. "Culture, State and Security in Europe: The Case of Citizenship and Integration Policy in Estonia." *American Ethnologist* 32.4: 676–94.

Hackmann, J. and M. Lehti. 2008. "Introduction: Contested and Shared Places of Memory. History and Politics in North Eastern Europe." *Journal of Baltic Studies* 39.4: 377–9.

Hallik, K., J. Kruusvall, I. Pettai, M. Pavelson, I. Proos and R. Vetik. 2002. *Integration in Estonian Society. Monitoring 2002*. Tallinn: TPÜ Rahvusvaheliste ja Sotsiaaluuringute Instituut.

Ivanov, S. 2008. "Viienda kolonni ehitamine" [Construction of the fifth column]. *Eesti Päevaleht*, 4 November.

Kase, K. 2008. "Vene kodakondsus peibutab Eesti omast rohkem" [Russian citizenship is more alluring than Estonian]. *Postimees*, 20 October.

Kasearu, K. and A. Trumm. 2008. "The Material Situation and Life Satisfaction of the Estonian- and Russian-speaking Population," in *Integration Monitoring of the Estonian Society 2008*, 7–23. Tallinn: Integration Foundation and Bureau of Population Minister.

Kionka, R. and R. Vetik. 1996. "Estonia and the Estonians," in G. Smith (ed.), *The Nationalities Question in the Post-Soviet States*, ed. G. Smith, 129–46. London: Longman.

Laitin, D. D. 2003 "Three Models of Integration and the Estonian/Russian Reality." *Journal of Baltic Studies* 34.2: 197–222.

Lauristin, M. 2008. "Citizens and Non-Citizens: The Different Integration Categories and Tendencies of the Russian-Speaking Population," in *Integration Monitoring of the Estonian Society 2008*, 142–63. Tallinn: Integration Foundation and Bureau of Population Minister.

Lauristin, M. and M. Heidmets (eds). 2002. "Introduction: The Russian Minority in Estonia as a Theoretical and Political Issue," in *The Challenge of the Russian Minority*. Tartu: Tartu University Press.

Lauristin, M. and P. Vihalemm. 2009. "The Political Agenda during Different Periods of Estonian Transformation: External and Internal Factors." *Journal of Baltic Studies* 40.1: 1–28.

Lauristin, M. and R. Vetik (eds). 2000. *Integration in Estonian Society: Monitoring 2000*. Tallinn: TPÜ Rahvusvaheliste ja Sotsiaaluuringute Instituut.

Leping, K. O. and O. Toomet. 2008. "Emerging Ethnic Wage Gap: Estonia during Political and Economic Transition." *Journal of Comparative Economics* 36: 599–619.

Pavelson, M., I. Proos, I. Pettai, J. Kruusvall, K. Hallik and R. Vetik. 2006. *Integration Monitoring 2005 Research Report*. Tallinn: MEIS.

Pettai, V. and K. Hallik. 2002. "Understanding Process of Ethnic 'Control': Segmentation, Dependency and Co-optation in Post-Communist Estonia." *Nations and Nationalism* 8.4: 505–29.

Semjonov, A. 2002. "Estonia: Nation-Building and Integration – Political and Legal Aspects," in *National Integration and Violent Conflict in Post-Soviet Societies, The Cases of Estonia and Moldova*, ed. P. Kolsto, 31–70. Rowman & Littlefield.

Smith, G., V. Law, A. Wilson, A. Bohr and E. Allworth. 1998. *Nation-Building in Post-Soviet Borderlands: The Politics of National Identities*. Cambridge: Cambridge University Press.

Steen, A. 2006. "Accessioning Liberal Compliance? Baltic Elites and Ethnic Politics under New International Conditions." *International Journal on Minority and Group Rights* 13: 187–207.

Teder, I. 2009. "Indrek Teder: Me ei saa sukelduda põhiseadusskleroosi" [Indrek Teder: We cannot plunge into a constitutional sclerosis]. Interview by Kärt Anvelt, *Eesti Päevaleht*, 10 October.

Vetik, R. 1993. "Ethnic Conflict and Accomodation in Post-Communist Estonia." *Journal of Peace Research* 30.3: 271–80.

_____. 2007. "Great Society," in *On the Boundary of Two Liberties*. Tallinn: Huma Press.

_____. 2008a. "Ethnic Domination in Estonia," in *Monumental Conflict: Memory, Politics and Identity in Contemporary Estonia*, ed. M. Tamm and P. Peterson, 112–26. Tallinn: Varrak.

_____. 2008b. "State Identity and the Cohesiveness of the Society's Public Sphere," in *Integration Monitoring of the Estonian Society 2008*, 164–79. Tallinn: Integration Foundation and Bureau of Population Minister.

Vetik, R., M. Lauristin, J. Helemäe, K. Korts, J. Kruusvall, G. Nimmerfeldt, E. Saar, A. Trumm, P. Vihalemm and T. Vihalemm. 2008. *Integration Monitoring of the Estonian Society 2008*. Tallinn: Integration Foundation and Bureau of Population Minister.

Vihalemm, T. 2008. "Language Skills and Attitudes," in *Integration Monitoring of the Estonian Society 2008*, 71–80. Tallinn: Integration Foundation and Bureau of Population Minister.

Wertsch, J. V. 2008. "Collective Memory and Narrative Templates." *Social Research* 75.1: 133–56.

Chapter 7

INTEGRATION PARLIAMENTS IN EUROPE AND LATIN AMERICA: EXPLAINING VARIATIONS

Juliana Erthal
Tübingen University

Integration Parliaments in Europe and Latin America

In the past decades, European efforts to build a strong supranational organization have been successful in many ways. Among other accomplishments, Europeans have implemented a monetary union and a supranational decision-making system. While in the "Old Continent" progresses in integration are often the target of criticism by both pro- and anti-Europe groups, on the other side of the Atlantic policymakers look at the European Union (EU) as an uncontested example of achievement. Since the first attempts to translate Latin American integration projects into institutions, the design of the EU has been more than a reference, serving as a source for institutional imitation.

It has been said that the empowerment of the European Parliament (EP) over the years would not have been possible had the founding members of the European Coal and Steel Community (ECSC) not included a parliamentary institution in the European institutional structure in the first place (Rittberger 2005, 73). While this is true, evidence from integration parliaments in Latin America show that integration parliaments[1] (IPs) can have very different fates after their creation: not only can they be empowered, they can also stagnate or even lose some of their initial powers. Even though the creators of Latin American IPs have attempted to follow the European model, the overwhelming distance between the actual functioning and the accomplishments of these different organizations is remarkable. A simple perusal of constitutional treaties already hints at the institutional limitations faced by the Latin American integration organizations and their respective IPs. What is even more distressing, observation of their actual functioning sometimes shows that the limited powers attributed to them in the treaties are in fact not translated into reality.

In order to explain the differences between international parliamentary institutions, Malamud and de Souza (2007) have developed a comparison between the Andean Parliament, the Central American Parliament, the European Parliament, the Latin American Parliament and the Joint Parliamentary Commission of Mercosur (the predecessor of the Mercosur Parliament). They have outlined five factors that are among those responsible for the difference in powers among parliaments. These are: time (the EP having started between two and four decades before the Latin American ones); sequence (the EU has followed the Monnet method, meaning function should precede form and incrementalism prevails over early institutionalization); level of economic integration; quality of domestic institutions of member states; and the influence of parliamentary, semi-parliamentary and presidential domestic regimes of member states (Malamud and de Souza 2007, 99–100).

If today there are great differences between the three IPs analyzed here, at the time of their creation they were already considerable. Each of them was created in a different context, as part of a different regional integration organization (RIO) and by different member states. The initial powers (or lack thereof) that characterized each IP is likely to condition their path of institutional development and therefore is a factor that must be taken into high consideration when explaining differences among IPs.

This article presents a brief account of the creation of the EP, the Central American Parliament (Parlacen) and the Andean Parliament (Parlandino), their initial parliamentary powers and their current competencies. Furthermore, it will focus on the moment of creation of each IP in order to analyze the specific factors that influenced how power was attributed to each one so as to contribute to the debate on the reasons for such different development paths among the three IPs.

Parliaments outside the Nation-State

An important part of the discussion on regional politics is the transfer of concepts developed within national frameworks to the international level. In order to evaluate parliaments at the regional level more comprehensively, we must understand the distinct functions that these institutions are expected to fulfill. The cases analyzed here all concern IPs, that is, parliamentary assemblies belonging to the institutional setting of a regional integration organization (RIO).[2] RIOs are defined by Van der Vleuten and Ribeiro Hoffmann (2007, 5–7) as a particular type of international cooperation which differ from others due to its distinct territoriality, identity and scope. In this sense, member states should belong to a certain geographical area, share "some combination of cultural, economic, linguistic or political ties," and the institution created should have an encompassing role which involves broad and diverse tasks, differentiating them from functional international organizations which focus on specific policy areas. These institutions also develop some kind of decision-making process that can be more or less intergovernmental or supranational. And it is precisely because of the creation of these decision-making institutions which encompass such diverse policy areas in a given region that the issues of democracy and legitimization emerge as sources of criticism for integration processes.

RIOs in Europe and Latin America were therefore designed so as to include a parliamentary institution as the main locus of democratic politics in the organization. However, the performance of these parliamentary assemblies around the world has generated debates about how effective or even how necessary IPs really are. In theory, the presence of a strong regional parliament in the institutional structure of a RIO stand for the possibility of development and well-functioning of regional democracy, since they potentially allow the citizens to vote, to participate in political organizations and to be elected to public office (Erthal 2007). Nonetheless, the usually limited powers of these institutions have led scholars to question their credentials as true "parliaments." This is the case of Malamud and de Sousa (2007, 100), who present a skeptic view on supranational parliaments other than the EP:

> ...regional parliaments may help to accomplish complementary goals such as nurturing a common regional identity among political elites, strengthening the symbolic presence of the regional organization in the minds of the public and third countries, and facilitating intraregional communication. They may also promote unexpected spill-over. However, these functions are neither exclusive nor characteristic of parliamentary institutions. If regional parliaments are to be enhanced, the distinction between their constitutive and complementary functions should not be neglected.

The authors approach the matter of what functions or powers an international parliament must have in order to be considered a real parliament and they adopt the same criteria that are used to define national parliaments.

In an interesting argument, Malamud and de Souza state that international parliamentary institutions must perform functions that are exclusive and characteristic of parliaments in order to deserve such a name. In his discussion concerning the definition of "parliament" Stefan Marschall (2005) begins by presenting Werner Patzelt's distinction of the parliament in its broad sense and the parliament in its narrow sense. The first one is a more open definition that embraces all representative bodies situated between the people and the executive and that brings considerable inputs from the society into the political system. The second of Patzelt's definition creates a subgroup of parliaments that can be distinguished from the first type; it only includes such parliaments (as defined previously) that are directly elected through periodical and free elections (Marschall 2005, 56–7). The author further elaborates this definition in order to specify what he understands as a democratic parliament: "Democratic parliaments are representation bodies in charge of representing the people. They are created by free, general, equal, secret and periodical elections. They comprise a plurality of individual representatives who have a free mandate" (Marschall 2005, 60).

The definition presented so far drives our attention to the fact that not all parliamentary institutions are composed of (directly or indirectly) elected members. But although this definition is useful, it does not clarify how a parliament should bring inputs from society into the political system – or in other words, represent the people. In order to understand how representation is supposed to take place, it is necessary to identify the functions that are required of a parliament.

Marschall presents a list of parliamentary functions, namely: electing government, legislation, control and communication. However, Marschall's list is explicitly inspired by the example of the German Bundestag (Marschall 2005, 138), making his definition hard to apply in comparisons involving RIOs composed by presidential governments as is the case with Latin American ones. In turn, Malamud and de Souza (2007) define parliaments as possessing classical parliamentary functions that exclude the "electing government" function, which is substituted by leadership selection and formation. Malamud and de Souza's definition is, in this sense, more useful since it allows us to evaluate parliaments in parliamentary and nonparliamentary systems.

The authors present parliament as an institution that evolved over the centuries to claim four main functions: representation (related to input legitimacy), legislation/decision making (output legitimacy), monitoring of the executive branch and the bureaucracy (control legitimacy) and leadership selection and formation. The authors use these functions as a reference to evaluate integration parliaments, adopting the same measures to assess the success of national and international parliaments.

Malamud and de Souza elaborate a comparison of international parliaments according to these criteria including the EP, Parlacen and Parlandino (Malamud and de Souza 2007, 98–9). The authors conclude that while the EP performs all four functions, Parlacen and Parlandino do not perform the legislation function. They argue that Parlacen partially performs the control, representation and leadership formation functions. In the next section I will argue that Parlacen's limited control powers have been nonexistent in reality so far, and therefore that this IP does not perform a control function. Nevertheless, Parlacen seems to be one step ahead of Parlandino in terms of classical parliamentary functions. Parlandino still does not perform the representation and control functions, only partially performing the leadership formation one.[3] Thus, our three cases present a variation in terms of their real functioning: while the EP performs all classical parliamentary functions, Parlacen has achieved limited success while Parlandino lags behind.

Based on the discussion presented above on the conceptualization of parliaments, it is possible to conclude that the EP could fit the concept of parliament, while Parlandino can be included in Patzelt's definition of parliament in a broad sense. Parlacen can be considered as an intermediary case.

To try to account for this state of affairs I will present a brief description of the creation of the three IPs, the political context in which they were embedded and the elements that influenced these processes. While the factors proposed by Malamud and de Souza presented above (time, sequence, economic integration, domestic institutions and parliamentary versus presidential regimes) aim at explaining the differences between international parliaments in a broader sense, the elements presented here refer specifically to the moment of creation of each parliament and the initial powers it has been provided with. While some of the elements identified here may coincide with those of the authors, some other elements will have a more prominent role.

Integration Parliaments: EP, Parlacen and Parlandino[4]

The European Parliament

The EP is part of the institutional structure of the EU, which at the moment has 27 members: Austria, Belgium, Bulgaria, Cyprus, the Czech Republic, Denmark, Estonia, Finland, France, Germany, Greece, Hungary, Ireland, Italy, Latvia, Lithuania, Luxembourg, Malta, the Netherlands, Poland, Portugal, Romania, Slovakia, Slovenia, Spain, Sweden, and the United Kingdom. Croatia, Iceland, the Republic of Macedonia and Turkey are candidate states. The EP today has 736 directly elected members,[5] and is provided with budgetary, control and legislative powers. Nonetheless, this configuration is the result of an impressive process of empowerment over the years, as governments of member states have progressively agreed to transfer it more and more powers. The EP as we know it today is the result of the ongoing institutional "evolution" since the creation of its forerunner, the Common Assembly (CA) of the ECSC. The ECSC in its turn is considered as the first step of an integration process that has been developing since its creation in 1951 (Weidenfeld and Wessels 2007, 186). In the following decades, the Treaty of Paris (or the Treaty Establishing the European Coal and Steel Community, its official name) would receive successive amendments,[6] and the ECSC would finally result in the EU and its current institutional structure.

The CA was created in 1951, and started functioning in 1952. At this first moment, it didn't have any legislative or budgetary powers; the CA's main role "was that of scrutinizing, controlling and, if deemed necessary, censuring a supranational institution, the (High Authority), forerunner of the Commission" (Rittberger 2005, 73). At that time, its members were not directly elected, but appointed by the national parliaments of the six founding member states (Nohlen 2004).

Although it can be argued that the CA's powers were very limited and that they were rarely used (Hix 2008), the very fact that *some* powers existed means that it had control powers over the High Authority (HA). This already creates a distance between the CA and the other IPs analyzed here.

The CA was created simultaneously with the ECSC. The Treaty of Paris had already established the CA as part of the institutional structure of the new European organization. The first efforts towards European integration were led by the Benelux countries shortly after the end of World War II. The process of establishment of a customs union between Belgium, Holland and Luxemburg started by the end of 1944 and became a reality in January 1948 when a customs tariff came into force. The political environment in the aftermath of the war was generally favorable to ideals of integration. But according to Spierenburg and Poidevin (1994), the push for further European integration initially came from the United States. Indeed, this was clearly manifested in the speech given by General George C. Marshall, secretary of state of the United States, when presenting the Marshall Plan on 5 June 1947.

The Marshall Plan was designed to help European countries to rebuild their economies and infrastructure and to provide immediate access to goods produced elsewhere (mainly in the US), as well as to perform strategic functions such as containing communist expansion[7] and helping to consolidate the American occupation of West Germany. But the primary aim of the plan was to "enforce peace in Europe" (Erixon 2008, 17), and this goal would be achieved through economic development and integration. It was in the interest of the US that Europe would become increasingly integrated and cohesive "not only against the Soviet Union but also, crucially, to restore economic ties" (Erixon 2008, 18).

The two first attempts to translate this impulse into a real organization were the Organisation for European Economic Co-operation (OEEC), created in 1948, and the Council of Europe (1949). The failure of these purely intergovernmental organizations to deal with the conflicts between multiple and strong national interests was perceived as a drawback for those who favored European integration (Rittberger 2005, 75) and led them to support the creation of an organization with limited attributes and influence, but with "exceptional" powers (Spierenburg and Poidevin 1994, 1).

Even though the creation of the ECSC and the CA lies more than half a century behind us, their initial characteristics were crucial to the fate of European integration since they conditioned the evolution of European institutions in the following decades. The institutional structure and decision-making mechanisms of the ECSC are by no means accidental. They are the result of intense debate and bargaining between its founding members, where different principles of institutional organization and ideas of representation were debated and negotiated (Rittberger 2009, 44–5).

If the role of the US was significant at the inception of the integration project, it was no less important during the negotiations for the creation of the ECSC. There was fear in Washington that the Europeans would create an international cartel, and that the US would suffer negative consequences from it. American diplomacy acted to weaken efforts coming from London to sabotage negotiations and even though the US was never a potential member of the ECSC, it participated actively in the talks between the six – making proposals, suggesting solutions and pushing for its favorite outcomes. As Spierenburg and Poidevin show in their account, "the Americans wanted Monnet's supranational concept to prevail and were against the idea of giving the Committee of Ministers power over the Authority" (Spierenburg and Poidevin 1994, 26–7).

Another striking example of US interference is found in their pressure on Germany to accept the ECSC in the French (supranational) model:

A request to participate in a European army (Pleven Plan) prompted the Germans to take a tougher line at the Paris negotiations on the Schuman Plan, but the Americans made it clear that without a German signature to the ECSC Treaty, there would be no general treaty amending the occupation arrangements, nor would there be any freedom of manoeuvre for Bonn in the field of foreign policy. (Spierenburg and Poidevin 1994, 27–8)

In addition to all this pressure, direct US financial support for the ECSC was envisaged by American authorities as early as November 1950, and the authors of the Schuman Plan were aware of the availability of funds (Spierenburg and Poidevin 1994, 27).

The negotiations resulted in the signing of the Treaty of Paris on 18 April 1951, creating the ECSC for the period of 50 years. It entered into force on 24 July 1952. The common market for coal, iron ore and scrap opened on 10 February 1953 and for steel on 1 May 1953. The resulting structure was composed by four main institutions: the HA, the CA, the Council of Ministers and the Court of Justice.

The CA was composed of "representatives of the peoples of the member states" (ECSC 1951). The representatives should be designated from among the members of national parliaments or directly elected by universal suffrage, depending on the decision of each member state. The distribution of seats in the CA was not equal for each member state: France, Germany and Italy had 18 seats each, Belgium and the Netherlands had 10 seats each and Luxembourg had 4. The CA held one session every year, and had "supervisory powers" over the supranational HA. These supervisory powers meant that it was the recipient of a yearly report produced by the HA that was to be presented to the CA before its session. The CA has the prerogative to censure the report. Article 24 clearly states how the motion of censure could be adopted and its consequences:

> If the motion of censure is adopted by two-thirds of the members present and voting, representing a majority of the total membership, the members of the High Authority must resign in a body. They shall continue to carry out current business until their replacement... (ECSC 1951)

Therefore from the very beginning, the CA effectively had the power to control the HA which, in its turn, had supranational powers from the moment of its creation. Although it can be argued that the CA's powers were very limited and that they were rarely used (Hix 2008), the fact that some powers existed already creates a distance between the CA and the other IPs analyzed here. It can be considered that the CA had control powers over the HA from the moment of its creation.

The Central American Parliament (Parlacen)

Parlacen is part of the institutional structure of the Central American Integration System (SICA). Member states of SICA are: Belize, Costa Rica, El Salvador, Guatemala, Honduras, Nicaragua and Panama. The Dominican Republic is an associate member. Despite being an official SICA institution, Parlacen's full members are not exactly the same of this RIO. El Salvador, Guatemala, Honduras, Nicaragua and Costa Rica participated in the creation of Parlacen. Costa Rica never ratified the treaty, while Panama (1999) and the Dominican Republic (2004) were later included.

Parlacen was created in 1987 and started its activities four years later in 1991 when its first assembly took place in Guatemala City, where its seat is located. Today the parliament is composed of 132 representatives, 22 for each country: 20 of which are directly elected plus two which are reserved for the countries' ex-presidents and ex-deputy presidents. Regarding direct elections, the exception was the Dominican Republic, which in May 2010 elected for the first time its representatives to Parlacen.[8] Prior to this date, the Dominican members of Parlacen were designated by the Dominican president. This recruitment method contrasted with the majority of other IP member states (for example, member states of Parlandino and Parlasur) that usually appoint members of national parliaments to act also as IP members. Despite the fact that Parlacen members are directly elected by citizens, it has no budgetary, legislative or control powers over other SICA institutions.

The SICA institutional structure is composed of the following main bodies: the Meeting of Presidents; the Council of Ministers; the Executive Committee; the General Secretariat; the Meeting of Vice Presidents; Parlacen; the Central American Court of Justice and the Consultative Committee.

The history of Central American integration is rather complex. The first attempts of uniting the small countries of the region go as far back as their independence from Spanish colonial domination in 1821. Since then, Central America has undergone many attempts to realize what many authors refer to as a project of "reintegration."[9] The Organization of Central American States (ODECA) was created in 1951 amidst the signing of the Charter of San Salvador, with the goal of advancing Central American integration. In 1962 a second charter was signed, aimed at reinforcing the integration process (SICA 2008b). The charter established the ODECA institutions, among them the Legislative Council, a consultative body composed by representatives appointed by national legislatives. But even though ODECA was created to offer an institutional structure to support regional integration, this structure was considered inefficient. As a result, Central American states decided to create the SICA. The Tegucigalpa Protocol was signed in Honduras in December, 1991 and incorporates the ODECA Charter.

Parlacen, however, had been created three years before SICA in the context of the peace process that was being negotiated to end the civil wars in Central America. The 1980s (that is, the decade during the creation of the Parlacen in 1987 and before the SICA in 1991) are known for protracted armed conflicts in the region which affected most directly El Salvador, Guatemala and Nicaragua while indirectly influencing all neighboring countries which would receive refugees from all sides of the conflicts who would continue their fights in foreign territory.[10] The armed conflicts resulted in terribly high costs for Central American society in the form of fatal victims (most of them civil) and human rights violations (García García 2002; Call 2003). Also, internal conflicts greatly hindered economic development (Rettberg, 2007). In 1987 the declaration of Esquipulas II entitled "Procedure for the establishment of a firm and lasting peace in Central America" was signed, opening way for the peace negotiations in each individual country and proposing the creation of Parlacen to ensure the sustainability of the peace arrangements. During the 1990s peace agreements were signed in Nicaragua (1990), El Salvador (1992) and Guatemala (1996) and, despite very high crime rates, today Central America is free from civil war.

Parlacen's Constitutive Treaty was signed one year after the meeting of Esquipulas I and two months after Esquipulas II. Parlacen was created with the aim of representing Central American citizens. The Constitutive Treaty establishes that Parlacen has the mission of promoting political debates on the economy, society and culture so as to achieve "the highest levels of cooperation" in the region (Parlacen 1987).

In this sense, Parlacen is the institutional expression of the efforts of peace and democratization that were carried out with the successful Esquipulas process. The connection between integration and the peace process is clear: during the negotiations of Esquipulas I and II, the presidents of Central American countries worked together to find a common solution to the problem. Internal security problems faced by the countries were perceived as a common threat that should be dealt with by all of them together. The result of this movement was the signing of the peace accords and the creation of the Parlacen. Thus, this IP is directly connected to the necessity of the member states to deal with their internal security problems, and is intended to promote the understanding between the citizens of the region. It has a strong symbolic connection to the peace accords.

Even though Parlacen only commenced activities in 1991 (that is, at the same time when the SICA was created) this fact had consequences that are relevant to the argument presented here. At the time of its creation, Parlacen was given the power to "elect, appoint and remove, correspondently, in accordance with the Internal Rules, the higher executives of all existing and future institutions of the Central American integration" (Parlacen 1987).[11] In this sense, Parlacen would have been an exception among other Latin American IPs, which otherwise have no control over the other institutions within the integration framework. However, observation of the actual functioning of this parliament shows that this power is nonexistent in practice. Parlacen has in fact lost its original (limited) control powers over the other SICA institutions, as established in the Constitutive Treaty. This situation is due to the fact that Parlacen's

Constitutive Treaty was signed before the creation of the SICA. When the SICA was created and Parlacen was merged into its institutional structure through the Tegucigalpa Protocol, it lost its control prerogatives to the Central American Commission. Furthermore, given its lack of budgetary or legislative powers, Parlacen became a solely deliberative organ with none of the classic parliamentary functions.

However, it is interesting to note that Parlacen is actively pursuing to reclaim its original competences. The beginning of the year 2008 was particularly significant as the Reform Protocol to the Constitutional Treaty of the Parlacen and Other Political Boards (Protocolo de Reforma al Tratado Constitutivo del Parlamento Centroamericano y Otras Instancias Políticas) was signed on 20 February in El Salvador by the SICA's heads of state. The protocol aims at conferring Parlacen more significant participation in the integration process through more initiative competences. According to members of Parlacen, the protocol is mainly a result of their long campaign for enhanced powers for their institution. Since the population in general, the media and academic experts seem to have played no significant role in this process – in general, citizens and the media have little or no knowledge concerning the integration process, and many oppose the very existence of Parlacen – it is clear that the push for empowering the Parlacen has come from the Central American parliamentarians with the support of national governments willing to foster integration.

Today, the protocol has already entered into force. Although the original power of appointing heads of other integration institutions (foreseen in the Constitutive Treaty) was not restored, the new protocol not only guarantees Parlacen's right to be informed of all appointments of directors of integration institutions, but also gives it the competence of swearing in high ranking SICA officials. Among the new competences, the most important one is the power of initiative: Parlacen can propose legislation on matters of integration and harmonization of legislation by sending proposals to the "respective Council of Ministers or to the competent organisms." The respective Council of Ministers must, in turn, consider the proposal and respond in no longer than 180 days. After this process, the proposal is submitted to the Meeting of Presidents. The protocol has brought Parlacen the possibility of a more significant participation in the integration process through more initiative competences.

The signing and ratification of the protocol by member states, as well as the expanded influence of Parlacen in the SICA, means a clear empowerment of this integration parliament. Although the support for empowerment came from a majority of member states, it is not homogeneous among SICA's member states. While some countries seem to be in favor of empowering

Parlacen, others, like Costa Rica and Panama, are still skeptical and appear to try consistently to hinder measures of empowerment.

The Andean Parliament

With its seat in Bogotá, Parlandino is part of the Andean Community (CAN), whose members are Bolivia, Colombia, Ecuador and Peru. Chile was also a founding member but left the group in 1976, being accepted in September 2006 as an associated member by the Andean Council of Ministers of Foreign Affairs – clearing the way for the reintegration of the country as a full member.[12] Venezuela joined in 1973, and left the CAN in April 2006.

Parlandino was created in 1979, and it started its activities in 1984. After Venezuela's withdrawal, it seated 20 deputies, 5 for each member state. With an absolute majority voting system, Parlandino does not participate in the decision-making process of the CAN and does not wield any of the classical powers. In other words, its decisions, recommendations, declarations and agreements do not obligate any other CAN institution. Parlandino also "is no formal receptor of suggestions or proposals, and does not have any authority over none of the other three main institutions" (Bustamante 2004). This means that its functions do not include decisions on budget, legislation or executive control.

Although Parlandino does not have any classical parliamentary powers, it does seem to be taken into consideration by the other community institutions. All other institutional bodies present report to the parliament and some even send their highest executive to present to it in person in front of the assembly. It is reasonable to say that Parlandino is then a well-informed institution, capable of producing well-informed decisions. It can also be argued that, when promoting activities to inform the population in general about the integration process, Parlandino will be able to deliver credible information and therefore conduct better information campaigns.

Direct elections for the Parlandino are stipulated in its Constitutional Treaty. However, not all countries conduct regional elections yet. Bolivia still sends representatives from the national legislative. Colombia elected its representatives for the first time in March 2010. But the Colombian case is distinct due to the fact that holding direct elections for the Parlandino has not automatically translated into true citizen engagement. The number of blank votes (1,445,999 representing 20.62 percent of the total of votes) surpassed the number of votes received by most voted party (Partido de la U, with 1,277,559 votes representing 18.22 percent of the total).[13] This situation is a symptom of a lack of interest in the Parlandino and a widespread lack of knowledge (if not complete unawareness) about this IP.

Following the Cartagena Agreement, the CAN is composed of the Council of Presidents, the Council of Ministers of Foreign Affairs, the Andean Commission, the General Secretariat, the Andean Court of Justice and the Andean Parliament, as well as of the Andean University Simón Bolívar and the so-called Consultative Institutions, Financial Institutions and Social Agreements.[14]

The CAN was created in the context of the Latin American integration efforts of the post–World War II period. In 1960, the Montevideo Treaty was signed and the Latin American Free Trade Association (ALALC)[15] was created by Argentina, Brazil, Chile, Mexico, Paraguay, Peru and Uruguay, and was joined by Venezuela in 1966 and by Bolivia in 1967. Nine years after its creation, ALALC was not proving capable of advancing trade liberalization among its members, and the 12-year program to remove trade barriers in the region had to be rescheduled. In that same year, "a group of six less developed Andean countries decided to go their own way, as they complained the big players (namely Argentina, Brazil and Mexico) were the main beneficiaries of trade liberalization" (Dabène 2009, 18). The Andean countries went on to develop a highly complex institutional integration structure "modeled after" the European project and that would eventually "not prove very efficient either" (18). In this endeavor, the Andean countries were supported by the Economic Commission for Latin America and the Caribbean (ECLAC). In the words of the 2001 ECLAC executive secretary José Antonio Ocampo:

> The broadest ideas of regional integration, fostered since the first years of our institution and crystallized in the document "A common Latin American market," elaborated in 1959, were the basis for the creation, one year later, of the Latin American Free Trade Association, ALALC, today the Latin American Integration Association, ALADI. CEPAL has equally supported the initiatives that lead to the signing of the Cartagena Treaty and its ambitious efforts to put in move a much deeper integration than that achieved in the context of the ALALC.[16]

The CAN had very ambitious goals from its beginning and aimed at being more than a project of economic integration. Its founders also understood it as a political union and sought to coordinate the economic and industrial policies of its member states as well as the policies governing extra-Andean foreign direct investment.[17] After being swept by several crises in the 1980s unleashed by the devastating debt crisis, the partners set out to relaunch it in the mid-1990s (the Trujillo Protocol was signed in 1996) with a new series of initiatives, new organs as well as a new name: the Andean Community

(Effner 2003 105ff.). When measured against the goals and objectives it set out to fulfill, both the Andean Pact and the CAN have achieved little. A common market (envisioned for 2005), the coordination of several policies and the establishment of a common foreign policy, among others remain a very distant reality. In addition, a crisis of the CAN unraveled with Venezuela's withdrawal in 2006 and was further deepened by the "tense" relationship between the Ecuador and Colombia in 2008.[18] All these problems have hampered the CAN's ability to act as an international actor. Negotiations with the EU for a biregional association agreement could not be completed until this moment because of disagreements between Andean countries.

During the decade that precedes the creation of Parlandino (that is, during the 1970s) most of the Andean countries – with the exception of Colombia – were experiencing periods of military dictatorships. Although during this period there was a considerable amount of internal instability and political turmoil in all these countries, escalated armed conflicts or civil war were avoided. The intense conflicts triggered by clashes with guerrilla movements and drug trafficking organizations did not reach a climax until the 1980s, after the negotiations for the establishment of the CAN. Since then the guerrilla conflicts in the region have been a source of constant insecurity, but have not affected all countries so as to be perceived as a "common menace." In this sense, Colombia and Peru were (and still are) especially affected by internal conflicts. While Peru's guerrilla movement, the Shining Path (Sendero Luminoso), all but disappeared during the 1990s, Colombia's efforts to deal with a variety of illegal violent groups generated during the years of conflict (guerrillas, independent paramilitary and drug cartels) is still an ongoing process.[19] Perhaps because the problem has not represented an equally serious menace to all the countries, the internal conflicts observed in the Andean countries did not generate an incentive for deeper institutional integration. On the contrary, it seems to encourage unilateral measures and cooperation with countries not belonging to the organization, as is the case both for Peru and Colombia and their close bilateral cooperation with the United States and with the EU on security matters.

Also, on the international front it is reasonable to say that there have been no major security threats to the Andean countries during the years of CAN negotiations. Aside from the atmosphere of general insecurity generated by the Cold War and occasional tensions involving border disputes (for example between Peru and Ecuador, who actually entered a conflict with each other from 1995 to 1999), it is once again reasonable to assume that no major common international security threat was perceived by the Andean countries as an incentive for integration.

Between Europe, Central America and the Andes: Explaining the Variation

Based on the accounts presented above of the creation of the three IPs, this section highlights five elements that seem to have influenced the initial powers that were attributed to them. These are: security threats as incentives for integration; the perception of a democratic deficit as a result of the creation of a supranational decision-making institution; the quality of domestic democracy; parliamentary and presidential political regimes; and external pressure from third parties.

Regarding common security threats,[20] accounts of politicians involved in the crafting of the HA of the ECSC, Europe's first supranational institution, clearly state the crucial role of the issue of security in the integration project during the first moments of European integration.[21] Security threats also served as fundamental incentives in the Central American integration process. But differently from the European post–World War II scenario, where threats came from external actors, Central American countries were fighting against internal enemies. Still, Andean countries did not seem to have the perception of a common security threat at the time of the creation of Parlandino.

The second factor that should be observed is the potential creation or the perception of a democratic deficit. In this case a democratic deficit is defined as the transfer of sovereignty to another (higher) level of government – whether it be international or regional – at the expense of the quality of democracy at the national level. A democratic deficit is usually linked to the creation of a supranational decision-making institution, such as the HA, and is a concern at the time of the creation of the ECSC and the EP. But it may also be argued that intergovernmental arrangements also generates constraints in the freedom of member states to, for example, negotiate trade agreements with third parties and therefore also represents a democratic deficit. In spite of this discussion, in Latin America the democratic deficit is far from being a serious political issue. This is due to the fact that in the SICA and CAN member states, there is no perception of such a deficit (even though there is evidence that some decisions are actually taken by majority vote at the ministerial level by the CAN). This is probably due to the low level of economic integration experienced by these RIOs and of the generally low impact of the policies produced at the regional level.

Whether a democratic regime or a dictatorship is in place at the national level also seems to play a role in the creation of IPs. The EP and Parlandino were created by groups of democratic countries (with levels of quality and stability of the democratic system varying considerably from the European to the Central American contexts). It is reasonable to argue that political elites who are elected as representatives by citizens will have in mind a model of democratic legitimacy not only in regard to national, but also to regional institutions. In the case of Parlandino, the countries of Bolivia, Colombia and Ecuador are identified by Cheibub (2007, 44–6) as presidential democracies in 1979. In terms of democratic regimes, the exception among Parlandino founding members seems to be Peru, as the country was then not classified as a democracy. Peru would only be included in the list of presidential democracies one year later, in 1980. Furthermore, if we are to take a closer look, at that time Bolivia was in between dictatorial periods and in 1980 it was no longer considered a democracy. In addition, Ecuador had recently come out of 15 years of dictatorship. So the real exception seems to be Colombia, which ended its last dictatorial period in the late 1950s, and was 21 years into its presidential democracy when Parlandino was created.

The fourth element is parliamentary and presidential political regimes of the member states. Like democracy, the existence of parliamentary or presidential institutions also shapes the notion of legitimacy of political elites. According to Cheibub, the main feature of parliamentary democracies is the ability of the parliamentary assembly to remove a government. In contrast, presidential democracies are defined as systems in which "governments cannot under any circumstances be removed by a vote of the legislative assembly" (Cheibub 2007, 37).[22] This is intriguing because while all founding members of the EP were parliamentary democracies,[23] all founding members of Parlacen and Parlandino were presidential democracies. Interestingly, the EP is the only IP that has de facto control powers. However, in the light of the different functions exercised by parliaments in different types of democratic regimes, the fact that Parlacen and Parlandino do not have control powers (and especially "government formation" and "government censure" mentioned by Malamud and de Souza) is not necessarily a sign of weakness, but it is coherent with the fact that they were created by member states that were presidential democracies.

Finally, the external influence of third parties was present in all cases, but in different forms: while in the case of the EP, the US pressured for the adoption of the French supranational model; in the Latin American cases the influence of the ECLAC and the inspiration provided by the European model cannot be underestimated.

Acknowledgments

For their useful comments on preliminary versions of this chapter I am thankful to Andreas Boeckh (who supervises the research on which this paper is based), Juan Albarracín, Antje Daniel, Patricia Graf, Jane Oispuu, Thomas Stehnken, and Daniela Theuer (in the context of extensive exchanges at the Tübingen University), to Simon Hix and Peter Mair (in memoriam) (in the context of the ECPR 18th Summer School on European Parties and Party Systems), as well as to Andrés Malamud. I would like to thank the German Academic Exchange Service (DAAD) and the Office for Gender Equality of the Tübingen University for financial support. I also thank all deputies and staff members of the Parlacen and Parlandino, as well as members of other Latin American organizations who provided me with interviews, documents and relevant information.

Notes

1 The term "integration parliament" was chosen in lieu of the term "regional parliament," often used in the literature. While "integration parliament" refers only to a parliament that is part of the institutional setting of a regional integration process, the term "regional parliament" is also used in reference to subnational parliaments, or to other kinds of international parliaments such as the Latin American Parliament (Parlatino).

2 For this reason I do not take into account other international parliamentary assemblies such as the Council of Europe or Parlatino. As these parliaments are not part of a RIO, they do not share the same institutional constraints and incentives typical of the EP, Parlacen and Parlandino. The history of the Mercosur Parliament (Parlasur) is too short and recent to be analyzed here.

3 The authors present a more detailed analysis of the specific elements that compose each function. Representation can be broken down into elections, national representation and political parties; legislation into the capacity to deliberate on regional budgets, law-making competencies and the right to take legislative initiatives and regulate decision mechanisms; control into government formation, government censure and bureaucracy oversight; and leadership formation involves the competencies developed in committees and hearings, salaries and immunity as well as socialization (Malamud and de Souza 2007, 98–9).

4 The subsections on the Parlacen and Parlandino are strongly based on information collected during field research conducted in Colombia and Guatemala in 2008 and in the Dominican Republic and Panama in 2011. This information includes interviews with members and staff members of both parliaments, official documents, unofficial work plans and my observations on the institution's activities.

5 With the Lisbon Treaty entering into force, in the next elections the EP will have 751 members.

6 For a complete list and chronology see http://europa.eu/legislation_summaries/ institutional_affairs/treaties/ treaties_ecsc_en.htm (accessed 17 January 2012).

7 "In essence, the Marshall Plan would be the initial push to apply the Truman Doctrine and suppress any communist uprising. The allied forces ultimately created the North Atlantic Treaty Organization in 1949 to coordinate efforts against the enemy." (Erixon 2008, 23)

8 Constitutional reforms were necessary to introduce direct elections, but these were accomplished in time for the 2010 elections. According to the amendment, Dominican members of Parlacen are named *Diputados de ultramar* (ultramarine deputies).

9 For a detailed account of the many efforts conducted in the region towards integration, see Dabène (2009, 39–59).

10 This is the case of Honduras, obtained from an interview with a Honduran parliamentarian of the Parlacen in Guatemala City, 2008.

11 This is my own translation from the original: "Elegir, nombrar o remover, según corresponda, de conformidad con el Reglamento Interno, al funcionario ejecutivo de más alto rango de los organismos existentes o futuros, de la integración centroamericana creados, por los Estados Parte de este Tratado."

12 See the historical summary available on the website of the CAN: http://www.comunidadandina.org/quienes/resena.htm (accessed 17 January 2012).

13 Numbers from the Registraduría Nacional del Estado Civil on 26 June 2010. Available from http://www.registraduria.gov.co

14 The "Consultative Institutions" are the Consultative Business Council and the Consultative Labor Council. The "Financial Institutions" are the Andean Development Corporation (CAF) and the Latin American Reserve Fund (FLAR). The "Social Agreements" are composed by the Andean Health Organization and the Simón Rodríguez Convention for social and labor matters.

15 It was relaunched in 1980 as the Latin American Integration Association (ALADI) with the signing of the second Montevideo Agreement.

16 The original excerpt reads as follows: "Las ideas más amplias de integración regional, impulsadas desde los primeros años de nuestra institución y cristalizadas en el documento 'Un mercado común latinoamericano,' elaborado en 1959, fueron una de las bases para la creación, un año después, de la Asociación Latinoamericana de Libre Comercio, ALALC, hoy Asociación Latinoamericana de Integración, ALADI. Desde la CEPAL se apoyaron, igualmente, las iniciativas que condujeron a la suscripción del Acuerdo de Cartagena y su ambiciosos esfuerzos por poner en marcha una integración mucho más profunda de la que se había logrado en el seno de la ALALC."

17 The goals set for the Andean Pact show the importance ascribed to import substitution industrialization (ISI) and related development concepts by the member countries. In fact, the withdrawal of Chile from the Andean Pact was to a large extent due to the incongruence between the economic and development policies followed by the pact and the military government of Chile after 1973.

18 Colombia's internal conflict has long been a source of tension in the region. In March 2008, Colombian troops attacked a FARC (Colombian guerrilla) outpost in Ecuadorian territory, killing one of its main leaders. This action by the Colombian government became a serious diplomatic incident. Despite all its limitations, the CAN offers its member countries a forum for cooperation and information exchange. At the time when two of its member states (Colombia and Ecuador) had very fractured diplomatic ties, the CAN was in fact one of the few arenas of permanent exchange between these two countries.

19 The following passage illustrates the difference between Central America and Colombia in this respect: "In the past decade peace negotiations with leftist insurgents took place in El Salvador, Guatemala and Colombia. The Central American talks resulted in peace accords (concluded in 1992 in El Salvador and 1996 in Guatemala), while the Colombian government's peace negotiations with the leftist Fuerzas Armadas Revolucionarias de Colombia (FARC) collapsed in 2002" (Rettberg 2007, 464). Despite the peace negotiations and the recent victories achieved by the Colombian government – such as the rescue of key hostages such as Ingrid Betancourt – a short-term solution to the conflict still seems unlikely.

20 Common security threats can also be seen as an incentive to construct strong RIO institutions in general (not only regional parliaments). This has been included in the group of explanatory variables for the differences between parliaments because of its positive effect in the specific case of the creation of parliamentary institutions. Other variables that are important to the explanation of other RIO institutions but not particularly for the parliaments are not included in the analysis. For example, socioeconomic interests – which play a significant role as incentives for integration in general – can function as hindering factors in the case of regional parliaments. In his analysis of the negotiations involving the creation of the CA of the ECSC, Rittberger (2005, 106) states that "Benelux countries accepted the principle of parliamentary accountability of the HA but only under the condition that the CA would not be able to exercise any form of legislative or policy-influencing powers (which...were viewed to be detrimental for the achievement of domestic socio-economic policy objectives)."

21 With the creation of the EC and the admission of new members, market integration gradually emerged as the main aspect of the process. The renovated momentum towards the building of a political union interestingly coincides with the also renewed security incentives generated by German reunification in 1989–90. Indeed, Jopp (1994) describes the reunification as having altered the internal balance in the EC, creating the "decisive impetus for political community-building," aiming at a deeper integration capable of embedding Germany in strong institutional structures. The German and French initiatives to discuss the political union led to the negotiations of Maastricht for the Treaty on European Union, which included not only the agreement on a monetary union and cooperation in policy, judicial and domestic affairs, but also provisions for the Common Foreign and Security Policy (CFSP). The fear of widespread armed conflicts in the continent is deeply ingrained in the European integration project, and it remains very present in today's Europe. French president Nikolas Sarkozy in his speech to the EP on 16 December 2008 stated that "the friendship between Germany and France is not an option, is a duty" because they had both been at the center of the conflicts that devastated the continent in the previous century.

22 Thus the argument does not imply an intrinsic weakness of parliaments in presidential regimes. It only acknowledges that parliamentary institutions in such contexts have different functions from parliaments in parliamentary regimes. This is a view supported by Cheibub, who argues that presidentialism does not necessarily generate unstable polities. According to this author, the source of instability in presidential regime is not institutional one. Rather, the unstable tendency of presidential systems is explained by their past military dictatorships. In this sense, presidential constitutions are in principle not worse than parliamentary ones in their ability to provide stable institutional settings: "the problem of presidential democracies is not that they are 'institutionally flawed.' Rather, the problem is that they tend to exist in societies where democracies of any type are likely to be unstable. Fears stemming from the fact that many new democracies have 'chosen' presidential institutions are therefore unfounded. From a strictly institutional point of view, presidentialism can be as stable as parliamentarism" (Cheibub 2007, 3).

23 Although France later changed its regime to a mixed democracy (or, in Shugart's nomenclature, a premier-presidential system), what is relevant in the context of this research is that in 1951 it was a parliamentary system.

References

Bustamante, A. M. 2004. "Desarrollo Institucional de la Comunidad Andina." *Aldea Mundo* 8.16: 16–28.

Call, Charles T. 2003. "Democratization, War and State Building: Constructing the Rule of Law in El Salvador." *Journal of Latin American Studies* 35: 827–62.

Cheibub, José Antonio. 2007. *Presidentialism, Parliamentarism, and Democracy*. New York: Cambridge University Press.

Dabène, Olivier. 2009. *The Politics of Regional Integration in Latin America*. New York: Palgrave Macmillan.

Effner, H. 2003. "Die Andengemeinschaft: Scheitern eines Integrationsmodells?" in *Lateinamerika im internationalen System: Zwischen Regionalismus und Globalisierung*, ed. Klaus Bodemer and Susanne Gratius. Opladen: Leske + Budrich.

Erixon, Fredrik. 2008. "The Marshall Plan, Institutional Design and Postwar Economic Development," in *The Marshall Plan at 60*, ed. Fredrik Erixon, Birgit Karlsson, Örjan Appelqvist and Mike Winnerstig. Falun: Timbro Publishers.

Erthal, J. 2007. "Discussing Regional Democracy," in *Closing or Widening the Gap? Legitimacy and Democracy in Regional Integration Organizations*, organized by Andrea Ribeiro Hoffmann and Anna van der Vleuten. London: Ashgate.

———. 2006. "Democracia e Parlamentos Regionais: Parlacen, Parlandino e Parlasul." *Observador Online OPSA* 1.9.

Erthal, J. and J. Albarracín. 2009. "Candidate Selection, Direct Elections and Democracy in Integration Parliaments: The Case of the Andean Parliament." Paper presented at the 21st IPSA World Congress of Political Science, Santiago, Chile, 14 July.

García García, Glenda Mabelyn. 2002. "Herederos de la Guerra: Ex paramilitares y víctimas de la contrainsurgencia en Guatemala." Final report for the competition "Movimientos sociales y nuevos conflictos en América Latina y el Caribe." Programa Regional de Becas CLACSO.

Hix, S. 2008. Lecture at the 18th Annual European Consortium for Political Research (ECPR) Summer School on European Parties and Party Systems at the European University Institute (EUI), Florence, 8–19 September.

Hix, S., A. Noury and G. Roland. 2007. *Democratic Politics in the European Parliament*. Cambridge: Cambridge University Press.

Jopp, Mathias. 1994. "The Strategic Implications of European Integration." *Adelphi Papers* 34.290.

Loth, Wilfried. 2007 "Der Weg nach Rom – Entstehung und Bedeutung der Römischen Verträge." *integration* 1/2007.

Mair, P. 2005. "Democracy Beyond Parties." Center for the Study of Democracy, Working Paper 05–06.

Malamud, A. and L. de Sousa. 2007. "Regional Parliaments in Europe and Latin America: Between Empowerment and Irrelevance," in *Closing or Widening the Gap? Legitimacy and Democracy in Regional Integration Organizations*, organized by Andrea Ribeiro and Anna van der Vleuten. London: Ashgate.

Marschall, Stefan. 2005 *Parlamentarismus: Eine Einführung*. Baden-Baden: Nomos.

Nohlen, Dieter. 2004. "Wie wählt Europa? Das polymorphe Wahlsystem zum Europäischen Parlament." *Aus Politik und Zeitgeschichte* B 17/2004, April.

Puertas, J. A. 2006. "La desintegración andina." *Nueva Sociedad* 204: 4–13.

Rettberg, Angelika. 2007. "The Private Sector and Peace in El Salvador, Guatemala, and Colombia." *Journal of Latin American Studies* 39: 463–94.

Rittberger, B. 2005. *Building Europe's Parliament – Democratic Representation Beyond the Nation-State*. New York: Oxford University Press.

———· 2009. "The Historical Origins of the EU's System of Representation." *Journal of European Public Policy* 16.1: 43–61.

Segovia, A. 2005. "Integración Real y Grupos de Poder Económico en América Central: Implicaciones para el desarrollo y la democracia de la región." Final report for "Las Economias y Sociedades de América Central a Principios del Siglo XXI," November.

Shugart, Matthew S. 1993. "Of Presidents and Parliaments." *East European Constitutional Review* 2.1 (Winter).

Spierenburg, D. and R. Poidevin. 1994. *The History of the High Authority of the European Coal and Steel Community*. London: Weidenfeld & Nicholson.

Van der Vleuten, A. and A. Ribeiro Hoffmann. 2007. "RIOs, Legitimacy and Democracy: A Conceptual Clarification," in *Closing or Widening the Gap? Legitimacy and Democracy in Regional Integration Organizations*, organized by Andrea Ribeiro Hoffman and Anna van der Vleuten. London: Ashgate.

Weidenfeld, Werner and Wolfgang Wessels (organizers). 2007. *Europa von A bis Z: Taschenbuch der europäischen Integration*. Bonn: BPB.

Official Documents and Speeches

CAN. 1969. Cartagena Agreement (Acuerdo de Cartagena).

———· 1996. Trujillo Protocol (Protocolo de Trujilo).

ECSC. 1951. Treaty Establishing the European Coal and Steel Community (Treaty of Paris).

Marshall, George C. 1947. "Marshall Plan Speech." NATO Online Library. http://www.nato.int/docu/speech/1947/s470605a_e.htm (accessed 10 October 2009).

Ocampo, José Antonio. 2001. "Palabras del Secretário Ejecutivo de la CEPAL, Con ocasión de la visita del Excelentísimo Señor Presidente de la República Bolivariana de Venezuela Hugo Chávez Frías a la CEPAL." http://www.eclac.org/cgi-bin/getProd.asp?xml=/prensa/noticias/noticias/5/7595/P7595.xml&xsl=/prensa/tpl/p1f.xsl&base=/prensa/tpl/top-bottom.xsl (accessed 16 January 2012).

Parlacen. 1987. Tratado Constitutivo del Parlamento Centroamericano y Otras Instancias Politicas.

Parlandino. 1979. Constitutive Treaty of the Andean Parliament (Tratado Constitutivo del Parlamento Andino).

———· 1997a. Additional Protocol to the Constitutive Treaty of the Andean Parliament (Protocolo Adicional al Tratado Constitutivo del Parlamento Andino), 1997.

———· 1997b. Additional Protocol to the Constitutive Treaty of the Andean Parliament on the Direct and Universal Election of Its Representatives (Protocolo Adicional al Tratado Constitutivo del Parlamento Andino Sobre Elecciones Directas y Universales de sus Representantes).

Republic of Colombia. 2007a. Ley No. 1157 del 20 de Septiembre de 2007: "Por cual se desarrolla el artículo 227 de la Constitución Política con relación a la elección directa de parlamentarios Andinos."

———· 2007b. Sentencia C-502/07 de la Corte Constitucional sobre el proyecto de ley estatutaria No. 34/05-SENADO Y No. 207/05-CAMARA.

Schuman, Robert. 1950. The Schuman Declaration. http://europa.eu/abc/symbols/9-may/decl_en.htm#top (accessed 10 October 2009).

SICA. 1991. Protocolo de Tegucigalpa a la Carta de la Organización de Estados Centroamericanos (ODECA).

――――. 2008a. Protocolo de Reformas al Tratado Constitutivo del Parlamento Centroamericano y Otras Instancias Políticas.

――――. 2008b. "Comemoran Día de la Integración Centroamericana." SG-SICA. http://www.sica.int/busqueda/Noticias.aspx?IDItem=28999&IDCat=3&IdEnt=1&Idm=1&IdmStyle=1 (accessed 14 October 2008).

Part III

IDEAS AND THE ROLE OF
ELITES AND ADVOCACY NETWORKS:
TRANSLATING AND LEGTIMATING
THE FRONTIERS OF INSTITUTIONAL
REFORMS

Chapter 8

MARKETING PROFESSIONAL EXPERTISE BY (RE)INVENTING STATES: PROFESSIONAL RIVALRIES BETWEEN LAWYERS AND ECONOMISTS AS HEGEMONIC STRATEGIES IN THE INTERNATIONAL MARKET FOR THE REPRODUCTION OF NATIONAL STATE ELITES

Yves Dezalay

CNRS and Maison des Sciences de l'Homme, Paris

Bryant Garth

American Bar Foundation, Chicago, and Southwestern Law School, Los Angeles

In the last ten years, the promotion of the rule of law has become one of the essential components of the politics of international developmental assistance. Paradoxically, the rather substantial investments that have taken place both financially and professionally, according to most commentators, have not had results proportional to the amounts invested. Recurring scholarly criticisms emphasize that the enduring forces of culture and legal tradition have led to the repeated failure of efforts to transplant features of one system to another.

The close relationship of the legal field to the institutions of the nation-state contrasts with the internationalization of the field of economics, where pretentions of a universal global science coexist with different national practices (Fourcade-Gourinchas and Babb 2002; Fourcade-Gourinchas 2006). The spread, content and modes of international transfer of these two types of governing expertise depend on logics tied to the specific history of these professional fields. This history determines how each field constructed its national autonomy, and more particularly, how it supports its claim to universalism played out through active transnational networks structured around the major institutions for the production and diffusion of expertise. The role and authority of degrees and expertise gained abroad contributes to a hierarchical division of labor that in turn leads to the reproduction both of the transnational expertise and of the national elites that promote it.

It is necessary, therefore, to work through national histories in order to understand the market for the import and export of state expertise. The national approach is essential whether that market in the import and export of governing expertise – such as human rights or the economic recipes for development – actually represents the beginnings of the global field of state power or whether it turns out to represent only a strategy of symbolic imperialism characterized by prescriptive discourses claiming universal value.

Working on the basis of a first line of research focused on relations between the United States and Latin America (Dezalay and Garth 2002a), we examined transfers of expertise through competitive battles between different professional elites in the North as well as the South. Our findings supported a hypothesis initially offered by Pierre Bourdieu (2002) to examine the international circulation of ideas. He pointed out that "texts circulate without their contexts," meaning that the importers of state expertise can adapt the texts according to their own positions in the field of state power. This double game strategy allows them to take advantage of the legitimacy of the imported expertise while using the expertise instrumentally in their local fights for power and influence.

Yet, in spite of local reinterpretations, international strategies deployed in palace wars do not always lead to major institutional or professional transformations. Our empirical findings show that it is the existence of a structural homology of positions – and interests – between importers and exporters that determines the success of a particular process of import-export. In order to present the data which led to the formulation of this core hypothesis, we will start by comparing the relatively successful transplantation of Chicago economics in Chile and other Latin American countries with the more ambivalent effects of the global campaign for human rights within this same region. Then, in a second part, we will sketch briefly some more general findings drawn from further research in Asia that allowed us to systematize our problematic concerning the earlier colonial genesis – and its later hegemonic restructuring – of the international markets for the import-export of competing forms of state expertise.

Imported Expertise in Latin American "Palace Wars"[1]

The "dollarization"[2] of economics

The Washington Consensus in the South and North was developed out of structural similarities in the position of a group of economists positioned outside the establishment. The first key ingredient was scholarly investment as a legitimating basis for what was then an "unholy alliance." The University of Chicago economists – almost all of whom were first or second generation immigrants – lacked the requisite social capital and connections for legitimacy and therefore invested in mathematics, public choice and media strategies. Early on they formed alliances with a then-marginal group of very conservative Republicans and business people hostile to the cozy relationships that made up the establishment. The Chicago economists also developed powerful mathematical arguments to build their position in "pure" economics against the position of Harvard essayists and the powerful position of the Eastern establishment. The fight staged on the terrain of economics was also a political battle against the Keynesian economists among the intellectuals from the Eastern establishment active in the Kennedy administration. They were denouncing governmental bureaucracies and policies as the product of rent-seeking behavior that led to inflation and economic stagnation.

In the 1950s, at a time when neoliberal economics was still relatively weak in the United States, Chicago economists invested internationally. Led by Arnold Harberger of the University of Chicago, they took advantage of the US's Agency for International Development (USAID) and the philanthropic foundations to invest in potential counterparts in the South, especially in the Catholic University in Santiago, Chile – the home of the original "Chicago boys" (Valdés 1995). The investment in Chile could be directed against the Comisión Económica para América Latina y el Caribe (CEPAL) – the UN organization in Santiago – and Raul Prebisch (himself the perfect embodiment of the well-bred cosmopolitan economist). The US investment was relatively even-handed between Keynesians and neoliberals, but Keynesian and developmentalist economics constituted the mainstream within the Chilean establishment at the University of Chile. The young economists at the Catholic University came in large numbers to Chicago, and they formed political alliances in Chile similar to those alliances that were being formed among conservatives in the United States. Thus, they were ready when Pinochet came to power in 1973.

They used their mathematical economics, their ties with the media (especially *El Mercurio*, the Chilean analogue to the *Wall Street Journal*) and their

---

1 See Dezalay and Garth (2002a).
2 See Dezalay and Garth (2002b).

connection to the Chicago economists who were rapidly gaining power within the economics profession in the United States to call for a "shock treatment" and a series of reforms that became the Bible for neoliberal attacks on the interventionist state elsewhere including Britain. The almost perfect parallel between Chicago and Catholic universities made for a remarkable story of export and import. This success, in turn, then helped to build the credibility of the emerging Washington Consensus and provided the basis for structural adjustment after the debt crisis and the Reagan election in the 1980s.

In Brazil, Delfim Netto, a first-generation economist who gained power with the military, used the state and developmentalism against the old establishment that had dominated the state. The second-generation descendants of the establishment, exemplified by Pedro Malan, built their base at the Catholic University in Rio de Janeiro. Since economics was still relatively new in all these countries, the new generation of economists could invest abroad and upon their return take over an economics department and align it with the emerging global market. This new generation used US economics and the legitimacy of mathematics against the strong state and relatively high inflation characteristic of the policies of Delfim Netto in the 1970s. The debt crisis further built their position.

Argentina's think-tanks – always well-connected internationally – did not need economics to challenge the establishment or the military, but economists led initially by Domingo Cavallo made their way into the international markets in economic expertise with relative ease. Mathematics could be used to challenge converted lawyers like Martinez de Hoz, the economics minister of Argentina. In Mexico, a new generation within the Partido Revolucionario Institucional (PRI) establishment exemplified by Mexican president Carlos Salinas de Gortari used economics to gain power within the state establishment and to build bridges to economists from the private schools and the private sector, as shown by former Mexican finance minister Pedro Aspe.

Groups of economists were able to enhance their domestic positions after the debt crisis of the 1980s. They got along perfectly with their negotiating counterparts. Drawing on their proficiency in English, their technical economics, their connections in the economics communities in the United States and their democratic sympathies (sympathies which the next generation of Latin American economists would also pick up while swimming in US academic waters), this generation of economists became the core of the "technopols" (Dominguez 1997) celebrated in the United States. Indeed, many of the most prominent economists in Latin America met and formed friendships in the United States, especially at MIT or Harvard where much of the post-Chicago generation was educated. They became the Southern side of the more democratic version of the Washington Consensus.

The market integration of economic expertise has only increased in the following years. It is not just that international degrees are required as a matter of course in order to make any credible claim to economic expertise, but also that it is increasingly necessary to have held a position in the United States that provides further professional credibility – including visiting professorships, or even tenure track appointments. One result is that there are quite a number of Latin American economists teaching and even holding tenured positions in US universities and there are many others who have had a stint at the World Bank or the International Monetary Fund (IMF). While the senior economists who have reached governmental positions in the South are monitoring the careers of their younger protégés teaching and publishing in the United States in order to determine their suitability for home positions, the most talented within this new generation are worried that this return home might "ruin their careers as economists." The globalization of economics thus contributes to create new incentives and channels of brain drain from the South to the North (Dezalay and Garth 2008a, 2008c).

The globalization of human rights and the brain drain of "moral entrepreneurs"

After Pinochet came to power in 1973 and began to persecute those who had worked with the Allende government, a few lawyers who had been sympathizers of this regime joined with the church – which still strongly reflected the social gospel – and sought the legal remedies to fight back. They had very few options in politics or the legal profession, and this alternative also provided little in the way of legal success. At that particular moment, however, Amnesty International was working assiduously to build the idea that human rights were not merely tools for political groups out of power, but reflected universals that proscribed torture and disappearance. A relatively marginal group of legal academics in the United States – linked to Amnesty and the International Commission of Jurists – had worked toward the same end by drawing on European principles and postwar developments such as the European Convention on Human Rights. They sought to build the credibility of human rights as international law (Dezalay and Garth 2006, 2008d).

The investment of these groups was recognized and augmented by the split in the foreign policy establishment in the United States. The breach in the US side of the Cold War opened up new possibilities. The Democratic doves held hearings in the United States following the Pinochet coup and sought to use this human rights expertise to challenge the hawks who had supported and aided the coup. The Cold War split could also be found in the Ford Foundation, where young idealists had decided after 1970 to work with the Allende regime despite the pressure of the CIA and the State Department. After the coup, they sought to protect the individuals in whom they had invested earlier. The Ford Foundation did not immediately invest in human rights, but they and the Democratic doves formed an alliance with reformers from the establishment who were now out of power. This international alliance brought together social groups which had converging interests because they occupied similar professional and political positions in the North and the South.

At first the alliance drew upon the shared investment in neutral social science. In Chile, human rights developed as a technical legal expertise, even if it was closely linked (personally and intellectually) to the social scientists who had worked with the Allende regime for land reform and other social programs. Both in the North and the South, the opposition actors joined with the media to build the credibility of human rights as a discourse that suited both sides perfectly. Amnesty thrived, winning the Nobel Prize in 1977 and Jimmy Carter became president in part as a result of his human rights platform. By 1977, after the Ford Foundation Board of Trustees had visited the Vicariate in Santiago, the Ford Foundation was willing to create a program in human rights and use the Vicariate model – which seemed "curiously legalistic" – to expand to other terrains. During the Reagan administration, (which was also the time of the debt crisis and the softening of the authoritarian regimes in Latin America) legally oriented human rights organizations thrived in the North and the South. Responding to the changing field of state power in the United States, additionally the Human Rights Watch challenged Amnesty International and emerged as the leading global human rights organization.

The model from Chile exerted a great influence around the world, in particular interacting with parallel developments in Brazil and somewhat similar developments in Argentina – where, however, the church offered no support and the Madres of the Plaza de Mayo were the only strong voice at the outset. The growing legitimacy of international human rights discourse in the late 1970s and 1980s meant also that it came to Mexico to be used by groups who aspired to employ legal expertise to challenge and to upgrade the PRI. Since "the model worked everywhere else," the philanthropic foundations also were available to help those who wished to try this international strategy in Mexico.

Human rights organizations were a thriving form of public interest law in the 1980s throughout Latin America and the United States. The international market in human rights expertise was a plausible counterpart to the international market in economic expertise. Both were centered in the North and especially in United States campuses. Both were closely connected to the media and had become increasingly competitive. The human rights movement helped to make the rules for the transitions to democracy and lawyers active in the human rights movements became key players in the new regimes.

Once the actors in the human rights movement succeeded in gaining power in Chile, Brazil and elsewhere, however, they abandoned institutions like the Vicariate in order to invest in the politics of the transition regime. The human rights movement hardly exists anymore in Chile in the sense of a movement seeking to hold the state accountable through legal institutions. The same conclusion in general could be reached for Argentina, Brazil and Mexico. For example, Raul Alfonsin in Argentina (the first president after the military dictatorship) came from a human rights background to elite party politics and the institutions of the state. In fact, in all the countries we studied, the investment of the first generation in human rights provided an excellent base for political activity after the transition. What was left behind was not replenished by a new generation eager to mimic the careers of their predecessors. The particular conjuncture that had united moral activism with law through the church and international actors did not continue. The newly created institutional structures that built the human rights nongovernmental organizations (NGOs) unraveled, revealing the structures that had been in place prior to the 1970s.

Nevertheless, once formed, local human rights organizations can continue to exist in the South even if they no longer resemble what they represented earlier. Many, for example, have converted to causes and issues such as the control of crime or the prevention of violence against women. There are many more outposts of international development assistance than activist legal institutions challenging the state. Legal professionals are involved, but it is hard to see these organizations as professional analogues to public interest law.

The patterns may change over time, however, and there may be some exceptions in the South involving institutions that continue to follow the approach of moral investment in law against the state. In Brazil, for example, Viva Rio (an NGO) is one example of a mix between social movements, religion, politics and law. Its activities, which grew out of the human rights movement, focus on crime, hunger and police violence in Rio de Janeiro and it draws on elite lawyers as well as social activists. In Chile, activities centered at the University of Diego Portales – a private university originally designed to produce business lawyers – continue to emphasize human rights and public interest law. Argentina seems to offer the most promise for cause lawyering, given the long tradition of professionals investing in institutions and organizations outside the state. Such entities as Poder Ciudadano and a recent and related entity termed the Association for Civil Rights (Associacion por los Derechos Civiles, or ADC), which is dedicated to the protection of civil liberties in Argentina and funded primarily by the Ford Foundation, provide examples (Dezalay and Garth, 2008d).

In contrast to the general pattern in the South, the leading international human rights organizations in the United States are thriving in the legal profession. Instead of abandoning their investment in legal expertise to join political parties and movements, human rights organizations continue to invest legal resources and techniques in the cutting edges of US foreign policy. As with power corporate lawyers in Washington DC, some enter the government on the basis of their experience and expertise, but the legal bases continue to thrive through their symbiotic relationship with the state.

Two further developments relate to the structural asymmetry of the present period. First, those lawyers who have continued to invest professionally in the field of human rights from the South have tended to go abroad, where their expertise and investment in international human rights remains validated and recognized. This legal morality and brain drain from the South to the North helps to legitimate the international human rights organizations based in the North. The Northern organizations can use their openness – and make certain modifications that come with that openness – to legitimate further their positions of leadership in the field of international human rights.

Structural homologies and the relative failure of transplants

The thriving of human rights organizations in the United States, in contrast to their absorption and reincorporation into the state in the South, is consistent with what our structural model would expect. New forms of symbolic capital tend to gravitate toward the more established and dominant symbolic banks where they can be better valued, guaranteed and exchanged. This means that in the United States, symbolic innovators continue to gravitate around the powerful and relatively autonomous professional *milieux* – especially given the fairly amorphous and porous configuration of the US state. In Chile, to make the obvious contrast, the state provides the dominant symbolic bank.

For structural reasons, therefore, the current situation reveals only a partial transplant of the US professional model of legal legitimacy. The partial transplant reinforces US hegemony and helps to sustain the long-term prosperity of the US professional model at home. International activities add a key dimension to a US legal elite that combines hired guns, reformers and public interest lawyers acting on the basis of legal noblesse oblige (Dezalay and Garth 2007). In the field of human rights (as well as that of the environment and of the movement to protect women against violence), the local prestige and power of US organizations draws extensively on international activities and expertise. Yet in national settings outside of the United States, there has been far more lasting success in transplanting US-style business law than US-style public interest law. Within the business law firms, there is a move parallel to that of the economists toward investment in the state and its institutions. The notion of professional strategies of using law against the state and business, which is a key ingredient of the legal field in the United States, has not, however, been able to thrive beyond a particular time period – when fractions of the establishment united against the authoritarian states which evicted them from power.

The processes of professional dollarization, and the dollarization of state knowledge (Dezalay and Garth 2002b), captured in the shift from gentlemen lawyers to technopols, are therefore highly uneven. Elite economists can make their professional careers locally through investment in and legitimacy from the international market of expertise centered in the United States. They legitimate their superiority to the rank and file economists of their own countries while drawing on the latest economics of the campuses in the North. The US professional ranking of economists outside the United States translates directly into professional prestige and recognition at home. There is a brain drain to the North, including to the World Bank and the IMF, but there is enough return traffic flows to maintain the crucial connections. We can trace the development of this international field through interactions between the North and the South that flourished in the development of the Washington Consensus. The relative newness of economics as an academic institution and profession and the need to develop autonomy from law and the legal establishment helped to facilitate these developments.

The same pattern of success does not hold true for public interest law, despite the remarkable professional and legal success that went into the construction of the field of human rights. The institutional prosperity of public interest law in the United States draws on the model of schizophrenic corporate lawyers that developed in the nineteenth century. It is closely linked as well to the role of courts and to the elite law schools in the United States. However, the professional role of "public interest lawyer," has not taken root in Latin America so far. The human rights movement fit parallel structural histories in the North and the South, but unlike the North, the South did not have institutions, such as the elite law schools and the dense networks of philanthropic foundations and professionalized NGOs, that could be used to direct public interest law into a more lasting indigenous path. It remains to be seen whether this "emancipatory side" of US professionalism will take root along side the successful business practice side – and whether a joint effort might mount a real challenge to the traditional positions of the courts and the law faculties.

In both law and economics, the criteria for legitimate expertise are set according to the international market centered in the United States. There is a new global hierarchy which places elite US professionals at the top (either home grown or immigrants selected through brain drain from the periphery) and within each country there is also a two-tier professional hierarchy. There is a small cosmopolitan elite who is able to circulate between various positions of power – as academics, politicians or entrepreneur – over which they have secured a quasi-monopoly. This first tier is surrounded by an increasingly provincialized mass of professionals in law, economics and other fields who have taken advantage of the expansion of educational opportunity in the postwar period. The combined effect of these international and national hierarchies undermines the possibility of building autonomous professional fields in these dominated states. These hierarchies can be challenged by all those who feel excluded, and the legitimacy of states and political regimes built out of this cosmopolitan expertise is therefore always fragile.

The Globalization of the Market of the Import-Export of State Expertise

Taking this finding on the importance of national settings on the processes of import and export as a starting point, we have enlarged our field of investigation to take into account Asian and European developments (Dezalay and Garth 2008a, 2008b, 2010; Dezalay and Madsen 2006). An expanded terrain brings the interplay of synchronic and diachronic dimensions to a larger historic and global canvas, leading to a more refined sociological approach having much in common with the "world system theory" developed by Wallerstein. Going beyond a comparative sociology of national professional fields, the Wallerstein-inspired perspective leads to analyses of strategies seeking to redefine the international hierarchy of expertise at the same time as they seek to build national dominance. Through this more holistic approach, international transfers of expertise appear to be determined by a double competitive logic: one which involves competing expertises seeking universal credibility (such as law versus economics) and another which represents a competition between imperialisms – where professional networks structured around the new hegemonic power compete with those built by the old "imperial societies" of Europe (Charle 2001). Therefore the competition in the export of expertise that is evident in the politics of development assistance is played out in a triangular dynamic, whereby the "imported states" (Badie 1993) from the periphery represent the stakes and a laboratory to try out new technologies of governance.

Wallerstein's world system theory provides lines of inquiry to build on the sociology of professional fields – including studies of the internationalization of the reproduction of the "state nobility" and on the genesis of the international field of state power (Bourdieu 1992, 2000). The hypotheses and issues that derive from this sociology of globalization nicely extend Bourdieu's observations made about the "Esprits d'État" (1993) and the reproduction of the "Noblesses d'État" in the French national setting (1989). In this international competition for the establishment of universals, the elites who dominate national professional fields mobilize resources of the national state – accumulated through more or less lengthy and successful investments in the construction and perpetual reactualization of the state. The authority of these professional expertises, and thus their value on the international market of symbolic import and export, is therefore quite dependent on their homologation by state institutions.

The confrontations between different hegemonic powers seeking to diffuse their model of the state to other countries as a basis for an emerging international field of state power must be analyzed as elitist fights contributing toward the acceleration of the internationalization of the reproduction of national elites. This internationalization helps to compensate for the increased competition among national university graduates by revalorizing the linguistic and cultural capital of the descendants of the old cosmopolitan elite (Dezalay 2004).

The diversity of the terrains and national histories upon which the struggles are fought for the recomposition of international and disciplinary hierarchies can only be summarized at the risk of seeming too simplistic. Brief descriptions can ignore, for example, the subtle ways that individual and collective strategies continuously produce micro adjustments mutually reinforcing each other. Furthermore, it is difficult to take into account strategies that play simultaneously on two registers: hegemonic politics and competition between expertise.

Towards a Sociological Problematic

Importers and exporters: Converging and complementary strategies...

Conforming to the hypotheses of the "international circulation of ideas," the first task of a sociology of the globalization of professional fields is to examine international transfers through the positions that operators occupy in their respective national spaces. Exporters utilize hegemonic strategies to develop new markets for their expertise on the periphery, as was the case notably in economics with the "Chicago boys" in Chile. On the other side, importers gain from opportunities to convert their social capital (as descendants of a cosmopolitan elite) into the most modern forms of state expertise. The acquisition of these competencies, made credible through international homologation, guarantees the importers access to leadership posts in state institutions – especially those that are at the crossroads of politics and scholarly capital, such as think-tanks or their equivalents.

...In a cyclical process

The combination of international financial support and imported international legitimacy is typically not enough to produce programmatic success, in part because the reforms often require support and resources linked to state clientelism or even authoritarianism. Such support does not come without compromises or even deals, either of which can lead imported institutions toward an unforeseen mode of operation and or even to the pursuit of unforeseen goals. This "half-failure," revealed in many cases through critical diagnoses made by international missions of experts, is also a reason for a new cycle of import-export ostensibly aimed at rectifying the errors of the prior efforts while mobilizing the same social, learned and political resources, and indeed benefiting essentially the same categories of agents thriving in the international market of import-export of state expertise.

This self-propelling process is also continued because it is supported by waves of investment in hegemonic power, by proliferating missionaries promoting law and democracy or by entrepreneurs on behalf of development and "good governance." Rivalries between competing expertise such as between law and economics help fuel the cyclical process of imported reforms – in which the interests of importers and exporters are perfectly complementary.

Hegemonical competition between national exporters

In order to complete this general scenario, it is necessary to specify the variables that influence the offerings on the international market of state expertise in more detail. The quantity and the diversity of available resources are functions of the intensity and level of competition between suppliers. The first level of competition is seen among major state powers competing for hegemony. This kind of competition is best exemplified by the Cold War conflict between the Soviet Union and the United States. Yet, even during the Cold War, this level of competition was also seen to a lesser degree in more subtle transatlantic rivalries – whereby traditional imperial societies continued to take advantage of the influence they gained through colonial ties. This level of state competition was also fueled by internal battles in aspiring hegemonic powers between different interest groups or expertises seeking to strengthen their position in their state by mobilizing disciples outside who, once trained, could become potential allies abroad. Within the United States, this internalized local strategy was pursued especially by NGOs supported by the resources of the philanthropic foundations seeking to build coalitions in the service of such causes as the protection of the environment or the defense of human rights (Dezalay and Garth 2008c, 2008d).

When examining the strategies of the exporters, it is important to take into account not only the interplay of oppositions and alliances structuring the field of power within the hegemonic powers, but also the institutions (state development organizations, philanthropic foundations, churches or producers of learned discourse) that facilitate multiple strategies to export internal fights. In this respect, the Europe–US comparison is especially revealing of the influence of specific institutional channels that provide the particular form – and also the structure and package – of the international offer of expertise.

Positions and interests of importers

An identical approach can specify the factors that influence the demand on the side of the importing countries. On one side, it is necessary to take into account the perceived strategic importance of a given country at a given moment of hegemonic struggle. For example, before the threat represented by Fidel Castro led the United States to multiply its investments in Latin America and notably in Chile, the politics of US philanthropic assistance had for a number of years tended to privilege Europe (Gemelli 1998) and Asia, especially countries considered critical outposts in the Cold War, such as Indonesia and South Korea (Ransom 1974).

A strict geopolitical logic, however, does not suffice to explain the North–South trade and exchange in symbolic products, even taking into account the colonial ties that also played a role different from the strict Cold War competition. In particular, internal fights between different groups contending for state power have much more marked effects in the dominated countries than in the exporting countries. The new peripheral states are imported states. Contests for state power are exacerbated by the weak autonomy of many of the states, largely because of their relatively recent origins (Badie 1993). Autonomy is further weakened in countries where relatively short histories of the state were interrupted repeatedly by revolutions or military coups. The expertise homologized in the hegemonic societies serves as critical and perfectly legitimate weapon in contests around state institutions in peripheral states.

Military regimes and the international promotion of newcomers and new technocratic expertise

Paradoxically, authoritarian, populist or nationalist regimes often were accompanied by an acceleration of the importation of new expertise (Dezalay and Garth 2008a, 2008c, 2010). One reason was simply that the leaders of the new government were frequently protégés of the United States, put in place to prevent or divert social movements suspected of harboring communist sympathies. Military leaders were also often newcomers to the international scene, needing to reinforce their legitimacy through the importation of new forms of expertise, especially linked to economic development. This alliance of newcomers and foreign expertise is well exemplified by the authoritarian alliances with economic technocrats. That alliance served also to justify putting aside particular predecessors and competitors, in particular the notable politicians of the law who, in most of these countries, once enjoyed a quasi-monopoly on the field of state power – and foreign relations.

Conclusion

Hegemonic logic, hierarchies of expertise, and the international division of labor of symbolic domination

This brief discussion should suffice to show that the international circulation of state expertise cannot be explained fully by analyses of the markets of import and export of ideas. Symbolic exchanges are the product of political hegemonies that depend, for their effectiveness, on their strict connection with strategies for the reproduction of national elites through and around state institutions. This logic explains why the markets of expertise in public politics continue unabated regardless of whether or not earlier transfers have been successful.

The stakes go well beyond success or failure. According to the logic of the diffusion of expertise of power, claims of universalism are central parts of efforts to legitimate strategies of symbolic imperialism. Simultaneously, expertise affects the reproduction of national elites by legitimating their privileges through the mechanism of state governing expertise (Bourdieu 1993). The two sets of stakes are closely connected. The markets in expertise assure the internationalization of the reproduction of state elites and the restructuring of national institutions – inserting both people and institutions in the new hegemonic order.

References

Bertrand, B. 1993. *L'État importé*. Paris: Fayard.
Bourdieu, P. 1989. *La noblesse d'État, Grandes écoles et esprit de corps*. Paris: Editions de Minuit.
———. 1992. "Conclusions d'un colloque sur 'L'internationalisation et la formation des cadres dirigeants,'" in *Les institutions de formation des cadres dirigeants*, directed by Monique de Saint Martin and Mihai D. Gheorgiu, 281–3. Paris: MSH.
———. 1993. "Esprits d'Etat, Genèse et structure du champ bureaucratique." *Actes de la recherché en sciences sociales* 96–97: 49–52.

_____· 2000. *Les structures sociales de l'économie*. Paris: Seuil.

Bourdieu, P. and L. Wacquant. 1998. "Sur les ruses de la raison impérialiste." *Actes de la recherche en sciences sociales* 121–122: 109–18.

Charle, C. 2001. *La crise des sociétés imperiales, Allemagne, France, Grande Bretagne 1900–1940*. Paris: Seuil.

Coicaud, J. M. 2008. "International Organizations as a Profession and Distribution of Power," in *Mobility of Talent*, ed. Andres Solimano. United Nations University–World Institute Development for Economic Research (UNU-WIDER).

Dezalay, Y. 2003. "Las ONG y la dominacion simbolica," in *Hacia una sociedad civil global*, directed by J. V. Beneyto. Madrid: Taurus-Unesco.

_____· 2004. "Les courtiers de l'international: Héritiers cosmopolites, mercenaires de l'impérialisme et missionnaires de l'universel." *Actes de la recherche en sciences sociales* 151–152: 5–35.

Dezalay, Y. and B. Garth. 2002a. *The Internationalization of Palace Wars: Lawyers, Economists and the Contest for Latin American States*. Chicago: University of Chicago Press.

_____· 2002b. "Dollarizing State and Professional Expertise: Transnational Processes and Questions of Legitimation in State Transformation, 1960–2000," in *Transnational Legal Process: Globalisation and Power Disparities*, ed. M. Likosky with B. Garth. London: Butterworths, LexisNexis.

_____ (eds). 2002c. *Global Prescriptions, the production, Exportation and Importation of a New Legal Orthodoxy*. Ann Arbor: University of Michigan Press.

_____· 2006. "From the Cold War to Kosovo: The Rise and Renewal of the Field of International Human Rights." *Annual Review of Law and Social Sciences* 2: 231–6.

_____· 2007. "Law, Lawyers and Empire: From the Foreign Policy Establishment to Technical legal Hegemony," in *Cambridge History of American Law*, directed by M. Grossberg and C. Tomlins. Cambridge: Cambridge University Press.

_____· 2008a. "National Usages for a 'Global' Science: The Dissemination of New Economic Paradigms as a Hegemonic Global Strategy and a National Strategy for the Reproduction of Governing Elites," in *Global Science and National Sovereignty*, ed. G. Mallard, C. Paradeise and A. Peerbaye. London: Routledge.

_____· 2008b. "Re-structuring States by Exporting Law: American Law Firms and the Genesis of a European Legal Market," in *Paradoxes of European Legal Integration*, ed. M. Madsen in collaboration with B. Garth. Aldershot: Ashgate Publishing.

_____· 2008c. "Lógicas hegemónicas, universalización de los saberes de Estado y reproducción internacional de las élites nacionales: Chile como laboratorio de la governanza de un nuevo Consenso de Washington," in *Chile: De país modelado a país modelo*, ed. M. De Cea, P. Diaz and G. Kerneur. Santiago, Chile: Editores Academicas.

_____· 2008d. "Las paradojas de un imperialismo de la virtud civica: De la internationalicion de los derechos humanos a la profesionalizacion del activismo juridico." In *Derechos humanos en América Latina. Mundializacion y circulacion internacional del conocimiento experto juridico*, edited by A. Santamaria and V. Vecchioli. Bogotá: Editores Academicas.

_____· 2010. *Asian Legal Revivals: Lawyers in the Shadow of Empires*. Chicago and London: University of Chicago Press.

Dezalay, Y. and M. Madsen. 2005. "La construction européenne au carrefour du national et de l'international," in *Les formes de l'activité politique. Éléments d'analyse sociologique (18ᵉ–20ᵉ siècles)*, directed by A. Cohen, B. Lacroix and P. Riutort. Paris: Presses Universitaires de France.

Dominguez, J. (ed.) 1997. *Technopols: Freeing Politics and Markets in Latin America in the 1990s*. University Park, PA: Penn State University Press.

Fourcade-Gourinchas, M. 2006. "The Construction of a Global Profession: The Transnationalization of Economics." *American Journal of Sociology* 112.1: 145–94.

Fourcade-Gourinchas, M. and S. Babb. 2002. "The Rebirth of the Liberal Creed: Paths to Neoliberalism in Four Countries." *American Journal of Sociology* 108.3: 533–79.

Gemelli, G. 1998. *The Ford Foundation and Europe (1950s–1970s) Cross-fertilization of Learning in Social Science and Management.* Brussels: European Interuniversity Press.

Ransom, D. 1974. "Ford Country: Building an Elite for Indonesia," in *The Trojan Horse: A Radical Look at Foreign Aid*, ed. S. Weissman, 93–116. San Francisco: Ramparts Press.

Valdés, J. 1995. *Pinochet's Economists: The Chicago School in Chile.* Cambridge: Cambridge University Press.

Chapter 9

IDENTITY, POLICY PREFERENCES AND THE PERCEPTION OF THE EUROPEAN INTEGRATION PROCESS AMONG THE HUNGARIAN ELITES[1]

György Lengyel and Borbála Göncz
Corvinus University of Budapest

Introduction

In this chapter we will be exploring how symbolic and pragmatic aspects of the perception of the European integration process are related in the opinion of Hungarian elites. We are interested in the intensity of Hungarian elites' supranational attachment as a symbolic form of identification. We will explore how the EU level of redistribution is perceived as a pragmatic measure of identification with the European Union. We will also describe how elites perceive the delegation of certain policy areas to the EU level and whether Hungary's EU membership is perceived as advantageous or not. Taking into account some of the theoretical approaches of the field, we will verify how identity, the positive perception of EU membership and policy preferences are interconnected.

Our analysis is based on the 2007 wave of the IntUne elite survey in Hungary where 80 members of parliament and 42 top business leaders were interviewed.

Theoretical Background

Several models for explaining support for the European integration process have been elaborated since the 1970s. Studies in this field often conceive the

---

1 A Hungarian version of this chapter was published in Gy. Lengyel (ed.), *A magyar politikai és gazdasági elit EU-képe* [The EU image of the Hungarian political and economic elites] (Budapest: Új Mandatum Könykiadó, 2008).

EU as an economic entity – according to this utilitarist logic the support for the EU is based on a rational cost–benefit calculation. Benefits of the EU and the ability to profit from these benefits can either appear at the individual or at the country level (Gabel 1998).

Other analyses approach the subject through the information deficit with regards to the EU. Their main suggestion is that, due to the low level of information, people use "cues" in order to be able to relate to the EU (Anderson 1998; Gabel-Anderson 2001). These cues are to be found in the domestic political arena, such as following the stance of a certain party, government's support of the EU or the general legitimacy of a regime and its attitude towards the EU. According to this logic, political elites play an important role in shaping public opinion.

Inglehart's approach is also based on the conception of the EU as an abstract and distant construct. Moreover, the information available concerning the EU is extremely complicated and requires special capacities to understand them (Inglehart 1970). According to this logic, cognitive mobilization capacities are an important element which would enable one to understand information on the EU and which also supposes a general interest in political matters.

Besides the mentioned utilitarist approach and the role of cues rooted in the domestic political arena, the role of identity and belonging to a group has returned into focus in recent works on the subject (Hooghe and Marks 2001, 2004). While in earlier studies no clear distinction was made between perception of the EU, perception of the European integration process and the attachment to Europe, recent works separate between rational or cognitive and affective attachment to the EU. The latter would stand for identification with Europe. Nevertheless, in some studies the affective aspect is not oriented towards Europe but towards the EU (Kritzinger 2005), meaning that the causal relation between European identity and support for the integration process can actually be inverted.

According to Hooghe and Marks, in the early years of European integration, political actors thought that the integration process itself would create identity. Nowadays, rather, the focus is on how multiple identities affect the perception of European integration. However, others argue that the EU by its mere existence will create identification (Opp 2005), or that a well-functioning and effective EU is able to generate affective attachment (Kritzinger 2005).

Not all students of identity accept that European identity exists – it usually depends on how one defines the concept. For those who share an essentialist approach, which defines national identity as based on common cultural roots, the concept of European identity is problematic. Anthony D. Smith argues that an identity based on common history, common culture, common myths and ancestor can't exist at the European level, while he admits that there are certain common traditions (e.g. Roman law, the Renaissance, humanism, democracy) (Smith 1992). Thus this essentialist perspective on European identity is considered pointless by Horolets, who rather emphasizes the elitist character of the integration process (Horolets 2003). She argues that European identity is difficult to define due to the lack of direct experience with the EU; in addition to the concept of democratic deficit she proposes the concept of affective deficit with regards to the EU which stands for the lack of symbolic attachment.

At the same time, the constructivist approach (e.g. Delanty 1995; Habermas 1998) doesn't focus on culture but rather conceives European identity as a more civic kind of belonging which is rooted in political participation, a European public sphere and a common lifestyle. Furthermore, democratic constitution is considered a common reference point when a common culture, state, territory or dominant ethnical tradition is lacking.

When dealing with elites, some special characteristics of this population need to be taken into account. The information deficit with regards to the European integration process is less accentuated and the cognitive mobilization capacities of this special group are also more salient than among the general public (Lengyel and Göncz 2006). What is more, they are also in a better position to be able to benefit from the advantages of the EU.

According to the functionalist/ neofunctionalist approach, the European integration process is an elite-driven process (Anderson 1998, 570). As such, it is interesting to note whether the leading position of the elites is met by an indifferent public or if public opinion is in accordance with the elites' position because of the latter's role in opinion formation. In previous studies it was found that while before 1992 there was a "permissive consensus" between the elites and the general public (Carubba 2001; Anderson 1998; Gabel 1998), nowadays we can rather speak of a "constraining dissensus" in which the public increasingly wants to make its voice heard (Steenbergen et al. 2007; Hooghe and Marks 2008). This will was manifested through the referenda on the Maastricht Treaty, then more recently through the French and Dutch "no" on the referenda on the European Constitution and nowadays through the referenda on the Lisbon Treaty in 2008 and 2009.

In some studies the comparison of elites' and the general public's opinions are made regarding the different policy content they imagine will fall to the EU (e.g. Hooghe 2003). Hooghe found in her analysis that there are important differences between the two groups regarding policies to be delegated to the EU level, although it is true for both that more costly policies would be rather kept within national competence. However, while the general public would rather welcome a more social and protective EU, delegating social policies to the EU level, elites would rather delegate policies connected with economic competitiveness and free market (Hooghe 2003; Gabel and Anderson 2001).

Figure 9.1. Identity-developing process from instrumental to affective orientations

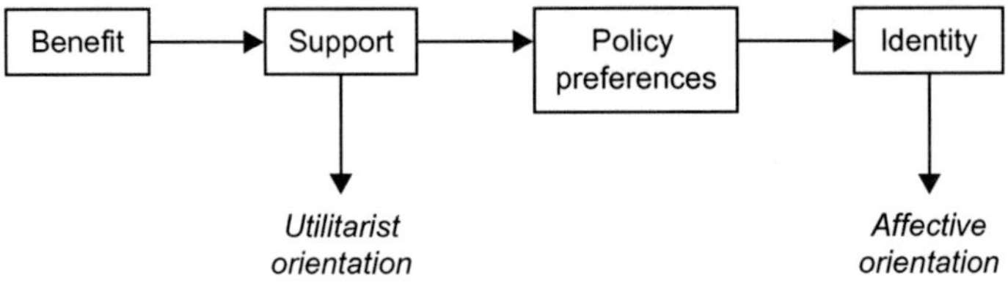

Source: Kritzinger (2005, 55).

In terms of how the content of EU policy preferences is connected to the overall perception of the EU and European identity, Kritzinger proposes a causal model (Kritzinger 2005).[2] The model proposes an inverse causal path between European identity and the perception of the EU as proposed by Hooghe and Marks. The model supposes that people decide on their policy preferences based on their perception of the EU, and the affective attachment to the EU will be based on how efficient they think the EU and its policies are (see Figure 9.1).

Structure of Attachment to Different Territorial Levels

European identity will be defined as territorial attachment to Europe in the current chapter. It can be said that half of the respondents consider themselves to be very attached to Europe – MPs of the governing party are more attached to Europe than those of the opposition, while top business leaders of Hungarian companies are more attached than those of international companies. However, it is imperative to place these results in a wider context taking into account attachment to other territorial levels. Overall, respondents are the most attached to their own country – political elites slightly more (94 percent) than economic elites (84 percent). Strength of country-level attachment is followed by attachment to respondent's localities, – here again political elites expressed a stronger attachment than economic elites.

The level which generates the least feeling of belonging is the region level – there is no significant difference in this respect among the different elite groups. However, it should be noted that attachment to the region was stronger than the attachment to Europe among the MPs in the opposition. This might be explained by considering that MPs in the opposition often tend to withdraw to subnational levels of power. As a result, this level generates a stronger feeling of belonging among them. It has to be noted too that top business leaders of

---

2 The model was elaborated for the general public but due to its general character it can also be applied for the elites.

Table 9.1. Attachment to different territorial levels among political and economic elites (%)

	N	Very attached to their own locality	Very attached to their own region	Very attached to Hungary	Very attached to Europe
MPs of a party in governance	47	89.4	44.7	91.5	55.3
MPs of a party in opposition	33	97.0	57.6	97.0	39.4
Political elites	**80**	**92.5**	**50.0**	**93.8**	**48.8**
Top leaders of international companies	24	29.2	25.0	62.5	33.3
Top leaders of Hungarian companies	18	66.7	38.9	66.7	77.8
Economic elites	**42**	**45.2**	**31.0**	**64.3**	**52.4**
Total	**122**	**76.2**	**43.4**	**83.6**	**50.0**
Cramér's V (N)		.39*** (122)	ns (122)	.26*** (122)	.29* (122)

Note: Measured on a 1–4 scale, 4 = "very attached" shown in the table. Statistical significance: *** < 0.01, ** < 0.05, * < 0.1.

Hungarian companies are the most attached to Europe, more than either the political elites or the leaders of international companies; this attachment was also stronger than attachment to any other territorial levels.

In previous theoretical and empirical studies there have been different views as to whether attachment to different territorial levels can strengthen or exlude each other. Our results confirm that sub- and supranational attachments in fact are mutually strengthening each other. Strong attachment to the locality and the country goes together most often – 71 percent mentioned that they were very attached to both of these territorial levels and 46 percent mentioned that they were very attached to both Hungary and Europe. However, it is worth mentioning that, compared to other public opinion surveys, more respondents mentioned to be strongly attached to all of the measured levels – in this case 21 percent.

Attachments to both Hungary and to the regional level are independent from each other. Although the attachment to Europe and the region was a statistically significant relation, only 25 percent of the respondents mentioned to be very attached to both levels. The reasons behind this fact is the divided opinion of elites on the matter – while MPs in the opposition withdraw to the regional level, top leaders of Hungarian companies are rather attached to Europe.

Table 9.2. Attachment to different territorial levels (%)

	Very attached to their own locality	Very attached to their own region	Very attached to Hungary	Very attached to Europe
Very attached to their own locality	–	40.2 (0.40***)	71.3 (0.321***)	40.2 (0.298***)
Very attached to their own region	–	–	40.2 (ns)	24.6 (0.27***)
Very attached to Hungary	–	–	–	45.9 (0.246**)
Very attached to Europe	–	–	–	–
Total	**76.2**	**43.4**	**83.6**	**50.0**

Note: Measured on a 1–4 scale 4 = "very attached" shown in the table. Cramér's V measure concerning the strength of the relationship between attachment to different territorial levels in parenthesis. Statistical significance: *** < 0.01, ** < 0.05, * < 0.1.

Symbolic and Pragmatic Aspects

This part of the chapter deals with the symbolic and pragmatic aspects of the relation to Europe. Our approach to the symbolic dimension of identification has already been dealt with in the previous section. We understand the pragmatic dimension as the role attributed by elites to the EU in terms of tax redistribution – that is, the share of the total tax revenues which would be transferred to the EU level.

Half of the respondents classified as part of the Hungarian elites mentioned that they are very attached to Europe and another 40% mentioned that they are somewhat attached. In the following tables we only considered those as having symbolic attachment those who replied having a strong attachment to Europe.

About half of the Hungarian elites would transfer at least 20 percent of the total taxes to the EU and delegate decisions on redistribution to that level – this share is considerably superior to the actual share which is around 1 percent. On the other hand, this pragmatic aspect of the relation to the EU is not significantly connected to supranational identity, thus symbolical and pragmatic aspects seem to be independent from each other.

Symbolic and pragmatic aspects follow a different trend across the different elite segments. Political elites of a party in governance show a more positive attitude both towards Europe and European redistribution than their counterparts in opposition. This trend is slightly more complicated among economic elites. Top leaders of international companies are less attached

Table 9.3. The symbolic and pragmatic aspects of the relation to the EU among Hungarian political and economic elites (%)

	N	Very attached to Europe	Would transfer at least 20% of the taxes to the EU level
MPs of a party in governance	*47*	55.3	58.7
MPs of a party in opposition	*33*	39.4	38.7
Political elites	***80***	**48.8**	**50.6**
Top leaders of international companies	*24*	33.3	52.2
Top leaders of Hungarian companies	*18*	77.8	22.2
Economic elites	***42***	**52.4**	**39.0**
Total	***122***	**50.0**	**46.6**
Cramér's V (N)		.29* (122)	.26* (118)

Note: Statistical significance: *** < 0.01, ** < 0.05, * < 0.1.

to Europe in a symbolical way but are more positive towards a European redistribution. This is just the opposite among top leaders of Hungarian companies, in which strong symbolic attachment goes together with a less accentuated pragmatic attitude.

Policy Preferences

Analyzing perception of the EU in terms of its "content" (that is, the different policy areas to be delegated to the EU level) is a more sophisticated approach to the question. For the analysis of policy preferences we included several policy areas recoded into binary variables where 1 stands for positive attitude towards the delegation of the area to European level (see Table 9.4).

There is a group of policy areas which requires a high level of European involvement and another one which is perceived to be more beneficial in national competence. Environmental protection, immigration and the fight against crime – all policy areas that are dealing with transnational or cross-border issues – would involve higher European participation. Whilst in the case of policy areas that are usually dealt with within a state such as taxation, social policy and health care questions (all of which do not involve as much cross-border coordination) would also be more beneficial in national competence.

In addition to EU involvement and the cross-border character of the issue, the other hidden dimension along which the different policy areas can

Table 9.4. Share of those among Hungarian elites who are positive about the delegation of certain policy areas to the European level (%)

Environmental policy	84.4
An army at the EU level	76.2
Fight against crime	67.2
More help for EU regions in economic or social difficulties	64.8
Immigration policy	61.5
Taxation	56.6
A single EU foreign policy toward outside countries	55.7
A common system of social security	44.3
Fighting unemployment	34.4
A unified tax system for the European Union	27.0
Health care policy	23.0

be grouped is the duality of integration and unification. For many the two concepts are equal – unification is in fact a phenomenon which strengthens integration; however, integration can happen without unification.

This duality might be behind the fact that the two questions regarding taxation generated different results. For the question concerning which level taxation should be dealt with, the share of answers favoring supranationality was higher than positive answers for the question concerning a unified tax system in ten years. The difference between the two questions on taxation was, on one hand, the term unification and, on the other hand, the concrete ten year period versus the general approach without a specific timeframe.

Overall, Hooghe's findings suggesting that elites favor an "economic" EU with the delegation of policy areas related to economic competitivity and free market instead of a socially oriented one seem to be fitting in the case of Hungarian elites as well (Hooghe 2003). However, the opinion of the elites is not homogeneous with regard to all policy areas. Regarding policy areas with both social and economic connotations, like unemployment or immigration, economic elites would be more open to EU involvement than political elites. In the case of the immigration policy, 73.8 percent of the economic elites would be willing to delegate policy in this area to the EU. In case of unemployment, this figure is lower: 47.6 percent. For the political elite the figures were 55 percent and 27.5 percent respectively. There was a significant difference between the two elite groups regarding the unification of the tax systems as well – 45.2 percent of the economic elites were in favor, against 17.5 percent of political elites. However, these issues concern the two elite groups in different ways, as the political elite would be possibly less eager to give up certain powers whereas economic elites are not that directly affected. Another question is why the economic elites are more open to delegate these issues to the EU level. The fact that this difference only appears in certain policy areas shows that it is not a general lack of trust in political elites that motivates these differences, but rather the different perception of the efficiency of the treatment of these specific policy areas.

The hierarchical cluster analysis we ran on the different policy areas showed that two main groups exist (see Figure 9.2). The first group consists of policy areas where a higher EU participation would be welcome and the second one of policy areas that would be rather kept within the national domain. The first one regroups those problems that are classified as cross-border and require cross-border or supranational treatment such as environmental issues, crime, taxation, a common European army and immigration. Regional policy and foreign policy are part of this group of policy areas, yet slightly isolated from the others. The second group of policies rather revolves around health care, unemployment and social policy. It is interesting that taxation as a general issue appears in the first group while a unified tax system appears in the second.

We have carried out a multidimensional scaling for the same variables (based on Euclidean distance) in order to explore further the underlying dimensions of the different policy areas. The first two dimensions explain 87 percent of the total variation of the measured items which is already acceptable.

Based on the results of the multidimensional scaling, the first (horizontal) dimension clearly stands for a European versus national level of policy treatment which is in line with the results of the cluster analysis and fits the two or three main clusters – the third cluster would include regional policy and foreign policy which are part of the first cluster but are still somewhat standing

Figure 9.2. Dendrogram of a hierarchical cluster analysis (average linkage between groups)

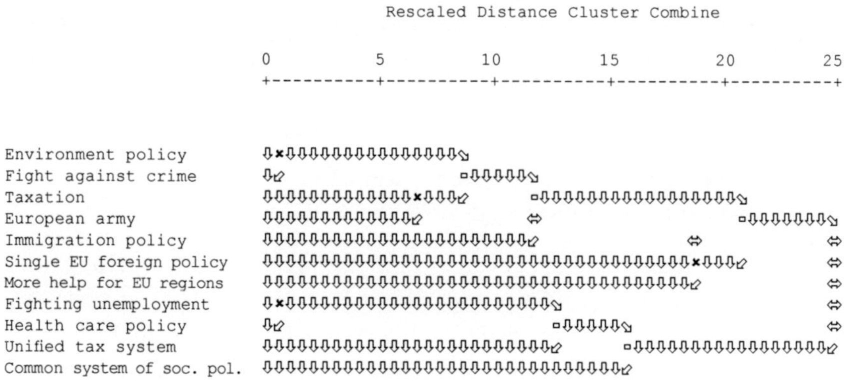

```
                          Rescaled Distance Cluster Combine

                    0         5         10        15        20        25
                    +---------+---------+---------+---------+---------+

Environment policy
Fight against crime
Taxation
European army
Immigration policy
Single EU foreign policy
More help for EU regions
Fighting unemployment
Health care policy
Unified tax system
Common system of soc. pol.
```

Figure 9.3. The placement of the policy areas in a two-dimensional space (multidimensional scaling)

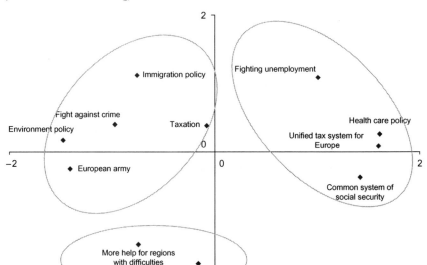

separately. Thus, the horizontal axis contains the European versus national dimension but also the efficiency vs. solidarity axis, in which the adequate and most efficient level of treatment of issues that are cross-border in nature is clearly the EU level (Kritzinger 2005; Opp 2005). Our results also suggest that national elites (especially political ones) would prefer to keep issues that might directly affect the social situation of their constituency in national competence and delegate issues with less of a direct impact to the EU level.

The second (vertical) dimension is more difficult to interpret. A possible interpretation could be a distinction between existing problems (immigration, unemployment, crime) as opposed to the prevention of potential issues yet to become evident (regional policy and foreign policy). The existence of this second axis could be the reason for the isolation of regional and foreign policy within the first group of policy areas.

How the Goals, Institutions and Benefits of the Integration Process are Perceived

It should be mentioned in advance that the majority of the Hungarian elites agree that overall the country has benefitted from EU membership, that integration should be further reinforced and that the main aim of the EU should be to make the European economy more competitive in world markets. About two-fifths of the elites think that there is a need for a common European army. The issues in which the elites' opinion is divided concern whether or not Hungary has benefitted from the EU membership and whether the member states ought to remain the central actors of the European Union. Regarding the latter, the political elites are is divided as well: only one-seventh of the MPs of the party in government favored this opinion against two-thirds among MPs of the party in the opposition. Regarding the perception of Hungary's EU membership, the differences in opinion are slightly less accentuated but follow a similar pattern. The causes of these differences can be rooted in actual political positions – whether in the government or in the opposition, and degree of access to power. This phenomenon is in line with those international experiences in which the perception of the European integration process is a function of domestic political debates (Gabel 1998).

Symbolic and pragmatic aspects of the relation to the EU are not only independent from each other as mentioned earlier, but are also independent from the perception of the institutional design and the benefits of the EU. The latter variable wasn't significantly associated with any attitude, meaning that utilitarianism explains neither the support for integration nor European identity as suggested by Kritzinger's model.

Increasing economic competition as the aim of the EU displays a weak positive relation to the opinion that integration should be strengthened and to the preference for a single European army. Support for further integration is positively linked with the perception of EU institutions regardless of whether they support an intergovernmental or a federalistic view of the EU: there is a positive link with maintaining the central role of member states but also with attitudes of strengthening the role of EC or EP. The concept of a single European army follows a similar trend and is positively linked with the wish of further integration.

Therefore, the assumption that the elites would either prefer an intergovernmentalist EU or a federalistic EU proved to be untrue. Our results don't support the idea that the wish for an enhanced role of member states would go against the support for central EU institutions either.

Connections between Identity, Policy Preferences and the Perception of the Integration Process

When analyzing the connection between European identity and policy preferences, we didn't make any assumptions concerning the causal character of this connection as there was no methodological possibility for checking the direction of this causality. However when interpreting the

Table 9.5. The perception of the aim, institutions and benefits of the EU among different subgroups of Hungarian political and economic elites (%)

	The main aim of the EU should be to make the European economy more competitive in world markets	European integration should be strengthened	We should have a single European army	The member states ought to remain the central actors of the EU	The European Commission ought to become the true government of the EU	The powers of the European Parliament ought to be strengthened	Hungary has on balance benefitted from being a member of the EU
MPs of party in government	76.6	61.7	76.6	14.9	29.8	31.9	93.6
MPs of party in the opposition	63.6	46.9	63.6	66.7	18.2	24.2	72.7
Political elites	71.3	55.7	71.3	36.3	25.0	28.8	85.0
Top leaders of international companies	79.2	65.2	87.5	37.5	29.2	29.2	100.0
Top leaders of Hungarian companies	88.9	83.3	83.3	27.8	38.9	22.2	83.3
Economic elites	83.3	73.2	85.7	33.3	33.3	26.2	92.9
Total	75.4	61.7	76.2	35.2	30.9	27.9	87.7
Cramér's V	ns	ns	ns	.437****	ns	ns	.315***
(N)	(122)	(120)	(122)	(122)	(122)	(122)	(122)

Note: Statistical significance: **** < 0.001, *** < 0.01, ** < 0.05, * < 0.1.

results we tried to follow Kritzinger's logic, placing the results in her model (Kritzinger 2005).

Thus three regression models were elaborated featuring policy preferences, European identity (symbolic attachment) and tax redistribution (pragmatic attachment) as dependent variables. In order to measure policy preferences, we produced a new variable based on the ones dealt with in part four of this chapter – in creating this one single variable we conserved mainly the European versus national dimension.[3] European identity was measured as already stated (those who felt "very attached to Europe"), pragmatic attachment was measured through the level of tax redistribution question. The regression models included the same explaining variables, as we didn't hypothesize a causal relationship between the dependent variables.[4] We also included a variable to measure the effect of the different elite groups in the models; as in the previous analysis, this proved to be the most defining factor of the different attitudes – together with variables concerning the perceptions of the EU aim and institutional design.

Regarding the explaining factors for political preferences, it can be said (see model A in Appendix) that those who would allocate more than 20 percent of the total tax money to the EU level are significantly more open to delegate policy areas to the EU level too. This finding is consistent with the fact that increasing solidarity as the main aim of the EU is also indicative of positive policy preferences at the EU level. At the institutional level, negative attitudes towards maintaining the leading role of the member states is also indicative of more Europeanized policy preferences. The regression model confirms that the opinion of different elite groups is not homogeneous. As showed earlier, the political elite are less open to delegate policy areas to the EU level than top leaders of Hungarian companies.

The results of the regression model explaining European identity or the symbolic attachment (see model B in Appendix) show that pragmatic attachment has a weak, but rather negative effect on it. Policy preferences do not have an impact on identity either, just as the perceived aim of the EU or the imagined institutional design. However, elite groups do not hold a single opinion in this case either. Top leaders of Hungarian companies show a stronger affective attachment to Europe than top leaders of international companies or MPs of a party in the opposition – this once again confirms our earlier results.

---

3 The binary variables referring to the level of preferred treatment of the policy areas were first standardised (z-scores), then summed up and rescaled into a 0–100 scale.

4 The first model is a linear regression model as the 0–100 scale dependent variable on policy preferences made the usage of this methodology possible. The other two are logistic regression models as the dependent variables are binary.

Table 9.6. The interconnections of the aim, institutions and benefits of the EU (%, Cramér's V)

	The main aim of the EU should be to make the European economy more competitive in world markets	European integration should be strengthened	We should have a single European army	The member states ought to remain the central actors of the EU	The European Commission ought to become the true government of the EU	The powers of the European Parliament ought to be strengthened.	Hungary has on balance benefitted from being a member of the EU
Total	75.4	61.7	76.2	35.2	27.9	27.9	87.7
Very attached to Europe	77.0 Ns	65.6 Ns	77.0 Ns	32.8 Ns	34.4 Ns	32.8 Ns	90.2 ns
Would transfer at least 20% of the taxes to the EU level	69.1 Ns	63.6 Ns	78.2 Ns	29.1 Ns	34.5 Ns	32.7 Ns	92.7 ns
The main aim of the EU should be to make the European economy more competitive in world markets	—	67.0 .196*	82.1 .182*	33.7 Ns	30.4 Ns	26.1 Ns	88.0 ns
European integration should be strengthened	—	—	85.1 .254***	27.0 .233**	36.5 .255***	37.8 .268***	89.2 ns

We should have a single European army	—	122	—	31.2 Ns	30.1 Ns	26.9 Ns	91.4 .2*
The member states ought to remain the central actors of the EU	—	—	—	—	20.9 Ns	20.9 ns	81.4 ns
The European Commission ought to become the true government of the EU	—	—	—	—	—	52.9 .348****	94.1 ns
The powers of the European Parliament ought to be strengthened.	—	—	—	—	—	—	79.4 ns
N	122	120	122	122	122	122	122

Note. Statistical significance: **** < 0.001, *** < 0.01, ** < 0.05, * < 0.1.

Based on the explaining model of pragmatic attachment (see model C in Appendix) one can see that symbolic attachment has no effect. However, policy preferences do have an impact. Greater openness to the delegation of policy areas also implies greater willingness to allocate tax money to the EU level. The different elite groups have a significant impact on the attitudes in this case too. MPs from the party in government are more open to delegate tax money to European level, which confirms results showed earlier.

Finally, as an experiment to fit our results in Kritzinger's model, we assumed that people would decide on their policy preferences based on their perception of the EU, and their affective attachment to Europe would be determined by their evaluation of how efficiently the EU works. The first causal relationship in this model would be how the perceived benefits of the EU influence the overall perception of the EU. Taking our results into account, namely that the majority (87.7 percent) of the respondents mentioned that Hungary has benefitted overall from being an EU member state and that this variable wasn't in significant relationship with any other variables (see Tables 9.5 and 9.6), we concluded that further analysis of the relationship would not add much to the results.

Two causal models were then tested: one measuring the effect of the perception of the EU on policy preferences and another measuring the effect of policy preferences on European identity (see models A and B in Appendix). As previously mentioned, the perception of the EU has a slight positive impact on policy preferences, but the latter has no impact on affective attachment. Thus, the causal model proposed by Kritzinger is only partially confirmed in the case of Hungarian elites – the perception of the EU as a cognitive attachment positively influencing political preferences, however, doesn't lead to an affective attachment as policy preferences and European identity are independent from each other. At the same time it should be mentioned that we have accepted causality as suggested by Kritzinger's model only as an experiment, however, the research design doesn't allow us to test the validity of this causal path.

Conclusions

Compared to previous studies which dealt with the subject of public opinion concerning European integration process, in this chapter we chose not to focus on the effect of phenomena such as information deficit, lack of knowledge, and special cognitive mobilization capacities required by the issue being targeted. We assumed that the influence of these factors would be negligible as elites are better informed, interested and concerned with regard to this topic compared to the general public. This group can also be considered much more homogeneous in terms of cognitive mobilization capacities.

In this chapter we analyzed both symbolic and pragmatic aspects of the relation to the European integration among Hungarian elites. We found that there is only a weak and rather negative link between the two aspects.

About half of the Hungarian elites targeted in this analysis claimed to be very attached to Europe and would transfer more than 20 percent of the taxes to the EU level, a figure which hugely exceeds the share currently in place. At the same time, the majority (87.7 percent) of the respondents were of the opinion that Hungary's membership in the EU was beneficial. This was especially true regarding the MPs of the party in government. These tendencies are somewhat different depending on which elite group is concerned. MPs of a party in government together with top leaders of international companies were more open to a higher share of tax redistribution at the EU level, while MPs of the party in government and top leaders of Hungarian companies claimed to be more attached to Europe. National and European identities appeared to strengthen rather than exclude each other, in line with several other previous studies.

The analysis of policy preferences showed that Hungarian elites – just as elites of other European countries according to previous studies – would prefer to delegate policy areas related to economic competitiveness to the European level. At the same time, top business leaders were also more open to delegate policy areas related to solidarity and social issues than the political elite. In addition to a European vs. national categorization, this generated a "prevention" categorization comprising the different policy areas where policy areas dealing with problems already manifested, as opposed to policy areas that revolved around the prevention of problems yet to become manifest or areas in which EU plays a more traditional role regionally and internationally.

Another interesting element revealed in the results pertains to the differentiation between the concept of integration and unification. This primarily appeared with regards to taxes: opinions on the delegation of this policy area to the EU level and the unification of the different tax systems were not consistent with each other. The support for unification was in line with opinions that would enhance the role of the European Commission and the European Parliament against the role of the member states.

The results of regression analyses aimed at understanding the factors which affect European identity, policy preferences and the overall perception of the integration show that pragmatic attachment (tax redistribution) is indeed positively linked with policy preferences. This means that positive perception of the EU implies openness to the delegation of policy areas to the EU level. On the other hand, pragmatic attachment and policy preferences do not have an impact on symbolic attachment. However, it should be mentioned that the strength and direction of impacts mentioned in this chapter should be interpreted as a measure of association and not as a causal relationship. The research design does not allow us to draw conclusions regarding the causality of these associations.

References

Anderson, C. 1998. "When in Doubt, Use Proxies." *Comparative Political Studies* 31.5: 569–601.

Carubba, C. J. 2001. "The Electoral Connection in European Union Politics." *Journal of Politics* 63: 141–58.

Delanty, G. 1995. *Inventing Europe: Idea, Identity, Reality*. New York: St. Martin's Press.

Gabel, Matthew. 1998. "Public Support for European Integration: An Empirical Test of Five Theories." *Journal of Politics* 60.2: 333–54.

Gabel, M. and C. Anderson. 2001. "Exploring the European Demos (or Lack Thereof): The Structure of Citizen Attitudes and the European Political Space." Jean Monnet Centre for European Studies (CEuS) Working Paper No. 2001/4.

Habermas, J. 1998. *The Inclusion of the Other: Studies in Political Theory*. Cambridge: Polity Press.

Hooghe, Liesbet. 2003. "Europe Divided? Elites vs. Public Opinion on European Integration." *European Union Politics* 4.3: 281–304.

Hooghe, Liesbet and Gary Marks. 2001. *Multi-Level Governance and European Integration*. Lanham, MD: Rowman & Littlefield.

————· 2004. "Does Identity or Economic Rationality Drive Public Opinion on European Integration?" *Political Science and Politics* 37.3: 415–20.

————· 2008. "A Postfunctionalist Theory of European Integration: From Permissive Consensus to Constraining Dissensus." *British Journal of Political Science* 39: 1–23.

Horolets, A. 2003. "Conceptualising Europe Through Metaphors: A Way to Identity Formation?" *Polish Sociological Review* 141/1.

Inglehart, Ronald. 1970. "Cognitive Mobilization and European Identity." *Comparative Politics* 3: 45–70.

Kritzinger, S. 2005. "European Identity Building from the Perspective of Efficiency." *Comparative European Politics* 3.1: 50–75.

Lengyel, Gy. and B. Göncz. 2006. "Integráció és identitás: hogyan ítélik meg a magyar társadalmi csoportok az európai integrációt és a szupranacionális identitást?" in *A magyarok bemenetele. Tagállamként a bővülő Európai Unióban*, ed. I. Hegedűs, 71–114. DKMKKA, Budapesti Corvinus Egyetem: Politikatudományi Intézet.

Opp, K-D. 2005. "The EU and National Identifications." *Social Forces* 84.2: 653–80.

Smith, A. 1992. "National Identity and the Idea of European Unity." *International Affairs* 68.1: 55–76.

Steenbergen, Marco R., Erica R. Edwards and Catherine E. de Vries. 2007. "Who is Cueing Whom? Mass-Elite Linkages and the Future of European Integration." *European Union Politics* 8.1: 13–35.

Appendix

A. Explaining model of policy preferences

(Dependent variable: Delegation of policy areas to the EU level) *(Linear regression)*	b	ß
Very attached to Europe	−4,35	−0,10
Would transfer at least 20% of the taxes to the EU level	9,82 **	0,22
European integration should be strengthened	−0,85	−0,02
Hungary has on balance benefitted from being a member of the EU	3,02	0,05
MPs of a party in governance	−15,80 **	−0,35
MPs of a party in opposition	−17,48 **	−0,35
Top leaders of international companies	−11,47	−0,21
Top leaders of Hungarian companies	−	−
The main aim of the EU should be to make the European economy more competitive in world markets	8,41	0,16
The main aim of the EU should be to provide better social protection for all its citizens	11,14 *	0,24
The member states ought to remain the central actors of the EU	−8,94 **	−0,19
The European Commission ought to become the true government of the EU	1,88	0,04
The powers of the European Parliament ought to be strengthened	4,90	0,10
Constant	54,30 ***	
R²	**0,21**	
Adj. R²	**0,12**	
N	**122**	

B. Explaining model of European identity

(Dependent variable: Very attached to Europe) *(Logistic regression)*	B	Exp(B)
Would transfer at least 20% of the taxes to the EU level	−0,65	0,52
European integration should be strengthened	0,02	1,02
Hungary has on balance benefitted from being a member of the EU	0,88	2,42
MPs of a party in governance	−1,11	0,33
MPs of a party in opposition	−1,79 **	0,17
Top leaders of international companies	−2,15 ***	0,12
Top leaders of Hungarian companies	−	−
Policy preferences	−0,01	0,99
The main aim of the EU should be to make the European economy more competitive in world markets	0,25	1,29

(Continued)

B. Continued

(Dependent variable: Very attached to Europe) *(Logistic regression)*	B	Exp(B)
The main aim of the EU should be to provide better social protection for all its citizens	0,43	1,54
The member states ought to remain the central actors of the EU	0,10	1,10
The European Commission ought to become the true government of the EU	0,48	1,61
The powers of the European Parliament ought to be strengthened	0,61	1,84
Constant	0,78	2,17
Correct prediction	**68%**	
R^2_L	**0,12**	
Adj. R^2	**0,15**	
N	**122**	

Note: Statistical significance: *** < 0.01, ** < 0.05, * < 0.1.
Reference categories in italics.

C. Explaining model of pragmatic attachment (tax redistribution)

(Dependent variable: Would transfer at least 20% of the taxes to the EU level) *(Logistic regression)*	B	Exp(B)
Very attached to Europe	−0,60	0,55
European integration should be strengthened	0,33	1,40
Hungary has on balance benefitted from being a member of the EU	0,57	1,76
MPs of a party in governance	1,88 **	6,52
MPs of a party in opposition	1,15	3,16
Top leaders of international companies	1,30	3,68
Top leaders of Hungarian companies	−	−
Policy preferences	0,03 **	1,03
The main aim of the EU should be to make the European economy more competitive in world markets	−1,05	0,35
The main aim of the EU should be to provide better social protection for all its citizens	−0,34	0,71
The member states ought to remain the central actors of the EU	0,05	1,05
The European Commission ought to become the true government of the EU	0,66	1,94
The powers of the European Parliament ought to be strengthened	0,02	1,02
Constant	−2,64	0,07
Correct prediction	**68%**	
R^2_L	**0,15**	
Adj. R^2	**0,18**	
N	**122**	

Note: Statistical significance: *** < 0.01, ** < 0.05, * < 0.1.
Reference categories in italics.

Chapter 10

CRITICAL JUNCTURES, INSTITUTIONAL LEGACIES AND EPISTEMIC COMMUNITIES: A DEVELOPMENT AGENDA IN BRAZIL

Carlos Henrique Santana
Instituto de Estudos Sociais e Políticos, IESP-UERJ

Introduction

The divergent paths of the diffusion of neoliberal reforms and the return of development agendas across countries in the last 30 years allow us to set aside the conventional view which states that there has been a tendency towards institutional convergence due to globalization, especially in its financial dimension. Thus, this chapter will explore which aspects of national path-dependency contribute to domestic narrow or expand the degree of freedom when it comes to adapting these globalization agendas to local scenarios. Given the centrality of monetary policy in Brazil, the state's role in creating an incentive structure capable of dealing with a more coordinated trajectory – like that identified by the concept of selective industrial policy (Chang 2003; Huber 2002) – is being delimited by a double-sided economic policy model. If, on one hand, floating exchange rate policies and the liberalization of capital flow restrict the sovereignty of the country for long-term planning, then on the other hand, the legacy of state capacities and the specific pattern of reform trajectory creates room for maneuvers in the formatting of public development policies.

In order to evaluate this process, this chapter combines a variety of theoretical perspectives that aim to comprehend the importance of the discourse produced in epistemic communities which was legitimized by the experience of indebtedness, rampant inflation in Latin America, and the normative coercion brought about by structural adjustment policies advocated by multilateral financial institutions. In this context, it seems suggestive to enrich the comparative political economy literature, especially the varieties of capitalism (VoC) literature, with the perspective of discursive institutionalism. More specifically, this chapter seeks to emphasize the Brazilian trajectory, relating it to the development agenda which succeeded in recovering state capacity; it also identifies the institutional complementarities within the scope of pension funds and the Brazilian Development Bank (BNDES). Furthermore, its purpose is to assess the emergence of new professional networks in response to a structure of incentives provided by new institutional linkages, highlighting the role of these networks in the consolidation of a new cognitive system capable of defining a normative basis that can sustain changes in development pathways.

Varieties of Capitalism and Institutional Changes

The literature on varieties of capitalism (VoC) has been gaining international relevance within the field of comparative capitalism studies since the pioneering work of Hall and Soskice (2001). The analytical advantage of this proposal has contributed with a series of comparative empirical studies that emphasize the importance of the historical path of national institutions as an endogenous explanatory variable of development in the context of globalization.

The main axis of the VoC literature is the idea of institutional complementarity – in other words, the concept of increasing returns over some of the modalities of institutional frameworks likely to promote endogenous adjustments without resulting in institutional convergence (Krasner 1988; Hall and Gingerich 2004; Höpner 2005). In the wake of this literature an institutionalist critique of this variant of historical institutionalism emerged. It suggested that the solution presented by VoC on how institutional changes occur is unsatisfactory, as there would be a static bias in this literature (Djelic and Quack 2007; Campbell 2004; Schmidt 2006). By and large, historical institutionalism has been seeking to circumvent these critiques through the concept of critical juncture, namely, contingent events playing an important role in the genesis of path dependence (Gourevitch 1986; Collier and Collier 1991; Pierson 2000; Mahoney 2000). The critical juncture disrupts the complementarities of national paths, forcing actors and institutions to rearticulate their frameworks and seek new mechanisms to reduce the incentives for exit and promote the resumption of coordination patterns with increasing returns. On the other hand, there are critiques that seek to deal with the difficulties of the VoC literature, responding through the expansion of the repertoire of varieties, such as the regulation school (Amable 2000; Boyer 2005), and studies that seek to emphasize the role of the state or hierarchical forms of coordination as mechanisms for the third or fourth variety of capitalism. (Schmidt 2003; Schneider 2009).

Despite the recent efforts of the key authors of the VoC literature to point out the dynamics of institutional change through adaptive and incremental adjustments, these adjustments tend to reconstruct the framework of equilibrium. This is the case of recent studies in which the institutions are conceived as resources (Aoki 2007; Hall and Thelen 2006; Streeck and Thelen 2005) in the regulation of the financial system (Culpepper 2005; Vitols 2005; Johnson 2002), of corporate governance (Gourevitch and Shinn 2005; Goyer 2006) and the labor market (Campbell and Pedersen 2007). The problem of institutional change is conditioned by contingent impasses to which the historical background of each country and the cyclical political game should offer a specific answer.

By emphasizing the incremental dimension of change, the VoC literature seeks to escape the concept of critical juncture or contingent events by highlighting how endogenous and incremental events produce from time to time far more historical institutional transformations and recovery of complementarity than sudden breaks or convergent isomorphic changes (Hall and Thelen 2006; Hall 2007; Streeck and Thelen 2005). The wealth of this analytical framework is immense, but it does not respond satisfactorily to how coalitions organize consensus among actors in search of a new development agenda.

Besides this difficulty, it is necessary to emphasize that almost all of the empirical research on VoC literature is concentrated in (Organisation for Economic Co-operation and Development) OECD countries – therefore around the modality of organized capitalism. An exception to this trend is some recent works of Schneider (2009) on what would be the Latin American variety of capitalism, characterized by what he calls hierarchic market economy (HME). However, the interpretation that this author elaborates for the region is far from encouraging. According to his diagnosis, Latin America (AL) suffers from institutional complementarities marked by decreasing returns, which is a coordination pattern that creates more obstacles than incentives for the development agenda.

Despite being one of the first systematic attempts to frame Latin America in the VoC literature, Schneider's approach suffers from generalizations of societies and economic and political systems aggregated under the label of "Latin America," without respect to the difference in their historical trajectories and institutional conjunctures. This bias neglects a major asset of the VoC literature, which is the attention to the diversity of institutional histories, and reinforces some institutional stigmas – almost historical atavisms – that supposedly only in Latin America have deleterious effects. The alternative to this analysis has been provided by Boschi (2007) and Boschi and Gaitán (2009) that emphasizes the aspect of production, innovation and social policies, highlighting the specific national trajectories from the point of view of so-called state capacities.

Given this framework it is necessary to assess analytical resources that meet the need of understanding recent institutional changes and, on the other hand, adjust the analysis to a context of disorganized or less organized capitalism than the OECD countries (Offe 1989). From this point of view, I would like to advance the proposal to incorporate the aspects of what has been called social constructivism or discursive institutionalism into the VoC approach and promote a cross-fertilization between these two fields (Schmidt 2006; Campbell 2001, 2004).

The discussion on the role of ideas in institutional change is not new, neither for the main advocates of VoC, nor for other strands of institutionalism. In general the issue of changing paradigms, intersubjective articulation and cognitive evolution are present in the discussions on the composition of coalitions, formulating consensus and inflections of the political agenda.

These topics have appeared in a fragmented way since the mid-1970s, when constructivist formulations started to point to the relationship between knowledge and technology in the constitution of international regimes and the role of epistemic communities in conditioning these articulations (Haas 1975; Ruggie 1975). Also in the mid-1980s, Gourevitch (1986) emphasized the role of ideological programs in the formation of coalitions that could respond to critical junctures. In the early 1990s, Hall (1989, 1993) and Dobbin (1993) signaled the importance of ideas and economic crises as a means of changing political paradigms and social learning; North (1990) and Goldstein and Keohane (1993) pointed to ideas as cognitive mechanisms, as *road maps*, *shared mental models* or *focal points*, behind the institutional construction and changes, whereas Haas (1992) and Adler and Haas (1992) emphasized the role of epistemic communities in the consolidation of intersubjective relationships capable of pointing to programmatic directions. More recently, various studies have been appropriating the constructivist approach in the sociology of science, influenced by Bourdieu (2000) and Latour (1987), to discuss forms of institutionalization of professional fields as mediators of development trajectories (Fourcade-Gourinchas 2006; Babb 2005; Dezalay and Garth 2002; Fourcade-Gourinchas 2001; Yonay 1998; Bockman and Eyal 2002).

In this context, a series of more systematic works have sought to consolidate an institutionalist focus on the role of ideas and discourse (Campbell and Pedersen 2011; Schmidt 2011; Ruggie, 1998; Blyth 2002). Certainly, these works will have reverberations in empirical comparative research and have obtained some success in addressing the earlier set dilemma: that of institutional change. The purpose of this chapter, however, is not to delineate a substitute for the other variants of institutionalism, but rather to employ ideas as a mechanism to counteract the tendency of punctuated equilibrium (Krasner 1984) of historical, rationalist and sociological variants, and propose discourse as one of the causal axes of the institutional change process.

The Brazilian Trajectory and Its Critical Junctures

Unlike heterodox plans of inflation stabilization during the 1980s implemented as surprise packages, the orthodox Plano Real was marked by gradualism and transparency, which supposedly gave economic players more political confidence and predictability (Mettenheim 2006). That is, the Brazilian Central Bank built a monetary authority ensuring more macroeconomic predictability to agents in the market through the development of a comprehensive regulatory framework, allowing it to concentrate high decision-making capacity and at the same time, constitute a link of credibility around the network of economists strongly connected to the agenda of market-oriented reforms.

It can be argued that the Plano Real strategy to stabilize inflation owes its success to its ability to reduce inflation, producing positive effects on the purchasing power of wages. The political legitimacy arising from this success was capable of guaranteeing policymakers greater freedom in reshaping the governance structure of monetary policy and thereby establishing an institutional legacy marked by insulation of decision making. However, the interest here is to emphasize that the part of the literature which deals with aspects of successful insulation of decision making concerning the control of inflation in Brazil (Pio 2001; Sola and Marques 2006; Sola and Kugelmas 2006) does not adequately consider the perverse aspects of this autonomy denoted by an oligopoly of private ownership of state assets by distributional coalitions with close ties with that community of policymakers (Schamis 2005), and the gradual naturalization of criteria of "financial performance" that legitimizes the same predatory practices (Grün 2007).

A clear example of this process of construction and insulation of fiscal and monetary authority can be verified in the occupation pattern of key macroeconomic policy decision-making structures. The National Monetary Council (CMN) – the body responsible for monetary policy in Brazil – was traditionally composed of all ministers in the economic field, several in the social area, all the presidents of public banks, five members of private enterprises, representatives of labor unions and the president of FEBRABAN (Brazilian Federation of Banks). After June 1995, with the consolidation of the Plano Real, the CMN became composed of only the minister of finance, the minister of planning and the president of the Central Bank (Santos and Patrício 2002). Researchers have further reported that the occupation of decision-making positions at the Central Bank and the Ministry of Finance has not been based on the technical criteria of distinction (which selected career employees), but on the relationships built within epistemic communities – both from within academic and market circles (Loureiro and Abrucio 1999; Loureiro 1998; Pio 2001). This process was largely facilitated by a shift in the management structure of currency whose spheres of negotiation and bargaining have been narrowed and weakened in terms of their relative capacity of coordinating interests.

From the standpoint of a critical juncture, one might consider this progressive insulation of state decision making on macroeconomic policies as a result of a combination of two factors: the legacy of debt and the inflationary inertia of the 1980s and frustration over the heterodox plans used to combat it; and the emergence of an ideological wave of promarket reforms in which structures of dissemination and translation stimulated an alignment of interest groups and epistemic communities through normative emulation, coercive pressures and competitive imitation (Henisz, Zelner and Guillén 2005; Powell and DiMaggio 1991).

This apparatus of dissemination and coercion has consolidated (that is, achieved hegemony in public opinion) a view that the problems of underdevelopment in the region have been related primarily to the mismanagement of economic policy, resulting from a vicious circle of "populism" and electoral conditions that would lead to a fiscal irresponsibility (Dornbusch and Edwards 1991). This resulted in the adoption of liberalization policies of capital flows through the deregulation of CC5 accounts,[1] fiscal restraint through the Fiscal Responsibility Law, the Revenue Enhancing Union (DRU) and primary surplus, valued exchange rate, privatization of state enterprises and exponential growth of public debt. This path constitutes a highly restrictive legacy in Brazil, consolidating a path dependency.

Institutionalization of Legacy

To understand how this legacy has taken root in Brazil it is necessary to avoid the view that naturalizes the market, such as those that assume that

---

1 Designed for Brazilians living outside Brazil, export and finance companies with securities abroad, the CC5 accounts were deregulated in 1992. According to Sicsú (2006), the net outflow of resources from financial institutions through CC5 during the period 1993–2004 was over USD 113 billion (according to the Brazilian Central Bank). According to the same author, this movement was the main cause of the six currency crises during the Fernando Henrique Cardoso's government. Between 1998 and 2002, the attorney general discovered that several companies had used the CC5 accounts for money laundering. After several cases of circumvention, the National Monetary Council changed the rules of CC5 accounts in 2005, restricting the access and increasing the control over money laundering.

measures of institutional alignment depend on the greater or lesser degree of macroeconomic weakness (Maxfield 1997). By borrowing the concept of actor networks of Latour (1987), the suggestion is that the reproduction of institutional forms does not have to be subjected to external forces. In contrast, the emphasis may be placed on an endogenous and historical dimension based on the work of network construction, establishment of ties between statements, effects demonstrated in the laboratory (for example, countries), financial resources, advice and support of allies. Although it seems that with this approach, the enforcement process of international financial constraints is less relevant, what this chapter intends to explore is the way this type of coercion becomes shadowed by local path-dependency, or, how it is semantically appropriated and translated for specific and cognitively delimited political ends (Fourcade-Gourinchas and Babb 2002; Bockman and Eyal 2002). Thus, certain institutional patterns are reproduced and disseminated according to the amount of resources mobilized through the network ties to strengthen certain positions and increase the capacity of stakeholders to hide the work required to maintain the network elements articulated – or what Latour also called "closing the black box."

What makes this approach interesting is the fact that the institutions coincide with the very same actor networks (that is, the institutional models are being reproduced through them). This involves giving a crucial role to certain professional networks, as it is they who control the flow of key resources for other core networks as well as mobilizing and appropriating the work of interpretation (Loureiro 1997 and 1998; Keck and Sikkink 1998; Foucarde 2006; Pio 2001; Dezalay and Garth 2002). Considering the role that economists have in the consolidation of actor networks, because of their prominence in key positions in decision-making structures of governments and businesses they have become the centerpiece for the formation of a normative basis, that through the production of value-laden consensus may elevate or reduce both the state's costs of exit and voice with regard to the rules of the international financial system in which they are inserted (Hirschman 1970; Santiso 2003).

Thus, combining the discursive and historical variations of neoinstitutionalism, it is possible to think about how the neoliberal program has defined the institutional legacy in Brazil, and based on that, identified the room for maneuvers to rebuild the development agenda. In this context, ideas have a crucial importance, as they can appear as a link of cohesion between different societal interest groups, adapting a policy to norms and values underlying society, serving as focal points – guidelines for reducing inflation, budget and trade imbalances and for the resumption of growth (Goldstein and Keohane 1993; Hall 1989 and 1993).

In this context, the power of ideas lies in the fact that they provide symbols and other discursive schemes that an actor network can employ to make their program more convincing and sustain the agenda of policymakers. For this, it is important to stress the relevance of professional networks (economists) to mobilize resources necessary to maintain a cohesive set of linkages and mechanisms for mutual support (called black-box) able to legitimize their political agenda and ensure the dominance in key decision-making arenas such as the Central Bank, the Ministry of Economic Affairs, public banks, media, finance, consulting firms, rating agencies, etc. This network is constituted as an epistemic community in that its members share a set of causal and normative beliefs, intersubjectively defined notions of validity, political initiatives capable of articulating diverse actors and interest groups, promoting a political innovation (Haas 1992; Adler and Haas, 1992). While the repertoire of ideas constrains the actors and limits the perception of options, the ideas may be subjected to a process of *bricolage* and translation through which the actors recombine available and legitimate concepts, and cognitive models and other cultural artifacts in their institutional environment (Adler 2005; Campbell 2004; Bockman and Eyal 2002). These artifacts are capable of elevating the costs of exit and rearticulating institutional complementarities.

The Protagonist Network and Degrees of Institutional Freedom

The group of networked actors that became the hegemonic epistemic community in Brazil was formed by those who had been directly involved in the implementation and administration of inflation stabilization policies since 1994. The majority of these actors held decision-making and policymaking positions and occupied posts in the Central Bank, BNDES and the Ministry of Finance. But this group was also supported by people who, even without occupying decision-making positions, shared a cognitive history and common interests, being shareholders in banks or consultancies or professors and experts with similar academic trajectories.

Based on a preliminary selection of professional networks, it is possible to evaluate illustratively what the educational institutions that have prevailed in the provision of bureaucratic cadres for strategic macroeconomic decision making are and what career paths offer greater incentives to secure such positions in a context marked by the institutional macroeconomic legacies of the inflation stabilization trajectory.

The results of the survey (Table 10.1) provide several relevant examples. Among the 92 selected economists, who are the key decision makers concerning the Brazilian national economy since the implementation of the Plano Real,

Table 10.1. The trajectory of Brazilian macroeconomic policymakers between 1995 and 2009

	Central Bank		The Ministry of Finance		BNDES	
	1995–2002 (n=17)	2003–9 (n=11)	1995–2002 (n=13)	2003–9 (n=19)	1995–2002 (n=16)	2003–9 (n=17)
PhD in economics in the USA	11	6	4	4	5	1
PhD in economics in England	0	1	1	1	0	4
Dr in economics UFRJ/Unicamp	0	0	0	4	2	4
Dr FEA-USP/FGV-SP/PUC-SP	1	0	3	1	0	0
Graduation in economics/IR/finance in Brazil	5	3	5	5	3	7
Graduation in economics/IR/finance in the USA	0	1	0	2	4	0
Prof. of economics at PUC-Rio/FGV-Rio	8	3	3	3	3	0
Prof. of economics at UFRJ, Unicamp	0	1	0	3	0	0
Prof. of economics at PUC-SP, FEA-USP and/or FGV-SP	1	1	5	2	1	5
Career employees (Bancen/Min. of Foreign Affairs/Min. of Finance/ IBGE/BNDES/IPEA	4	3	5	6	4	7
Directors and/or economists of IMF/ WB/IDB	4	4	7	4	0	0
Directors of consultancy and/or of domestic and/or foreign private banks	13	8	8	5	12	3
Party-political articulation	0	0	0	6	0	3

Source: Institutional sites of the Ministry of Finance and the Central Bank, in addition to personal sites.
Note: The study included 92 cadres that between 1995 and 2009 occupied the presidency and/or the management of economic policy, international issues, monetary policy of the Central Bank; ministries and executive secretaries of political economy, inland revenue, national treasury of Ministry of Finance, and presidents of BNDES.

it is possible to observe four types of professional and academic origins: in addition to career civil servants in high-level federal bureaucracies, it has become essential to hold a PhD in economics at prestigious US universities (known as the Ivy League,[2] but not limited to these); most professors are graduates of the principal school that shaped neoliberal thinking in Brazil – PUC-Rio – and were or are consultants and/or directors of domestic or foreign private banks, multilateral financial institutions like the IMF, Inter-American Development Bank (IDB) and World Bank and investments funds. It was possible to verify at least two basic patterns of trajectories which constituted the construction of the confidence game essential to select the cadres of macroeconomic decision arenas: (1) academic training abroad – mostly PhD in economics in the US (mostly from academic ties originating from PUC-Rio) – followed by internships in multilateral organizations such as the World Bank/IMF or careers in domestic or foreign private banks, until reaching a key position in the national macroeconomic decision-making sphere, followed by a return to a relevant position in a private bank or by the setting up of one's own investment bank – a phenomenon known prosaically as the "revolving door." (2) The second path provides fewer resources to build the game of international confidence and follows the circuit of more eclectic academic training in economics at home, followed by an open competition in high federal bureaucracy until reaching a decision-making position in some key post, with more residual circulation in the private financial system.

It is possible to notice a reduction of the participation of the staff with orthodox background in key decision-making positions when comparing two periods: 1995–2002 and 2003–8. In the Central Bank the percentage of professors from PUC-Rio fell from 49 to 27 percent, while in the BNDES (the historical birthplace of development policies) the professors of PUC disappeared. Both in the Ministry of Finance and in the BNDES, the change of epistemic communities has been relevant with the entry of economists from the UFRJ/Unicamp/PUC-SP/FGV-SP – schools with a more eclectic academic tradition, inclined to heterodox theoretical strands in line with ECLAC's and neo-Keynesian background. Another parallel development is the importance of party-political contacts and, to a lesser extent, of the career staff in the definition of policymakers between 2006–9, which occurred at the same time as a significant reduction of the involvement of private financial circles in the Ministry of Finance and the BNDES – which secured a lower incidence of the "revolving door" pattern during Lula's government. Although academic training in the US is still a

2 The Ivy League is a group of eight universities located in the northeastern United States – Harvard, Yale, Princeton, Columbia, Cornell, Brown, Dartmouth and Pennsylvania, known for their academic and social prestige (Babb 2005).

prerequisite, it is possible to observe a greater variety of personal trajectories in the Ministry of Finance and the BNDES than in the Central Bank which had 65 percent of its staff trained in the United States between 1995–2002, which ensured extraordinary normative and cognitive cohesion.

In the second survey conducted between 2006 and 2008, a group of fifty one columnists of two major newspapers (Valor Econômico and Folha de S. Paulo) who are not directly employed by the media groups for which they collaborate was selected. Based on these initial conditions, their academic training, private and public professional trajectory, the variety of newspapers and number of times published per month were accounted for. Taking this into consideration, one can verify that for example, 51 percent of columnists published at least once every two weeks, 40 percent of them obtained their PhD in economics at top schools of the United States, 50 percent were directors of the BNDES, the Central Bank or the Ministry of Finance at some point and 38 percent were or have been consultants or directors (or both) of national or foreign private banks, of rating agencies and multilateral financial institutions like the IMF, IDB or World Bank.

Among the selected columnists, it can be said that there is a greater diversity of academic and professional careers despite the repetition of the same "epistemic triangulation": PhD in a US academic institution, macroeconomic policy related decision-making positions and ties to the financial system as significant features in the institutionalization of the hegemonic discourse. Another aspect is that before or after holding positions in public institutions of macroeconomic regulation in Brazil and national and foreign private institutions, most had stints in international financial institutions such as the IMF, WB, IDB and fund managers.

Thus, it is possible to say that the agenda of macroeconomic reforms in Brazil has counted on a network of professionals who share the bonds of trust and programmatic identity that has enabled them to consolidate a legacy. In this context, the internationalization of the economic field is a link that supports a new principle of access to power and legitimacy of the ruling cadres of the country. Global social structures sustain these communities by means of a transnational socialization of economists, for which the academic degree in the US is the prerequisite for entrance in political and intellectual power circuits (Fourcade-Gourinchas 2006; Biglaiser 2002; Loureiro 1998).

In the context of strong insulation, this protagonist network mobilized resources able to consolidate links to support and strengthen bonds of trust and loyalty and build and legitimize a new normative grammar from which a series of values came to establish the preconditions for any decision: country risk, fiscal balance, inflation control etc. and a number of references to high normative power which was built discursively in the 1990s and until today serves as a "natural" criterion for any "stable" or "responsible" government. The predominant diagnosis of alternatives to the financial vulnerability of Brazil is still deeply dependent on the view that it is impossible to escape the confidence game of financial markets (Santiso 2003), supported by this actor network that still today guarantees these ties through the strategic posts in the Central Bank and the Ministry of Finance, for example. This combined process is embedded in the context of greater short-term integration of exchange rate and financial markets than the integration of markets for goods and long-term capital or productive processes, given the residual position of Latin America (3 percent) and of Brazil (1.1 percent) in the world trade of goods and services. In this respect, the state and national governance maintain an important regulatory role in national productive systems in the region in the context of globalization (Chang 2003; Vogel 1996; Weiss 1999; Helleiner 1994).

At the same time, the strategies to control inflation are not discussed nor compared with other global experiences, becoming a semantic property legitimately mobilized only by the members of actor networks who manage monetary policy. In other words, unlike other central banks like the US Federal Reserve (FED) – which have a mandate to control inflation, but also to ensure growth rates and employment – the Brazilian Central Bank is merely fulfilling a mandate directed exclusively to control inflation. The network that manages monetary policy claims not only the expertise of financial markets, building a confidence game (Santiso 2003), but also the access to instances of reproduction of institutional practices in the national and international context. These instances can be prestigious academic centers, multilateral financial institutions, banks, consultancies, rating agencies, columns in prestigious journals, brokerage firms and decision-making positions in government, built on the basis of an academic and professional career that consolidates previous bonds of trust and loyalty and reinforcing the establishment of a black-box, whose legacy restricts the domestic degrees of freedom.

In this respect, my perspective follows the direction opposite to this optimistic outlook (Pio 2001; Sola and Marques 2006; Sola and Kugelmas 2006) with regard to the path for the formation of the monetary authority. Rather, it questions the idea that the success of the Plano Real was related to the capacity of the cadres of the hegemonic epistemic community to ensure the very bureaucratic enclosure to implement the "correct" economic program. In this respect, Loureiro (1997) seems more coherent by inverting this argument and suggesting that the lack of coordination of political actors caused by watertight positions of this insulated bureaucracy would have resulted in the failure of stabilization plans in Brazil and Latin America. It is also possible to observe perverse effects deriving from low responsibility or accountability of results of the agents responsible for the privatized sectors, as has been emphasized by Boschi and Lima (2002) and Melo (2001).

The image of the "revolving door" used to illustrate the circulation patterns of this epistemic community, while suggesting promiscuity as something compelling, may hide the incentives for predatory mechanisms underlying the bargaining that the market agents employ to arbitrate the key prices of the economy such as the exchange rate, interests and fiscal surplus. The bureaucratic insulation that should protect public policies against particular pressures has become susceptible to capture due to the absence of mechanisms that would regulate the "revolving door." At the same time, the understanding of the patterns of movement of such cadres can contribute to the comprehension of a stabilization narrative, or how it rationalizes and presents a package of macroeconomic policies that benefits organized economic interests and contributes to a concentrated appropriation of a share of national income by these interests as common sense.

However it would be an exaggerated, if not spurious, to establish a causal relationship to identify these epistemic communities as instruments of those interests. The ideas and their organizers end up developing proper incentives and allow economic and social actors to distinguish opportunities and alternatives for integration and cooperation, but ideas do not necessarily determine the interests (or vice-versa). With his allusion to the metaphor of a switchman, Weber had already called attention to the role of ideas as facilitators (systematized and rationalized world images) of new coalition routes for the combination of interests – introducing to this end the notion of elective affinity between the two spheres (2001). In this sense, where is the elective affinity between the community of economists, the organizer of the stabilization plan and the new internationalized financial class that emerged in the course of privatization policies? Moreover, in the face of a significant shift in the routes of former trajectory, which new affinities were established between the epistemic communities and relevant economic actors such as pension funds and public banks?

As observed in Table 10.1, this trajectory has been redesigned as of 2003, with a slow and gradual loss of space of this community in the spheres of the federal government. Such a transition can especially be verified since 2005 when Guido Mantega took office in the Ministry of Finance, combining his ministry with the Executive Office (Casa Civil) and Ministry of Planning in the organization of the Growth Acceleration Plan (PAC).[3]

---

3 Launched at the beginning of 2007 Brazil's national Growth Acceleration Program (PAC) aims at furthering a concentrated investment strategy and consistent incentives until 2010. PAC addresses social and infrastructural development, regulation, financing, taxation and specific measurements to accelerate Brazil's sustainable growth. In this context, it stipulates investments of more than USD 254.4 billion on infrastructure, including areas of sanitation, habitation, water resources, energy and transportation.

The cadres that come from academic centers of heterodox tradition, such as Unicamp, FGV-SP and PUC-SP, are replacing the economists of PUC-Rio in positions of decision making and formulation of macroeconomic policies. Additionally, recent changes in the board of directors of the Central Bank have given priority to career officials with more diverse – and not necessarily orthodox – academic backgrounds. There is also evidence that the new generation of economists is beginning to change the focus of its research agendas, replacing the issue of inflation by the concern for the long-term development and strategies to achieve it, including educational policies and investment in technology and skills.[4]

With the launching of the Industrial, Technological and Foreign Policy (PITCE) in 2004, the Growth Acceleration Plan (PAC) in 2007 and subsequent institutional coordination of long-term planning strategies through the Productive Development Policy (PDP) released in 2008, the government aims to integrate fixed investment rates, volume of private spending on research and development and a higher degree of external policy integration as national development policy objectives.[5] Headed by the BNDES and the Ministry of Development, Industry and Foreign Trade (MDIC), the PAC integrates state institutions, which in association with public banks and pension funds have created ties to formulate a new more centrally coordinated policy. With the reelection of Lula and the consolidation of a broad political-party coalition, it was possible to forge a stable internal and external macroeconomic environment with signs of renewed economic growth, formalization of the labor market and real increase in salary, with the consequent resumption of the role of internal market as a structuring variable.

To assess the scope of this new emerging path, it should be noted that the path-dependency of institutional capacities of the Brazilian state allows it to return to an agenda of more coordinated investment and greater degree of freedom, where public banks (especially the BNDES) and pension funds can play a key-role in the establishment of an incentive structure to a new discursive coalition that would reinforce the neodevelopmental and/or post-neoliberal policies (Boschi and Gaitán 2008; Diniz and Boschi 2007; Diniz 2007; Bresser-Pereira 2006; Sicsú, Paula and Michel 2005). That is, just as the incentive structures to delegate the decision making of these agencies of macroeconomic coordination were crucial for the internationalized epistemic communities could consolidate their stabilization and liberalization program,

---

4 Sergio Lamucci, "Outra agenda para a economia," *Valor Econômico*, 15 August 2008.
5 Executive Secretary of the PDP, "Relatório de Macrometas: Política de Desenvolvimento Produtivo" (2009).

it is possible to imagine that the observed trend of path-dependence in state capacities as embedded autonomy (Evans 1995) may now be appropriated and translated by a new actor network to build neodevelopmental coalitions.

* * *

As it has been possible to observe by now, institutional changes can be identified based on their incremental transformation. That is to say that the dimension of institutional complementarities as a reinforcement of preceding trajectories stresses the static aspect of the VoC literature and loses the capacity to capture the long-range changes that could be reached through the accumulation of changes and adjustments, or what Pierson (2004) also called *tipping points*. The critiques that have been made targeting the static dimensions of the VoC literature, as was stressed in the beginning of this article, have brought a sequence of methodological contributions to increase the explanatory capacity of the theory with regard to the institutional changes. Discursive institutionalism sustains the role of ideas as a normative map of collective action and of coalition formation. This approach enables us to consider the institutional transformation from the incremental perspective that finds strong parallels in variations of historical institutionalism that also searches for capturing incremental changes. In that particular case, institutions are seen as open regimes or systems that suffer from gradual but cumulatively transforming changes (Becker 2009; Djelic and Quack 2007; Streeck and Thelen 2005; Campbell 2004).

The next section, based on the analysis of the role of the BNDES and pension funds in the new agenda of productive restructuration and of internationalization of enterprises, aims to call attention to how the new coalition of interests has consolidated around the new institutional regime, where not only the new epistemic community has come to constitute a new distinct structure of incentives, but also how these changes alone can be perceived as *tipping points*, which is to say, responses to the transforming and continuous incremental rearrangements.

BNDES and Pension Funds: New Translation of Institutional Legacies

During the 1990s, the Brazilian Development Bank (BNDES) and pension funds played a crucial role in the privatization process. The BNDES didn't act anymore as a development bank, but instead began to play the role of an investment bank and became a principal source of credit for national and foreign consortiums involved with privatizations. Yet, the pension funds were submitted to a cognitive siege referring to the idea of the "collapse" of the pension system, having to convert the investment logic run by the principle of distribution – in accordance with development policies – to precepts of capitalization within the composition of consortiums of privatization during the period (Grün 2005). Despite this trajectory, there are signs that the role of the BNDES and pension funds of public banks and of state companies has been crucial for the stabilization of macroeconomic variables that affect the labor market and important sectors of Brazilian industry, guaranteeing them the innovative capacity and competitive insertion into the world trade and a space for interest intermediation that permits consolidating the agenda capable of opening the space for formation of new productive coalitions (BNDES 2006 and 2007).

It is worthwhile emphasizing, for the purposes of this chapter, that these state credit and investment institutions compose one of the institutional legacies that have become the objects of a new translation of development policy and that contradict the hegemonic diagnosis (Wolf 2007) around the autochthonous role of market forces in this recent dynamics of economic expansion in Brazil. Since 2003 BNDES has been realigned as a development bank, especially after the launching of a new industrial policy (PITCE), and pension funds have started to act in a restructuration of shareholdings of strategic sectors of industry and infrastructure. This dynamics helps to explore the limits of the diagnosis centered exclusively upon coordination through market and the role of these two entities as instruments of institutional complementarity capable of providing degrees of freedom of a development agenda.

Associating these favorable indicators to previous studies (Santana 2005) that show the role of Brazilian public banking institutions in promoting PITCE, it is important to explore how a specific credit policy has contributed to this new international insertion and made it possible to respond satisfactorily to a new favorable – and in a way competitive – external setting. It is from this perspective that it will be possible to question the current bias according to the dynamics of external trade and the very capital market that exclusively explains the performance of economic sectors and at the same time stresses the impact of institutional legacies and the role of epistemic communities in the change of the trajectory.

BNDES

BNDES has mapped its future investments and they show that a set of segments of the manufacturing industry and infrastructure will receive twice as much investment between 2007 and 2010 as between 2002 and 2005 (BNDES 2007). This new perspective in Brazil is different from the rest of the Latin American countries in so far as the institutional legacy of Brazilian public banks and their presence in the whole set of the country's banking assets have remained relevant even after the privatization period that has guaranteed comparative institutional advantages to resume the development agenda (Stallings and Studart 2006; Santana and Kasahara 2007). In order to evaluate the role of credit policy and the relevance of public banks in this new dynamics, it is necessary to stress that since 2003, after the period of strong shrinking of credit due to the inflation stabilization policies, Brazil has been experiencing a new cycle of credit expansion and recently recovered levels of investment last recorded in 1995. The current governmental coalition has broadened the room of maneuver of the macroeconomic policy for several reasons: the volume of total credit increased by 23 percent in 2003 and reached 40 percent of GDP in 2008 due to directed credit policies geared towards agriculture, housing, consignation and industrial policy; the government adopted a policy of valuing the minimum salary that doubled its nominal value between 2002 and 2008 and produced a real increase of 58 percent between 1998 and 2008; and the unemployment rate fell from 20.8 percent in 2003 to 15.5 percent in 2007 (see Table 10.3). It has happened because the internal market has become the principal responsible for the economic recovery. This can be seen in the data of investments of enterprises (FBCF), imports and family consumption (Table 10.2) on the rise with ascending mobility among social classes and the widening of the middle class (Neri 2008). We can add the fact that international reserves have increased fivefold between 2001 and 2007 (Table 10.5), which has guaranteed a higher degree of domestic freedom within the scenario of external restrictions, motivated especially by the international banking financial crisis.

Despite this context, a set of hegemonic arguments backed by the orthodox epistemic community suggests that: (1) the capital market is overlapping the role of bank credit as a source of funds for business investments to the extent that credit transactions with debentures have been growing exponentially; (2) Brazilian exports owe its growth to the increase of international demand for, and prices of, commodities; and that (3) this new international insertion would be based on a kind of a regressive specialization or deindustrialization where sales to foreign markets would be concentrated in natural resources intensive sectors. At the same time, there would be a substitution of domestic production by imports, justified to a large extent by overvalued exchange rate.

Whereas the emission of debentures accounted for 58 percent of transaction in the primary market of capital during the period of 1998 and 2007 (and since this was the segment that had also had the highest growth rates in recent years) it would be advisable to evaluate the profile of this performance in relation to the predictions of the supposed new centrality of capital markets in

Table 10.2. Real annual variation of Brazilian components of aggregate demand (% per year)

	Gross domestic investment rate	Family domestic consumption	Public administration consumption	Export	Import
1995	7.29	8.62	1.35	−2.03	30.68
1996	1.50	3.39	−1.83	−0.42	5.59
1997	8.73	3.04	1.25	11.2	14.60
1998	−0.34	−0.61	3.22	4.91	−0.06
1999	−8.2	0.34	1.69	5.71	−15.09
2000	5.03	3.93	−0.15	12.86	10.80
2001	0.44	0.67	2.74	10.05	1.51
2002	−5.23	1.82	4.75	7.42	−11.82
2003	−4.59	−0.65	1.15	10.4	−1.62
2004	9.12	3.81	4.09	15.29	13.3
2005	3.63	4.52	2.30	9.33	8.47
2006	9.96	5.20	2.54	4.66	18.34
2007	13.44	6.30	4.73	6.61	20.65
2008	13.77	5.38	5.64	−0.60	18.49

Source: IBGE.

corporate financing. The average annual emission of debentures[6] from 2005 to 2007 reached R$52.5 billion, which is six times more than the average from 2002 to 2004; however it still less than the annual average of R$54.4 billion disbursed by BNDES between 2005–7 (Table 10.7).[7] Therefore, it is not fair to suggest that the capital market would be overriding the bank credit in intermediating the financing of the investments of domestic companies in the sense of converging to an Anglo-Saxon financial system. At the same time, in the last four years the proceeds from the debenture sale have been concerned primarily with the increase of working capital and extending debt under conditions of securing and indexing of interest rates unfavorable to long-term investments, both in industry and infrastructure.

With regard to the second hegemonic bias, studies[8] show that the growth of Brazilian exports is outpacing the global rate two to one. Thus, the international dynamics only explain half the gain in volume of Brazilian exports while the

---

6 According to Andima (National Association of Institutions of Financial Market), debentures are mobile assets representative of medium and long-term debts.

7 http://www.debentures.com.br/dadosconsolidados/comparativovaloresmobiliarios. asp (accessed 17 January 2012).

8 Fernando Puga, "Por que crescem as exportações brasileiras," *Visão do Desenvolvimento* (Rio de Janeiro: BNDES, 2006).

Table 10.3. Total public sector net debt (% of GDP), total unemployment rate in metropolitan areas (%),* tax burden (% of GDP) and real minimum wage (R$ in April of 2008) deflated by INPC**

	Public debt	Unemployment	Tax burden	Real minimum wage
1995	29.1		28.4	238
1996	29.6		28.6	249
1997	30.4		28.6	255
1998	35.4	18.7	29.3	266
1999	45.5	20.2	31.1	268
2000	45.5	18.7	30.4	277
2001	47.8	18.8	31.9	302
2002	52	19.5	32.4	309
2003	52.1	20.8	31.9	312
2004	49.8	19.6	32.8	324
2005	47.8	17.9	33.8	346
2006	46.7	16.8	34.1	395
2007	44.7	15.5	35.3	419
2008	41.2	15.2	35.8	432

Source: DIEESE, Central Bank and IPEA.
* DIEESE.
** National Index of Consumer Prices.
Note: For an estimate of the values presented in Brazilian currency (real R$), the exchange rate in Sept 2008 was USD 1 = R$1.70. Three months later after the international bank crisis, the exchange rate changed to USD 1 = R$2.50. In December 2009 the exchange rate returned to USD 1 = R$1.70.

Table 10.4. Credit operations of the Brazilian financial system (% of GDP)

	Public banks	National private banks	Foreign private banks	Total
1995	19.1	12.7	2.6	34.4
1996	16.9	10.3	3.2	30.4
1997	16.1	8.9	4.0	29.1
1998	14.5	8.6	4.3	27.4
1999	13.5	7.7	5.0	26.3
2000	12.5	7.8	5.3	25.6
2001	9.7	9.4	6.5	25.7
2002	8.6	9.2	6.1	24.0
2003	9.0	8.7	5.2	22.9
2004	9.2	9.2	5.2	23.6
2005	9.9	10.6	5.8	26.3
2006	10.6	11.9	6.5	29.0
2007	11.2	13.5	7.1	31.9
2008	12.9	16.3	8.0	37.2

Source: Elaborated by the author based on the data of the central bank – Estfin (Ministry of Finance, Economic and Financial Statistics).

Table 10.5. Balance of trade, foreign direct investment and foreign exchange reserves (USD millions)

	Balance of trade	Foreign direct investment	Foreign exchange reserves
1995	−3,465	4,405	51,840
1996	−5,599	10,791	60,110
1997	−6,752	18,992	52,173
1998	−6,574	28,855	44,556
1999	−1,198	28,578	36,342
2000	−697	32,779	33,011
2001	2,650	22,457	35,866
2002	13,121	16,590	37,823
2003	24,793	10,143	49,296
2004	33,640	18,145	52,935
2005	44,702	15,066	53,799
2006	46,456	18,822	85,839
2007	40,028	34,584	180,334
2008	24,745	45,060	206,805

Source: Brazilian Central Bank.

rest can be considered as gains of Brazilian industry's participation in world trade, which is the consequence of internal dynamics possibly resulting from modalities of strategic coordination anchored by institutional incentives that have led to productivity gains. In that sense, it is plausible to consider that the role of internal market and overvalued exchange rate have been crucial to private investment strategies. Exports constitute only 14 percent of the GDP in Brazil and the commodities account by half of this percentage. Public policies to reduce social inequalities and stimulate internal demand, as can be observed in Tables 10.2 and 10.4, suggest that we should focus on the internal market in order to understand the export profile. On the other hand, Table 10.6 shows that the pattern of industrial sectors' insertion into international trade, according to their technological intensity, follows the pace of well balanced growth with all the segments growing at similar rates when comparing the two periods of 1998–2002 and 2003–7: (I) – 47 percent, (II) – 149 percent, (III) – 139 percent, (IV) – 96 percent, (V) – 154 percent. The exception in this dynamic was the segment of high-technology while there has been a higher gain in volume in the areas of medium-high, medium-low technology and nonindustrialized products.

Therefore, the diagnosis that the Brazilian industry has been going through a phase of deindustrialization is perhaps too hasty because the import volume, despite having intensified sharply over the past year, is still small in absolute terms and has risen in sectors – especially medium-high technology that have

Table 10.6. Brazilian export and import in industrial sectors by technological intensity (USD millions FOB)

	High technology (I)		Medium-high technology (II)		Medium-low technology (III)		Low technology (IV)		(V) – Nonindustrialized products	
	Export	Import	Export	Import	Export	Import	Export.	Import	Export	Import
1998	3,240	12,078	12,977	25,347	8,846	7,496	16,154	6,717	9,923	6,126
1999	4,126	11,782	10,874	20,856	8,511	6,599	15,775	4,604	8,724	5,460
2000	6,838	14,180	12,751	21,446	10,227	8,793	16,152	4,716	9,118	6,714
2001	6,982	13,824	12,317	23,036	9,985	8,260	18,464	4,099	10,474	6,383
2002	5,935	10,460	5,935	19,870	10,650	6,671	19,132	3,651	11,709	6,590
2003	5,135	10,431	16,694	19,987	13,394	6,800	23,281	3,319	14,580	7,789
2004	6,610	14,158	22,295	24,743	18,847	8,665	29,384	4,060	19,339	11,210
2005	8,757	17,134	28,912	28,418	22,741	10,484	33,606	4,744	24,292	12,819
2006	9,364	21,203	32,403	33,311	27,252	14,339	38,300	6,216	30,150	16,281
2007	10,241	25,284	36,519	46,645	31,599	19,649	43,549	8,372	38,741	20,671

Source: SECEX/MDIC.
Note: Classification extracted from the OECD Directorate for Science, Technology and Industry's STAN Indicators Database (2003).

also take advantage of higher growth of export coefficient. This movement, then, suggests that industrial sectors have invested in improving productivity by importing capital goods aimed at import substitution, and therefore, qualifying as a case of complementarity.

This position is opposed to what has normally been said: the rise of world trade flows is inferior to the pace of Brazilian export; commodity prices affect only a small portion of the growth of Brazilian flow; the increasing role of the capital markets is restricted to capital turnover and does not meet the needs of long-term investments, so it is not a substitute for bank credit. It is too early to talk about regressive expertise or deindustrialization, as the rise of export coefficients has reached all sectors – especially those with higher added values. This implies that path-dependency of domestic institutions can play a significant role in explaining the current dynamics of investments, contrary to the current viewpoint that the market is the main if not the only relevant cause.

One of the main institutional legacies of Brazil to understand this new phase of economic expansion is the federal public banks, among which the BNDES stands out. Besides being the main long-term funder of the manufacturing industry and infrastructure, the BNDES plays a strategic role in stabilizing the credit supply in the face of cyclic changes arising from international financial crisis, providing that economic adjustments to these crises had less deleterious effects on the rates of investment, employment and growth. The countercyclical action of federal banks in the context of the banking crisis in the US in 2008, for example, is one of the strongest indicators of rapid recovery of current Brazilian macroeconomy.[9]

The BNDES accounts for 20 percent of all the credit of Brazilian banks in the private sector. In 2009, this figure represented, together with other public banks, a relative volume of credit equal to the domestic private banking sector, or about 18 percent of GDP. Altogether, federal public banks account for

---

9 The volume of federal public bank credit between 2008 and 2009 grew exponentially because of a political decision by the government to compensate the lack of international credit due to financial crisis. Since October 2008 the public sector banks now account for 83 percent of the increase in the stock of credit to the private sector. To cite some examples, between 2008 and 2009 the Caixa Econômica Federal increased its loan volume by 56 percent (due to the housing program); in the same period the Banco do Brasil raised its loan portfolio by 32 percent, and for persons this increase was 69 percent; on its turn, the BNDES increased by 65 percent the volume of disbursements in the first half of 2009 compared to the same period in 2008. (For details, see Barbosa 2010) It can also be noted (Table 10.6) that the BNDES disbursements have peaks in the periods of financial crises (1999 and 2002) when Brazil had difficulties in obtaining foreign loans. According to Table 10.4, after the reduction of the public sector banks' loans during the neoliberal period in the 1990s, they resumed their relevant role in credit supply in real terms as a percentage of GDP in 2000s.

Table 10.7. Annual disbursements of BNDES (% of GDP)

	Agriculture	Industry	Trade and services (infrastructure)	Total	Total (R$ millions)
1995	0.10	0.58	0.33	1.01	
1996	0.09	0.52	0.54	1.15	
1997	0.15	0.72	1.04	1.91	
1998	0.14	0.76	1.04	2.18	18,990
1999	0.12	0.79	0.78	1.87	18,051
2000	0.16	0.88	0.91	1.98	23,045
2001	0.21	1.01	0.72	1.98	25,216
2002	0.31	1.18	1.05	2.59	37,419
2003	0.27	0.95	0.75	2.06	33,533
2004	0.36	0.81	0.89	2.07	39,833
2005	0.19	1.09	0.91	2.19	46,980
2006	0.14	1.14	0.88	2.21	51,318
2007	0.19	1.02	1.29	2.50	64,891
2008	0.19	1.35	1.60	3.18	92,251

Source: BNDES.

38 percent of the total credit offered by the banking system. The BNDES has maintained its disbursements at an increasing rate; throughout 1999–2002 it almost doubled the volume of disbursements and increased it by 175 percent between 2003 and 2008. At the same time, the institution is the largest Brazilian bank focused on long-term loans (the average recovery time is 96 months), while other banks work with a term of 9 months. The profile of its lending to the domestic market is basically aimed at restructuring or expansion of productive capacity – with an emphasis on manufacturing and infrastructure – while the growing participation in the financing of exports has particularly benefitted the industry of capital goods and services in accordance with industrial policy.

Pension Funds

Next to the BNDES, the so-called pension funds linked to Brazilian public banks and state enterprises have played a central role in the productive restructuring process in Brazil since privatizations. They stand out in the financial market due to their long-term horizon appropriate to development policies that receive privileged fiscal treatment from the state. It should be emphasized that these pension funds are significantly represented in the boards of all internationalized domestic industries in which they hold shares.

Unlike other countries, pension funds in Brazil are part of a system where the access to capital markets is still very much limited when it comes to long-term investments. However, other studies have shown that the Brazilian financial system is even closer to that found in Continental Europe – in other words, to a model centered on a long-term interlocking between national public banks and enterprises, which supports the model of competitive entry (Mettenheim 2005; Stallings and Studart 2006). Thus, globalization does not point to the convergence of funding models as suggested by its enthusiasts. While acknowledging that the volume of transaction-oriented financial resources has grown exponentially over the past 25 years, this process is still highly concentrated in some regions of the world. That is, they are still associated with assets constrained by national regulation and innovation systems, where the state has maintained a leading role (Stiglitz 2003; Chang 2003; Vogel 1996; Zysman 1996).

In the context of capital markets, the pension funds are key actors. Until 2007, the Brazilian pension funds had assets in the order of R$413 billion, or about 17 percent of GDP. While the asset values are significant, the investment growth has been even more extraordinary, reaching approximately 300 percent among the 20 largest funds from 2001 to 2007. While in 2002 the entire complementary pension system[10] had accumulated a deficit of R$20 billion, between 2003 and 2007 the situation became a surplus of R$43.5 billion. For the purpose of this paper, it is important to highlight that from this set, three funds linked to federal public banks (Banco do Brasil and Caixa Econômica) and to a state oil enterprise (Petrobras) that controlled 42.2 percent of total assets of pension funds alone, whereas only Previ – the largest institutional investor in Latin America – ended 2007 with a net worth of R$137.1 billion.

This dominant group of federal pension funds links the savings of important segments of middle-class workers whose union base is the most organized and mobilized among the workers and is one of the mainstays of the Workers' Party, which is the leader of the current coalition government. Just as they had a strategic role in the privatizations of the 1990s, now their main administrative cadres are composed of ex-union leaders who have given a very different orientation to the role of funds.

---

10 Closed private pension entities are nonprofit organizations that can be established on a single-employer or multi-employer basis and by labor unions. The accumulated assets are legally separated from the sponsoring undertaking. In addition to the closed approach, which is predominantly chosen by large employers, authorized financial institutions provide complementary pension provision through open private pension entities. http://www.pensionfundsonline.co.uk/countryprofiles/brazil.aspx (accessed 5 May 2010).

A fact that shows the change in policy stance occurred in 2003 when the BNDES acquired a block of shares of Investvale, preventing one Japanese company from increasing its stake in Vale (second-largest mining company in the world), which would have made it a binational company. Vale is controlled by the holding Valepar, which has 60 percent of its voting shares controlled by national pension funds Previ, Petros and BNDESPAR. More recently, after taking administrative control of Brasil Telecom, Previ was articulating strategically with the government and the BNDES to enable the merger of Brasil Telecom with Oi/Telemar and thereby constitute a third telecommunications conglomerate of national capital, ensuring – through the golden share – strategic coordination to leverage national private groups to compete for a position (internally and externally) with other foreign groups of the sector.[11]

In short, it is necessary to explore the extent to which these state or para-state arms of credit and investments have been instruments of institutional complementarities concerned with the model of corporate governance and of productive regime capable of providing increasing returns and guaranteeing industrial sectors with better insertion in international competition, based on the coordination arrangements that emphasize the strategic interaction between different actors (Deeg 2007; Hall and Gingerich 2004). In that sense, recent statements made by key state policymakers have pointed to the need to return to the capitalist role, in the Schumpeterian sense,[12] which emphasizes the need for a closer reading of the role of institutions such as BNDES and pension funds in the mediation of strategic interaction.

A preliminary survey of the data about the ownership of the three principal pension funds in several sectors of Brazilian industry shows that its investments are focused primarily in the sectors of energy infrastructure and transport, telecommunications, mining, pulp and paper, capital goods, steel, civil aviation and petrochemicals, all of which are highly internationalized aligned with BNDES disbursements. Previ, Petros and Funcef have contributed decisively to the long-term investments of the leading companies in each sector, which also means that these funds have a role in the administrative policies of those companies where the funds have a seat. In particular, the state pension funds and the BNDES itself have been attempting to establish criteria for investment and credit such as the adoption of environmental practices, incentives for technological innovation, creation and preservation of jobs and corporative

---

11 For details about this process more recently see Santana (2010).
12 Claudia Safatle and Cristiano Romero, "Governo quer companhias fortes e globais, diz Dilma"; "Governo é contra reestatizar setores da economia, diz Dilma," *Valor Econômico*, 24 September 2007.

governance rules – for example the stimulus to the adoption of international standards of information disclosure (proxy statement) and the sustainability index of Bovespa.[13]

It is worth emphasizing that this shift of pension funds towards greater capitalization combined with a worldwide trend of fund participation in corporate governance may lead to greater coordination of entrepreneurial action with an agenda of administrating the savings of a significant segment of middle class or civil servants, around which the state is able to build a directive.

Notably, the managers of pension funds – even during the Fernando Henrique Cardoso government (1995–2002) – sought to mitigate the effects of the reckless use of their saving in the consortia of privatizations carried out during his period. Thus in the new corporate law passed in 2001, they included clauses to protect the rights of minority share holders in whose formulation the party base of the Workers' Party, linked to the union of bank workers, played an important role. This path seemed to suggest that there was a consolidation of a pattern of coordination by the market according to a *transparency coalition* type of a coalition model (Gourevitch and Shinn 2005), where the workers (read as employees of state companies and banks) would assume an interested position in the stock market through a leading position of its pension funds.

In countries like the United States, France, Germany and Italy the pension funds associated with the trade union base of center-left parties have played a strategic role in encouraging the spread of state asset stock thus expanding the market through the coordination of procedures of the protection of minority share holders, which has contributed to a greater capitalization of funds (Cioffi and Höpner 2006). In Brazil the largest capitalization of outstanding pension funds appears not to result from a policy of dismemberment of *blockholders* – with a view to policy changes with respect to privatizations – but from the strengthening of strategic coordination patterns where the assets of state companies and banks (and pension funds linked to them) play a crucial role of veto. For Grün (2003), pension funds of public banks and state companies would meet requirements to be thought of as an interface between industry segments and employees with resources that can be the "central network nodes." In the context of Growth Acceleration Plan (PAC), a lot has been suggested with regard to the possibility to integrate such funds as funding sources for investments in infrastructure. Moreover, little is known about the financing instrument, its importance and capillarity in the financial system and its relation to industrial economic groups.

---

13 The largest stock market in Latin America, Bovespa is a São Paulo–based stock exchange.

Conclusion

It was observed that the institutional constraints arising from cross-fertilization between the isolation paths of the arenas of decision making for the macroeconomic coordination along with the epistemic community that has founded the criteria of legitimating this stabilization agenda have consolidated their legacy and partially delimited the room for state maneuver. However, the change in the coalition government in 2003, and the employment of the BNDES and pension funds as instruments of a new type of investment and international integration, has suggested that there is a significant room for the return of the development agenda.

The literature of comparative political economy, especially those influenced by the models of VoC, has emphasized the research on the OECD countries. At the same time, comparative studies in the peripheral regions of the world today emphasize the aspects related to institutional weaknesses of these democracies, which result in analyses that freeze the paths of these societies and atavistically condemn their immediate futures into some perverse historical past. This results in diagnoses that incorporate the vocabulary of populism, patronage and other types of political pathologies, to describe and generalize, anachronistically, other institutional contexts emerging in the periphery of capitalism. What is intended here is to avoid this common practice of sterile generalization of area studies, and emphasize how recent institutional paths – marked by critical junctures – have also varied in the Global South. Therefore, it is important to adopt the approach of the VoC to understand this variation also in the periphery and semi-periphery of the capitalism system, seeking to understand how institutional change has been gaining ground from endogenous changes derived from a correlation between path dependency and cognitive systems.

If we recall the lessons of Polanyian literature, one can see that the economic liberalization period – which began with the stabilization of inflation – was not consolidated due to the absence of state regulation of the market sphere, but because of it. The Central Bank has consolidated its monetary authority through the bureaucratic insulation of the National Monetary Council and the COPOM, permitting the new epistemic community to consolidate its game of trust with the international financial community and close the black box in relation to cognitive control of the agenda. To accomplish the neoliberal economic agenda of growth with foreign savings, the decision makers of the Central Bank administered high interest rates combined with fixed exchange rate. They withdrew money from circulation by raising the so-called compulsories, which produced a progressive decrease in the volume of available credit from 34.4 to 24 percent of GDP between 1995 and 2002.

The Ministry of Finance consolidated its fiscal authority by promoting a law that sought to contain the current expenses of government, such as the DRU[14] (which hit especially the social resources) and the Law of Fiscal Responsibility, besides administering increasing doses of primary surplus to tackle the progressive public debt and raising the tax burden by approving new taxes, such as the CPMF.[15] If during the consolidation period of the Plano Real the state had its arenas of coordination emptied and the coalition that drove it gave up a national development project, the government had to equip certain decision-making arenas so that they would have the capacity to make a neoliberal policy, as a typical Polanyian case of *freer market, more rules* (Vogel 1996; Polanyi 2000).

In what sense does the new coalition that took office in 2003 differ from that of the preceding period? Although the bureaucratic insulation of the monetary authority of the Central Bank has stayed intact and the confidence game of the epistemic community with the international financial community remains untouched, the current coalition has brought back the development agenda with social inclusion. It significantly expanded the state capacities and macroeconomic room of maneuver. It also kept inflation under control, ensuring a gradual return of liquidity in the credit market – particularly through directed credit policies where public banks and pension funds returned to play an important role and provided real gains in wage income. This resulted in a significant distribution effect and reduced the public debt, the interest rate and the primary surplus, thus the return of public investments through the PAC. This set of measures has ensured ample room for domestic macroeconomic maneuver, and therefore more autonomy against external shocks – something quite impossible during the previous coalition. In short, one of the hypotheses that this chapter seeks to sustain refers to a scenario in which market relations are further embedded in a new political and social development that is still in the process of consolidating.

There is a legacy of institutions that characterizes the variety of Brazilian capitalism particularly through the BNDES, public banks and

---

14 Desvinculação das Receitas da União is fiscal restriction law that subtracts 20 percent of the Federal Social Budget intended for education and health care that was approved in the beginning of the establishment of the new Brazilian currency, the real, in 1994. The objective of it was to reduce the public expenditures to contain inflation. As of 2008, the DRU no longer subtracts the resources of education.

15 Provisional Contribution on Financial Transactions was originally instituted in 1993 as a "temporary" tax measure to help fund the country's public health care system. While in place, CPMF submited every financial transaction accomplished at a Brazilian bank to a tax of 0.038 percent, which provided up to R$22 billion per year to the Brazilian tax coffers.

pension funds. It would not be productive to seek a new label for this modality but certainly Brazil has preserved a significant state capacity that guarantees levels of strategic coordination, important in the times of global crisis. At the same time, the role of ideas to understand the formation of coalitions and macroeconomic frameworks through the role of epistemic communities – and how they have appropriated this legacy – provides good evidence for understanding the process of institutional change that has occurred incrementally over the recent years. Unveiling the most relevant aspects of the room for maneuver that these institutions bequeathed, and the chances of fertilizing new epistemic communities, are the most central concerns to avoid dismaying readings of the capacities of policy intervention in the routes of economic globalization.

Acknowledgments

Former versions of this paper were presented at the 6th Meeting of the Brazilian Political Science Association (ABPC), at Universidade de Campinas (UNICAMP), Campinas (SP), 29 July – 1 August 2008; and at the Comparative Perspectives of Development Experiences in South America and Eastern Europe International Conference organized by NEIC-IUPERJ and the Estonian Foreign Policy Institute in Tallinn, 9–10 October 2008. I would like to thank my colleagues and professors from Berkeley, where I was as visiting researcher supported by a CNPq scholarship from 2008–9, for their fruitful remarks. I am especially grateful to John Zysman, Peter Evans, Harry Makler and Daniel Buch. At the IESP/UERJ, I am indebted to Renato Boschi, my supervisor, Eli Diniz and Flavio Gaitán, all of them brilliant researchers. I would also like to express my gratitude to Krista Lillemets, Thiago Nasser and Rebecca Tarlau, who helped me improve the readability of this text. Needless to say, I am solely responsible for any probable mistakes.

References

Adler, Emanuel. 2005. *Communitarian International Relations: The Epistemic Foundations of International Relations*. London and New York: Routledge.
Adler, Emanuel and Peter Haas. 1992. "Conclusion: Epistemic Communities, World Order, and the Creation of a Reflective Research Program." *International Organization* 46.1: 367–90.
Amable, Bruno. 2000. "Institutional Complementarity and Diversity of Social Systems of Innovation and Production." *Review of International Political Economy* 7.4: 645–87.
Aoki, Masahiko. 2007. "Endogenizing Institutions and Institutional Changes." *Journal of Institutional Economics* 3.1: 1–31.

Babb, Sarah. 2005. "Del nacionalismo al neoliberalismo: El ascenso de los nuevos Money Doctors en México," in *Políticas de economía, ambiente y sociedad en tiempos de globalización*, coordinated by Daniel Mato. Caracas: Facultad de Ciencias Económicas y Sociales, Universidad Central de Venezuela.

————· 2002. "Neoliberalism and the Globalization of Economic Expertise," in *Managing Mexico: Economists from Nationalism to Neoliberalism*. Princeton: Princeton University Press.

Barbosa, Nelson. 2010. "Latin America: Counter-cyclical Policy in Brazil: 2008–09." *Journal of Globalization and Development* 1.1: art. 13.

Batista, Paulo Jr. 2005. *O Brasil e a Economia Internacional: Recuperação e Defesa da Autonomia Nacional*. Rio de Janeiro: Campus-Elsevier.

Becker, Uwe. 2009. *Open Varieties of Capitalism: Continuity, Change and Performances*. London: Palgrave Macmillan.

Biglaiser, Glen. 2002. "The Internationalization of Chicago's Economics in Latin America." *Economic Development and Cultural Change* 50: 269–86.

Blyth, Mark. 2002. *Great Transformations: Economic Ideas and Institutional Change in the Twentieth Century*. Cambridge: Cambridge University Press.

————· 2003. "Structures Do Not Come with an Instruction Sheet: Interests, Ideas, and Progress in Political Science." *Perspectives on Politics* 1.4: 695–706.

Bourdieu, Pierre. 2000. *Les structures sociales de l'économie*. Paris: Éditions du Seuil.

BNDES. 2006 and 2007. *Visão do Desenvolvimento*, organized by Ernani T. Torres Filho and Fernando P. Puga. Rio de Janeiro: BNDES.

————· 2007. *Perspectivas do investimento 2007/2010*, organized by Ernani T. Torres Filho and Fernando P. Puga. Rio de Janeiro: BNDES.

Bockman, Johanna and Gil Eyal. 2002. "Eastern Europe as a Laboratory for Economic Knowledge: The Transnational Roots of Neoliberalism." *American Journal of Sociology* 108.2: 310–52.

Boschi, Renato. 2007. "Idéias de pelica na América Latina: Os 'ismos' comparados." *Insight Inteligência* X.37: 126–36.

Boschi, Renato and Maria R. Lima. 2002. "O executivo e a construção do estado no Brasil – do desmonte da era Vargas ao novo intervencionismo regulatório, " in *A democracia e os três poderes no Brasil*, organized by Luiz W. Vianna. Rio de Janeiro/Belo Horizonte: IUPERJ/UFMG.

Boschi, Renato and Flavio Gaitán. 2009. "Legados, política y consenso desarrollista." *Nueva Sociedad* 224 (November–December).

Boyer, Robert. 2005. "How and why Capitalisms Differ." *Economy and Society* 34.4: 509–57.

Bresser-Pereira, Luiz Carlos. 2006. "The New Developmentalism and Conventional Orthodoxy." *São Paulo em Perspectiva* 20.1, Special Issue on Developmentalism. http://www.networkideas.org/featart/jul2006/Developmentalism_%20Orthodoxy.pdf (accessed 16 January 2012).

Campbell, John. 2001. "Institutional Analysis and the Role of Ideas in Political Economy," in *The Rise of Neoliberalism and Institutional Analysis*, ed. John Campbell and Ove Pedersen. Princeton: Princeton University Press.

————· 2004. *Institutional Change and Globalization*. Princeton and Oxford: Princeton University Press.

Campbell, John and Ove Pedersen. 2011. "Knowledge Regimes and Comparative Political Economy," in *Ideas and Politics in Social Science Research*, ed. Daniel Béland and Robert H. Cox. Oxford: Oxford University Press.

Chang, Ha-Joon. 2003. *Globalisation, Economic Development, and the Role of the State*. London and New York: Zed Books.

Cioffi, John and Martin Höpner. 2006. "The Political Paradox of Finance Capitalism: Interests, Preferences, and Center-Left Party Politics in Corporate Governance Reform." *Politics & Society* 34.4: 463–502.

Collier, Ruth B. and David Collier. 1991. *Shaping the Political Arena: Critical Junctures, the Labor Movement, and Regime Dynamics in Latin America*. Princeton: Princeton University Press.

Culpepper, Pepper. 2005. "Institutional Change in Contemporary Capitalism: Coordinated Financial Systems Since 1990." *World Politics* 57: 173–99.

Deeg, Richard. 2007. "Complementarity and Institutional Change in Capitalist Systems." *Journal of European Public Policy* 14.4: 611–30.

Dezalay, Yves and Bryant Garth. 2002. *The Internationalization of Palace Wars: Lawyers, Economists, and the Contest to Transform Latin American States*. Chicago: University of Chicago Press.

Diniz, Eli (ed.) 2007. *Globalização, Estado e Desenvolvimento: Dilemas do Brasil no novo milênio*. Rio de Janeiro: FGV.

Djelic, Marie-Laure and Sigrid Quack. 2007. "Overcoming Path Dependency: Path Generation in Open Systems." *Theory and Society* 36: 161–86.

Dobbin, Frank. 1993. "The Social Construction of the Great Depression: Industrial Policy During the 1930s in the United States, Britain, and France." *Theory and Society* 22: 1–56.

Dornbusch, Rudiger, and Sebastian Edwards (eds). 1991. *The Macroeconomics of Populism in Latin America*. Chicago: University of Chicago Press.

Evans, Peter. 1995. *Embedded Autonomy: States and Industrial Transformation*. Princeton: Princeton University Press.

Fourcade-Gourinchas, Marion. 2001. "Politics, Institutional Structures, and the Rise of Economics: A Comparative Study." *Theory and Society* 30.3: 397–447.

————. 2006. "The Construction of a Global Profession: The Transnacionalization of Economics." *American Journal of Sociology* 112.1: 145–94.

Fourcade-Gourinchas, Marion and Sarah Babb. 2002. "The Rebirth of the Liberal Creed: Paths to Neoliberalism in Four Countries." *American Journal of Sociology* 108.3: 533–79.

Goldstein, Judith and Robert Keohane. 1993. "Ideas and Foreign Policy: An Analytic Framework." *Ideas and Foreign Policy: Beliefs Institutions and Political Change*. Ithaca, NY: Cornell University Press.

Gourevitch, Peter. 1986. *Politics in Hard Times: Comparative Responses to International Economic Crises*. Ithaca, NY and London: Cornell University Press.

Goyer, Michel. 2006. "Varieties of Institutional Investors and National Models of Capitalism: The Transformation of Corporate Governance in France and Germany." *Politics & Society* 34.3: 399–430.

Grün, Roberto. 2003. "Fundos de pensão no Brasil do final do século xx: Guerra cultural, modelos de capitalismo e os destinos das classes medias." *MANA – Estudos de Antropologia Social* 9.2.

————. 2005. "O 'nó' dos fundos de pensão." *Novos Estudos* 73: 19–31.

————. 2007. "Decifra-me ou te devoro! As finanças e a sociedade brasileira." *MANA – Estudos de Antropologia Social* 13.2.

Gourevitch, Peter, and James Shinn. 2005. *Political Power and Corporate Control: The New Global Politics of Corporate Governance*. Princeton: Princeton University Press.

Haas, Ernst B. 1975. "Is There a Hole in the Whole? Knowledge, Technology, Interdependence, and the Construction of International Regimes." *International Organization* 29.3: 827–76.

Haas, Peter M. 1992. "Introduction: Epistemic Communities and International Policy Coordination." *International Organization* 46.1: 1–35.

Hall, Peter (ed.) 1989. *The Political Power of Economic Ideas*. Princeton: Princeton University Press.

––––––· 1993. "Policy Paradigms, Social Learning and the State: The Case of Economic Policymaking in Britain." *Comparative Politics* 25.3: 275–96.

––––––· 2007. "The Evolution of Varieties of Capitalism in Europe," in *Beyond Varieties of Capitalism*, ed. Bob Hancke Mark Thatcher and Martin Rhodes. Oxford: Oxford University Press.

Hall, Peter and David Soskice. 2001. *Varieties of Capitalism: The Institutional Foundations of Comparative Advantage*. Oxford: Oxford University Press.

Hall, Peter and Daniel Gingerich. 2004. "Varieties of Capitalism and Institutional Complementarities in the Macroeconomy: An Empirical Analysis." MPIfG discussion paper, presented 4 May.

Hall, Peter and Kathleen Thelen. 2006. "Institutional Change in Varieties of Capitalism." Paper prepared for presentation to the Europeanists Conference, Chicago, March.

Helleiner, Eric. 1994. *States and the Reemergence of Global Finance*. Ithaca, NY and London: Cornell University Press.

Henisz, Witold, Bennet Zelner and Mauro Guillén. 2005. "The World Diffusion of Market-oriented Infrastructure Reform, 1977–1999." *American Sociological Review* 70.6: 871–97.

Höpner, Martin. 2005. "What Connects Industrial Relations with Corporate Governance? Explaining Complementarity." *Socio-Economic Review* 3.2.

Huber, Evelyne. 2002. "Conclusion: Actors, Institutions and Policies," in *Models of Capitalism: Lessons for Latin America*. Pennsylvania: Pennsylvania University Press.

Johnson, Juliet. 2002. "Financial Globalization and National Sovereignty: Neoliberal Transformations in Post-Communist Central Banks." Paper presented at the American Political Science Association annual meeting, 29 August–1 September, Boston, MA.

Latour, Bruno. 1987. *Science in Action*. Cambridge, MA: Harvard University Press.

Loureiro, Maria and Fernando Abrucio, 1999. "Política e burocracia no presidencialismo brasileiro: O papel do Ministério da Fazenda no primeiro governo Fernando Henrique Cardoso." *Revista Brasileira de Ciências Sociais* 14.41.

Loureiro, Maria. 1997. *Os economistas no governo: Gestão econômica e democracia*. Rio de Janeiro: Editora da Fundação Getúlio Vargas.

––––––· 1998. "L'internationalisation des milieux dirigeants au Brésil." *Actes de la Recherche en Sciences Sociales* 121.1.

Loureiro, Maria and Fernando Abrucio, 1999. "Política e burocracia no presidencialismo brasileiro: O papel do Ministério da Fazenda no primeiro governo Fernando Henrique Cardoso." *Revista Brasileira de Ciências Sociais* 14.41.

Keck, Margaret and Kathryn Sikkink. 1998. *Activists Beyond Borders: Advocacy Networks in International Politics*. Ithaca, NY and London: Cornell University Press.

Krasner, Stephen. 1984. "Approaches to the State: Alternative Conceptions and Historical Dynamics." *Comparative Politics* 16.2: 223–46.

––––––· 1988. "Sovereignty: An Institutional Perspective." *Comparative Political Studies* 21.1: 66–94.

MacKenzie, Donald. 2005. "Opening the Black Boxes of Global Finance." *Review of International Political Economy* 12.4: 555–76.

Mahoney, James. 2000. "Path Dependence in Historical Sociology." *Theory and Society* 29.4: 507–48.

Maxfield, Sylvia. 1997. *Gatekeepers of Growth: The International Political Economy of Central Banking in Developing Countries*. Princeton: Princeton University Press.

McNamara, Kathleen. 1999. "Consensus and Constraint: Ideas and Capital Mobility in European Monetary Integration." *Journal of Common Market Studies* 37.3: 455–76.

Melo, Marcus. 2001. "A política da ação regulatória: Responsabilização, credibilidade e delegação." *Revista Brasileira de Ciências Sociais* 16.46: 56–68.

Mettenheim, Kurt von. 2006. "From the Economics of Politics to the Politics of Monetary Policy," in *Statecrafting Monetary Authority: Democracy and Financial Order in Brazil*, organized by Lourdes Sola and Laurence Whitehead. Oxford: Centre for Brazilian Studies, University of Oxford.

———. 2005. "Commanding Heights: Para uma sociologia política dos bancos federais brasileiros." *Revista Brasileira de Ciências Sociais* 20.58.

Neri, Marcelo (ed.) 2008. *The New Middle-Class*. Rio de Janeiro: Centro de Políticas Sociais, FGV. http://www3.fgv.br/ibrecps/M3/index_eng.htm (accessed 16 January 2012).

North, Douglass. 1990. *Institutions, Institutional Change and Economic Performance*. Cambridge: Cambridge University Press.

Offe, Claus. 1989. *Capitalismo desorganizado: Transformações contemporâneas do trabalho e da política*. São Paulo: Brasiliense.

Pierson, Paul. 2000. "Increasing Returns, Path Dependence, and the Study of Politics." *American Political Science Review* 94.2: 251–67.

———. 2004. *Politics in Time: History, Institutions, and Social Analysis*. Princeton: Princeton University Press.

Pio, Carlos. 2001. *A construção política da economia de mercado no Brasil: Estabilização e abertura comercial (1985–1995)*. Rio de Janeiro: Tese (doutorado), Ciência Política, IUPERJ.

Polillo, Simone and Mauro Guillén. 2005. "Globalization Pressures and the State: The Global Spread of Central Bank Independence." *American Journal of Sociology* 110: 1764–1802.

Powell, Walter and Paul DiMaggio. 1991. "The Iron Cage Revisited: Institutional Isomorphism and Collective Rationality in Organization Fields," in *The New Institutionalism in Organizational Analysis*. Chicago and London: University of Chicago Press.

Ruggie, John. 1975. "International Responses to Technology: Concepts and Trends." *International Organization* 29.3 (International Responses to Technology): 557–83.

———. 1998. "What Makes the World Hang Together? Neo-utilitarianism and the Social Constructivist Challenge." *International Organization* 52.4.

Santana, Carlos Henrique. 2005. *Política industrial do governo Lula – limites da mudança*. Rio de Janeiro: Dissertação de mestrado em Ciência Política, IUPERJ.

———. 2007. "Redes de profissionais na definição da agenda de políticas macroeconômicas no Brasil." Paper presented at the 31st National Meeting of the Brazilian Association of Graduate Studies and Research in Social Sciences (ANPOCS), Caxambu, 22–26 October.

———. 2010. "BNDES e fundos de pensão: padrões de reestruturação acionária e graus de internacionalização" [Pensions Funds and Brazilian Development Bank: Ownership Restructuring Patterns and Degrees of Internationalization]. Paper presented at the 7th Workshop Empresa, Empresários e Sociedade, Florianópolis, 25–28 May.

Santana, Carlos Henrique and Yuri Kasahara. 2007. "Os limites da integração financeira e políticas de crédito na América do Sul: Um novo modelo de desenvolvimento regional?" in *Globalização, Estado e Desenvolvimento: Dilemas do Brasil no novo milênio*, ed. Eli Diniz. Rio de Janeiro: FGV.

Santiso, Javier. 2003. "The Confidence Game: Exit, Voice and Loyalty in Financial Markets," in *The Political Economy of Emerging Markets: Actors, Institutions and Financial Crises in Latin America*. New York: Palgrave Macmillan.

Santos, Fabiano and Inês Patrício. 2002. "Moeda e poder legislativo no Brasil: Prestação de contas de bancos centrais no presidencialismo de coalizão." *Revista Brasileira de Ciências Sociais* 17.49.

Schamis, Hector. 2005. *Re-forming the State: The Politics of Privatization in Latin America and Europe*. Ann Arbor: University of Michigan Press.

Schmidt, Vivien A. 2000. "Democracy and Discourse in an Integrating Europe and a Globalising World." *European Law Journal* 6.3: 277–300.

———. 2003. "French Capitalism Transformed, Yet Still a Third Variety of Capitalism." *Economy and Society* 32.4: 526–54.

———. 2006. "Bringing the State Back into the Varieties of Capitalism and Discourse into the Explanation of Institutional Change." Paper presented at the annual meeting of the American Political Science Association, Philadelphia, 31 August–2 September.

———. 2008. "Discursive Institutionalism: The Explanatory Power of Ideas and Discourse." *Annual Review of Political Science* 11: 303–26.

———. 2011. "Reconciling Ideas and Institutions through Discursive Institutionalism," in *Ideas and Politics in Social Science Research*, ed. Daniel Béland and Robert H. Cox. Oxford: Oxford University Press.

Schneider, Ben Ross. 2009. "Hierarchical Market Economies and Varieties of Capitalism in Latin America." *Journal of Latin American Studies* 41: 553–57.

Sicsú, João. 2006. "Rumos da liberalização financeira brasileira." *Revista de Economia Política* 26.3.

Sicsú, João, Luiz F. de Paula and Renaut Michel (organizers). 2005. *Novo-desenvolvimentismo: Um projeto nacional de crescimento com equidade social*. Rio de Janeiro: Manole/Fundação Konrad Adenauer.

Sikkink, Kathryn. 1991. *Ideas and Institutions: Developmentalism in Brazil and Argentina*. Ithaca, NY: Cornell University Press.

Simmons, Beth, Frank Dobbin and Geoffrey Garrett. 2006. "Introduction: The International Diffusion of Liberalism." *International Organization* 60: 781–810.

Sola, Lourdes and Eduardo Kugelmas. 2006. "Crafting Economic Stabilization: Political Discretion and Technical Innovation in the Implementation of the Real Plan," in *Statecrafting Monetary Authority: Democracy and Financial Order in Brazil*, ed. Lourdes Sola and Laurence Whitehead. Oxford: Centre for Brazilian Studies, University of Oxford.

Sola, Lourdes and Moisés Marques. 2006. "Central Banking, Democratic Governance and Quality of Democracy," in *Statecrafting Monetary Authority*, ed. Lourdes Sola and Laurence Whitehead. Oxford: Centre for Brazilian Studies, University of Oxford.

Stallings, Barbar, and Rogerio Studart. 2006. *Finance for Development: Latin America in Comparative Perspective*. Washington DC: Brookings Institution Press/CEPAL.

Stiglitz, Joseph. 2003. *The Roaring Nineties: A New History of the World's Most Prosperous*. New York: Norton.

Streeck, Wolfgang and Kathleen Thelen (eds). 2005. *Beyond Continuity: Institutional Change in Advanced Political Economies*. Oxford: Oxford University Press.

Vitols, Sigurt. 2005. "Changes in Germany's Bank-Based Financial System: Implications for Corporate Governance." *Corporate Governance* 13.3: 386–96.

Vogel, Steven. 1996. *Freer Markets, More Rules: Regulatory Reform in Advanced Industrial Countries.* Ithaca, NY: Cornell University Press.

Weber, Max. 2001. "The Social Psychology of the World Religions," in *From Max Weber: Essays in Sociology*, ed. H. H. Gerth and C. Wright Mills. London: Routledge.

Weiss, Linda. 1999. "Globalization and National Governance: Antinomies or Interdependence?" in *The Interregnum: Controversies in World Politics 1989–1999*, ed. Michael Cox, Ken Booth and Tim Dunne, 59–88. Cambridge: Cambridge University Press.

Wolf, Martin. 2007. "Unfettered Finance is Fast Reshaping the Global Economy." *Financial Times*, 18 June.

Yonay, Yuval. 1998. *The Struggle Over the Soul of Economics: Institutionalist and Neoclassical Economists in America between the Wars.* Princeton: Princeton University Press.

Zysman, John. 1996. "The Myth of a 'Global' Economy: Enduring National Foundations and Emerging Regional Realities. *New Political Economy* 1.2.

Part IV

ECONOMIC REFORMS, PUBLIC POLICIES AND DEVELOPMENT

Chapter 11

DEVELOPMENT AND CITIZENSHIP IN THE SEMI-PERIPHERY: REFLECTING ON THE BRAZILIAN EXPERIENCE

Krista Lillemets
Freie Universität Berlin

Introduction

Sociological and comparative studies on Latin America produced in Western European and North American academic centers explain the sociopolitical contexts of peripheral regions and create explanatory models that are very often arbitrary. Since World War II, the modernization theory tried to interpret the underdevelopment of the region by relating it in a perverse manner to the cultural and institutional legacy of the colonial period. Catch-all culturalist typologies, which related the region's "historical handicap" to its heritage of Latin traditions and Iberian culture, were standard in explaining the causes of backwardness and stunted social, political and economic development. Modernization theory suggested that it would suffice to remove the elements of cultural heritage – which had created the inadequate cultural values – to clear the way for capitalist and democratic development. Autonomous thought on modernization in Latin America, best represented by dependency theory and the works produced by members of the Comisión Económica para América Latina (CEPAL) referring to the perverse consequences of capitalist development (as for example the widening of social and global inequality), did not take roots in mainstream academic centers of the core countries and were overthrown by globalization theories in the 1990s with the triumph of neoliberalism.

Neither the modernization theories nor the globalization theories permit to comprehend satisfactorily the production of inequalities and the ways to overcome them, which nonetheless remains the main challenge in the so-called modern semi-peripheral countries,[1] such as Brazil. Semi-peripheral modernization has been *contradictory*, combining, on the one hand, the precapitalist relations, which engender exclusion and marginalization, and on the other hand, substantive democratization and construction of citizenship rights. In the attempt to understand this contradictory process, the emphasis placed on cultural traditions as principal explanatory elements has tended to disguise the importance of underlying social dynamic, which is above all related to the material base and the power relations.

Moreover, it seems contradictory when today globalization theories pronounce the supremacy of transnationalism and the diminishing relevance of the state, as well as the deterritorialization of social relations, and then we look at a semi-peripheral country such as Brazil in which the state has played a leading role during its history to guarantee citizenship and development – even if selectively. It may explain why the state continues to be the main object of dispute over material and ideological hegemony and legal and social recognition.

The task of this chapter is to show that the selective modernization in Brazil has been implanted by the expansion of capitalist institutions rather than shaped by colonial heritage, as typically purported from the perspective of modernization theories. Furthermore, in the course of modernization, excluded segments of society have been incorporated into society during the *longue durée*. In this light, the chapter aims to explore the Polanyian "double movement" between the expansion of the capitalist system and the expansion of the sphere of citizenship, and how state power has been used to carry out these processes. Growing legal and social recognition of parcels of society has changed the state–society relations and legitimized the political system. The expansion of the sphere of citizenship will be analyzed as an action against the "accumulation by dispossession" (Harvey 2005, 2007a, 2007b), which implies commodification of labor and social life taking place through planned marketization.

By using the sociological-historical approach this chapter explores this social dynamics during the critical transformations in Brazilian history: industrialization and urbanization (1930–80), democratization in the 1980s which coincided with economic liberalization (1990s) and a "left turn" in the beginning of the 2000s. The legacy of the role of the state in national

---

1 From the economic perspective, the category of the semi-periphery within the world-system lies between the core (the dominant "Western" capitalist countries) and the periphery (developing countries in the South), and refers to the countries with industrial capacity (Wallerstein, 2000). These categories should not only be looked at from an economic nor political perspective, since the basic attributes tend to structure the whole social systems (Domingues 2008).

development is well expressed by the politics that have prevailed since the so-called left turn that took place in the beginning of 2000. In that context the chapter will explore the attempts of the current left-wing government to resume the development agenda in order to invert the dependency conditions in relation to the core countries. Furthermore, the paper discusses recent changes in social and development policies and asks whether it is possible to witness a new countermovement in terms of new modality of social protection.

Theoretical Reflections on Peripheral Modernization in Latin America

Latin America has been considered one of the first laboratories of "underdevelopment" (Love 1996). In the 1950s and 60s the theories that were most commonly used to explain development, backwardness and underdevelopment of Latin America were modernization theories and dependency theory. In the 1990s the modernization theories made a come-back under a new guise as a theory of globalization. After World War II, modernization theories developed in the US academic centers rested on several assumptions regarding progress: that modernization is a global and irreversible process concerning all the societies all over the world, whereby the traditional societies must catch up with the modern Western societies. The division between the core and the periphery was based on culturalist typologies which included values that were favorable or not to the construction of modern political-economic structures. In peripheral societies the dominant values were supposed to be personalism, collectivism, particularism and ascription, while in the core countries secular, individualistic and scientific values were prevalent (Knöbl 2003, 97). The revival of modernization theories in the 1990s repeated but also modified the original arguments. The modernization theories in the 1950s and 60s argued that in time socioeconomic development in peripheral countries would result in a transition from traditional to modern values which would enable them to follow capitalist development. The updated modernization theories emphasized that despite socioeconomic developments, the cultural traditions would endure and shape the economic and political behavior of these societies (Inglehart 2005). In spite of socioeconomic development, the cultural heritage, religion and colonial history of developing and underdeveloped countries form a distinct cultural tradition that continues playing a decisive role in influencing the economic, political and cultural development – giving rise to hybrid forms. For example in Latin America, the Iberian colonial heritage, the permanence of Catholic culture and the incorporation of indigenous elements would make it the "Other" of the West.

However, the modernization theories overstrain Weber's argument concerning the "elective affinity" between protestant ethics and the capitalist spirit by placing immense emphasis on cultural heritage and the origins of cultures and treating them as structuring factors in the configuration of the market, state and society (Feres and Eisenberg 2006).

Other theoretical approaches have contested this overstated importance given to cultural heritage within the process of reproduction of unequal development and have rather emphasized the relevance of the material base and of power relations in the capitalist system. Semi-peripheral countries have produced some alternatives to the evolutionist assumptions of modernization theory by stressing the need to adopt a *social-structuralist perspective*. One of the most known and widely recognized of these approaches is dependency theory, developed in the 1960s as a response to modernization theories (Cardoso and Faletto 1979). This perspective sustained that *underdevelopment* was not a phase apart of capitalist development, but rather one of the very elements of a single unitary system of capitalist development. In other words, underdevelopment should be examined within the framework of a *center–periphery* relationship. However, this diagnosis viewed the inclusion of peripheral societies and their national economies into the international capitalist division of labor in a more pessimistic light as a possible continuation of the colonial condition – only this time just at another level. This subordinated mode of development would integrate the social inequality of peripheral societies into the broader context of the employment of cheaper labor work in underdeveloped countries, which corresponds to a significant improvement of the welfare of the working classes in the core countries. That is to say that international development is unequal and accompanied by marginalization, the idea that is summoned up by the notion of "combined and associated development" (Cardoso and Faletto 1979).

Within this context emerged another viewpoint regarding the peripheral conditions of the integration to the world society, especially within the framework of systems theory. This perspective abandoned the view that peripheral societies are marked by premodern characteristics, which makes them the "Other" of the West and emphasized the need to reject exemplar and absolute models based on fixed notions of progress or backwardness. Instead, it is important to qualify peripheral modernity itself within the capitalist world system (Souza 1999).

The theorists that represent a more systemic view emphasize the need to overcome the "essentialist culturalism" which separates culture from institutions. Instead, the discussion over culture should be related to the *institutional logic* (economic and political) in a capitalist system. In that sense the persistence of inequality cannot be related causally to colonial heritage, but is the product of the modernization process which has been implanted by capitalist expansion itself and unfolds as a result of the interaction between external factors and internal social structures (Souza 2005).

In semi-peripheral countries the case has been modernization under the leadership of the state. The state was conferred the responsibility to guarantee modernization, integrate territory, support economic development and forge collective identity based on citizenship (Reis 1999, 118). However, neither the state nor the market in the periphery has been able to guarantee full inclusion and social integration of the entire population. Modernization in the periphery has been accompanied by "marginalization" or "exclusion" of large social segments. In a semi-peripheral country like Brazil, we can consider it the result of the "accumulation by dispossession,"[2] politically orientated. In this context, the institutionalization of citizenship has been unequal and selective.

Brazil Facing Rapid Social Transformations

Brazilian development unfolded under what has been called by various social scientists as "conservative modernization" (Vianna 1994 Reis 1998), which originated from the accord between big land owners and the industrial bourgeoisie. This accord led to industrialization and consequently, urbanization. As a "late, late industrializer," its industrialization started in the beginning of the twentieth century. By the end of the century, Brazil was a middle-income country – with per capita income of more than 7,000 USD, while income was highly unequally distributed. During the period from 1930 to 1980 the socioeconomic structures in Brazil were completely modified. The importance of the primary sector in the economy diminished more than twofold: from 65.9 percent to 29.9 percent, while the industrial sector grew from 19.4 to 24.4 percent and tertiary sector from 19.9 to 36.7 percent. Whereas in the 1930s Brazil was exclusively agrarian, in the 1980s it had become predominantly urban and industrial. The urban population during the years between 1930 and 1980 had more than doubled, growing from 31.2 to 67.6 percent of the

---

2 It implies dispossession of the affected from the means of producing their subsistence. By this concept, Harvey (2007b) refers to the continuation and proliferation on accumulation practices which Marx treated as of "original" during the rise of capitalism. These include commodification and privatization of land and labor and forceful expulsion of peasant populations; conversion of various forms of property rights into exclusive forms of property rights; suppression of rights to the commons. What is most curious is that the state with its monopoly of violence and definitions of legality plays a crucial role in both backing and promoting these processes. Commodification, privatization of public assets and state redistribution (upwards) has been a signal feature of the neoliberal project to open up new fields for capital accumulation.

entire population. During the period from 1965 to 1980 Brazilian economy grew at an average rate of 8.8 percent a year (Santos 1994).

These structural changes which took place after World War II were driven by the developmentalist ideology of economic nationalism, according to which the state had the power to intervene in the economy in order to promote domestic industry. The strategy chosen by the state was the policy of import substitution industrialization (ISI) (Kohli 2004). This policy was sustained by a social corporatist pact established between ruling classes, land owners, middle classes and a modern working class who were taken under the protective wing of the state (Domingues 2008; Avritzer 2002; Sader 2008). This developmentalist ideology combined populism and autonomous economic development, which prevailed in all of Latin America between 1930 and the 1960s and created opportunities for new reembeddings among peasants and the industrial working class – which is to say that they were integrated to economic development and provided with social rights (Reis 2000). While in Western Europe neocorporatism was developed under liberal or social democracy, in Latin America it followed a pattern of co-optation–repression that implied fewer rights and more state control over workers organizations and movements (Domingues 2008, 8).

During the period spanning from 1964 to 1985, Brazil was under a military dictatorship supported by the US administration as part of its imperialist intervention in Latin America after the national-popular revolution in Cuba.[3] The military government (which came to power with the support of the antipopulist and antisocialist national and international dominant bourgeoisie classes) changed the ideological basis of the national project, although preserving its corporatist structures. Labor was disorganized completely, the rural sectors particularly (Love 1996, 189).

With the military regime there was a substantive shift from a relatively inward-looking country to a more outward looking country, that is to say that import substitution industrialization was combined with the promotion of foreign exports and heavy borrowing of foreign capital (Kohli 2004). The authoritarian regime continued the nationalist project, which implied no direct rupture with the previous path placed on track by President Vargas.[4] The military regime did not destroy the interventionist apparatus of the state; on the contrary it strengthened the existing state institutions – for example the oil

---

3 Ironically enough, the military *coup d'état* in Chile took place on 11 September 1973. Other similar September 11ths supported by the US government emerged like mushrooms after the rain: in Brazil and in Bolivia in 1964, in Argentina in 1966 and 1976 and in Uruguay and Chile in 1973 (Sader 2008).

4 Brazilian president between 1930–45 and 1951–4.

company Petrobras – and created various others. Furthermore, it strengthened the Brazilian Development Bank (BNDES), created in 1952 (Velasco e Cruz and Moraes 2008, 6). At the same time, the alliance with foreign capital became the basis of the economic development model, whereby capital accumulation was directed to internal investments and urban consumption – not benefitting all the social sectors in an equal manner (Cardoso and Faletto 1979, 152).

Integration with the world economy became a main goal during the military regime. The dependency on foreign capital increased, which also resulted in growing foreign control over the economic decisions and capital flows. According to Cardoso and Faletto (1979), the complexification of the industrial economy required external capital, technology and organization which would lead to the reorganization of the economy thus making the (semi)periphery more dependent on the core. Although production and marketing was taking place in the (semi)peripheral countries, the revenues and profits served the growing consumption in the center. This however cannot be considered a natural process, but a result of the expression of economic and political interests of ruling groups within the state institutions whereby the "populist state became the state of entrepreneurs." It can be said that the state became even more autonomous in the face of the societal interests, which permitted it to carry out profound structural changes in the agrarian and industrial sphere.

The military regime decreased political liberties suppressing any kind of dissension in the society. Economic growth took place at the expense of social distribution, which deepened social inequality and suppressed the demands for redistribution. The economic strategy relied basically on imports and foreign debt, which meant that by the beginning of the 1980s Brazil had reached extremely high indebtedness.

The development models envisage certain citizenship models. The terms that are used to describe the state capitalism in Brazil are: "regulated citizenship" and "selective modernization," meaning that granting citizenship was regulated by the state unequally (Reis 1999; Santos 1979; Souza 2000). During the dictatorship, populism was no longer the ideology of state policy although a certain modified version of paternalism continued to legitimate the government (Reis 1999). All in all, the developmentalist project in Brazil was rather elitist, since the ruling groups favored income concentration and had little interest in including the masses that served rather instrumentally the industrialization (Kohli 2004).

In terms of class structure, Alejandro Portes (1985) shows how the Latin American import substitution-based economic model favored income concentration in the hands of upper and middle social classes and curtailed formal employment in modern sectors of the economy. Nonagricultural employment in Latin America had increased from 13 to 36 million persons between 1925 and 1960, but only 5 million of the 23 million additional employees were absorbed by industrial work. The migrating peasants that moved from the countryside to cities were only partly absorbed by the growing industrial sectors. While the industrial output in the 1950s had been 6.2 percent per year, industrial employment increased only 1.6 percent per year during this period.

The emerging informality and marginality of rural and urban masses was theorized in the "mode of production" debate during the 1960–70s as a phenomenon belonging to the dynamic interrelationship between precapitalist and capitalist modes of production (Love 1985). Marginalization, represented by the presence of an informal proletariat[5] and informal petit bourgeoisie in urban and rural areas, accompanied the capitalist restructuring in Latin America. These dynamics could be well understood in the context of agro-industrial development and Amazonian integration with the Brazilian national economy in the 1970s, which resulted in violence against squatters and peasants and their expulsion to agricultural frontiers. On one hand it has been argued that the state had a strategic role in integrating the national market system based on precapitalist agricultural labor relations, which contained violence and coercion. On the other hand it has been alleged that capitalist modernization was slow and restricted; peasants were only partly proletarianized, continuing to face coercion. Although the informal sector in rural areas was shrinking mainly because of the expansion of agro-industrial relations in the countryside, the informal sector as a whole did not decrease – representing only the dislocation of workers from countryside to cities. One of the conclusions arising from the modes of production debate was that the noncapitalist mode of production was not a remnant from the colonial period but part of the dynamics of capitalist development (Love 1985, 207).

At the same time it can be noticed that profound social changes taking place in the countryside and in the cities resulted in a highly diversified and plural society, rich in new interest groups and movements of free associations, being that up to 70 percent of them were created in 1960–1988.[6] Moreover, the electorate grew from 16 percent of the population in 1945 to 25 percent in 1962, reaching 51 percent in 1986 which made the Brazilian electorate

---

5 The informal proletariat is the social class that (1) does not receive regular money wages; (2) does not receive social security; and (3) its relation with employers is not contractual (Portes 1985).

6 The most spectacular data can be verified in rural areas, where 96 percent of the associations of rural workers were created within the same period, which implied, in theory, incorporation of the rural workers into the public arena.

in 1982 inferior only to Japan, the US, India and Indonesia (Santos 1994). Nevertheless, the illiterate were not granted political rights until 1988 when the new constitution was adopted. All in all, it meant that the incorporation of the sectors of the population into the political arena opened access to social welfare rights. Large strata were incorporated into wage relations, and as a result were partly freed from personal relations of domination prevalent in the countryside, expanding social rights to rural masses (Reis 1999, 2000).

The acquisition of social rights by the working class under the corporatist regime remained limited to formal and modern workers and the political and economic empowerment of those not incorporated was constrained due to restrictions imposed upon their capacity to develop an autonomous political organization that could challenge the ruling elites (Oxhorn 2003).[7] But informally, mainly towards the redemocratization era, labor organization became more frequent. At the same time new labor leaders started to emerge independently of state-controlled arenas. The stratified access to rights during the modernization process had created plural demands that were impossible to control (Domingues 2002).

The 1980s marked the transition to democracy for Latin American countries. In Brazil, the transition lasted 11 years, culminating with the election of a civilian government in 1985 and the introduction of the debate on expanding social and political rights to all citizens, including minorities and indigenous peoples, to the agenda. Democratization implied restoring formal democratic institutions (with the establishment of rules of competition and freedom of opinion), expanding political rights (in 1985 the right to vote was also given to the illiterate, and all political parties became legal) and adopting a new constitution (Fausto 1999, 317).

Several factors contributed to democratization. One could emphasize the emerging opposition and change in the political culture which was, ironically enough, related to the unintended structural changes triggered by the modernization process itself during the military regime – like the expansion of the salaried middle-class and industrial working class and urbanization which altered lifeworlds, thus opening new horizons and redefining expectations and worldviews, giving rise to new social forces (Velasco e Cruz and Moraes 2008). Other factors were also important such as conflicts between military forces and state authorities due to repressions, the abolishment of censorship, economic downturn, foreign debt that had grown to stratospheric levels – from USD 43.5 billion in 1978 and to USD 91 billion in 1984 – and the flourishing of autonomous labor unions in rural and urban areas, including the white-collar unions (Fausto 1999).

---

7 See Portes (1985) about the change of social structure.

Democratization set the stage for greater changes within the ruling groups in society, but also for new social and political demands that had emerged, whereby multiple social actors – unions and popular movements – demanded political incorporation and social rights. Diverse disembeddings and the growth of informal sector had given the excluded masses the incentive to mobilize politically through community-groups, popular parties and church-financed associations. The demands which galvanized the informal proletariat were not related to the control of the means of production but rather to collective reproduction – demands for minimal access to public transportation, housing and other services. These new demands were derived from the acceleration of migration from the countryside to the cities and the consequent aggravation of the housing crisis, the breakdown of public services and pressure on public transport as well as violations caused by the threat of removal of urban slums (Portes 1985, 31–2).

The social thought of the Catholic Church guided by liberation theology had an important role in supporting the popular movements, the emerging movement of landless peasants and new workers' unions.[8] In the automobile industry a new type of union emerged, the ABC SP–São Bernardo,[9] which became the main social and political base of the Workers' Party (founded in 1980). The transition to democracy did not mean only the emergence of the sphere of civil society, but also the construction of new actors and political projects which played a significant role in the undermining of the hegemonic authoritarian project. Various actors and movements gathered around the Workers' Party (PT) in the 1980s, including unions, social movement activists, leftwing Catholics, Marxists and progressive intellectuals (Dagnino 2006).

The new emerging social actors started to redefine their political role, as well as the aims and ways of politics by occupying the political space and manifesting themselves based on an axis of interests, rights and citizenship (Avritzer 2002; Vianna 2004; Oliveira 1999). One of the most visible actors has been the Landless Farmworkers' Movement (MST).[10] All in all, it can be said

---

8 About the role of Catholic social thought and the role of the church in the struggle against authoritarianism and organizing the poor see Paiva (1995). The author demonstrates how Russian populism in the nineteenth century had influenced populist movements within the Catholic Church in Brazil in the middle of the twentieth century.

9 Much of the foreign capital invested in Brazil resulted in the establishment of the automobile industry in São Paulo, since the economic model was based on the exports and luxury-goods sector. A big part of the growth in the 1960s was directed to car and domestic appliance production. This is where unofficial unionism developed and where the political career of Luiz Inacio Lula da Silva started, culminating in 2002 with his election as president of Brazil (Sader 2005).

10 The MST was founded in 1985 and is the largest social movement in Latin America with an estimated 1.5 million members (see www.mst.org.br).

that political democratization and new progressive constitutions represented a huge opportunity structure for a variety of social actors to place their social and political demands in the public arena.

Capitalist Modernization in the Neoliberal Molds in the 1990s

The transition from authoritarianism to democracy in Brazil took place during major transformations in the modern world and within the context of change of the political agenda. First of all, to most the Latin American countries the 1980s represented a "lost decade" because of the debt crisis and growing inflation.[11] Secondly, new political coalitions emerged in the 1980s that were oriented by market values and by the subordination of the social dimension to a new rationality derived from the necessities of capitalist modernization (Vianna 2004, 23). Responsibility returned from the state to the individual sphere, and the developmentalist projects – whose basis had been the state's active interference in the economy and society – had lost its credit, making room for antistate ideologies (Reis 1999, 122).

The economic agenda emphasized the monetary stabilization, which included regressive policies and resulted in a restructuring of productive sectors. From the 1980s on there were several attempts to resolve the profound debt crisis and tame high inflation, but without significant success. The solution, as described by Rocha (2002), was provided in the form of a new plan – the Plano Real – which was, according to her, much more ambitious than just striving for stabilization. One of the principal purposes of the Plano Real was to tame inflation in order create the economic environment for foreign direct investments (FDI) and attract foreign capital to guarantee economic growth. FDIs were presented as a panacea for the modernization of Brazilian economy; they were seen as a structural need in order to finance balance-of-payments deficits, modernize industrial structures, develop advanced technology, promote productivity and boost the international competitiveness of Brazilian exports. Foreign companies' access to natural resources was facilitated and multinationals were allowed to participate in the privatization process of state companies in the sector of infrastructure. The justification of the plan was based on the widely known neoliberal mantra that stabilization and liberalization of capital flows should increase the confidence and reliability of investors, efficiency, productivity and competitiveness.

The amount of foreign capital in the country increased from USD 14.3 billion in 1994 to USD 34.2 billion in 1996, while annual net FDI had grown

---

11 In 1984 233.8 percent and in 1985 235.5 percent per year (Fausto 1999).

from USD 3.9 billion in 1995 to USD 30.5 billion in 2000. The result of the Plano Real was that inflation decreased from 23.29 percent in 1995 to 1.79 percent in 1998 – a fact that played an important role and ensured the plan's architect with the victory in the 1994 presidential elections. The Plano Real was accompanied by trade liberalization which resulted in a dramatic increase in imports, which in turn lead to the overvaluation of currency. In 1995 this model brought some short-term fruits – domestic market had gained some nine million additional consumers that had left absolute poverty;[12] the average real wage increased significantly for all the societal groups. Nevertheless, in the long run and by the logic of the model, it was an economic and social disaster. The external debt almost trebled from USD 95 billion in 1984 to USD 236.8 billion in 2000, while the public debt in total reached 28.1 percent of GDP, making Brazil one of the most indebted countries in Latin America after Argentina and Nicaragua. It meant that in 2000 interest payments amounted to 20.5 percent of total public expenditure (Rocha 2002, 9).

One of the main strategies to attract foreign capital was privatization of state companies along with mergers and acquisitions,[13] all of which were liberalized after the Brazilian Congress amended the constitution in 1995. Between 1996 and April of 2002, FDIs worth of USD 30.9 billion, were channeled into the purchase of privatized state enterprises in such sectors as electricity, telecommunications, gas, finance etc. Foreign acquisitions happened mainly in such sectors as auto parts, steel, banks, food, drinks, dairy products, hygiene and cleaning, electronics and chemicals, which resulted in the disappearance of various Brazilian companies between 1995 and 2001. The rapid liberalization of imports and elevated interest rates has been the most important means of displacing local capital.

Some Brazilian financial and industrial interest groups in association with international capital have earned a monopoly in the domestic market and profited enormously during the privatization process. The examples of this "newly internationalized bourgeoisie" include the huge state mining company Vale, which is today the biggest exporter in Brazil, or Odebrecht, a huge company in the fields of engineering, construction, chemicals and petrochemicals, or private banks such as Bradesco and Itaú. One curious exception in Brazil is the oil company Petrobras, which stayed in the state's hands (Flynn 2007).

---

12 The number of people living in absolute poverty decreased from 41.7 percent of the population (59.4 million people) to 33.9 percent (50.2 million).

13 Rocha's study (2002) indicates that between 1995 and 1999 there were 1,233 mergers and acquisitions, whereby the multinational corporations acquired control or participation in Brazilian industries.

It must be said that the neoliberal logic of "creative destruction" (Harvey 2007a) contained a whole ideology that penetrated into the common sense and political setting. The increasing submission of public policies to the economic liberalization agenda, in which states are forced to employ a larger portion of budgetary income to pay debts and decrease the control of capital flows, has resulted in narrowly targeted public policies as the chosen remedy for state's fiscal crisis. At the same time, after the privatization of the state infrastructure sector there was an expectation pension, and health care systems would also follow the same market logic under the control of banks and insurance companies – motivated by profit and not by the principle of justice. In everyday social fabric, the discourse of privatism, or in other words, "subjective experience of apparent irrelevance of the public" prevailed (Oliveira 2000, 57). It had become the norm of the everyday life of the bourgeois, then of middle and working classes in the 1990s. The Brazilian experience as well as the experience of other South American countries, undermines the long-believed hypothesis that an open economy and foreign direct investments would decrease inequality in the long-run (Huber 2006).

Capitalist modernization in the neoliberal molds had a profound influence on class structure (Portes and Hoffman 2001). While import substitution industrialization expanded the class of state bureaucrats and formal workers, the neoliberal adjustments shrunk both the public sector as well as formal labor but increased the informal workers[14] from 37.5 percent of the economically active population (EAP) in the beginning of 1980s to 48.1 percent in the end of the 1990s. During the period 1979–1997 the percentage of formal proletariat in the EAP had decreased from 49.7 percent 44.6 percent. While observing the effects of capitalist restructuring on inequality and income, the report of the Comisión Económica para América Latina (2000) shows that the income of formal workers declined from 4.8 times the poverty line in 1979 to 3.9 in 1997. Between 1999 and 2001 the average real wage diminished by 10 percent. In 1999 more than half of the population earned less than 50 percent of the mean income. Although the economic adjustments implied diminishing income for all the classes, there was substantial income concentration in the upper strata of the population. The inequality in Brazil widened. While the income for the bottom 40 percent of the population increased 1.3 times during 1990–1996, it increased 1.5 times for the top 20 percent of the population. This difference between the classes was not as big in Brazil as it was in Argentina, where the bottom 40 percent had their income increased for 3.5 percent while the percentage for the top 20 was 6.8 percent,

---

14 In Portes and Hoffman (2001) the category "informal workers" includes microentrepreneurs, those working on own accounts and domestic servants.

or Mexico where the indicators were -0.2 and 3.8 respectively. However, in Argentina the inequality rate increased less than in Brazil. While in 1990 the inequality coefficient[15] in Brazil was 19.2 and in 1996 it was 21.5, in Argentina the same indicators were 7.0 and 8.0 for the same years respectively (Portes and Hoffman 2003).

The numbers demonstrate that the logic of the economic model was based on "accumulation by dispossession" (Harvey 2007b) whereby wealth from the poorer classes was redistributed to richer classes. The shrinking working class and stagnant informal working class show that the new economic model was not able to absorb labor and diminish poverty, making the popular sector even more heterogeneous. In this context a new situation emerged, namely the provision of universal political rights with social rights in decline (Oxhorn 2003, 47). In that context the state–society relations established during the corporatist era were transformed significantly. The "regulated citizenship" was exhausted, giving the way to a "liberal-informal" welfare state (Barrientos 2009).

The restructuration of the productive system, growing unemployment and diminishing labor rights also weakened the mobilization capacity of the society – especially the labor movements. At the same time other actors emerged on the public sphere to contest the neoliberal policies, demand new reembeddings, basic rights, justice and democracy. The principal novelty in the 1990s was the Landless Farmworkers' Movement (MST) that emerged as a response to the commodification and concentration of land and in defense of agrarian reform. In the 1990s the movement also positioned itself against neoliberalism, defending a stronger intervention of the state in the economy and incorporation of the excluded sectors into the sphere of citizenship that would be achieved through the access to land. On the national scale one could also observe various forms of protest in the 1990s, especially on the second part of the decade. The topics that inspired the manifestations were related especially to the social question such as unemployment and social exclusion. In the following we will observe how these social demands have found a response during the "shift to the left" of 2003.

"The Shift to the Left": Striving for Autonomous Global Policies and Social Inclusion

The neoliberal adjustment created a favorable environment for the election of left-center governments in Brazil. In this "shift to the Left," in 2002 the

---

15 The ratio of nominal average income of the top quintile of the population to the bottom two quintiles.

Workers' Party[16] headed by Luis Inácio Lula da Silva gained an electoral victory. In all Latin American countries[17] in which left-center governments came to power, the national development agenda has returned more or less to the political arena as a countermovement to the homogenizing agenda of globalization and the social crisis it created. From the geopolitical perspective,[18] according to Wallerstein (2005) the semi-peripheral countries in the South with progressive governments play a significant role in challenging consolidated power relations and politicizing trade negotiations for the benefits of the less favored nations.

In order to respond to the increasing and diversified demands for social rights left-center governments aim at building more autonomous economic and political relations by giving the state back its role in the mediation of a variety of social interests within the national development, strengthening the regional integration through supranational regimes like Mercosul and Union of South American Nations (UNASUL) to create favorable conditions for the global trade relations. It has been argued by various researchers that the new developmentalist agenda is not the exact reproduction of the developmentalist agenda that prevailed in the 1950–80s, but it can be considered a neodevelopmentalist response to the neoliberal agenda that swept the entire region in the 80s and 90s (Boschi and Gaitán 2008).

The social question emerged as a central element in the new developmentalist project, which is related to the political pressure by variety of subaltern groups. Poverty and inequality have always been the cost of economic development and no government has been able to

---

16 It can be said that the arrival of the Workers' Party (PT) to power symbolized the consolidation of the decades of popular struggle for the democratic-popular societal-political project. The new PT government, forming a wide alliance of developmentalism, hence represented new hopes for a future with more equality. However, it faced a situation in which almost half of the economically active population was occupied in the informal sector with diminished incomes as well as a variety of social groups placing their demands.

17 Hugo Chavez in Venezuela, and an Aymara Indian and the leader of the *cocalero* movement – Evo Morales – in Bolivia, Kirchner in Argentina, Correa in Ecuador, Fernando Lugo in Paraguay and Tabaré Ramón Vázquez Rosas in Uruguay.

18 From the perspective of systems theory, Wallerstein (2005) argues that in the geopolitical arena there are currently three global cleavages: 1) a struggle for capitalist accumulation in the capitalist world economy; 2) a struggle between North and South for control over the distribution of the world surplus; and 3) a struggle involving the structural crisis of capitalism, which doesn't strictly follow a geographical divide, but rather a class and moral divide between commodification and decommodification of social and public life to build a new political culture.

combine equality[19] and development. The response of the new left-center government to the marginalization caused by market-oriented reforms involves a wide range of compensatory policies. The social program for those living in extreme poverty implemented by the Workers' Party in Brazil is the expanded form of the programs created by the previous government and united under the catch-all Bolsa Família program. This income transfer mechanism[20] is provided on the condition that the beneficiaries attend their regular medical examinations and maintain children and youth at school.

Income transfer mechanisms with various conditionalities are the main form of social policy that has spread in Latin America (Argentina, Bolivia, Brazil and Mexico). It is a policy which targets extremely poor sectors of society, those which suffered most with the neoliberal wave. This kind of targeted policy is being criticized by some analysts for being mere mechanisms of administrating poverty without aiming at overcoming it, losing from sight the policy's importance within the dimension of universal right and depoliticizing the social question when it comes to poverty and inequality. Its role as far as decommodification is concerned is still questionable, principally because the value of the transfer is very low and may not protect the poorest from the perverse market forces. For that reason, it is still problematic to treat it as a "social right," although the scale of beneficiaries is expanding, already reaching 50 million people all over Brazil.

However, the program represents a step forward in the integration to the state of those suffering from long-term unemployment, social exclusion and low self-esteem. The study carried out by the researchers of the Institute of Social Policy of the Fundação de Getúlio Vargas has shown that six years of this policy have decreased poverty and inequality and contributed to the expansion of the domestic market and the emergence of the so-called "new middle class,"[21] which

---

19 There is an enormous resistance to equality politics by the upper classes as well as the mainstream media together with the legitimization of almost aristocratic meritocratic values (Souza 2005), as a mechanism of social control of the poorer social strata to express themselves politically. The conservative judiciary power contributes to the maintenance of privileges by being tightly engaged with oligarchic interests. For example, the initiatives of agrarian reform and popular protest against the corporatist interests are met by Judiciary repression in all parts of the country (Velasco and Cruz and Moraes 2008, 19).

20 The criterion of inclusion to the program is based on a monthly family income of R$140 cap (around USD 70) per person. There are currently 11 million families being benefitted by the program.

21 The criteria to measure class "C" is related to such consumption and symbolic goods as access to housing, cars, computers, TV sets, radios, washing machines, refrigerators and freezers, credit, the level of education of the head of the household and formal employment. The low-middle class household income is between R$1,064 (USD 591) and R$4561 (USD 2,633). The study was carried out in six metropolitan areas of Brazil (Neri 2008).

has grown by 22.8 percent between 2003 and 2008, comprising 33.19 percent of the population in 2002 and 51.89 percent in 2008. Besides the role played in this change by the Bolsa Família program, other factors have been influential as well such as the social security transfers related to the adjustments in the minimum wage as well as the structural changes taking place in the economy – more specifically the increase of formal employment with formally registered jobs (Neri 2008).

The demands of the urban working class for the right to housing have been responded by the program called "Minha Casa Minha Vida" that also has played an important role as a political economic instrument in containing the economic crisis. After decades of absence of investments in this area, the state returns to assume the role as a promoter of urban development, assuming it as a principal element of national development. However, it does not resolve the housing deficit; 90 percent of the housing deficit is composed of the families that earn less than three minimum salaries, but the program directs only 40 percent of the resources for these families.

When it comes to social demands from the rural world, where the most burning conflicts are concentrated today, the main rural policy towards the *campesinato* and rural workers is related to the democratization of the access to financial markets. The National Program for Strengthening the Family Agriculture (PRONAF)[22] supports family agriculture and the resettled families through the land reform. These interventions have reverberated in the social movements both in urban and rural contexts (Boito, 2010). The movements without housing, the Landless Farmworkers' Movement (MST) as well as the labor movements have intensified their social mobilization. Moreover, current economic and political context has, arguably, decreased the defensive strikes and instead has privileged the demands for new rights and better working conditions.

Increasing its autonomy to act, the Brazilian government has diversified its foreign trade, partly explained due to the new industrial development program (PITCE – Industrial, Technological and Foreign Trade Program) and the Growth Acceleration Program (PAC). In addition, the government has considerably promoted the regional integration and South–South cooperation. The trade policy shows how the export of Brazilian capital in abroad has been integrated to the world market (Boschi and Gaitán 2008).

The export strategy in Brazil favors big corporations actively engaged in international commerce. The enterprises that are responsible for the largest share of export are the ones that were internationalized with the support of

---

22 http://comunidades.mda.gov.br/portal/saf/programas/pronaf (accessed 9 December 2009).

international capital, making them "global players," especially in such sectors as oil, petrochemicals, mining, steel industry, civil construction, cellulose and agriculture (Santana and Kasahara 2007). These include state-owned oil and energy-producing company Petrobras, a high-tech company Embraer, which produces commercial aircrafts of fewer than 110 seats, Vale (mining) and Gerdau (steel industry). Although they are present in all the regions of the world, they are concentrated mostly in Latin America. Two of the sectors that have the greatest participation in the exports are mining products as well as agricultural commodities such as processed meat, oil, cellulose and paper, sugar, juices etc. (Flynn 2008).

Agribusiness[23] has emerged powerfully in the entire region as a strategy to promote foreign trade, but also as a central motor of accumulation. Besides the agricultural commodities, one of the areas that has significantly grown in recent years and draws great attention of foreign capital is sugarcane production.[24] Its growth has taken place mainly due to the elevation of domestic ethanol[25] consumption.[26] In 2007 consumption of ethanol reached 9.2 billion liters, which was 50 percent more than the previous year. It has been predicted that sugarcane production will double by 2014[27] in comparison with 2007 when the production was 475 million tons. The export of ethanol increased six fold between 2005 and 2007 and the main destination countries were the US, Japan, Holland and Sweden.[28] The growth of supply is related to the expected growth of demand in the long run. The EU, for example, has set an objective to replace 10 percent of gasoline production by ethanol by 2020.[29] Critical voices claim that the expansion of sugarcane cultivation will contribute to the

---

23 Agribusiness constitutes 30 percent of Brazilian export and exports responds to 50 percent of the turnover of the sector.

24 Brazilian Agricultural Research Cooperation and various other research institutes are developing endogenous agricultural technologies for rice, soy, sugarcane, beans, etc. (EMBRAPA, http://www.embrapa.br/).

25 Three quarters of the ethanol produced (roughly 45 billion liters) in the world in 2006 was generated in the US (maize) and Brazil (sugarcane).

26 Eighty-five percent of produced ethanol is used for domestic consumption and 15 percent is directed for export.

27 Doubling the production is will replace 50 percent of the gasoline (Goldemberg and Guardabassi 2009).

28 REBRIP (Brazilian Network for the Integration of Peoples) and FASE (Federation of Organs for Social and Educational Assistance), "Quem ganha e quem perde com as exportações brasileiras" [Who gains and who loses with Brazilian export], 2009. http://www.rebrip.org.br/projetos/clientes/noar/noar/UserFiles/20/File/Publicações REBRIP/Exportações Brasileiras - REBRIP-FASE.pdf (accessed 15 December 2009).

29 It will require 14.8 million cubic meters of ethanol per year by 2020 (Goldemberg and Guardabassi 2009).

consolidation of a dominant economic model in Brazilian agriculture based on large-scale property, single crops, the artificialization of activities through transgenic crops, industrial fertilizers, intensive use of fertilizers, pesticides and herbicides, automization and heavy mechanization.[30] Another issue is how sugarcane production will influence family agriculture and land prices as well as how and in which sense it will aggravate rural conflicts[31] and deepen regional inequalities since most of the production of ethanol is concentrated to the south and southeast regions of Brazil. On the other hand it is expected that by replacing gasoline with ethanol, there will be a drastic decrease of carbon emissions[32] in the future (approximately by 57 million tons per year) (Goldemberg and Guardabassi 2009). Whether for economic or environmental reasons, the government has actively promoted ethanol abroad. Currently ethanol still faces high import duties in the EU and the US.

The expansion of Brazilian capital abroad represents only one side of Brazilian integration with global capitalism. Another important aspect in the integration with the world economy is the institutional and regulatory framework provided by the Brazilian state through public institutions such as the National Bank for Economic and Social Development (BNDES)[33] founded in 1952 to finance the state-led industrialization. It has played a strategic role in furthering development through financing productive sectors, infrastructure and credit and microcredit policies. During the Cardoso's government it was used as a mechanism to finance many foreign acquisitions of privatized firms at very low interest rates (Boschi and Gaitán 2008). In Lula's government the ideological orientation of BNDES changed favoring domestic industrial policies. This change was related with the shift in the top management from investment bankers to development-oriented progressive economists related to the PT (Flynn 2007, 20).

---

30 REBRIP and FASE, "Quem ganha e quem perde com as exportações brasileiras" [Who gains and who loses with Brazilian export].

31 Coerced labor is still a present phenomenon in agribusiness. Expansion of the agricultural frontier for soya, sugarcane or eucalyptus production has intensified conflicts in rural areas, leading to the criminalization of social movements, for example. On the other hand monitoring and the discovery and release of slave labor in the countryside have also increased. Recently the government launched the Plan for Combating Violence in the Countryside.

32 Ethanol made from sugarcane is more effective in reducing greenhouse gas emissions, producing approximately 80 percent less CO_2 per energy unit than gasoline and biofuels made from maize (producing only 20–40 percent less emissions).

33 The source of its capital comes partly from the Fund for Workers' Assistance (FAT), created by the 1988 constitution. Between June 2008 and June 2009 its disbursements reached of R$96.6 billion (approximately USD 57 billion); the majority of it was destined to industry and infrastructure http://www.plataformabndes.org.br/documento_plataforma.pdf (accessed 8 September 2009).

BNDES also supports regional integration, which is part of the trade policy and development as well as part of the broader South–South cooperation strategy. It aims to lift the region to a better position in international trade negotiations in order to invert commercial asymmetries and obtain greater autonomy within the global economic and political hierarchy. One of the most known regional blocs is the Common Market of the South (Mercosul) founded in 1991 by Brazil, Argentina, Paraguay and Uruguay. Chile, Bolivia and Venezuela eventually became members as well. In December 2004, Mercosul and the Andean Community of Nations agreed to create a region-wide free trade zone called the Comunidad Sudamericana de Naciones (South American Community of Nations – CSN). All of these regional blocs have been concentrating on opening markets by creating common tariffs regimes (Oliveira 2006).

While regional integration has advanced, global free trade negotiations have been put on hold. The conflation of various societal interests[34] has played a strategic role in hampering the advancement of the construction of Free Trade Area of Americas (ALCA). The Doha Round negotiations under the World Trade Organization (WTO) have also come to a halt. Within the WTO negotiations, Brazil has had an outstanding role in trying to block further liberalization of trade until the demands and different conditions of the developing countries are taken into account. Strengthening the bargaining power of the peripheral and semi-peripheral countries was the main motivation in the creation of the G-20, a coalition of developing countries that also integrates India, China and South Africa and whose main message is: "free trade works both ways" (Wallerstein 2005). The main bone of contention has been the agricultural subsidies of the EU and the US. Brazil and other peripheral countries have been rejecting the negotiations over intellectual property rights, services and government procurement and will continue to do so unless the US and the EU agree to diminish the agricultural export subsidies and antidumping mechanisms. The core countries – especially the US – are willing to make limited tariff concessions on agricultural and low-value industrial goods produced in Southern countries; at the same time it tries to guarantee its monopolies (so-called intellectual property) and access to financial institutions. The future bilateral trade relations between the

---

34 A variety of societal groups have stakes in the negotiations. National entrepreneurs have not been straightforward at all regarding the free trade. In addition to entrepreneurs, labor unions and civil society organizations especially the Brazilian Network for the Integration of the Peoples (REBRIP) have played a role in trade negotiations. The most outstanding has been the role of civil society organizations represented by the initiative of Brazilian National Conference of Bishops (CNBB) and other groups with ties to the PT with the support of some members of Congress, who organized a national but unofficial plebiscite in which millions of Brazilians rejected FTAA (Armijo and Kearney 2008).

EU and Brazil[35] will be based on the Mercosul–EU free trade agreement. As this agreement is directly dependent on the Doha negotiations and since they have reached an impasse, the Mercosul–EU[36] negotiations are on hold as well.[37]

There is evidence suggesting that Brazil's economic elites are not subordinate to foreign capital, but have become part of an emerging transnational capitalist class. The expansion of Brazilian capital shows that the country does not have relations only of dependency. Its exports are restricted neither to basic commodities or low-tech manufacturing nor are they geographically limited to South America (Flynn 2007, 23). Globalization theorists argue that the role of state power in national development is diminishing and that as a result of neoliberal reforms, state institutions have been dedicated to the global accumulation (Sassen 2007). The Brazilian case exemplifies a controversial trend in that the state continues playing its traditional role of integrating the economic elite to global capitalism but also affirms its role as a coordinator of a national development project. At the same time articulating social and political interests at the national as well as international level in order to revert the economic commodification and asymmetries in international relations.

Conclusion

Through the sociological-historical approach it has been shown that selective modernization has been accompanied by the gradual expansion of the sphere of citizenship during the *longue dureé* of the twentieth century, notwithstanding the intervention of occasional conservative counterrevolutions. Rapid social transformations, that took place through industrialization and urbanization within the scope of the national-popular development model striving for national autonomy, permitted to incorporate formal and modern working classes and middle classes into the sphere of social rights. The developmentalist ideology that oriented the development project based on the import substitution industrialization diminished poverty but preserved inequalities, creating rather large masses of urban and rural informal workers. The repressive military government continued

---

35 The institutional relationship between Brazil and the European Union is fairly recent, having begun in 1992. The strategic partnership was established in 2007.

36 Currently Mercosur is the EU's main trade partner in Latin America, and the European power bloc corresponds to one quarter of imports and exports of Mercosur. The commercial relations between the European Union and Brazil or even Mercosur have been and still are asymmetric, which brings to the forefront the issue of justice in international trade. For example, direct investments in services have taken place unidirectionally, from the EU to Mercosul, mostly to Brazil and Argentina.

37 http://ec.europa.eu/trade/issues/bilateral/countries/brazil/index_en.htm (accessed 17 January 2012).

the development policy within the molds of the "corporatist-developmental" project, but gradually integrated the Brazilian national economy to the global economic system. Excluded social groups, with their unanswered political and social demands, found a variety of means to become reembedded in social life. Vast changes in the 1970s gave rise to associative movements, informal unionism and social movements that demanded the expansion of social and political rights and recognition using the language of interest, rights and citizenship. The democratization wave universalized political rights.

"Creative destruction" (Harvey 2007a) put forth by the capitalist modernization in neoliberal molds under the guise of globalization in the 1990s coincided with the most powerful democratization process in Brazilian history, partly aimed at delegitimizing the role of the state to the benefit of the self-regulating global market. However, the commodification of social life and the discrediting of the public by "accumulation by dispossession" (2007b) were challenged by the new wave of subaltern politics. In this respect, there emerged what has been described as a "turn to the left," or countermovement in Polanyian terms, in the wake of the leftist electoral victories in various countries all over the subcontinent during the last decade. As a countermovement to the neoliberal trend and consequent aggravation of inequalities, the Brazilian state has returned as the main sphere responsible for guaranteeing social solidarity and more autonomous and less dependent economic and political relations in the global arena. The examples of this endeavor for more autonomous and more developmentalist and rights-oriented national politics expresses itself in the rearticulation of the state and society through the expansion of social rights – in regional integration and in various global steps to democratize asymmetric trade relations.

It can be argued that two simultaneous "modernizing gears" have been in dispute during the last twenty years in Brazil: "democratic and progressive," and "neoliberal" (Domingues 2008). According to the latter, in this new capitalist turn the state and society value extreme individualism and efficiency ultimately promoting a conception of citizenship based on "private egotism" as well as practices of social control expressed in the criminalization of the poor or of movements that struggle for inclusion. This project presents a minimalist view of politics, reducing the societal actors into typical third sector organizations; political issues are treated technically and philanthropically, and as a result the issues of poverty and inequality are removed from the public arena. The subordination of the state to the predatory appropriation of private oligopolistic groups that benefitted from privatizations, in addition to the reduced permeability of the state to social movements and interests, weakened the state's legitimacy in the eyes of society.[38]

---

38 See more about this neoliberal project in Dagnino (2006).

As a response to the commodifying policies of the 1990s, countermovement from the society has started unfolding. It aims to contribute to the deprivatization of the state, making it more responsive to public interests and therefore less subordinated to private interests. The central element of this public-democratic project has been to construct more equal social relations, redistribute socially constructed wealth and expand the sphere of social rights – and thereby also the citizenship.

The new social actors becoming present in Brazil express an urgency motivated by extreme levels of inequality that deepened during the 1990s. As it has been possible to perceive by now, the expression of those new social actors in the political scene has drawn considerable interest and imposed on the state, and the classical institutions related to it, the necessity to incorporate in its agenda new forms of articulating diverse interests. In this sense it is possible to say that the Brazilian society has begun to denaturalize the liberal myths of self-regulation of economy and identify the power of the state as a strategic mediator of social interests in any development project. Hence, democracy and its institutional spheres are apt to acquire the status of a dynamic process and permeable to demands not exclusively linked to mercantile interests. What occurs in an intense manner in Brazil is not a new separation between state and society, but, rather a new articulation in which social movements depend on the normative capacity of the state to stabilize and consolidate its interests in policies; the state and parties need these movements to renew its legitimacy.

Acknowledgments

This chapter is the result of lectures given at the Institute of International and Social Studies at Tallinn University during the academic year 2008–9 and research completed at the Estonian Foreign Policy Institute. I would like to thank Carlos Henrique Santana and Ricardo Nobrega for their valuable comments on the previous versions of this paper.

References

Armijo, Leslie Elliott and Christine A. Kearney. 2008. "Does Democratization Alter the Policy Process? Trade Policymaking in Brazil." *Democratization* 15.5: 991–1017.

Avritzer, Leonardo. 2002. *Democracy and the Public Space in Latin America*. Princeton: Princeton University Press.

Barrientos, Armando. 2009. "Labour Markets and the (Hyphenated) Welfare Regime in Latin America." *Economy and Society* 38.1: 87–108.

Boito, Armando, Andréia Galvão and Paula Marcelino. 2009. "Brasil: O movimento sindical e popular na década de 2000." *OSAL* 26 (October).

Boschi, Renato and Flavio Gaitán. 2008. "Gobiernos Progresistas, Agenda neodesarrollista y capacidades estatales: la experiencia reciente en Argentina, Brasil y Chile." *Análise de Conjuntura* 1 (January).

Cardoso, Fernando Henrique and Enzo Faletto. 1979. *Dependency and Development in Latin America.* Berkeley: University of California Press.

Dagnino, E., A. J. Olvera and A. Panfichi. 2006. "Para uma outra leitura da disputa pela construção democrática na América Latina," in *A disputa pela construção democrática na América Latina*, organized by Evelina Dagnino, A. J. Olvera and A. Panfichi. São Paulo: Paz e Terra, e Unicamp.

Domingues, José Mauricio. 2002. "The Dialectic of Conservative Modernization Revisited and the Third Phase of Modernity." *Dados* 25.3: 459–82.

———. 2008. *Latin America and Contemporary Modernity: A Sociological Interpretation.* New York and London: Routledge.

Economic Commision for Latin America and the Carribean (ECLAC). 2000. "Social Panorama of Latin America, 1999–2000." Annual report. Santiago, Chile: ECLAC.

Fausto, Boris. 1999. *A Concise History of Brazil.* Cambridge: Cambridge University Press.

Feres, João and José Eisenberg. 2006. "Dormindo com o inimigo: crítica ao conceito de confiança." *Dados* 49.3: 457–81.

Flynn, Matthew. 2007. "Between Subimperialism and Globalization: A Case Study in the Internationalization of Brazilian Capital." *Latin American Perspectives* 34.9: 9–27.

Goldemberg, José and Patricia Guardabassi. 2009. "Are Biofuels a Feasible Option?" *Energy Policy* 37: 10–14.

Harvey, David. 2007a. "Neoliberalism as Creative Destruction." *The ANNALS of the American Academy of Political and Social Science* 610: 21–44.

———. 2007b. "In What Ways is 'The New Imperialism' Really New?" *Historical Materialism* 15: 57–70.

Huber, Evelyne, Francois Nielsen, Jenny Pribble and John D. Stephens. 2005. "Politics and Inequality in Latin America and the Caribbean." Paper prepared for the annual meeting of Research Committee 19 of the International Sociological Association, Northwestern University, Evanston, IL, 8–10 September.

Inglehart, Ronald and Christian Welzel. 2005. *Modernization, Cultural Change, and Democracy: The Human Development Sequence.* Cambridge: Cambridge University Press.

Kohli, Atul. 2004. *State-Directed Development: Political Power and Industrialization in the Global Periphery.* Cambridge: Cambridge University Press.

Knöbl, Wolfgang. 2003. "Theories That Won't Pass Away: The Never Ending Story of Modernization Theory," in *Handbook of Historical Sociology*, ed. Gerard Delanty and Engin F. Isin, 96–107. London and Thousand Oaks, CA: Sage.

Love, Joseph L. 1996. *Crafting the Third World: Theorizing Underdevelopment in Rumania and Brazil.* Stanford: Stanford University Press.

Neri, Marcelo Cortes. 2008 *The New Middle Class.* Rio de Janeiro: FGV/IBRE, CPS.

Oliveira, Francisco de. 1999. "Privatizacao do publico, destituicao da fala e anulacao da politica: O totalitarismo neoliberal," in *Os sentidos da democracia: Politicas do dissenso e hegemonia global*, ed. Francisco de Oliveira and Maria Célia, 55–79. Petrópolis: Editora Vozes.

Oliveira, Henrique Altemani de. 2006. "As perspectivas de cooperaçao Sul–Sul no relacionamento Brasil–China." *Nuevo Sociedad* 203 (May–June).

Oxhorn, Philip. 2003. "Social Inequality, Civil Society, and the Limits of Citizenship in Latin America," in *What Justice? Whose Justice? Fighting for Fairness in Latin America,* ed. Susan Eva Eckstein and Timothy P. Wickham-Crowley. Berkeley: University of California Press.

Paiva, Vanilda. 1995. "Catholic Populism and Education in Brazil." *International Review of Education.* 41.3–4: 151–75.

Polanyi, Karl. 2001. *The Great Transformation: The Political and Economic Origins of Our Time.* Boston: Beacon Press.

Portes, Alejandro. 1985. "Latin American Class Structures: Their Composition and Change During the Last Decades." *Latin American Research Review* 20.3: 7–39.

Portes, Alejandro and Kelly Goffman. 2003. "Latin American Class Structures: Their Composition and Change During the Neoliberal Era." *Latin American Research Review* 38.1: 41–82.

Reis, Elisa Pereira. 1998. *Processos e Escolhas: Estudos de sociologia política.* Rio de Janeiro: Contra Capa Livraria.

Rocha, Geisa Maria. 2002. "Neo-dependency in Brazil." *New Left Review* 16: 5–33.

Sader, Emir. 2005. "Taking Lula's Measure." *New Left Review* 33: 59–79.

———. 2008. "The Weakest Link? Neoliberalism in Latin America." *New Left Review* 52: 5–31.

Santana, Carlos Henrique and Yuri Kasahara. 2007. "Algo de novo no front? O retorno de estado e seus impactos sobre a integracao sul-americana." *Observador On-Line* 2.4.

Santos, Wanderley Guilherme. 1979. *Cidadania e justiça: A política social na ordem brasileira.* Rio de Janeiro: Editora Campus.

———. 1994. *Razões da Desordem.* Rio de Janeiro: Rocco.

Sassen, Saskia. 2007. *A Sociology of Globalization.* New York and London: W. W. Norton & Co.

Souza, Jessé. 1999. "A Ética Protestante e a Ideologia do Atraso Brasileiro," in *O Malandro e o Protestante:e a tese weberiana e a singularidade cultural brasileira,* organized by Jessé Souza, 17–54. Brasília: UnB.

———. 2000. *A Modernização Seletiva: Uma Reinterpretação do Dilema Brasileiro.* Brasília: UnB.

———. 2005. "The Singularity of the Peripheral Inequality," in *Imagining Brazil,* organized by Jessé Souza and Valter Sinder. Lanham: Lexington Books.

Velasco e Cruz, Sebastiao and Reginaldo C. Moraes. 2008. "A construcao retomada: Desafios politicos e perspectivas internacionais." *Nueva Sociedad* (October).

Vianna, Luis Werneck. 2004. *A revolução passiva: iberismo e americanismo no Brasil,* 2nd ed. Rio de Janeiro: Revan.

Wallerstein, Immanuel. 2000. "The Rise and Future Demise of the World Capitalist System: Concepts for Comparative Analysis," in *The Essential Wallerstein,* ed. Immanuel Wallerstein, 71–105. New York: The New Press.

———. 2005. "After Developmentalism and Globalization, What?" *Social Forces* 83.3: 1263–78.

Chapter 12

THE PERIPHERY PARADOX IN INNOVATION POLICY: LATIN AMERICA AND EASTERN EUROPE COMPARED

Rainer Kattel
Tallinn University of Technology

Annalisa Primi
OECD, Science and Technology Policy Division[1]

Introduction

The interest in innovation as a driving factor for a growth, competitiveness and well-being is a vision shared among countries in different levels of development. Most countries in the world have a national agenda for innovation, with fairly similar priorities and objectives. This, at least, is true at the rhetorical level. Or to use the words of Gerad De Graaf, head of unit in charge of the Lisbon Strategy at the European Commission, "Everybody agrees that there should be more innovation. I have never met anybody in my life who says that 'I am against innovation.' Is anybody against panda bears? Or against Santa Claus?" This does not mean that countries all share the same view regarding what is innovation, why public policy should support it and how to do it. But this means that we are in a "proinnovation" era, even in nonfrontier regions where in the recent past innovation and technological development were expected to appear naturally through trade and foreign investments (ECLAC 2008a, 2008b; Radosevic 2009; OECD 2009; UNIDO 2009).

---

1 Research for this chapter was partially funded by Estonian Science Foundation (grant no. 8418). The opinions expressed in this chapter are those of the authors and do not necessarily reflect those of their respective organizations.

This generalized interest in innovation derives in part from the current context shaped by recently established (information communication technology – ICT) and radically new (biotech and nanotech) technological paradigms which are transforming the way agents (individuals, firms and countries) produce, trade and invest – thus creating a situation in which the possibilities and spaces for innovation are multiple and different from the previous age (think for example about the wide variety of successful business models or the new ways of doing health-related research). In the global knowledge economy, innovating has become imperative.

Latin America and Central and Eastern Europe are fairly different regions in terms of size, political dynamics and prevailing economic specialization and trade patterns. However, both regions underwent similar reforms patterns since the 1990s, influencing the evolution of science, technology and innovation policy in a similar way. The Washington Consensus recipe marginalized science and technology (S&T) policies and instead aimed at targeting inflation and at the reestablishment of macroeconomic stability through openness, privatization and deregulation.[2] In the 2000s both regions faced a slow return of policies supporting innovation and competitiveness. However, besides the different reforms and the design of S&T plans and policies, both regions are still marginal actors in the S&T game. The reasons behind the persistence of scientific, technological and production backwardness are manifold. Among them are the dynamics of the evolution of S&T policies and the "stop and go" approach induced by each wave of reforms. These are key issues usually not addressed by the innovation policy literature. Cumulativeness and path dependency do not affect innovation dynamics exclusively; they also influence the evolution of policies.

In this chapter we are interested in analyzing the dynamics of innovation policy in nonfrontier countries, and their relationship with structural change and development. In the current context in which global powers are being redefined as new actors such as China, India, Russia and Brazil gain ground in the knowledge game, frontier countries are reflecting on how they can support innovation and which type of innovation strategy they should pursue in the next decades to sustain their competitiveness and avoid losing ground with respect to emerging economies. Also, we can witness increasing efforts at generating better innovation policies to respond to emerging challenges such as environment and sustainability, pushing the innovation policy discourse back into a systemic approach of policy mix to support the varieties of capabilities needed for innovating in the new economic era. In addition, the financial crisis has, on the one hand, steepened the catching-up climb for many

---

2 For the discussion of the Washington Consensus see Williamson (2002), Kregel (2008) and Rodrik (2006).

developing countries as they lack the resources for fiscal stimulus programs to counterbalance the loss of export demand while at the same time advanced economies increasingly recognize scientific capacities and entrepreneurial innovation capabilities as key assets for a successful way out of the crisis.

The pressure on developing economies to create capabilities for innovation is rising. Peripheral countries (and those catching up) face a more challenging task in creating and implementing effective innovation policies. For them, beyond the rhetoric that innovation matters for development, it is crucial to identify which types of innovations to support and how to do it – given the constraints posed by budgetary reasons and by trade incentives that tend to push towards specialization in low value-added activities (ECLAC 2008a). Analyzing the shortcomings of the past processes of reforms in S&T and innovation policies might help to avoid repeating the same errors and it could help in relinking innovation policies to production development and in bringing the issue of the sectoral differences in science, technology and production back into the policy debate – which has been missing in the innovation policy discourse since the structural reforms of the nineties.[3]

Production Structure and Incentives for Innovation

When it comes to innovation, the stories of Latin America (LA) and Central and Eastern Europe (CEE) are somewhat different. CEE is largely seen as a success story, especially in relation to the ICT boom. For instance, at the end of 2005, *Business Week* ran a cover story titled "Central Europe – Rise of a Powerhouse."[4] LA, on the contrary, is generally seen as a region still struggling with catching-up and is at the margins of global knowledge economies (Cimoli et al. 2005; ECLAC 2008a, 2008b).

However, besides the divergent perceptions, the two regions display similarities in terms of persistent gaps with frontier economies in terms of production structure specialization and low aggregate innovation performance. In addition, both regions are characterized by high intraregional heterogeneity and both contain a country which due to size, political strategy and accumulated capacity plays at a higher level: Brazil and Russia, respectively.

The experiences of Latin America and Central and Eastern Europe are particularly interesting because the two regions have followed relatively similar development paths since the 1990s, including increasing integration into global trade and rising foreign direct investment (FDI), and in the last decade, rising

---

3 Radosevic (2009) offers a very good summary discussion on the topic.

4 Below we use CEE for the EU member states in the region – namely Bulgaria, the Czech Republic, Hungary, Estonia, Latvia, Lithuania, Poland, Romania, Slovakia and Slovenia.

interest in innovation as a driver for economic growth. In addition, although coming from different experiences in the pre–Washington Consensus era (i.e., import substitution and the Soviet system), both regions were – at the time of liberalization – in the process of building and consolidating endogenous capabilities for science and technology.

Currently, despite the public policy efforts, which remain low in comparison to frontier countries, both regions display a persistent gap in innovation capabilities and efforts. Investment in R&D is not on a rising trend; investment in human resources for S&T is marginal, while production indicators are not encouraging either as the low number of scientific publications and patents suggest, for example.

A comparative look at R&D investment trend shows the asymmetry between Latin America, Central and Eastern Europe and the rest of the world (see Figure 12.1). Early industrializers such as the US and the "old" European countries show almost stable expenditure in R&D as a percent of GDP since 1990. Relatively recent catching-up countries like Finland and South Korea have markedly increased their R&D efforts. This growth has been the result of a deep structural change that transformed those economies into high

Figure 12.1. R&D investment as a percentage of GDP, selected countries and regions

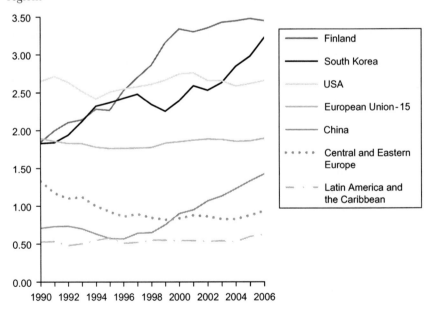

Source: OECD-MSTI database, RICYT.
Note: Central and Eastern European data consists of the average of the Czech Republic, Hungary, Poland, Slovak Republic, Romania and Slovenia.

technology producers and exporters thanks to the implementation of policies tailored to strengthen domestic technological capabilities.[5] On the contrary, Central and Eastern European countries decreased the intensity of R&D investments due to the change in the prevailing policy model. In turn, Latin American countries show persistence in the marginal R&D effort, which is consistent with the marginal changes that occurred in its production structure along the last two decades.

The asymmetry with frontier countries persists when we look at the expenditure on R&D by sector of performance. In frontier economies firms carry out the majority of R&D activities, followed by higher education institutes and the government. Similarly, in Central and Eastern Europe the private sector delivers the majority of R&D activities, however, the involvement of the private sector in R&D is lower than in more industrialized countries.[6] The pattern in LA differs; the majority of R&D is executed by the government or by the higher education sector (Table 12.1).

As for trends in higher education, more similarity appears with respect to frontier economies. Both LA and CEE substantially increased the stock of skilled human resources form the 1970s onwards; however the gap in relation to advanced countries persists, as shown below in Figure 12.2.

Within the region there are differences which international cross-country comparisons hide. In Latin America, the more proactive countries in terms of R&D spending are Brazil, Mexico, Argentina, Chile and Cuba, which as a whole account for almost 80 percent of regional spending. R&D expenditure in Latin America is mostly carried out by the state in contrast to more advanced economies; however patterns differ. In Argentina, Brazil, Mexico, Paraguay and Uruguay enterprises carry out more than 30 percent of total R&D spending, while in Ecuador and Colombia the participation of the private sector in R&D execution is extremely low. The three countries with the highest ratio of researchers per million habitants in the region are Cuba, Argentina and Chile, while the ranking for absolute numbers of researchers is as follows: Brazil in first followed by Mexico and then Argentina. As for the mobility of graduate and postgraduate students, Argentina and Chile are the preferred destination within the countries of the region even though the US, the UK and Spain are the top foreign destinations for Latin American students (ECLAC 2008b).

---

5 Hobday (2009) offers an excellent discussion of evolution of East Asian industrial and innovation policies in response to changing technological paradigms during the last five decades. On Finland, see Ylä-Anttila and Lemola (2006).

6 The CEE picture changes quite significantly when one adds the Baltic countries and Bulgaria and Romania, as the private sector share decreases.

Table 12.1. R&D expenditure by sector of performance, 2006 (%)

Latin America and the Caribbean	Government	Enterprises	Higher education	Private non-profit
	20	40.9	37.1	2
Argentina	40.7	30.4	26.5	2.5
Bolivia (2002)	21.0	25.0	41.0	13.0
Brazil (2004)	21.3	40.2	38.4	0.1
Chile (2004)	23.0	26.6	41.8	8.6
Colombia	8.3	22.2	52.8	16.7
Costa Rica (2004)	17.0	28.0	34.0	21.0
Ecuador	75.5	19.0	4.2	1.3
Mexico (2005)	23.2	46.9	28.7	1.1
Panama (2005)	37.1	..	8.6	54.2
Paraguay (2005)	14.6	38.5	35.4	11.5
Peru (2004)	25.6	29.2	38.1	7.1
Trinidad and Tobago (2004)	54.3	23.7	21.9	..
Uruguay (2002)	19.4	49.0	31.6	0.0
Central and Eastern Europe				
Czech Republic	17.5	66.2	15.9	0.4
Hungary	25.4	48.3	24.4	..
Poland	37.0	31.5	31.0	0.4
Slovak Republic	32.8	43.1	24.1	0.1
Slovenia	24.1	60.2	15.1	0.2
Russian Federation	27.0	66.7	6.1	0.3
United States	11.3	71.0	13.5	4.2
Total OECD	11.4	69.1	17.2	2.6
EU-15	12.7	63.9	22.3	1.2
Finland	9.3	71.3	18.7	0.6
Japan	8.3	77.2	12.7	1.9
Korea	11.6	77.3	10.0	1.2
China	19.7	71.1	9.2	..
Singapore	10.3	65.7	23.9	3.7
Israel	5.3	77.2	13.7	0.3

Source: RICYT, OECD-MSTI database and UNESCO.

Figure 12.2. Tertiary enrollment ratio

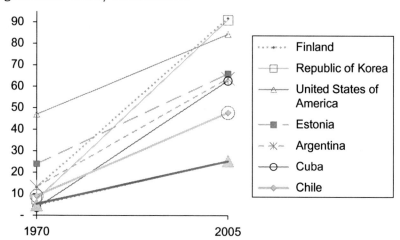

Source: UNESCO, *Global Education Digest 2009*. http://www.uis.unesco.org/Library/Pages/ DocumentMorePage.aspx?docIdValue=80&docIdFld=ID (accessed 16 January 2012).

In CEE there is a clear divide between countries in the EU and those outside of it.[7] The former exhibit relatively homogenous rates of change (e.g. in high-tech exports or FDI inflows – see Kattel, Reinert and Suurna 2012) – whereas the latter, however, (with the exception of Russia perhaps) have seen enormous declines in technological development (World Bank 2008).

In general, LA and CEE show features typical of the periphery: the coexistence of islands of technological excellence with a generalized low-tech and low-skilled labor production structure and marginal positioning in global production chains (ECLAC 2004; ECLAC 2008a; Kattel, Reinert and Suurna 2012). In Brazil and Russia, due to accumulated scientific and technological capabilities and for current political strategies, sustaining production development might play the role of regional geese. Although for the CEE European Union (EU) members, Russia plays an increasingly smaller role in trade; in particular, Central European countries such as Slovakia, Hungary and the Czech Republic have achieved high levels of integration with the EU: merchandising exports in worth of up to 60 percent of GDP in these countries goes to the EU (IMF DOTS database). These countries have become the main trading partners for Germany.

Latin American and Eastern European countries spend comparatively less on R&D (with respect to frontier economies) and invest less in the generation of

---

7 Besides Russia, these are the former Soviet republics: Ukraine, Belarus and Moldova, and former Yugoslavian republics not in the EU (Croatia, Serbia, Bosnia-Herzegovina, FYR Macedonia, Montenegro, Kosovo).

Figure 12.3. Technological specialization and innovation effort

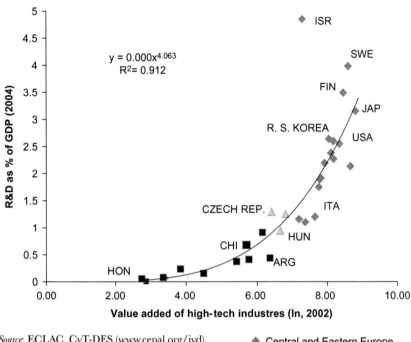

Source: ECLAC, CyT-DES (www.cepal.org/iyd).

human capital for scientific and technological activities. Latin America shows higher intraregional heterogeneity in terms of technological specialization of the production structure with respect to Eastern Europe, which also appears to be relatively more specialized in high-tech activities. This is not surprising considering that higher levels of R&D investments are generally associated with a higher weight of high-tech industries in domestic production structure (see Figure 12.3).

Different industries produce and innovate in different ways. An increase in R&D expenditure with a production structure oriented towards low technology industries is unlikely. The specialization pattern determines the prevailing innovation effort. Hence, incentives to increase R&D investments need to be coupled with policies supporting production and entrepreneurship in key R&D intensive sectors.

The Evolution of Innovation Policy

The evolution of innovation policies in LA and in CEE followed similar patterns. In both regions the efforts related to the creation of domestic scientific and technological capabilities date back to around half a century ago, even though they were framed by two different policy models: the import substitution strategy and the Soviet planned economy. During those years, both regions experienced a period of deliberate state intervention focused on the construction of domestic scientific and technological capabilities.

As a consequence of the debt crisis, both regions experimented similar reform patterns. During the 1990s the two regions followed the Washington Consensus market-oriented approach to development. State intervention was almost banned and markets were supposed to take the lead for structural change and development. It was believed that increased integration into international trade and openness would bring about the right incentives and competition to support modernization and innovation, rationalizing investments and prompting efficiency. However, this was not the case and liberalization clearly proved not to be enough for catching-up.

Microeconomic adjustments required more than openness and competition to transform production structures. The free market approach showed its limits in generating the right incentives for innovation, and specific policies for innovation and development once again gained legitimacy. The 2000s signaled the transition to the post–Washington Consensus strategy (Peres and Primi 2009; Radosevic 2009). Innovation policies returned to the agenda, usually framed under the umbrella of the national innovation systems approach or as plans supporting competitiveness. The 2008 financial crisis might induce a new phase in innovation policy, as countries are urged to redefine investment plans. A brief description of innovation policy in LA and in CEE follows.

Latin America[8]

During the 1950s and 1960s, government actions – which nowadays would be labeled S&T policies – aimed at creating the institutional infrastructure for S&T and at fostering the generation of endogenous scientific and technological capabilities in national priority areas, in line with the industrialization strategy of local production capacities expansion. Government action targeted the creation of scientific and technical knowledge in priority areas for national development. State-owned firms were responsible for carrying out R&D activities in strategic sectors such as transportation and telecommunication, while public research institutes supported research in agriculture, energy, mining, forestry and the aeronautics sector (ECLAC 2004; Cimoli et al. 2005).

Governments invested in the creation of the basic scientific and technological infrastructure to support the national industrialization effort in key scientific and technological areas. For instance, Argentina instituted the

---

8 This subsection draws on Cimoli, Ferraz and Primi (2005).

National Atomic Energy Commission (CNEA) in 1954 and in the Institute for Industrial Technology (INTI) in 1957. Its main function was to provide technology services to state-owned companies.[9] Correspondingly Mexico opened the National Institute for Nuclear Research (ININ), the Electronics Research Institute (IIE), the Mexican Institute for Water Technology (IMTA) and the Mexican Petroleum Institute (IMP). Consistently with a selective industrial focus, Brazil created a series of sectoral institutions. In the early 1950s it established Aerospace Technology Centre (CTA) and almost twenty years later, in 1973, the Agricultural Research Enterprise (EMBRAPA) was created (Burlamaqui et al. 2007). According to the predominant logic of state intervention as an engine of growth, many public enterprises established their own research centers. Those specifically worth mentioning are ELETROBRAS's Electrical Energy Research Centre (CEPEL) and the Leopoldo Américo M. de Mello Research and Development Centre (CENPES) run by PETROBRAS (ECLAC 2004; Pacheco 2003).

This policy model contributed to the creation of S&T infrastructure, creating the basis for future technological upgrading. At the same time, the model was weak in coordinating different sectoral agencies leading to overlapping initiatives and a consequent waste of resources (Capdevielle et al. 2000; ECLAC 2004; Yoguel 2003).

In the 1980s, the debt crisis and the "lost decade" diverted the attention from the long-term industrialization effort. Short-term inflation targeting policies prevailed. Macroeconomic stability was the priority and there was not much room left for policies to foster capability accumulation. In addition, the out-of-crisis recipe (proposed by international financial institutions and well accepted by most of the governments of the region) transformed state intervention into the less desirable tool for technological development.

Open and global markets were supposed to guarantee efficient allocation of resources and ultimately to provide the region with a technological upgrade. Capital goods imports, technology licensing and the need to compete with foreign and more technologically advanced firms would place enough pressure on domestic firms for modernization and innovation. Effectively, Latin American countries modernized their production apparatus as a result of these channels. However, modernization remained circumscribed to leading and larger firms and did not trickle down to the rest of the production structure, contributing to increasing the structural heterogeneity within and between

---

9 For additional information about Argentina, see Yoguel (2003); for Mexico, see Casalet (2003); and for Brazil see Pacheco (2003) and Burlamaqui et al. (2007).

the countries of the region (ECLAC 2008a). Furthermore, Washington Consensus reforms partially deepened macroeconomic problems inherited from the 1970s. As Kregel (2008) stated:

A rapid increase in external financing (much of which was not used for import substitution at all), such as the one that occurred in the 1970s, places a heavy burden on a country's balance of payments that can only be financed by increased foreign borrowing. This appears to have been the case in Latin America in the 1970s as increased borrowing was used to meet increasing debt service in a sort of Ponzi scheme... The problems that were faced by import substitution industrialization were caused as much by the inappropriate and potentially incendiary mix of financing domestic import substitution industrialization through private external financial flows as in the inherent difficulties in building sufficiently large domestic markets to support competitive domestic industry and avoid rent-seeking behavior.

These changes favored the generation of an industrial structure which alone had a low demand for knowledge, implicitly limiting the potential positive stimuli effect towards technological catch up of liberalization and increased competition. In contrast, the Asian economies like Korea and Taiwan followed by Malaysia, Thailand and Indonesia, were successful in creating expanding capabilities in technology intensive industries and production stages, combining selective import substitution policies with aggressive but gradual export-oriented strategies.[10]

The rationalization of regional production processes resulted in "truncated" modernization because the leapfrog towards effective domestic technological upgrading never really happened. Technological upgrading entails the development of endogenous capabilities through complex, dynamic and collective trial and error processes which need to be backed up by targeted policies. In the new global knowledge economy with increasingly powerful foreign actors and weak domestic scientific and technological infrastructure, market incentives increasingly push firms to rely on foreign sources of knowledge. At the same time, the few local results of innovation and technological upgrading tend to be transferred abroad, rather than appropriated locally.

---

10 The literature on the "Asian miracle" is vast; for analysis sustaining the role of policies, see Amsden (1989); Jomo (1997) and Wade (1990). For a comparative analysis of the evolution of industrial development and technological capabilities between Latin American and Asian economies, see Cimoli et al. (2006).

The rising prices of commodities in recent years, the improvement in the terms of trade for natural resources and the consequent appreciation of regional exchange rates have reduced the incentives for the production diversification which favors technological capabilities, undermining S&T policy effectiveness and implementation. A self-reinforcing process of concentration in fewer activities took place, reducing the incentives to learn and invest in other sectors (ECLAC 2008a).

The science and technology policy model of the 1990s emphasized the role of market incentives and of demand-side economics in priority setting. The support to technological upgrading and to private sector innovation focused on areas where market failures occurred, i.e. public policy priority merely consisted of correcting information asymmetries between economic agents. This stance towards public policy meant placing knowledge and innovation on an equal footing with information accessibility. In effect, a conceptual linearity associated with the process of knowledge generation and technology diffusion persisted. Knowledge was supposed to follow a bottom-up, nonhierarchical pattern in a setting in which the engine for innovation generation would supposedly be constituted by the spontaneous demand of the private sector.

The shift in policy models entailed institutional and organizational changes. New management styles were introduced and new institutional bodies were created. In Argentina, for instance, the restructuring of S&T institutional infrastructure led to an increase in coordination among different bodies, partly overcoming what represented a structural limit of the previous period. In Mexico, the priority was the decentralization of S&T institutional management, according to the different technological and specialization patterns of various Mexican regions.

Beyond peculiarities of each country, the reorganization of institutions generally brought about: (1) increments in resources and in the relevance of those S&T agencies dedicated to capture private sector demand for technology and knowledge; (2) an incipient interest towards greater articulation and coordination between the private and public sectors, resulting in greater interest in universities-enterprises connections in all countries; and (3) changes in competencies and objectives of agencies. S&T priorities shifted from basic research to the provision and commercialization of technological services, mainly oriented to support production process management and quality control. Reward systems and management styles of S&T institutions changed as well, moving towards practices that are more in line with market mechanisms and incentive schemes, privileging performance-based models of evaluation and allocation of priorities. Accordingly, the role of international financial institutions as sources of financing for S&T augmented.

In more recent years, policies gradually started to regain a certain degree of legitimization, usually under the label of policies for competitiveness or cluster development. Such policy evolution naturally entailed a nationally based focus of policies and instruments. The primary effort of building domestic capabilities and infrastructure as well as the focus on competitiveness required a national consensus and a primary look at the country's needs and priorities.

The management of policies for science technology and innovation follows different institutional arrangements in the countries of the region. Argentina, Brazil, Cuba, Costa Rica and Venezuela have ministries for S&T, while in the other countries the policy responsibility is placed in national councils that, in general, respond to the presidency, the Ministry of Education or to the Ministry of Economy. Beyond asymmetries in institutional infrastructure, there are considerable differences among countries in terms of origins of funds, magnitude of administered budgets, objectives and priorities. Each country establishes its own science and technology policy that is more or less formalized and contextualized according to the institutional development, the complexity of the production apparatus and articulation of the national innovation system.[11] The sets of instruments for S&T policies are well known in the countries of the region. Usually the bottlenecks appear more frequently at the level of implementation and management than at the level of policy design. In short, three main issues are the instruments for supporting human capital formation and public private partnership, technology funds and the rising topic of IP management.

An area of general consensus is the support for human capital formation for S&T. Brazil, with its articulated system of grants and loans for financing university postgraduate studies, produces around 7,000 PhDs per year and scores the highest in domestically formed PhDs in the region – accounting for more than 70 percent of total Latin American PhDs, according to RICYT's estimates. Almost all countries have (at least at the level of policy design) some measures to support human capital formation. In Argentina, the 2004 Argentine National Plan for Technology and Production Innovation put the strengthening of national scientific and technological base through supporting PhDs formation in its forefront. In Chile, the National Commission for Scientific and Technological Research (CONICYT) supports postgraduate

---

11 In November 2007, a group of countries of the region signed a protocol agreement expressing the political support for the generation of a regional dialogue for S&T policies for increasing cooperation in S&T policy formulation and implementation in the frame of the ECLAC activities for S&T policies. The issue of regional cooperation in S&T policy represents a key element in the management of S&T policies in global knowledge economies (Primi 2009).

training through a series of articulated ad hoc programs oriented to assist PhD formation within the country and through international networking. The Bolivian National Secretary for Science, Technology and Innovation, the Colombian National Program for Industrial and Technological Development 2000–10 and the Uruguayan National Service for C&T (SENACYT) and FUNDACYT support graduate and doctoral human capital formation through credit and grants systems. In Costa Rica, support to graduate and postgraduate studies is mainly coming from private universities, while in Mexico the National Council for Science and Technology (CONACYT) allocates public funds for sustaining high-level human capital formation and the public research centers (CPI) directly intervene in human capital formation and subsidize it through grants which are financed by specific CPI funds. According to a selective intervention strategy, in Peru the Genome Program finances graduate formation in genetics, while the Paraguayan 2002 National C&T policy prioritizes formation in the engineering and mining sectors, for example.

Resources to finance S&T activities are channeled for the most part through technology funds. At the country level, deep differences emerge in terms of beneficiaries and targets (research centers, enterprises, and special treatment given in certain cases to SMEs), source of financing i.e. (national – private or public – and international) and in terms of access mechanisms – basically supply or demand-side mechanisms or mixed. Since the structural reforms, technology funds have been fostering the promotion of consultancies and technical assistance services aiming to reinforce R&D in universities, research centers and enterprises. Two main categories of funds exist in the region, one is oriented towards demand and the other emphasizes the coordination between demand and supply.

The demand subsidy scheme which prevails in Argentina, Chile, Costa Rica and Mexico, channels public funds or loans from international organizations to S&T activities, subsidizing the demand by following a horizontal logic based on the evaluation of proposals and applications directly presented by potential recipients (enterprises or research centers). For instance, the Argentine Technological Fund (FONTAR) prioritize 5 areas in S&T development: (1) technological development of new products, services or production processes; (2) technological modernization, i.e. improvement of products and processes, training; (3) promotion of the technological services market, supporting research laboratories and business research centers activities; (4) training and technical assistance; and (5) technological advisory assistance programs especially to strengthen small and medium-sized enterprises' technological performance. The fund, which allocates resources on the basis of a demand-pull mechanism, is made up of national financial resources originating from the national budget, fiscal credit law, credit lines offered by public banks and resources originating from international loans (IADB loans according to the Argentine Modernization Plan).

The FONTAR assigns financial resources to demanding beneficiaries principally in the form of nonrepayable contributions, loans, subsidies and fiscal credit according to specific objectives and prospective beneficiaries. This kind of system, where access to incentives for innovation depends upon a direct initiative of potential targets, may lead to increasing heterogeneity in technological behaviors because it could ingenerate adverse selection mechanisms among recipients. In the demand subsidy scheme, incentives to resort to financial assistance for innovation are biased. More proactive agents, which perhaps have a comparative advantage in technological upgrading and that could probably master technological innovation without resorting to public funds, will be more prone to submit projects for evaluation while more technologically backward actors will face higher barriers to participate in this scheme. A further weakness of the demand subsidy model is that a proper information dissemination policy is needed in order to allow beneficiaries to be aware of the possibility offered by the financing schemes. The main reason for the subutilization of technological funds managed under a demand-oriented mechanism is that potential beneficiaries lack information.[12]

The Brazilian system of sectoral technology funds, introduced in 1999, overcomes the limits of a purely demand-based or technology-pushed incentive scheme. It represents a step forward in regional technology policy design on two accounts, first regarding mechanisms to finance S&T and second in terms of operational management. 12 industrial technological funds were set up through 12 sectoral laws that identify the amount of the income generated in each industrial sector that has to be devoted to support S&T development in the corresponding industry. These 12 industrial funds then collectively contribute to sustain S&T and R&D in three priority non-industry-specific areas for which three respective funds are set up (cooperation among universities, research centers and enterprises, maintenance and improvement of R&D infrastructure and development of S&T activities in the Amazonian region). The Brazilian sectoral technology fund scheme entails a strategic collective management approach. Representatives of academies and research centers, industrial ministries, members of the Ministry for Science and Technology, the business sector and regulatory bodies constitute a mixed management committee that run each technological fund according to a coordinated and consensual strategy. This mechanism – which has the great advantage of

---

12 See Casalet (2003), Jaramillo (2003), Pacheco (2003), Vargas Alfaro and Segura Bonilla (2003) and Yoguel (2003).

promoting coordination and stimulating interaction between the private and public sectors in technological management – is hard to manage and could originate serious governance troubles which could lead to a subutilization of the funds.

In addition to funds there are the fiscal incentive schemes, which essentially take the form of tax credits and deductions for different types of R&D activities according to the categories of involved actors and public development bank loans. Both mechanisms are marginal in terms of use, even though information on fiscal incentive laws is quite easily accessible in many cases. Fiscal incentives are powerful tools to foster selective development of S&T activities because they allow prioritizing in a simple way.[13] Risk capital is an indirect form of fostering science and technology development. Public institutions act as a convoy for private financial resources that flow through risk capital operations to business activities consenting to convert technologically advanced projects into operating production entities.[14] Despite their worldwide-recognized role in favoring technological development, risk capital businesses are hardly found in Latin America and the Caribbean.[15] Scant development of financial markets and institutions and strong uncertainty and volatility of regional macro setting could partly account for the low presence of risk capital operations in Latin America due to the close linkage existing between this form innovative and risky business support and financial markets.

A rising topic related with S&T policy is intellectual property (IP) management. There have been several changes in this domain in recent times. On the one hand, there have been changes in international IP management – such as the TRIPS agreement in 1994 – and the wave of bilateral free trade agreements (FTA) and bilateral investment treaties (BIT) containing IP provisions.[16] On the other hand, a changing attitude towards patenting

---

13 In effect they are being used to foster institutional infrastructure development and maintenance, as in the case of Mexico, and to promote patenting related activities as this has been happening in Brazil since the year 2002 when tax deductions for enterprises that carry out R&D activities were doubled if the business units were granted the patent for which they applied for.

14 Risk capital industries are based on private capitals but need public policies to create a favorable environment, to foster liquidity in financial markets, promote adequate regulatory and incentive systems and to encourage the involvement of public and private agents in innovation and technological upgrading.

15 The Argentine program to support technology based enterprises and risk capital, the Brazilian INOVAR project and Risk Capital Portal, the Colombian fund for risk capital investments, the risk capital initiative of the multisectoral investment bank in El Salvador and the Mexican capital risk fund for technological development are some regional initiatives in terms of risk capital financing.

16 See Cimoli et al. (2009) for an analysis of recent changes in IP regimes.

and privatization of knowledge has emerged. In the US, the Bayh–Dole Act of 1980 introduced the possibility for universities to patent discoveries obtained through federal funds.[17] After the adoption of TRIPS, most Latin American and Caribbean countries introduced substantial changes in IPR (intellectual property rights) regimes. The expansion of IPR resulted in the introduction of minimum standards, the increasing number of products and processes eligible for patents and in the license to import already patented products by means of including this activity under the umbrella of "sufficient exploitation."

More recently, countries started to recognize the relevance of IP for their catching-up. They have pushed for a change in IP governance – both at the bilateral and multilateral level – rather than for a change in terms of the organizational behavior of institutions dealing with IP management.[18] IP systems are a complex governing arena whose operating mechanisms are not easily manageable. Effective IP management requires proper infrastructure and institutions, actor preparedness, a suitable legal architecture and adequate enforcing mechanisms. Countries need to define their own policy towards the subject matter of patents (this is as especially relevant in the case of biotechnology and biopharmaceuticals as it is for publicly funded research) and they need to develop an IP policy in line with their production and innovation development policy.

In recent times, another common feature of S&T policies in the countries of the region is the increasing concern in fostering interaction and coordination between the public sector (mainly universities and research laboratories) and the private sector (essentially enterprises) in research and development. Most financing mechanisms emphasize articulation and coparticipation of supply and demand in technological upgrading, establishing incentive schemes to foster cooperation between them through various channels. Private–public partnerships might be a prerequisite for applying for financial support, otherwise additional mechanisms might favor the transfer of capacities between the different agents. An example is the new Brazilian Innovation Law in which

---

17 Beyond the reflection that this provision would foster the dissemination of university research to production, various analysts have raised concerns regarding the drawbacks of the so-called "privatization of scientific activities," which entails rising costs to access basic research results, augmented patenting overheads and amplified risks and costs of legal controversies (Correa 2003). In reality, the "public nature" of knowledge is definitively shifting towards the private and club goods domain, where access is ruled by given market mechanisms, thus incrementing access barriers to basic research's results.

18 For a critical discussion on the development agenda presented to WIPO see De Beer (2009).

greater degree of freedom is given to university researchers for undertaking temporary research at private sector institutions. These initiatives, however, are yet to gain strength and economic significance as budgets remain low and practices are still not in accordance with the behavior of production agents. In effect, the poor results of these regional S&T supporting mechanisms could be due to the asymmetry between this attention to coordination and the characteristics of regional production specialization, alongside reduced budgets. The Latin American and Caribbean production pattern induces the private sector and enterprises to express a meager demand for knowledge, and additionally leads domestic agents to seek mostly outward-oriented linkages, privileging foreign companies and research laboratories that already have sound reputations and worldwide recognized experience in effective and efficient S&T efforts. Thus, a mismatch ensues between demand side needs and supply side offerings, hampering the impact of policies.

Policies to support the creation of research consortia, science parks and public–private partnership for research have been designed – although seldom implemented – in almost all the countries of the region.[19] Although this recent shift in the policy model overcomes the drawback of linearity in policy conception, allowing interaction and cooperation between public and private sector, this new model seems to be a kind of "soft" policy approach. The linkage with sectoral differences and industrial priorities is still missing, and neutrality prevails over selection. Latin America needs to go beyond good intentions in policy formulation and to avoid the typical mismatch between supply and demand in public policy intervention.

The most notable example is the newly launched (May 2008) Brazilian production development policy, which represents the most advanced effort in Latin America in terms of policy design and articulation. The policy is under the general coordination of the Ministry of Development, Industry and Trade (MDIC). Above this ministry, there is a consultative body responsible for identifying the policy's main priorities (the National Industrial Development Council, CNDI). This well-articulated, albeit complex, institutional design also comprises an executive secretariat composed by the representatives of National Economic and Social Development Bank (BNDES), the Ministry of Finance (MF) and the Brazilian Industrial Development Agency (ABDI). The creation of the executive board responds to the need to reduce institutional bottlenecks that hamper the operation of even well-designed industrial policies, which usually tend to be managed by ministries which are less powerful than

---

19 For a review of policy instruments to support S&T development by country for Latin America and the Caribbean see the ECLAC-GTZ database, available at www.cepal.org/iyd.

institutions in charge of disbursing the financial resources. Ministries in charge of specific issues are responsible for the identification of their strategies and for coordination with the production development policy – the Ministry of Science, Technology and Industry, the Ministry of Health, etc. (Peres and Primi 2009). This institutional design allows for linkages between science and technology policies aimed at production development, thus overcoming the chronicle mismatch between policies fostering innovation and policies fostering production.

Central and Eastern Europe[20]

We can boil down the existing scientific and policy-analytical literature to the identification of two fundamental problems that persist in the innovation systems of CEE countries since a decade (if not for a longer period).[21] First, in most CEE countries there is a long-standing and strong mismatch between R&D and education system outcomes and industry needs. This mismatch has, in turn, two mutually enforcing aspects. Innovation policies in CEE tend to focus on high technology (for instance, commercialization of R&D results, technology parks, incubators, etc.); furthermore, actual economic and industrial structure is characterized by low productivity growth and dominated by outsourcing activities with very low demand for R&D or indeed for most outcomes targeted by innovation policies. Second, in most CEE countries innovation policies suffer from double fragmentation. On the one hand, there is a strong fragmentation and divide between various actors in the innovation system (universities, companies and governments); on the other hand, also within the public sector, fragmentation between various policy areas (education, industry, energy etc.) is strong. Such double fragmentation leads to massive systematic coordination failures in policy design, implementation and evaluation. Clearly, the two challenges are connected and mutually enforce each other. In this section, however, we intend to show how these challenges originate from the application of Washington Consensus policy toolbox to CEE economies. Moreover, as the European Union recognized and emphasized these problems throughout the accession talks and during the negotiations for implementation of EU's structural funding in the 2000s, its influence has perversely consolidated or

---

20 This subsection builds on Kattel et al. (2009) and Karo and Kattel, (2009).
21 For detailed country overviews see the European Commission's Innovation TrendChart, 2006 and 2007; see also Radosevic (2004 and 2006); Reid and Peter (2008); and Kattel et al. (2009). Best research on the CEE innovation systems from the late 1990s also covers the earlier transition period, see in particular Radosevic (1998, 1999).

even deepened these challenges. At the same time, it is a clear step towards much more coherent innovation policies in CEE. In addition, there are success cases, Slovenia for instance, which have followed from the outset a rather different approach to innovation policy strongly focused on local capacity building, (Drahokoupil 2007).

Restructuring the Soviet R&D system and industry

By the end of the 1980s, Eastern European and former Soviet economies were generally highly industrialized and many of these economies were seemingly on the same path of industrialization and growth as the East Asian economies. According to the World Bank data, countries like Estonia, Latvia and Hungary were ahead of Korea in the early 1980s in terms of industrial value added per capita. However, the industrialization of CEE countries was widely understood to be highly artificial and ineffective, meaning that excessive resources and other inputs were being employed to produce goods. Thus, after becoming independent once again, restructuring the economy (and in particular the industry) was at the top of the agenda for all CEE countries. In fact, in many ways what was desired was not so much restructuring as was outright replacement of the old Soviet industrial complex with one similar to the Western industries.

Washington Consensus policies offered a very coherent and relatively simple set of policies to deliver the restructuring and replacement. As all CEE countries set out to implement reforms inspired by the Washington Consensus, Drahokoupil (2007, 90) offers a very interesting categorization of group different strategies followed by CEE countries in 1990s: "The competition states in the Visegrád four can be called Porterian, aiming at attracting strategic FDI through targeted subsidies... The Baltic competition states can be called macroeconomic stability-driven neoliberal states with monetary institutions at their core... Finally, Slovenia has developed a distinct type of competition state, which can be characterized as a balanced neo-corporatist." However, as Weissenbacher (2007, 71) argues, Hungary, Poland and Yugoslavia already had experiences of dealing with IMF during 1980s when they borrowed from it and applied standard austerity programs. Thus, while there are clearly differences in accents, the general framework offered by the Washington Consensus was applied in all CEE countries throughout the 1990s; indeed the policy sets were actually converging during this time (Drahokoupil 2007).

Furthermore, Washington Consensus–inspired policies were considered by most CEE countries as *the* innovation and industrial policy measures and in essence there were no other policy initiatives during 1990s. During this period, almost all economic policies were directed towards macroeconomic competencies (being led therefore by central banks, ministries of finance and think-tanks). This was greatly helped by the advice and assistance from the Washington institutions such the World Bank and IMF, but also from OECD. Innovation policy was considered as secondary to transition related concerns. As there were no proper innovation policies, there was essentially no institution building for or in innovation systems. Washington Consensus-inspired policies were understood to deliver the economic stability to attract foreign direct investments that should become vehicles of delivering actual restructuring and replacement of Soviet industry. In other words, market demand was understood to deliver economic restructuring and would lead to the reform of the innovation system (R&D, educational systems, labor policy etc.). Building up capacity in specific areas of innovation systems seemed superfluous; indeed, the R&D system was seen in many ways as too big (employing too many people) and ineffective (too far from the private sector) (Radosevic 1998, 1999).

In reality, the Washington Consensus policies were ultimately too effective in destroying the old industrial structure. After the fall of the Berlin Wall, most CEE and other former Soviet economies watched their growth rates plummet. It took more than a decade for most CEE countries to reach the growth and development levels of 1990 (see Tiits et al. 2008). This is particularly so in the case of former Soviet republics. According the World Bank's (2006) calculations, the recession that many former Soviet republics (e.g. Ukraine) experienced during 1990s, and are still experiencing, is worse than the Great Depression in the US and World War II in Western Europe (in both cases, recovery was considerably quicker).

This cognitive dissonance between promise of reforms and actual developments was caused by one of the most striking features of post-Soviet development in the 1990s: the rapid primitivization of industrial enterprises or even the outright destruction of many previously well-known and successful companies. This happened because of the way Soviet industrial companies were built up and ran in a complex web of planning and competition (Radosevic 1998). A sudden opening of the markets and abolition of capital controls made these industrial companies extremely vulnerable. The partially extreme vertical integration that was the norm in such companies meant that if one part of the value chain ran into problems due to the rapid liberalization, it easily brought down the entire chain or complex. However, foreign companies seeking to privatize plants were almost always interested in only part of the value-chain (a specific production plant, infrastructure or location) and thus privatization turned into the publicly induced attrition of companies and shedding of jobs (see Frost and Weinstein 1998; Young 1994).

Such a drastic change made it relatively easy to *replace* Soviet industry; with the macroeconomic stability and liberalization of markets followed by a rapid drop in wages, many former Soviet economies became increasingly attractive as privatization targets and destinations for the outsourcing of production. Indeed, one of the most fundamental characteristics of CEE industry (and services) since 1990 has been that the majority of companies have engaged in process innovation (i.e. in the form of acquisition of new machinery and mastery of production capabilities) in seeking to become more and more cost-effective in the new market place (Tiits et al. 2008).

Perversely mirroring the "cluster"-like characteristic of Soviet industrial activities described above, the Soviet R&D system was based on similar vertical integration of R&D into specialized institutions: "Under socialism, most technical change was pushed from one institutional sector…which was essentially a grouping of R&D institutes and other related activities… This sector involved in activities far beyond R&D including design, engineering and often trouble-shooting activities" (Radosevic 1999, 282). These institutions also were usually the originators and carriers of patents and forms of intellectual property rights (285). This means that the Soviet-style R&D system had very low levels of in-house R&D (Radosevic 1998, 80–1). Industrial conglomerates were effectively cut off from various potential learning and feedback loops; production and actual innovation (in particular in form of new products and processes) took place in different institutions – both however highly concentrated and integrated. Thus, in general the system was highly linear and supply based.

Once carried out within local enterprises and institutions, the complex tasks of engineering, designing (or similar) were very rapidly replaced by significantly simpler commodified support activities as many companies were wiped out, privatized or restructured. The former R&D institutes could have played a key role in bridging academic research with industry needs as they were essentially the only existing link between the two. With the collapse of the institutes system, the link between academy–industry became, as Radosevic suspected in 1998, the weakest link in the CEE R&D system (1998, 90). Indeed, in "conditions of high uncertainty and prolonged privatization, the intangible assets and know-how of industrial institutes, primarily embodied in R&D groups, probably erodes much faster than production skills in industry" (1998, 100).

Massive onslaughts of FDI, in particular after the second half of the 1990s, and the privatization of enterprises gave foreign enterprises a key role in industrial restructuring and innovation. This, in turn, only reinforced the severing of linkages between former R&D institutes and enterprise sector (See also Radosevic 1999, 297).

Thus, we can sum up the key features of CEE innovation systems before the accession into the EU as follows:

- privatization programs and other measures to attract foreign direct investments;
- emphasis on macroeconomic stability;
- erosion and partial disintegration of the previous Soviet R&D system;
- market demand as key force of restructuring and reform of innovation system.

Europeanization of innovation policy in CEE since 1998

While the EU's importance for CEE countries economic policies was visible already during the early 1990s, the change that increased the EU's impact considerably was the beginning of accession talks with most CEE countries in 1998 and later. Indeed, Havlik et al. (2001) argue that the adoption of the EU's *acquis communautaire* has had a much stronger impact on the modernization of CEE industry than official (often rudimentary) innovation policy during 1990s. The introduction of new regulation (usually with significantly higher safety, health and other standards) meant that CEE industry "was forced to choose whether to modernize their products and production facilities rather drastically, to subject themselves to mergers with bigger players with greater economies of scale, or to close down altogether" (Tiits et al. 2008, 76–7). In essence, the harmonization process was a continuation of restructuring processes that started during the previous period and were even significantly enforced. Likewise, through so-called prestructural funding and its management, many CEE countries started to develop strategic documents and policies related to innovation and R&D proper. In this sense the EU integration played an enormously positive role in all CEE countries and their innovation policies.

However, similarly to Washington Consensus–inspired reforms in 1990s, harmonizing with the EU was by and large deemed to legitimize the CEE's path further. Thus, the end itself (accession to the EU) became much more important than what was being harmonized and how it being harmonized. Due to considerable self-imposed time pressure – harmonizing the legal infrastructure and preparing for accession in six years – the adoption the of EU's legal infrastructure was done hastily and without much attention to local context (Phare Consolidated Summary Report 2004, 2007; see also Schimmelfennig and Sedelmeier 2004; Goetz 2001).

There were two main vehicles of harmonization, the Phare funding mechanism and later prestructural funding. Phare was launched in 1989 as the EU's financial instrument to assist the CEE countries (initially only

Hungary and Poland) in their political and economic transition from a centralized communist system to a decentralized liberal democratic system. In the late 1990s, due to the progressive decentralization of the PHARE management structures as well as EU requirement for creation of regional and local institutions to administer the EU funds after the accession, a system of implementation agencies/administrative agents linked to the National Fund was created and pursued in CEE (European Commission 2003; Grabbe 2006, 82). This marks the first step in CEE towards managing economic policy, thus innovation and industrial restructuring in a distinctly different manner from the previous period where the free market and external forces were seen as key drivers of change. However, it is also important to note that these newly established agencies were created mostly in order to manage external funding – policy creation and respective capacity building plays almost no role in these agencies. The compartmentalized and structured nature of EU support (Phare Consolidated Summary Report 2007) and the lack of a tradition of partnership and interinstitutional coordination and cooperation between administrative levels meant that most positive effects of such agencies were not reaped and that in some cases they created more difficulties and problems than they solved (ESPON 2005).

In sum, in many ways the harmonization with the EU rules is a period in which policies supported the restructuring of the industry that began in 1990s under the Washington Consensus policies. Nonetheless, during this period the EU's influence on funding and administrative schemes led to the creation of novel governance structures that still play a key part in innovation policy in CEE to this day.

While harmonization with the EU legal infrastructure was important both in terms of actual changes it brought to industry and in terms of policy implementation/administrative agencies that were created to manage EU's financial help, the key changes in innovation policy proper came with EU structural funding,[22] which started in 2004 and is set to continue at least until 2013. Indeed, as we will see below, the EU structural funding significantly changed both the policy content and implementation. However, key problems that emerged during the 1990s (low networking, weak coordination and significant cooperation problems) have in fact been deepened during the current period.

The key content for many innovation policy initiatives in the CEE emerging after the accession was the underlying assumption that similarly to "old" European countries, the new members also need to overcome the so-called

---

22 For a general overview, see the EU's official homepage for structural funding http://ec.europa.eu/regional_policy/funds/prord/sf_en.htm.

"*European paradox*" (good basic research, low commercialization of the research results).[23] Thus, CEE innovation policies emerging in the early and mid-2000s tend to concentrate on high technology sectors, commercializing university research, technology parks for start-ups and similar efforts (Radosevic 2002, 355; Radosevic and Reid 2006, 297; see also the INNO-Policy TrendChart country reports for 2006 and 2007 for comprehensive overviews of the CEE countries' policies and challenges) In terms of content, an overwhelming number of policy measures concentrate on innovation programs and technology platforms (Reid and Peter 2008). At the same time, the CEE emerging innovation policies are characterized by their horizontal nature; policy measures typically do not specify sectors but rather are rather to all sectors. Arguably, this has to do with the way CEE policymakers understood EU state aid regulations (Reid and Peter 2008). We argue that this has to do with both the general neoliberal outlook inherited from the 1990s (i.e. market demand is seen as the key driver for the R&D system) internalized by most CEE policymakers by early the 2000s and also with their particular skills which emphasized macroeconomic management (see also Drahokoupil 2007).

In addition, as the majority of CEE measures are financed through EU structural funds; these instruments are mostly competition and project-based. Such aspects – project-based implementation, a multitude of horizontal measures – point to high fragmentation of the entire innovation policy field as well as to the lack of policy priorities or the ability to set the latter. It is also evidence of the strongly market-driven understanding of innovation that is at odds with underlying assumptions that innovation policies need to alleviate the "European paradox." That is, typical CEE innovation policy measure aims to commercialize a certain R&D result, typically in the high-tech sector, but the result and thus the initiative has to come from the market. This, however, has scarcely any justifications in reality: first, CEE R&D systems and their performance disintegrated heavily during 1990s; second, this was complemented by the strong specialization in the low-end of various value-chains, meaning that the demand for R&D and skills remains relatively low.

In terms of implementation, the trend initiated during the harmonization period through creation of financial and management agencies has been intensified with the structural funds (see the INNO-Policy TrendChart country reports for 2006 and 2007 for an overview). It is fair to say that the problems with these agencies that started during the harmonization period have partially deepened since 2004. Indeed, it can be argued that most problems summarized above in CEE innovation policies go in one way or another back to the institutional framework of agencies. Almost all CEE innovation policy

---

23 An excellent discussion of the paradox is Dosi et al. (2005).

implementation problems go back to very weak and disorganized actors, while coordination problems are rampant in policy design and implementation (see also Radosevic 2002, 355). On the one hand, there is a clear separation of policy responsibility between education/science and innovation/industry at the ministerial level and its delivery system (also see the INNO-Policy TrendChart country reports for 2006 and 2007). On the other hand, this kind of fragmented policymaking system has, in its turn, resulted in the lack of interlinking and cooperation between different innovation-related activities and actors such as research organizations, government and industry (see the INNO-Policy TrendChart country reports for 2006 and 2007).

Thus, with the introduction of structural funds and through strong influence from the European Commission, CEE innovation policies have been significantly changing since the mid-2000s, yet there are also serious problems that emerged with this trend. First, as we argued, the emerging innovation policies tend to be based on a rather linear understanding of innovation (from lab to market) whereas most CEE countries are specialized into low end production activities virtually void of any research and with low demand for high skills; in addition, the R&D system, as such, has been under constant pressure since the transition and its performance has been clearly lacking. Thus, CEE innovation policies tend to solve problems that do not in fact exist in the respective economies and in this context, the problem of misunderstanding of the Soviet R&D and industry in 1990s is replicated in the policymaking model of the 2000s.

Second, through creation of innovation policy implementation/administrative agencies (for structural funding and beyond), the innovation policy landscape is fragmented and previous problems in policy creation (lack of strategic skills and capacity, networking and coordination nonexistent) and implementation (competitive grant-based programming that relies on market signals without being able to follow set priorities and goals) are only deepened. One can argue that the innovation policies emerging in the process of Europeanization are based on the assumption that policy design and implementation follow a public–private partnership model, yet in reality CEE countries singularly lack the ability to implement such a model and, what is more, actual developments in industry seem to suggest that such a model is particularly ill-fitted to the CEE context.

In addition, there is an essential problem that CEE economic and innovation policymakers ignored throughout 1990s and 2000s when devising policies to deliver economic restructuring and growth. Stable macroeconomic environments envisioned to enable FDI inflow – in which CEE were indeed spectacularly successful – also encouraged massive private foreign lending (mostly through foreign banks settling into CEE markets that borrowed in foreign currency). This prompted consumption and real-estate booms in all

CEE countries, in particular after the mid-2000s (see Fitch Research, 2007a, 2007b, 2007c). Indeed, most CEE countries were highly dependent on foreign investments and private borrowing and thus were caught in a macroeconomic dead-end with appreciating exchange rates, negative current account balances and growing private indebtedness. This led to increased financial fragility through deteriorating balance of payments account and left CEE countries starving for new foreign lending and investments that however stopped in the aftermath of the global financial meltdown in 2008. In essence, the CEE industrial restructuring and innovation model became a giant Ponzi scheme. As global and especially inner-EU demand slows, so do CEE exports and by early 2009 most CEE currencies saw massive drops in their value and foreign investors seemed to flee en masse. As a result, debt deflation looks like a very probable scenario for the coming years. The fragmented innovation policy scene, inherited from the accession into the EU, paralyzes CEE countries into inaction as there seems to be no serious policy evaluation capacity present, and coordination problems prevent quick reaction to radically changed environment.

Thus, we can sum up the influence of the EU upon CEE innovation systems as follows:

- a much more active role of the state in structural and innovation policies;
- policies that concentrate on commercialization and other R&D aspects; high technology bias certified;
- increasing fragmentation of the policy arena through agencies resulting in substantial coordination problems;
- growing mismatch between R&D system, high-tech biased innovation policy and actual industry needs.

Policy Models in a Comparative Perspective

It is possible to identify three main phases in the evolution of innovation policy in LA and in CEE (see Table 12.2). During the import substitution phase in LA and the Soviet administration in CEE, a linear supply policy regime prevailed. The state was actively involved in the generation of the basic scientific and technological infrastructure (national research institutes and public research laboratories in strategic areas) as a support to the generation of production capacities in sectors such as the mechanical, nuclear, transportation and telecommunication. The linear supply model implicitly assumed that scientific progress would automatically be converted into technological innovation. Policy measures were selective in terms of targeted sectors and the provision of knowledge was centralized and basically in the hand of public laboratories. S&T policies were a component of the industrialization strategy and ultimately

Table 12.2. Evolution of innovation policy models in LA and CEE: A comparative perspective

Period	LA : Post–Washington / CEE: Soviet system	Washington Consensus	LA : Post-Washington Consensus / CEE : Accession to the EU	Post-2008–9 financial crisis
Policy regime	Linear supply model	Linear demand model	Public–private partnership model	
Main perspective	Public sector as main S&T provider	Private sector as main source of T&I	Public–private partnership as main source of knowledge and technology transfer	
Pattern of knowledge diffusion	Hierarchical: top-down	Hierarchical: bottom-up	Systemic	Towards a new policy model?
Main policy measures	Selective and centralized supply S&T policies	Horizontal and demand-oriented innovation policies + technology transfer via FDI	Public–private partnership and multidisciplinary-oriented T&I policies	
Management criteria of S&T institutions	Predominance of criteria coming from the scientific community and the state-owned companies	Predominance of private sector and market mechanisms	Increasing orientation towards participatory approach in policy management and creation of agencies fostering public–private interaction	

Source: Own elaboration based on Cimoli et al. (2005) and Kattel et al. (2009).

supported the creation of basic capabilities for supporting production in key strategic sectors. The model was not perfect in itself, as all models are not – but it served the purpose of creating the institutional infrastructure and the basic capabilities for the transition towards industrialization. Some drawbacks of the model were the lack of coordination between different activities and the lack of mechanisms for avoiding the capture of rents by incumbents.

In the 1990s both regions followed the Washington Consensus and embraced a series of market-led reforms. However, while it was sure that reforms were needed in the management of policies to support production development and the accumulation of technological capabilities, the obsession with macroeconomic stability led to marginalization of policies directed to microeconomic behavior. Reforms of the previous linear supply model were needed; however the change in policy model induced by the Washington Consensus failed to target and correct the shortcomings of the previous model. Instead they introduced a radical shift concerning the policy model adopted. State intervention was minimized, and a linear demand-oriented policy regime was introduced. The market logic ruled the innovation policy discourse, and the private sector was seen as the primary repository of knowledge and innovation capabilities. Getting the framework conditions right, simplifying mechanisms for technology transfer (especially North–South in the case of LA) and establishing funds and credits for innovating firms were the mostly accepted policy tools. The reforms favored the modernization of the production apparatus through rising capital imports and FDI. However, in the case of LA the modernization strengthened already established actors and did not trickle down to the rest of the production apparatus; in the case of CEE the reforms led to fast and furious replacement of Soviet industry with low value-added outsourcing production. In addition, the reforms delinked the efforts for strengthening S&T capabilities from the industrialization effort. Implicitly, S&T started to be considered as "neutral" and the policy regime turned into a demand-oriented one with stimulus packages for innovation and technological upgrading offered through open calls to firms.

One of the drawbacks of the policy model was the persistent linearity in addressing innovation; in addition, the countries of the regions would have required policies supporting industrialization and the creation of production capacities together with the support for innovation instead of importing good practices from the "North" which, however, had little impact in a context in which the demand for innovation from domestic agents was scant due to structural conditions.

Slowly, while the market-led approach showed its limits in the capacity to support catching-up and technical change, and in line with changes in policy attitude in frontier countries both LA and CEE entered a post–Washington

Consensus phase, which for CEE has been marked by the process of accession to the EU. In those years a new language became to be adopted by the innovation policy community and a systemic approach prevailed. Public–private partnerships and cooperation between the agents of the national innovation system were advocated as the main drivers for innovation. Multidisciplinarity was included as a key driver for fostering the generation and application of new ideas and efforts to design policies through a participatory approach were developed. Clearly, the transition to a nonlinear policy model which recognizes the systemic dimension of innovation represents a positive step; however, the reform failed to address the main problem posed by the previous generation of reforms: the detachment between innovation and industrial structure. In essence, both LA and CEE countries have experienced a "stop-and-go" trajectory in innovation policy in the past two decades; each new policy model has tried to target problems inherited from previous policy generation but has mostly failed to do so and in fact created additional problems in policy implementation and coordination. This leads to what we call the periphery paradox in innovation policy; despite growing importance attributed to innovation policy in LA and CEE economies, actual policy capacity and policy effectiveness does not rise accordingly. One of the explanations we adduce in the evolution of the political economy of innovation policy in the "periphery," is the missing link between the production side and the innovation policy.

The financial crisis urged countries to redefine priorities and investment strategies; it also left countries to face key production challenges such as social and environmental sustainability of current consumption and production patterns. Advanced countries deepened the debate on which types of innovation they should foster and through which mechanisms. A shift towards a greener, fairer and more knowledge-based policy agenda seems to be forthcoming. Peripheral regions will probably face the same transition; however, they should avoid pursuing this spiral of moving the innovation policy target without solving the problems caused by previous policy efforts. Policy learning proceeds through trial and error, but errors need to be identified and corrected in order to engender a virtuous policy process. Overcoming the current mismatch between innovation policy and production development is a must for peripheral regions. There are no blueprints for linking back innovation policies with an industrialization strategy aimed at creating domestic capabilities in key sector; each country should identify how to do it and through which institutions and mechanisms. A regional dialogue could support this process and ease the transfer of good practices and experiences between countries.

While in frontier countries there are already industrial constituencies lobbying for innovation policy, developing countries still face the challenge of building production capacities which will represent the targeted audience of the innovation policy and in addition, they need to respond to the global demand (pressure) coming from foreign companies operating in peripheral countries. Innovation policy is not a neutral policy, it is a policy with strong sectoral components and in developing economies this means that it needs to be coupled with policies supporting production development. It is in this mismatch between the production structure specialization and the innovation policy discourse that we identify a similarity between LA and CEE which goes beyond the vision of innovation "failure" versus "success." Both regions need to increase productivity, employment and well-being and a modification in the prevailing specialization pattern towards more knowledge intensive activities coupled with modernization of average production techniques and organization is needed.

A generalized call for innovation, detached from policies supporting structural change and the creation of domestic production and scientific capabilities, will not suffice. Currently, LA and CEE both suffer from the "periphery paradox" in innovation policy – i.e. rising political attention towards innovation detached from efforts devoted to strengthen the actors (firms, universities, institutions) which demand and offer the knowledge required for innovation. The detachment of the innovation policy from the dynamics of the real economy is particularly dangerous in peripheral countries which need to create a consensus for supporting innovation policies. Supporting innovation without creating and strengthening the actors whose job it is to innovate is a costly mistake not only in budgetary terms, but because this attitude contributes to delegitimize policies augmenting the impression that "policies do not work." And in fact they do not work or their impact is limited because most of the time, no matter how well they are designed, they address a missing actor. This is prevalent especially in the case of technology transfer policies and the policies supporting patenting activities. In contexts in which firms carry out basically incremental innovations and modernization of production, a policy which promotes patenting basically misses its target: a firm for which patenting could be a good corporate strategy. Hence, those policies should be a support and should be ancillary to policies fostering the creation of innovative production agents.

The "Proinnovation" Momentum: A Way Out of the Periphery Paradox?

After the 1990s, the decade in which "no policy" was the best policy, currently innovation policies are back on the development agenda in LA as well as in CEE. The political conjuncture of the last years has been particularly favorable to innovation, at least at the rhetorical level. However, countries face serious barriers in implementing policies and in matching innovation with structural change and industrialization.

The financial crisis led frontier countries to prioritize innovation as a way out from the crisis. In peripheral economies – which were in the process of creating endogenous technological and production capabilities – short-term competitive pressures would lead firms to reduce investments in R&D and in risky and uncertain innovations. This reduces the technological base with which those economies will face the postcrisis scenario. A sort of lock-in process emerges, in which countries which should invest the most in supporting the creation of endogenous technological capabilities are led to invest less as a result of short-term pressures. Redefining S&T priorities as a response to the crisis within a short-term perspective would reinforce peripheral marginal position in the global economy. A proactive response is needed. However, responding to the crisis is easier said than done. Readaptation and change are costly and require time and resources. The speed and the direction of change with which the firm responds to the shock are crucial to remain competitive in the market. And, obviously, not all firms will be able to respond swiftly enough. The effects of the readaptation of capabilities and production and investment strategies on productivity will not be immediate. There will be a time-lag, and during this time the economy will necessarily experience a slowdown in productivity growth. Clearly, the time for readaptation depends on many factors such as the specificities of the assets of firms, the kind of routines in the firm's management strategy and the general characteristics of the human capital – i.e. there is some degree of stickiness in technological and production capacities of firms which determines the time and direction of the readaptation process. A smart policy mix could support a smooth transition.

Research and knowledge capabilities are difficult to reconvert and recover and the perception that knowledge will be the assets that will determine the repositioning of powers after the crisis justify maintaining investments in those assets even in a crisis scenario. Of course it is not a matter of "spending for the sake of spending" as could happen in a "bonanza" momentum. It is time for "smart spending." But "smart" in this context is, more than ever, synonymous to technology, knowledge and intangible asset, not cost-effectiveness and efficiency in investment.

However, looking at the crisis as a moment of "creative destruction" in the current capitalistic development should not lead to a naïve comprehension of the crisis as a straightforward opportunity. Opportunities will be strictly linked with capabilities in new paradigms and technologies. Countries which master relevant knowledge in the new paradigms, countries that possess the human capital in those areas and countries with large high-tech firms will have an easier way out of the crisis compared to countries which were at the margins of the knowledge game in the precrisis scenario. Likewise, there will be windows of opportunities for all, but they will be identified and possibly taken advantage of only by firms (and countries) which follow a knowledge-centered development strategy prioritizing the construction of scientific and technological capabilities also within in this crisis context. It is highly probable that in the future, the basis for competitiveness of firms will be largely redefined. New demands will ensue, and it is likely that there will be a redefinition of production with a shift of priorities towards environmental sustainability and welfare concerns, in contrast to the technological race of past years.

The ongoing financial crisis and the nondeferrable challenges of climate change, energy and sustainability of production revitalized the debate on the role of the state in the economy in advanced economies. There is mounting interest in new forms of innovation which should better respond to the needs of citizens and increasingly respect the environment and an efficient use of energies and resources. A window of opportunity opens for LA and CEE to support innovation and elaborate policy models which overcome current bottlenecks. However, profiting from the reorganization of powers and the potential state of equilibrium which will emerge after the crisis will not happen through market forces alone. The (sometimes) oversimplified innovation discourse of recent years has led to the elaboration of national plans which are seldom or partially implemented but which have at least generated certain institutional learning in terms of policy management. Efforts should be tailored to implementation and effective support to production development.

The current "proinnovation" momentum – at the regional and the global level – represents an opportunity to capitalize on past experiences and to overcome some of the limits of the previous science and technology policy models.

A lesson that can be learned is that policies modify agents' behavior through incentives which then need to be incorporated into policy design in order to adapt policies to the new scenario. Also, policies require institutions for their management and implementation. Furthermore, the introduction of new policies requires an analysis of which kind of institutional set up will support the policy implementation and identify the adjustment mechanism needed to support the translation of policy design to implementation.

Learning, path dependency and cumulativeness affect the dynamics of policies and they should be taken into account when introducing reforms. Currently both in LA and in CEE, there are success stories of policy evolution which avoided the "stop-and-go" trap of continuous reforms which only partially addressed the shortcomings of a model and engendered new problems which then needed to be solved by a new reform.

Brazil, for example, is a success case in this respect. The various political administrations supported the generation of scientific and technological capabilities with certain continuity, allowing the country to capitalize on previous experiences in policy design and management. The dynamic of innovation policy followed a more cumulative approach rather than a "stop-and-go" logic and in recent years, there have been several efforts to design comprehensive policies which link innovation capacities to production development. Launched in 2004, the Industrial, Technology and Trade Policy (PICTE) represented the first return of industrial policies in the agenda and it institutionalized the need to look at technology policies within the frame of a more complex policy mix; the production development policy launched in 2008 capitalizes on the previous experience, and goes a step further in elaborating a policy mix which articulates support to industries with the need to create capacities in key strategic sectors. Innovation is not "neutral" in the current Brazilian policy; innovation is sought and supported in given sectors and according to strategic priorities. This of course requires negotiations between actors and strong capabilities in policy management in order to move from policy design to implementation.

In CEE, the EU has had enormous influence in redirecting CEE countries' attention to industrial upgrading and some countries have been exemplary in building policies that correspond to industry needs, as in the case of Slovenia. While Slovenia has been able to focus innovation policies towards upgrading existing industry and skills from the early on in 1990s, it serves as an exception and not as a rule of CEE developments. Indeed, it can be argued that there are strong historical reasons for Slovenia's success (e.g. partial private property prior to independence) that are not replicable in the other CEE countries).

Policy capacities are built over time through a cumulative process just as scientific, technological and innovation capacities. There are multiple policy approaches and models. Some are better fits in certain contexts while others are more appropriate for more advanced countries. However, a "best policy model" should not be the goal. Rather, there should be a quest for a possible policy regime which takes into account policy management capacities and production structure bettering order to respond to the need of fostering innovation and structural change. Policy fine tuning is probably more desirable than a radical shift in the prevailing policy approach which will undermine the process of policy learning and accumulation of capacities.

Conclusions

There are no generic blueprints for an optimal technology policy. Policy goals, instruments and capabilities must be tailored to country-specific context and time requirements and they have to cope with local financial constraints. The mix of suitable policies should take into account regional specificities and should be designed on the basis of a renewed and more pragmatic technology policy model which needs new institutional settings for policy management and implementation.

Disposing of a well-designed policy is not a sufficient guarantee. A key factor of success for any technology policy is the matching of its goals with production structure needs and effective demand. Path dependent and cumulative processes form key features of policy processes that should be taken into account when devising new or revising existing initiatives. The design and implementation of innovation policies requires mechanisms for policy follow up. Establishing mechanisms for identifying success and failure factors in policy implementation and the creation of institutional mechanisms for fine tuning policy accordingly are required.

The process of construction of capabilities for innovation is costly in terms of time, resources and institutional experiments needed. While it is normal to progress along this track by trial and error, it has to be recognized that errors are not always easily reversible. Identifying factors which engender failures in the process of policy design and implementation matters for improving the capacity to develop new policy solutions, which actually respond more adequately to the challenges posed by the changing context and nature of innovation – but which limit the generation of "new problems" which will need new policies to deal with. Usually a policy (whether "good" or "bad") will engender changes in the scenario in which it was adopted and also in the agents' responses. As a result, new or modified policies will probably be needed to deal with the reshaped scenario. However, while advanced countries usually concentrate their policy efforts in identifying new trends for implementing policies which are able to deal with those trends and whose ultimate goal is to support the country's competitiveness and well-being, in the periphery it happens that the policy dynamic tends to be trapped by a sort of Red Queen effect – "Now, here, you see, it takes all the running you can do to keep in the same place."[24] As a result when new policies are introduced, basically following foreign good practices, their impact is reduced due to the mismatch with the demand side thus engendering a "periphery paradox." In contrast to the European paradox (excellence in research yet poor capacity to translate research outcomes into production), which we described then dismissed, in the periphery there seems be a paradox in which innovation is part of development agendas but the moving target addressed by policies in the last decades has been dominated by a "new problem – new policy solution" approach rather than by incremental efforts for building endogenous capabilities.

---

24 Lewis Carroll, *Through the Looking Glass and What Alice Found There* (London: Macmillan, 1872).

References

Amsden, A. 1989. *Asia's Next Giant: South Korea and the Last Industrialization.* New York: Oxford University Press.

Burlamaqui, Leonardo, Jose A. P. de Souza and Nelson H. Barbosa-Filho. 2007. "The Rise and Halt of Economic Development in Brazil, 1945–2004: Industrial Catching-up, Institutional Innovation, and Financial Fragility," in *Institutional Change and Economic Development*, ed. Ha-Joon Chang, 239–59. London: Anthem Press.

Capdevielle, M., M. Casalet and Mario Cimoli. 2000. "Sistema de innovación: El caso mexicano." Institutions and Markets Project, CEPAL/Sociedad Alemana de Cooperación Técnica (GTZ).

Casalet, M. 2003. "Políticas científi casy tecnológicas en México: Evaluación e impacto." Mexico City: FLACSo.

Cimoli, Mario and Annalisa Primi. 2004. "Las políticas tecnológicas para la creación y difusión del conocimiento en América Latina y el Caribe." División de Desarrollo Productivo y Empresarial, CEPAL. Mimeo.

Cimoli, M., J. C. Ferraz and A. Primi. 2005. *Science and Technology Policies in Open Economies: The Case of Latin America and the Caribbean.* Santiago, Chile: ECLAC.

Cimoli, M., M. Holland, G. Porcile, A. Primi and S. Vergara. 2006. "Growth, Structural Change and Technological Capabilities: Latina America in a Comparative Perspective." LEM Working Paper Series, November. http://www.lem.sssup.it/WPLem/files/2006-11.pdf (accessed 17 January 2012).

Cimoli, M., B. Coriat and A. Primi. 2009. "Intellectual Property and Industrial Development: A Critical Assessment," in *The Political Economy of Capabilities Accumulation: The Past and Future of Industrial Policies for Development*, ed. M. Cimoli, G. Dosi and J. E. Stiglitz. Oxford: Oxford University Press.

Correa, M. 2003. "Políticas para Propiedad Intelectual." Paper presented at the "Reunión Regional OMPI-CEPAL de Expertos sobre el Sistema Nacional de Innovación: Propiedad Intelectual, Universidad y Empresa." Santiago, Chile.

De Beer, J. (ed.) 2009. *Implementing the World Intellectual Property Organization's Development Agenda.* Ottawa/Waterloo, ON: Laurier University Press.

Dosi, Giovanni, Patrick Llerena and Mauro Sylos Labini. 2005. "Science Technology-Industry Links and the 'European Paradox': Some Notes on the Dynamics of Scientific and Technological Research in Europe." LEM Working Paper Series, February. http://www.lem.sssup.it/WPLem/files/2005-02.pdf (accessed 17 January 2012).

Drahokoupil, Jan. 2007. "From National Capitalisms to Foreign-Led Growth: The Moment of Convergence in Central and Eastern Europe," in *Dollarization, Euroization and Financial Instability*, ed. Joachim Becker and Rudy Weissenbacher, 87–108. Marburg: Metropolis.

ECLAC. 2004. *Productive Development in Open Economies.* LC/G.2234 (SES.30/3). Santiago, Chile: ECLAC.

———. 2008. "Structural Change and Productivity Growth, 20 Years Later. Old Problems, New Opportunities." Santiago, Chile: ECLAC.

———. 2008b. *La economía del Conocimiento, Espacios Iberoamericanos.* Santiago, Chile: CEPAL/SEGIB.

ESPON (Institut für Regionalentwicklung und Strukturplanung). 2005. *ESPON 2.2.2 Pre-Accession Aid Impact Analysis.* Final report. http://www.espon.eu/export/sites/default/Documents/Projects/ESPON2006Projects/PolicyImpactProjects/PreAccessionAid/2.ir_2.2.2.pdf (accessed 17 January 2012).

European Commission. 2003. Decision (C) No 4906/2003 of 23 December 2003 on the Review of the Guidelines for Implementation of the Phare Programme in Candidate Countries for the Period 2000–2006. Application of Article 8 of Regulation 3906/89.

Fitch Research. 2007a. "Risks Rising in the Baltic States?" Special report, 6 March.

————. 2007b. "Bulgaria, Croatia, Romania – How Sustainable are External Imbalances?" Special report, 20 March.

————. 2007c. "The Baltic States: Risks Rising in the Trailblazers of Emerging Europe?" Special report, 8 June.

Frost, A. and M. Weinstein. 1998. "ABB Poland." Richard Ivey School of Business, University of Ontario.

Goetz, K. H. 2001. "Making Sense of Post-Communist Central Administration: Modernization, Europeanization or Latinization?" *Journal of European Public Policy* 8.6: 1032–51.

Grabbe, H. 2006. *The EU's Transformative Power: Europeanization through Conditionality in Central and Eastern Europe.* Basingstoke: Palgrave Macmillan.

Havlik, P., M. Landesmann, R. Stehrer, R. Römisch and B. Gilsätter. 2001. "Competitiveness of Industry in CEE Candidate Countries Composite Paper." Vienna Institute for Economic Studies Research Reports 278.

Hobday, Michael. 2009. "Asian Innovation Experiences and Latin American Visions: Exploiting Shifts in Techno-Economic Paradigms," in *Techno-Economic Paradigms: Essays in Honor of Carlota Perez,* ed. W. Drechsler, R. Kattel and E. Reinert. London: Anthem Press.

INNO-Policy TrendChart. 2006. *European Innovation Progress Report 2006.* European Communities. http://www.proinno-europe.eu/index.cfm?fuseaction=page.display&topicID=264&parentID=52 (accessed 17 January 2012 – subscription required).

————. 2006–7. *INNO-Policy TrendChart Annual Country Reports for Czech Republic, Estonia, Hungary, Latvia, Lithuania, Poland, Slovakia, Slovenia, Bulgaria and Romania.* European Communities. http://www.proinno-europe.eu/index.cfm?fuseaction=page.display&topicID=263&parentID=52 (accessed 17 January 2012 – subscription required).

Jaramillo Salazar, H. 2003. "Políticas científicas y tecnológicas en Colombia: Evaluación e impacto durante la década de los noventa." Bogotá: CEPAL.

Jomo, K. S. 1997. *Southeast Asia's Misunderstood Miracle: Industrial Policy and Economic Development in Thailand, Malaysia and Indonesia.* Boulder, CO: Westview Press.

Karo, Erkki and Rainer Kattel. 2009. "The Copying Paradox: Why Converging Policies but Diverging Capacities for Development in Eastern European Innovation Systems?" The Other Canon and Tallinn University of Technology Working Papers in Technology Governance and Economic Dynamics, No. 24.

Kattel, Rainer, Erik S. Reinert and Margit Suurna. 2012. "Industrial Restructuring and Innovation Policy in Central and Eastern Europe Since 1990," in *Learning, Knowledge and Innovation: Policy Challenges for the 21st Century,* ed. M. Cimoli, G. Dosi, and A. Primi. Oxford: Oxford University Press. Forthcoming.

Kregel, Jan A. 2008. "The Discrete Charm of the Washington Consensus." Working Paper No. 533, Levy Economics Institute of Bard College. http://www.levy.org/pubs/wp_533.pdf (accessed 17 January 2012).

OECD. 2009. *The OECD Innovation Strategy: Draft Interim Report.* Paris: OECD.

Pacheco, C. 2003. "As reformas da Política Nacional de Ciência Tecnologia e inovaçao no Brasil, 1999–2002." Campinas, Brazil: CEPAL.

Peres, W. and A. Primi. 2009. "Theory and Practice of Industrial Policy: Evidence from the Latin American Experience." Production Development Series No. 187. Santiago, Chile: ECLAC-United Nations.

Phare Consolidated Summary Report. 2004. "From Pre-Accession to Accession: Interim Evaluation of Phare Support Allocated in 1992–2002 and Implemented until November 2003." European Commission.

———. 2007. "Supporting Enlargement – What Does Evaluation Show? Ex-post Evaluation of Phare Support Allocated Between 1999–2001, with Brief Review of Post-2001 Allocations." European Commission. http://ec.europa.eu/enlargement/pdf/financial_assistance/phare/evaluation/consolidated_summary_report_phare_ex_post_eval.pdf (accessed 17 January 2012).

Primi, A. 2009. "Regional Cooperation in S&T Policies: A View from Latin America." Conference proceedings of a CGEE international seminar on "International Cooperation in the Knowledge Era," Rio de Janeiro, Brazil.

Radosevic, Slavo. 1998. "The Transformation of National Systems of Innovation in Eastern Europe: Between Restructuring and Erosion." *Industrial and Corporate Change* 7.1: 77–108.

———. 1999. "Transformation of Science and Technology Systems into Systems of Innovation in Central and Eastern Europe: The Emerging Patterns and Determinants." *Structural Change and Economic Dynamics* 10.3–4: 277–320.

———. 2002. "Introduction: Building the Basis for Future Growth – Innovation Policy as a Solution." *Journal of International Relations and Development* 5.4: 352–6.

———. 2004. "A Two-Tier or Multi-Tier Europe? Assessing the Innovation Capacities of Central and East European Countries in the Enlarged EU." *Journal of Common Market Studies* 42.3: 641–66.

———. 2006. "The Knowledge-based Economy in Central and Eastern Europe: An Overview of Key Issues," in *The Knowledge-based Economy in Central and Eastern Europe: Countries and Industries in a Process of Change*, ed. K. Piech and S. Radosevic, 31–53. Basingstoke: Palgrave Macmillan.

———. 2009. "Policies for Promoting Technological Catch Up: Towards a Post-Washington Approach." *International Journal of Institutions and Economies* 1.1: 22–51.

Radosevic, S. and A. Reid. 2006. "Innovation Policy for a Knowledge-based Economy in Central and Eastern Europe: Driver of Growth or New Layer of Bureaucracy?" in *The Knowledge-based Economy in Central and Eastern Europe: Countries and Industries in a Process of Change*, ed. K. Piech and S. Radosevic, 295–311. Basingstoke: Palgrave Macmillan.

Reid, Alastair and Viola Peter. 2008. *Sectoral Innovation Systems: The Policy Landscape in the EU25*. http://archive.europe-innova.eu/index.jsp?type=page&previousContentId=9741&cid=9945&lg=EN(accessed 17 January 2012).

Rodrik, Dani. 2006. "Goodbye Washington Consensus, Hello Washington Confusion? A Review of the World Bank's Economic Growth in the 1990s: Learning from a Decade of Reform." *Journal of Economic Literature* 44: 973–87.

Schimmelfennig, F. and U. Sedelmeier. 2004. "Governance by Conditionality: EU Rule Transfer to the Candidate Countries of Central and Eastern Europe." *Journal of European Public Policy* 11.4: 669–87.

Tiits, M., R. Kattel, T. Kalvet and D. Tamm. 2008. "Catching Up, Forging Ahead or Falling Behind? Central and Eastern European Development in 1990–2005." *Innovation. The European Journal of Social Science Research* 21.1: 65–85.

UNIDO. 2009. *Industrial Development Report 2009. Breaking In and Moving Up: New Industrial Challenges for the Bottom Billion and Middle Income Countries*. http://www.unido.org/fileadmin/user_media/Publications/IDR_2009_print.PDF (accessed 17 January 2012).

Vargas Alfaro, L. and O. Segura Bonillla. 2003. "Políticas industriales, científicas y tecnológicas en Costa Rica y Centro América." Centro Internacional en Política Económica para el Desarrollo Sostenible (CINPE). Costa Rica: Universidad Nacional, Hereida.

Wade, R. 1990. *Governing the Market: Economic Theory and the Role of Government in East Asian Industrialization*. Princeton: Princeton University Press.

Weissenbacher, Rudy. 2007. "Historical Considerations of Uneven Development in East Central Europe," in *Dollarization, Euroization and Financial Instability*, ed. Joachim Becker and Rudy Weissenbacher, 35–83. Marburg: Metropolis.

Williamson, John. 2002. "What Washington Means by Policy Reform." Updated version of 1990 article. http://www.iie.com/publications/papers/paper.cfm?ResearchID=486. (accessed 17 January 2012).

————. 2008. "Williamson Versus the Washington consensus?" http://wayback.archive-it. org/2180/20101029231805/http://www.growthcommissionblog.org/content/williamson-versus-the-washington-consensus (accessed 17 January 2012).

World Bank. 2006. *Economic Growth in the 1990s: Learning from a Decade of Reform*. http://www1.worldbank.org/prem/lessons1990s/ (accessed 17 January 2012).

————. 2008. *Science, Technology, and Innovation. Capacity Building for Sustainable Growth and Poverty Reduction*. http://go.worldbank.org/GEYA2NRGW0 (accessed 17 January 2012).

Ylä-Anttila, P. and T. Lemola. 2006. "Transformation of Innovation System in a Small Country – the Case of Finland," in *Creative Destruction Management: Meeting the Challenges of the Techno-Economic Paradigm Shift*, ed. T. Kalvet and R. Kattel, 85–99. Tallinn: Praxis Center for Policy Studies.

Yoguel, G. 2003. "La política científica y tecnológica argentina en las últimas décadas: Algunas consideraciones desde la perspectiva del desarrollo de procesos de aprendizaje." Buenos Aires: CEPAL.

Young, A. 1994. "Gerber Products Company: Investing in the New Poland." Harvard Business School case study.

Chapter 13

THE LULA GOVERNMENT AND THE SOCIAL DEMOCRATIC EXPERIENCE IN BRAZIL

Fabiano Santos

Instituto de Estudos Sociais e Políticos, IESP-UERJ

Introduction

In this chapter I will propose a few lines of *reflection* on the current partisan political struggle in Brazil and how this can be read in the light of international experience of contention between liberals and social democrats.[1] Many wonder why the PT and the PSDB/ DEM coalition have been the most successful options in recent presidential elections in Brazil.[2] Indeed, no matter how complex the political life in modern societies may seem, there is basically a single and fundamental cleavage which pits electorally viable political forces against each other in nations structured according to the dictates of the capitalist order: the political actors who organize around the social democratic movement and the actors that organize around the liberal movement. The replication of this ideological divide is expressed in the famous ideological left-right continuum along which parties, leaders, voters, interest groups and opinion leaders seek to position themselves or somehow are inevitably drawn into. The point here is not exactly to determine, for example, whether or not the Partido Social Democratica Brasileiro (PSDB) is a liberal or genuinely social democratic association, but rather to point out that starting in the 1990s with the introduction of market-oriented reforms in Brazil, the PSDB in association with the former Partido da Frente Liberal (PFL) renamed the Democrats (DEM),

---

1 The present ideas have been developed in Santos (2006).
2 PT – Work's Party; PSDB – Brazilian Social Democratic Party; DEM – Democrats.

has become the most competitive and reliable option for voters with rightist or center-right inclinations. The reverse of this last statement, a far less controversial assertion by the way, is that the PT has been the most competitive and reliable option from the perspective of leftist voters.

Once we accept this point of departure, then the naked truth of Brazilian politics is that the PT together with its traditional partners on the left: the PSB, PCdoB and PDT[3] and the PSDB – usually accompanied by the DEM – are the respective options, which are able to amass votes from the left and right of the ideological spectrum and are in the best position to attract voters in the center (who are those usually responsible for clenching the win in a majority election). The reasons that led to this result would merit a lengthy discussion, but that regarding the PT will be limited here to the fact its roots lie in trade unions and social movements and that it never adopted an official ideology. Thus it allowed for the coexistence of various strands of leftism within its cadres, leading to its adoption of sophisticated strategies of organizing and mobilizing, besides strict internal rules of recruitment. Concerning the PSDB/DEM, what stands out is the coalition's capacity to attract (since the beginning) excellent technical staff as well as it's a strong support base – particularly the PSDB in São Paulo.

One criticism that has been made of this state of affairs is that, in essence, these parties are similar in every way – the electorate being unable to distinguish between them, much less find an alternative representing a genuine change in priorities and agenda within government. I will argue that the similarity between major contenders for presidency in Brazil (as in much of so-called "mature democracies" in the world) does not derive from a common essence inherent to parties, let alone the willingness, interests and ideas of the leaders of such organizations. Electoral competition requires the assembly of complex and multifaceted coalitions and also implies that the issues which most concern voters will have to be the same prioritized by the candidates (in other words, the candidate able to confront these issues most aptly will garner most credibility and will therefore be the winner).

Importantly, the key items on the agenda of Brazilian voters generate, to some extent, contradictory pressures on the government: while they demand monetary stability, they also wish economic growth and more jobs. At the same time that they push for social spending, they also oppose higher income taxes. Thus, it is understandable that successive governments appear to promote somewhat similar policies. Nevertheless, this appearance of continuity

---

3 PSB – Brazilian Socialist Party; PCdoB – Brazilian Communist Party; PDT – Labor Democratic Party.

collapsed in view of what has happened during the current government and what happened during the eight years of the previous government.

First, it is undeniable that there are major differences between parties like the PT, PSB and PCdoB on the one hand, and PSDB and DEM on the other, in regard to the means to achieve development; such differences correspond exactly to the differences pointed out between social democratic and liberal parties in contemporary Europe. While the first group of parties proposes a more proactive public sector, the second includes in its agenda the strengthening of policies of privatization, downsizing the public sector and reform of labor relations. Second, while the first set of parties has a foreign policy agenda oriented toward regional integration and opening markets in Third World countries, the second one has a distinct orientation focusing on strengthening historical ties with developed nations, especially the US. Third (as will be discussed ahead in a specific section of this chapter), there are, on one side, radical policies focused on income transfer benefitting the poor and very poorest – as adopted by the current government; on the other side there is opposition to distribution policies, which are criticized as a form of a populist handout.

For the reasons stated above, the hypothesis which posits that the PT and the PSDB/DEM are essentially the same is untenable, although it is true that the macroeconomic policy – identical in its fundamentals in the current administration to that in much of the previous period – impose significant limits to what government can or cannot accomplish. Furthermore, the persistent gap between expectations and what was actually achieved in terms of growth and social inclusion might have generated the impression of similarity between the parties to which the two latest incumbents, Fernando Henrique Cardoso and Luiz Inácio Lula da Silva, belong. Yet this impression fades after careful scrutiny of the evidence in terms of policies and their results. This evidence should be considered in light of the challenges, differences and similarities faced by social democracy in the current context of global capitalism.

Social Democracy: Theoretical Issues

In this chapter, as mentioned, I will reflect on the current political moment in Brazil, making use of concepts and practices from the experience of social democracy in Europe. Throughout the discussion, it seems useful to allude to the trajectory of the democratic socialist tradition – especially the disputes it engaged in with the liberal tradition both in the field of ideas and in the political and partisan spheres.

I will use the terms "liberalism" and "social democracy" to express the currents of political thought which respectively stem from the liberal tradition and the socialist tradition. The terms also distinguish the opposing political forces organized in political parties positioned on opposite sides of the political spectrum in Western Europe and Brazil. In other words, I argue that although there have been important confluences in terms of political practices of liberal and socialist political parties in the postwar period, fundamental differences remain – differences that relate not only to doctrines concerning the state's role in social life, but also concerning the concrete interests of actors who are affected on a day-to-day basis by policies that result from either direction. These are differences that confer meaning to the persistent political and doctrinal dispute between liberals and social democrats in the context of contemporary representative democracies.

The following discussion focuses on the definition of liberalism and social democracy, emphasizing, in the latter case, the historical path of formation of political forces that orbit around the social democracy. Next, I will present the more general outlines of the party-political struggle waged between liberal and social democracy in the postwar period until the beginning of the era of globalization. The terms according to which this struggle is being expressed today, after the effects of globalization have altered the relationship between the state and the economy, are the subject of the next topic before proceeding to a discussion on the contemporary political context in Brazil. The main emphasis will be on the major public policy implemented during the two terms of President Lula, the Bolsa Família (Family Grant) program, with a focus on the electoral coalitions that he mobilized and the conceptual basis on which it is grounded.

Let us begin by addressing some terminology issues. When talking about liberalism, few questions as to what the term designates are made. Liberalism is a broad concept that refers to a body of doctrine with several ramifications. It nevertheless possesses a well-defined common core: the idea of individual freedom as the basis of political and social order. Economic liberalism characterizes arguments, policies or theories that support free enterprise, the quest for individual material welfare as the best way to achieve collective economic development and the expansion of aggregate wealth. Political liberalism is based on the ideas of free expression of opinions and free organization for the protection and propagation of such views.[4] The term social democracy can not be exposed as easily, but it is worth the challenge because even through the reflection on the concept itself, several crucial questions can be raised concerning the relationship between the two streams under consideration in this chapter.

---

4 For a clear and succinct summary of the liberal arguments, see Merquior (1982).

Let us refer now to socialism. This doctrine comprises a broad set of theories and arguments concerning the normative social order whose ballast is the idea of equality – not just in terms of opportunities for action, but also in terms of results. At the same time, the economic theories of a socialist bent share the perception that an economic order based on private ownership of goods and services leads to the undesirable distinction of wealth. Thus, in the political sphere, socialism supports the idea according to which the government must act to minimize the distributional inequality resulting from individual efforts to increase material well-being.

The discussion gains in complexity when we add "democracy" to the term socialism, thus arriving at the concept of social democracy. Indeed, the relationship between representative democracy and social democracy are at the very core of social democracy since the political and doctrinal debate that occurred within the socialist parties and intellectual circles in late nineteenth-century Europe.[5] This debate was critically shaped by the confrontation between theorists affiliated to the Marxist tradition, which considered representative institutions as a political manifestation of bourgeois ascendancy, characteristic of the capitalist order, and thinkers, publicists and activists who believed representative democracy to be the essential form of political organization of an order based on socialism.

Historical hindsight suggests that had socialist representative democrats emerged victorious from this debate things would have been quieter, without major ups and downs. Reality however was quite different and there are nuances worth a digression.[6] Firstly, it is important to note the differences that occurred with respect to the constitution of left-wing parties in different national contexts. If the Labour Party in England was initiated by an active union movement and emerged in an intellectual context marked by utilitarianism and absent nationalism in Germany and in several other countries in Continental Europe, the Social Democratic Party was born in parallel and in conjunction with the formation of labor unions and in an intellectual context largely hostile to liberalism and receptive to nationalism. In England, the format of electoral political disputes as well as Parliament as the site of government formation was already long established and their legitimacy went unquestioned. Meanwhile, in Continental Europe national state building was a more painful and tortuous process, meaning that democratic rules faced a higher degree of verbal and factual confrontation.

Secondly, it is relevant to recall that just after World War II socialist parties completed the abandonment of the principles that had guided them since

---

5 For an excellent presentation of the intellectual origins of social democracy, see Kloppenberg (1986).

6 In which I follow Przeworski (1985) and the volume by Bergounioux and Manin (1989).

their founding – principles that denied the normative validity of representative democracy. Essentially, the principles that had driven socialist actions were: (1) the revolutionary character of the seizure of power by the proletariat; (2) the single-class character of the party; and (3) the collectivization of the means of production.

As a result of this first shift, workers and leftist intellectuals started agreeing that the appropriate way to achieve socialism was indeed the electoral route. In other words, they adopted the idea of a peaceful revolution through the ballot. Economic conflict would inevitably lead to the rise of socialists to power, for in a class society based on the capitalist mode of production they would obtain the support by the majority of the electorate. The truth, however, was that capitalist societies did not engender the sort of polarization predicted in which the owners of the means of production would be massively outnumbered (and therefore outvoted) by a majority of workers. Based on this sobering realization, socialists reached out for electoral support, promoting coalitions with average income sectors, small farmers and professionals. Consequently left parties no longer could claim to be an instrument of the workers in their struggle to seize power. They had in fact become machines specialized in electoral competition and the political socialization of candidates for the exercise of political representation and management of the state. But the expansion of the electoral appeal and attempt to form coalitions with sectors other than the workers restricted policy proposals of the Left, especially the beloved idea of collectivization of the means of production – which had to be dropped.

It is important to note that the abandonment of such principles was not the result of a clear-cut and straightforward decision taken after evaluating the best theoretical directions for socialism available. Rather, it occurred as a consequence of the confrontation with political and economic reality and its very narrow limits to what can be achieved. It was not simply an abandonment of dogmatic principles, but rather an adaptation of such principles to the terms under which the political struggle of socialists has developed since its inception – namely, the terms set by the capitalist order combined to representative democracy.

The goal here is not to narrate the history of social democratic parties and how it accommodated to the terms of capitalist order, but rather more broadly to define more accurately what it means when the concept of social democracy. Today when we speak of social democracy we are referring to the parties and intellectual movements that originated from socialism and workers' struggle for political inclusion and government control, but which eventually ended up moderating their pretensions, adapting to the context of political pluralism and market economies that characterize the capitalist order associated with representative democracy.

But this sort of adaptation also occurred in the context of liberalism. When the representative system was hatched, the notions of freedom of opinion, expression and organization were linked to the idea of a government under control, its action limited to the extent of the intervention needed to preserve individual freedoms. The institutionalization of parliament, as well as the emergence of the concept of political opposition, was a product of the struggle for the imposition of limits on the exercise of power by the state. The elimination of barriers to political participation – particularly of restrictions tied to income criteria as a result of the claims of the underprivileged classes for political incorporation – changed the nature of government intervention in social life. In other words, the political participation of groups and individuals with lower incomes (a phenomenon that resulted from the democratic reforms of the early twentieth century) eventually created a new conception of the role of state in the economy – something that was reflected by the creation of welfare states and the organization of the apparatus of state economic intervention under the inspiration of Keynesianism.

Liberalism, Social Democracy and Political Competition in the Postwar Era

The model of political competition which was established at the end of the World War II in Western Europe (and to a great extent also in the United States) can be understood as a struggle between two visions concerning state intervention in social and economic life: the relationship between state and society – in short, the very functioning of the institutional politics. In the following I will analyze each of these aspects but prior to doing so, it is worth returning to some of the conclusions that we reached at the end of the previous section.

Representative democracy as a political system that deals with the conflicts that emerge between social actors and economic groups in a capitalist market-based industrial order is the product of a two forms of accommodation. On one hand, the socialists gradually gave up of some basic principles that guided their formation as an intellectual and political movement. This abdication was at first only perceptible due to the suspicious and instrumental adherence to representative democracy, but afterwards this shift became clear as statutory programs of parties and political theory textbooks formalized the new guideline, establishing political institutions of democracy as the only legitimate means of gaining and exercising power. On the other hand, liberals and the social and economic forces that supported it as an intellectual and political movement accepted the reality of a state intervening at the micro level in the economy to mitigate the distributional effects arising from the operation of the market order and at the macro level to prevent that the business cycles and the ups and downs (characteristic of the capitalist economy) sharply affect employment, wages and in sum, the welfare of disadvantaged populations.

Despite several points of convergence, deep differences remain between liberals and socialists – being that the latter now go by the social democrat label in relation to the crucial issues of relationship between government and society, government and economy. As said at the beginning of this section, there are at least four fundamental disjunctions.

The first disjunction is related to the social policy model adopted in countries with a stronger tradition of social democracy vis-à-vis the traditional forms of social intervention in countries where liberalism is more influential.[7] In the social democratic model, the state must be equipped to prevent the manifestation of unequal outcomes. The income transfer system, the apparatus of taxation, public services of health and education and the pension system are based on the principles of universalism and de-commodification. Regardless of social and occupational status, all individuals are entitled to minimum income levels, and the same health and educational services. In contrast to this model, according to the model of liberalism intervention is only residual – meaning that the state is called upon to minimize the effects of more acute poverty. The diversification of the nature of health services and education, robust private educational services and less generous systems of retirement are the hallmarks of this model. The idea here is to create minimal conditions for the individual to develop their own capacities to fight for the expansion of material welfare.

A second major disjunction concerns macroeconomic objectives pursued by social democratic governments versus governments inspired by liberalism.[8] In the first type of government there is an emphasis on the "employment" variable, while in the second type the emphasis is on inflation. Trade-offs are different in the two cases: while the social democrats accept higher levels of inflation in exchange for lower levels of unemployment, liberals accept the decrease of employed population in exchange for greater stability in the price level.

A third disjunction concerns the societal model, i.e. the modes of interaction between state and society. One could say that there is an affinity between liberalism and the societal model called "pluralism" in several modern political analyses, and this model is, moreover, the central axis of American political culture.[9] In this model, freedom and equal opportunities

---

7 Esping Andersen (1990) being the main reference here.

8 The classical article in this respect is Hibbs (1977).

9 Once again the reference here is Bergounioux and Manin (1989).

come together to protect the individual interests that are in accordance with the laws of nature. Individuals form interest groups that are dispersed in the political world, compete against each other in search of supporters and exert pressure from outside the government whose role in this model is to serve as an arbiter of social conflict. The importance of conflict, in turn, is precisely to temper the exercise of power by government – the dispersion of interests, the multiplication of divisions and the strict separation of public and private spheres all conspire towards a peaceful coexistence between liberty and equality, this being understood as equality of opportunities.

Therefore it is arguable that the moderation of the exercise of power, a fundamental goal of the liberal-pluralist societal model, derives from social structure itself. The complex web of overlapping interests and multiple cleavages underscoring the capitalist social order which is based on division of labor gives rise to the diversity of groups and associations – the essence of pluralism. Policy in this context is understood as an open space, occupied by interest groups to the extent that public policy issues affecting such groups become subject to governmental decision. Once the decision is taken, groups disband and give way to the representation of alternative interests. The clash and competition among groups vying to shape governmental action guarantees that no essential interest is irrevocably harmed in the political process, thus preserving the fundamental freedoms of the individual by the state.

The societal model or the model of state/society relationship, typical of social democracy, has also been labeled neocorporatism. In this model, the moderation of the exercise of political power takes place according to a face-to-face logic. The key idea here is the inclusion and creation of spaces of deliberation in which conflicting interests are represented. It is a basic principle that minorities should be part of the decision-making process and that actors can never fully fulfill their political projects.

In order for this model to be minimally effective, some assumptions must be observed. First of all, it is impossible to assume that groups will form only when issues are important and disband when they become less prominent in the public debate. Actors must keep some sort of permanent standing in negotiating forums. Second, groups negotiating public policies with the government must simultaneously hold the monopoly of representation of the interests they represent. According to this face-to-face logic one must assume that there is no competition within groups that are part of the deliberative forums. Finally, one cannot conceive of a strict separation between public and private spaces. Government and groups have a symbiotic relationship – with the former delegating responsibilities to the latter – while the government is a participant in the process of negotiating as well, with its own interests and views as to the direction of public decisions.

This discussion brings us to the last disjunction between liberalism and social democracy. It concerns the assembly and formation of governments with varying political leanings – that is, the different approaches to the perennial problem of governability. Once again following the line of analysis suggested by Bergounioux and Manin (1989), it is reasonable to assert that the tradition of government-inspired social democrats is to share power with minorities, and the solution to the problem of governability lies in a conception of power based on the idea cohabitation. Contrarily, the liberal tradition follows a distinct approach, which asserts that power to govern should be concentrated on those who received the majority of votes, i.e. the majoritarian conception of democracy. The solution to the problem of governance, according to this view, lies in building parliamentary cartels according to the model posited by Cox and McCubbins (1993) in their analysis of the years of democratic dominance in Congress of the United States.

These models are expressed, in the first case, either through the assembly of minority governments in which the participation of opposition and independent parties is crucial for the adoption of the governmental agenda or through supermajoritarian governments, ideologically heterogeneous and with high transaction costs of intraoffice. In the second case, strictly majoritarian offices in which the opposition is not required to cooperate in the definition of matters submitted by the government to the legislature tend to be the predominant.

These four disjunctions during several decades marked the dispute between liberals and social democrats in the political economic sphere, as well as in the academic and intellectual debate and in the press. Since the oil crises and the apparent failure of Keynesian economic management, the lines along which this dispute occurred started to change. At the same time, financial globalization, the intensification of international trade flows and demographic changes in the productive structure of firms diminished the capacity of national states and their governments to independently define political and economic models of social intervention – especially without taking into account of economic processes and decision making established in other countries (both commercial partners, as in the financial field). Such changes and their impacts on the competition between liberals and social democrats are the subject of the following section.

A New Outline for Political Conflict in the Era of Globalization

The distinction between leftist parties and conservative parties has become somewhat controversial in the European context where the socialist experience of reaching power through elections first occurred. Even more evident is the American two-party system, where the difference between Democrats (whose profile is more liberal) and Republicans (more conservative) is often called into question. What is it that gives rise to this controversy?

The term globalization serves to synthesize the phenomena that are thought to have caused the blurring of the differences between liberals and social democrats. Major changes in the world of labor – with equally significant impact on the structure of occupations – have contributed to the reduction of the bargaining power of unions. Demographic changes (with the aging of the population reducing the ratio of between the economically active population and the population at retirement age) have increased the tax burden of the state, already overburdened by the set of responsibilities assumed by decades of welfarism. Intensification of the flow of international trade has imposed increasing productivity demands of the sectors related to exports vis-à-vis the sectors engaged in activities related to the domestic market which sharpens the distributive conflict within groups that once were on the same side in negotiations concerning income policies. The internationalization of finance has imposed the need for greater coordination in monetary policies, drastically mitigating the freedom governments once had to effect changes by altering exchange rates, encouraging exports and thereby the level of economic activity.

In short, globalization has undermined the effective functioning of the assumptions that guided the actions of social democratic parties during the period immediately after WWII until the mid-1980s. The crucial questions that intellectuals and political leaders made were: Is there still room for significant differences between liberals and social democrats in the context of global capitalism? Would the neocorporative societal model have chances of survival in this new context? Has the homogenization of macroeconomic policies led to a final dilution between the governments of liberal inclination and the governments of social democrat inclination? Isn't the welfare state doomed to disappear? Many said yes, but the history continued providing evidence to the contrary.

What recent studies show is that significant differences between the left and the right governments in Europe remain, especially regarding the manner in which they are facing the challenges posed by globalization.[10] It is true that this (understood as a context of greater mobility of financial capital and the entire ensemble of phenomena listed above) brought restrictions to the ability of national governments to combine monetary policy and public debt with the aim of stimulating the economy. In other words, the most important

---

10 The main references here are: Boix (1998), Garret (1998) and Iversen (2005).

political consequence of globalization has been to render classical Keynesian intervention untenable, something that had been adopted for decades by the social democrats as a tool to achieve growth and full employment. This resulted in greater uniformity in terms of macroeconomic policies characterized in general by the orthodoxy in dealing with the currency. The similarities, however, end here.

The response of social democratic parties in the face of risks and uncertainties arising from the new scenario has been the maintenance of social spending, expansion of the tax burden and investment in physical and human capital while the liberal parties, once in power, have reduced the tax burden, relieve companies from labor charges and transferred to the private sector the responsibility for training and improvement of manpower.[11] In other words, in the period of classic Keynesianism, the differences between macroeconomic therapies focused on management tools to stimulate and restrict demand; now governments distinguish themselves according to the intensity of policies that aim to stimulate supply – supply-side economics as it has been termed.

Beyond the fact that the evidence concerning the decay of neocorporate societal models and the decline of the welfare state might be considered weak, it is important to note that the alternatives in dispute relate, in their distributional impacts, to social interests and the essential normative tenets of liberal and social democratic movements. If increasing the tax burden and public investment serves the interests of actors related to social democracy, tax cuts, increased private investment in infrastructure and transferring the task of training the workforce to the private sphere corresponds to the liberal ideals of the state intervention in the economy – just as when the government was allowed to manage the politics of demand. In this case the political and intellectual liberals and social democrats have adapted to the context in which the representative democracy and the capitalist order must be combined.

The Recent Brazilian Context: Public Policies in the Light of Social Democracy

Let us now examine the recent political scene, in particular the years after the Workers' Party (the PT) achieved victory in the presidential elections of 2002. It is important to recall some key moments of the European social democrat trajectory in its dispute with what I have called more generally the liberal field, in order to contextualize what I am calling social democratic experience in Brazil.

A first key point relates to the context of party competition in which the PT was formed and developed into a major party. In this sense, there is no

---

11 Once again the main references here are Boix (1998) and Garret (1998).

single and essential definition of what is social democracy – there are political forces that are organized around the interests of workers and low-income populations, relatively articulated in unions and socialist ideas, more or less markedly doctrinal. In each specific national experience, the party or coalition of parties committed to these interests and ideas define strategies taking into account the distribution of political forces in the electorate and the world of organized economic sectors. It is not my goal to narrate the history of the PT and in particular how this party became the main electoral option for the left-wing voter in Brazil. For the time being, it suffices it to say that Lula was elected president backed by a large and complex of political network, a party and social network in which his party and other leftist parties are one among many, actors.

In this respect, the argument I would like to advance is precisely that the Brazilian experience of social democracy has been similar to the European in that both have faced and are facing the double-sided task of balancing the contradictions within such a network and, second, nevertheless remaining faithful to some of its basic principles and thereby shifting the status quo of public policies to the left.

A second key point, associated to the first one, refers to the societal context in social democratic experiment unfolds at the government level. In neocorporatist contexts in which economic actors are highly organized into worker and employer unions which monopolize the representation of these interests in the state, there are fewer restrictions for governments to pursue expansionary macroeconomic policies. These policies are an important component in the history of European social democracy because Keynesian measures against the cycles of expansion and recession – typical of capitalism – are credited for the success of the Left in Europe in articulating more inclusive government agendas: an agenda that includes the demands of workers in the maintenance and expansion of employment and, at the same time, preserved the property rights and profits of business sectors.

It is known, however, that expansionary economic policies are inflationary and increase the public deficit – particularly in the absence of restraint by workers and employers when they are fighting for the expansion of, respectively, earnings and margins profit. In countries where it has deeper roots, the corporatist societal model contributed to the moderation of demands and coordination of economic policy with the policy of income. It should be noted that Brazil is far from having a neocorporatist societal model. The country is closer to being a hybrid model with huge pluralistic circuits coupled with the important legacy of more corporatist states in the past as well as some marginal experiments of neocorporatism. The most important consequence for the purposes of this analysis was that Lula's economic policy, at the moment when he was sworn in 2003, facing sharp currency devaluation, capital flight and soaring inflation, had to assume an assuredly orthodox character.

A final key point is the belief that the adoption of a certain set of public policies, such as economic Keynesianism and the social welfare state, was only possible due to the arrival of social democracy to power policies. Historical does not authorize such an interpretation. Such policies (which admittedly have become the hallmark of social democracy) have been implemented at several moments of the process of continuous adaptation and political experimentation, sometimes with conservative parties in power, in others by left-wing governments, but rarely just as a result of socialist dogma. In the biggest and most important cases, policies have arisen as a result of urgent and concrete demands placed in certain countries in specific historical moments. As soon as the program to respond to the issues that emerge is launched, coalitions are formed in its support and adjustments are made to give it a more or less universal or permanent character – depending on the strength of socialist parties in each case and the nature of political alliances that allowed the arrival of the left government.

The important lesson to draw is that policies to combat poverty in the Lula government should be observed from the same perspective. These are not policies extracted from a perfectly designed body of principles and whose implementation would be a prerequisite for leftist credentials. Reality is that government actions are a continuation of previously initiated state processes and which are intended to overcome emergencies in specific political situations, conditions that impose restrictions on what can be done by a leftist government.

However, several examples can be cited as potential targets of investigation in order to test my general argument, which is that the priorities of action of the Brazilian state have experienced a significant change since the election of President Lula in 2002:

(1) Investment in physical capacity policy: The Growth Acceleration Program (Programa de Aceleração do Crescimento – PAC) stipulates expenses that total R$1.148 trillion by 2010 of which 11.5 percent will be allocated in logistics, 22.4 percent in social infrastructure and 66.1 percent in energy. It is jointly funded by the public and private sectors, with the public sector contributing with somewhere around 54 percent and the private sector 46 percent. The investments in transportation logistics focus on highways, although they will also benefit rail, ports and airports, waterway projects and the construction of ships. In terms of energy, the priority is certainly the oil and gas sector, which accounts for 65 percent of the amount of investment in energy projects, while the electric system accounts for 28.5 percent of the total, and the remaining projects for renewable fuels. With regard to social infrastructure, planning

provides for investments in sanitation and water resources, including expenses in the amount of 22.5 billion and R$12.6 billion, respectively. It should be noted that the social infrastructure heading comprises the pilot project agreed with the IMF whose aim is to exclude spendings in basic sanitation from primary surplus calculation.

(2) Regional integration policy: One of the main components of the Lula foreign policy is the strengthening of political, economic, social and cultural ties among the countries of South America. But currently the concept of integration involves more than just trade liberalization and the intensification of economic transactions – which involves the integration of the physical infrastructure of the countries in order to establish common platforms for the production and export of products, services and commodities with high value. The integration of infrastructure in turn implies a strong state presence both as a coordinator of the efforts of private enterprise or as loan guarantor.

(3) A policy of coordination with social movements and a policy of creating a condominium partisan coalition of support in Congress: The creation of the Council of Economic and Social Development (Conselho de Desenvolvimento Econômico Social – CDES), which has a ministerial status, is an organ of deliberation and consultation on major issues in the public agenda. It is composed of government leaders, union leaders, employers, the financial world, members of civil society organizations and members of top state bureaucracy. Besides this initiative, it is worth mentioning the multiplication of the Conferences of National Councils linked to several fundamental issues of social life – the National Health Council only being one of them. In terms of party politics per se, it is worth noting the condominium character of legislative coalition of support for Lula which includes eight to nine parties from across the ideological spectrum.

Each of these policies deserves more detailed and specific studies. In fact, many analysts have been working on some of them and have drawn conclusions that support the perception that at various times an inflection occurred with the arrival of the PT to the presidency, with shifts in the direction that would be expected with a government change to the left of the party spectrum.

Family Grant: Conceptual Basis and Electoral Impacts

This section focuses on the main antipoverty program adopted by the present government, the Family Grant Program (Bolsa Família). This examination will take place from two distinct points of view: the conceptual and the political one with the latter one considering the social and electoral coalitions mobilized.

The Bolsa Família is a program focused on poverty, like many around the world, but the Brazilian has distinguished itself for its broad scope. It is a heritage from other programs adopted during the government of Fernando Henrique Cardoso but magnified in terms of the scale, values involved and population covered. Its origin dates back to conceptual studies and suggestions from World Bank policies in the context of reforms in developing countries by the IMF orientation. In order to counter state downsizing and the adoption of orthodox monetary and fiscal tightening aimed at the resolution of debt problems, compensatory social programs capable of mitigating the harmful effects of adjustment were prescribed. There short-term programs consisted of direct cash transfers to people in extreme poverty on the condition of keeping their children in schools and providing them with basic health care.

From the conceptual point of view, the direct income transfer amounts to what the European social democracy has traditionally understood as social rights. Programs such as the Bolsa Família also bring to the fore the notion of assistance. It is important to remember that the subject of social rights is *the worker* and these rights are continuously being negotiated with entrepreneurs and the state. As discussed earlier (see "A New Outline for Political Conflict in the Era of Globalization"), we have seen how the criticism by liberals and the political right in the broadest sense directly affected the institutional framework which supported the welfare state. At the same time this inspired market reforms and fiscal adjustment in developing countries, such criticism ultimately benefitted the idea of focused programs – being that social rights of the welfare state consist of a privilege for unionized and formalized workers, who therefore live in relatively favorable social conditions. Nothing seems fairer given the need for fiscal adjustment rather than restricting the scope of security systems, encouraging the adoption of private health and welfare and further measures of support for people undergoing extreme poverty.

It was not until the 1980s when capitalist economies became more market oriented that focalized policies became staple suggestions of the World Bank. Transfer policies were not just one way of pressuring the debtor countries in the periphery, but rather a set of transformations that the industrialized countries were going through – with profound implications on the conceptual basis of social policies. Social democratic analysts such as Esping-Andersen (2000) admit that the conditions for the development of pure welfare states no longer exist, primarily as a result of changes in the structure of employment and demographic variables and that therefore new policies should be adopted to mitigate the exposure of low-income populations to risks and uncertainties characteristic of a market economy. In other words, the concept of decommodification is retained, although adapted to new circumstances of global capitalism.

The income transfer programs adopted by the Fernando Henrique Cardoso administration, whose scope was admittedly restricted, are explicitly mentioned by Esping-Andersen as examples of policies that needed to develop a new conception of the welfare state. A program that is not aimed at the worker as such – i.e. an actor endowed with a certain identity arising from her insertion in the productive process – but focused on children, specifically, to their empowerment and protection during the entire cycle of life. In the Lula government, however, the Bolsa Família (based on the same conceptual foundation) reaches 11 million households, 29 percent of the population, and recent government decisions have extended the program to the landless (who only received food donations), the indigenous population, the garbage collectors and to the homeless. If we are to cite the figures relating to the north and northeast of Brazil, the picture is even more impressive – the assisted population amounts to more than 50 percent in the states of Maranhão, Piauí, Ceará, Alagoas, Paraíba and Pernambuco and 40 percent in Bahia, Roraima, Acre, Tocantins, Rio Grande do Norte and Sergipe.

Like other policies adopted throughout the trajectory of social democracy in the world, the Bolsa Família has caused real transformation in the structure of voting and social coalitions in support of the Workers' Party (PT). In other words, it is impossible to deny the program's positive effect on the lives of lower income sectors of the population. Moreover, it is also a fact that it has brought about the inclusion of these segments into the market and has given their social existence a more institutionalized profile.

In order to illustrate the point of the electoral realignment, the maps below compare the distribution of electoral support for Lula by different mesoregions of the country. All shades (five in all) indicate a percentage range of votes obtained by the PT candidate in that mesoregion. For example, in Figure 13.1, the regions shaded in the lightest tone indicate that Lula received from the minimum percentage of votes obtained in a mesoregion up to 37.5 percent of the votes within the same mesoregion. In the regions shaded in the darkest tone, Lula received between 49.4 to 70.5 percent of votes in a mesoregion, the maximum reached by him in any of the mesoregions.

In the 2006 elections, Lula was reelected with electoral results very similar to those observed in the 2002 election. However, a striking difference emerged regarding the geographical distribution of the vote. In his first victory, the votes were more evenly distributed among the population, with a slight predominance in the coastal strip (where the major cities are concentrated); this did not occur in 2006. A comparative reading of the maps clearly shows that while this year represents a remarkable rise of the PT in the north and northeast, as remarkable

Figure 13.1. Presidential election 2002 – Results by percentage, PT

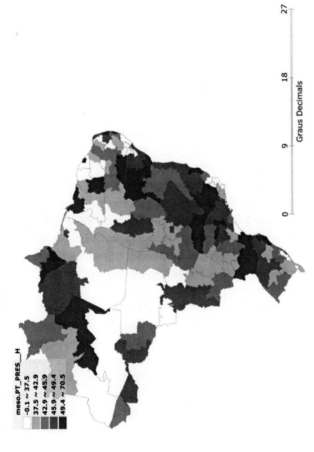

Figure 13.2. Presidential election 2006 – Results by percentage, PT

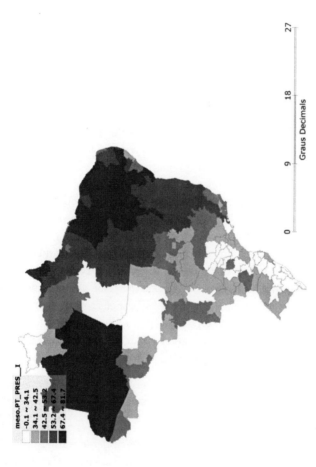

Note: These maps were constructed based on 139 meso-Brazilian regions so that a more reasonable viewing of the units could be obtained. The legends refer to five categories of quintiles. The stronger the shading tone the larger proportion of votes the candidate has. Additionally, we used data from IPEADATA for the regions, which were processed in TerraView Social Policy.

is the loss of strength in the south, southeast and midwest of Brazil. We know that the regions where the PT becomes dominant bear the highest rates of poverty, percentage of population with no education, infant mortality and, therefore, these are precisely the regions where investments from the Bolsa Família program are concentrated. Lula obtained more votes in places which benefitted from the main antipoverty program by the government. These happen to be the places where income transfer, employment and GDP per capita grew the most during the first term of the current government and also where the DEM (the party which was part of the center-right coalition which ruled Brazil before the rise of Lula to the presidency) lost significant electoral support.

This shift in the geographical pattern of PT votes cannot be underestimated. Prudence and caution should mark any effort to analyze – especially if we consider that the results refer to only two points in time – and it is not known whether the votes given to Lula tend to stay with the PT when he stops competing. Only time can provide the answers in this case. However, if the direction of the main argument in this chapter is correct, it is a reasonable bet that we are facing a more permanent phenomenon. The Bolsa Família has become the symbol of inclusion policy of the government; both the electorate directly benefitted by the policy as well as those ideologically committed to the idea of a public sector responsible for handling the problem of poverty and inequality has responded when deciding their vote and expressing their opinion about the performance of the administration. In this sense, the argument is that in Brazil the program ended up being the synthesis of a broader phenomenon which occurred along the trajectory of European social democracies – that is, the redefinition of party loyalties of the Brazilian electorate, especially the identity politics of lower income strata. At this point, the concept and electoral efficiency are combined, precisely the great virtue of the left-leaning social welfare state in Europe and to some extent also in the United States.

Conclusion

My goal in this chapter, in a sense, was not ambitious. After all, to argue that a government in any country can be defined as social democratic profile does not seem to take us very far in terms of a political analysis. However both in public debate as in the current academic discussions, Brazil is a specific manner; but also in South America, the question of what is the best definition of the governments that have recently governed the majority of countries in the continent is quite controversial. Categories such as populism, personalism, corporatism and co-optation are used abundantly in the attempt, at times to disqualify political opponents, while in others to analyze the phenomena that at first sight seem not to fit frameworks with which they are accustomed.

I think that this chapter may help clarify some terms of the debate. Let us first deal with the Brazilian case specifically. The perspectives according to which in the Brazilian political system parties have little meaning to voters are well-known. Also according to this perspective, the personal interests of politicians outweigh anything else and government activity takes place through trade-offs between presidents and lawmakers, and not by corporate bodies constituted by broader interests and ideas. In this context, little room is left for programmatic shifts in the status quo of public policies. However, the government's characterization of the PT as an adaptation of social democracy in Brazilian soil is not trivial. To defend such an idea is also to argue that Brazilian politics are guided primarily by programmatic conflicts between political forces clustered into parties that do, in fact, make a difference for both elites and voters in the broadest sense.

It is not trivial either that most analysts of Brazilian politics identify the Lula government – especially his first term – as an additional example of policy switching (Stokes 1999), common in Latin America in times of globalization. According to this argument, as a result of external pressures and the imminence of an economic and administrative catastrophe, several leftist governments in developing countries would have to betray promises and the interests of followers to embrace historical and orthodox policies of fiscal adjustment. Through this strategy, such government managed to stay in power through a diffuse support of a population that was the most vulnerable to the rigors of inflation, but at the cost, however, of dismantling the party framework and the transmutation of the concept of accountability.

The reassessment of the historical trajectory of social democracy and its recent adaptation to the Brazilian case once again help to clarify the terms of debate. From this perspective, what happened to Lula when he took office and was forced to promote strong fiscal adjustment coupled with orthodox monetary policy was not exactly "just another case" of policy switching but a classic example of a social democratic government at the helm of a broad coalition party in a context not so favorable for the coordination between monetary, fiscal and income policies in order to stimulate output growth without generating inflationary pressures. This is a context in which the explicit pact between players for moderation and the extension in time of their demands are out of question, leaving the government with no other choice but to administer the bitter medicine of orthodox monetary and fiscal tightening, in view of the main objective of a leftist government for satisfying the poorer strata of the population.

But the reconsideration of the conceptual and historical trajectory of social democracy is not useful to understand the Brazilian case only. It may also help to redefine our view of what happens in other parts of the continent of South America. In this sense, two results of previous analysis should be remembered: first of all, it is essential to note the context of party competition. It is perhaps facile and unhelpful to classify governments as populist, demagogic, etc. before determining the past history of competing parties in a given country, especially the strategies and rhetoric of the forces on the right of the political spectrum. To a great extent, the left group in one country is not only a result of a societal model developed there, but also of the political choices of their liberal opponents. Secondly, it is necessary to observe carefully the public policies and alliances that are built around them. Policies aimed at benefitting the lower income strata and which define the terms of realignment of loyalties and voting behavior are the hallmark of the social democratic path, and to some extent, wherever it occurs the same historical processes of institutionalized dispute between labor and capital will also come into play.

References

Bergounioux, A. and Bernard Manin. 1989. *Le régime social-democrate*. Paris: Presses Universitaires de France.

Boix, Carles. 1998. *Political Parties, Growth and Equality: Conservative and Social Democratic Economic Strategies in the World Economy*. Cambridge: Cambridge University Press.

Cox, Gary W. and Matthew D. McCubbins. 1993. *Legislative Leviathan: Party Government in the House*. Berkeley: University of California Press.

Garrett, Geoffrey. 1998. *Partisan Politics in the Global Economy*. Cambridge: Cambridge University Press.

Esping-Andersen, Gøsta. 1990. *The Three Worlds of Welfare Capitalism*. Princeton: Princeton University Press.

Glyn, Andrew. 2001. *Social Democracy in Neoliberal Times: The Left and Economic Policy since 1980*. New York: Oxford University Press.

Hibbs, Douglas A. Jr. 1977. "Political Parties and Macroeconomic Policy." *American Political Science Review* 71: 1467–87.

Iversen, Torben. 2005. *Capitalism, Democracy and Welfare*. Cambridge: Cambridge University Press.

Keohane, Robert and Helen Milner. 1996. *Internalization and Domestic Politics*. New York: Cambridge University Press.

Kitschelt, Herbert. 1994. *The Transformation of European Social Democracy*. New York: Cambridge University Press.

Kloppenberg, James T. 1986. *Uncertain Victory: Social Democracy and Progressivism in European and American Thought, 1870–1920*. New York: Oxford University Press.

Merquior, José Guilherme. 1982. *A Natureza do Processo*. Rio de Janeiro: Nova Fronteira.

Przeworski, Adam. 1985. *Capitalism and Social Democracy*. New York: Cambridge University Press.

Rodrik, Dani. 1997. *Has Globalization Gone too Far?* Washington DC: Institute for International Economics.

Santos, Fabiano. 2006. "Integração Regional e as Eleições Presidenciais de 2006 no Brasil." Analysis survey, OPSA/IUPERJ.

Scharp, Fritz. 1991. *Crisis and Choice in European Social Democracy*. Ithaca, NY: Cornell University Press.